THE AMERICAN LAW INSTITUTE

THE WTO CASE LAW OF 2004–2005

LEGAL AND ECONOMIC ANALYSIS

This book is the fourth report of the American Law Institute (ALI) project on World Trade Organization Law. The project undertakes yearly analysis of the case law from the adjudicating bodies of the WTO. These studies cover a wide range of WTO law: this volume focuses on the years 2004 and 2005. Each case is jointly evaluated by well known experts in trade law and international economics. The contributors critically review the jurisprudence of WTO adjudicating bodies and evaluate whether the ruling 'makes sense' from an economic as well as a legal point of view, and, if not, whether the problem lies in the interpretation of the law or the law itself. The Studies do not cover all issues discussed in a case, but they seek to discuss both the procedural and the substantive issues that form the 'core' of the dispute.

HENRIK HORN, Professor of International Economics, is Senior Research Fellow at the Research Institute of Industrial Economics (IFN), Stockholm. He is a member of the Editorial Board of the *World Trade Review* and is a member of the Centre for Economic Policy Research. He has previously worked for the Economic Policy Research and Analysis Division of the World Trade Organization, and has been a judge on the Swedish Market Court (supreme court for competition law).

PETROS C. MAVROIDIS is Edwin B. Parker Professor at Columbia Law School, Professor at the University of Neuchatel, and a member of the Centre for Economic Policy Research. He was previously Chair of Competition Law, EUI, Florence, and a member of the Legal Affairs Division of the World Trade Organization.

THE AMERICAN LAW INSTITUTE

THE WTO CASE LAW OF 2004–2005

LEGAL AND ECONOMIC ANALYSIS

Edited By

HENRIK HORN

AND

PETROS C. MAVROIDIS

CAMBRIDGE
UNIVERSITY PRESS

CAMBRIDGE
UNIVERSITY PRESS

Shaftesbury Road, Cambridge CB2 8EA, United Kingdom

One Liberty Plaza, 20th Floor, New York, NY 10006, USA

477 Williamstown Road, Port Melbourne, VIC 3207, Australia

314–321, 3rd Floor, Plot 3, Splendor Forum, Jasola District Centre, New Delhi – 110025, India

103 Penang Road, #05–06/07, Visioncrest Commercial, Singapore 238467

Cambridge University Press is part of Cambridge University Press & Assessment, a department of the University of Cambridge.

We share the University's mission to contribute to society through the pursuit of education, learning and research at the highest international levels of excellence.

www.cambridge.org
Information on this title: www.cambridge.org/9780521730761

A catalogue record for this publication is available from the British Library

ISBN 978-0-521-73076-1 Paperback

CONTENTS

Foreword

This volume, containing analyses of decisions rendered by the adjudicating bodies of the World Trade Organization in 2004 and 2005, is The American Law Institute's most recent contribution in its continuing examination of the developing law of world trade. As with our previously published volumes analyzing decisions rendered from 2001 through 2003, each study is the joint work of a lawyer and an economist, and each study has been subjected to additional review and analysis by the other contributors and by an international group of experts at an invitational conference in Geneva in March 2007. The studies are the work of the individual authors and not of The American Law Institute.

With five years of WTO case law studies now to our credit, we have begun the second phase of our world trade work, seeking to draft general principles of world trade law based on that developing body of case law. The Chief Reporters for this phase are Henrik Horn of Stockholm University and Petros Mavroidis of the University of Neuchâtel and of Columbia University School of Law. We also hope to continue our reporting and analysis of individual WTO decisions.

We are grateful to the economists and lawyers who contributed the studies in this volume and to those who reviewed and constructively criticized their earlier drafts. We also express our appreciation to the Jan Wallander and Tom Hedelius Foundation and the Milton and Miriam Handler Foundation for their continued and generous financial support of this endeavor.

LANCE LIEBMAN
Director
The American Law Institute

Introduction

HENRIK HORN AND PETROS C. MAVROIDIS

This is the fourth round of Reporters' Studies undertaken in the context of the American Law Institute project 'Principles of World Trade Law: The World Trade Organization'. The aim of the project is to provide systematic analysis of WTO law based in both economics and law. This year's focus has been on disputes that came to an administrative end during the years 2004 and 2005, either because they were not appealed or because the appeal process had come to an end. Each dispute has been evaluated jointly by an economist and a lawyer. Their general task has been to evaluate whether the ruling 'makes sense' from an economic as well as a legal point of view, and, if not, whether the problem lies in the legal text or in the interpretation thereof. The teams of lawyers and economists do not always cover all issues discussed in a case, but they seek to discuss both the procedural and the substantive issues that form the 'core' of the dispute as they see it.

Earlier versions of the Reporters' Studies were presented at a meeting at the WTO in Geneva in February 2007. The comments provided by discussants and other participants have been very helpful in the preparation of the final version of the papers in the volume, and we want to thank discussants and other participants for their efforts. We would also like to thank the WTO for providing a venue for the February meeting.

This project would not have existed had it not been for the efforts and commitment of Professor Lance Liebman, Director of the ALI. We have also benefited greatly from the support of ALI President Michael Traynor, ALI Deputy Director Elena Cappella, and former ALI Deputy Director Michael Greenwald. We would also like to thank Judy Cole, Sandrine Forgeron, and Marianne Walker of the ALI's staff for very efficient administrative and editorial help. Finally, we are extremely grateful for financial support from Jan Wallander's and Tom Hedelius' Research Foundation, the Milton and Miriam Handler Foundation, and Svenska Handelsbanken of Stockholm.

The Reporters' Studies on the WTO Case Law of 2004–2005

In this edition, we discuss Appellate Body (AB) reports only.

Horn and Howse discuss the *EC-Chicken Cuts* customs classification dispute. Superficially, the dispute thus only concerned the meaning of 'salted', and, in particular, whether it subsumed a long-term preservation condition. The parties, the Panel, and the AB all dealt with this issue as a question of treaty interpretation, the central task being to decide the meaning of 'salted' in accordance with the canons of treaty interpretation to be found in Articles 31 and 32 of the Vienna Convention on the Law of Treaties. Horn and Howse disagree with the determination by the Panel and the AB on several core issues. First, the courts bias the outcome against the importing country due to the interpretation of the burden of proof in cases where two customs classification headings can be argued with equal force as the appropriate classifications. Second, in their view the case is about customs classification (despite the arguments by the parties and the courts to the contrary). For this determination, the Panel should have asked for expert opinion by the WCO. Third, they argue against the conclusion that the result of an EC violation of Art. II of the GATT could be justified on the basis of the evidence presented in this dispute. But Horn and Howse still believe that the actual outcome of the case might be justified on other grounds.

The comment by **Meagher** addresses several of the points made in Howse and Horn's paper. In tariff-classification cases, it is important to strike a balance between ensuring that exporting Members may benefit from the tariff concession in question and still permitting importing Members to protect their tariffs. In the WTO context, this case raised not just issues of customs classification, but also the interpretation of treaty provisions in the form of the EC's tariff schedules. As such, the WTO panel was compelled to accept jurisdiction and resolve the issue. The comment also disagrees with the authors' suggestion that the issue should properly have been addressed under GATT Article X:3.

Hoekman and Trachtman discuss the *Canada–Wheat Exports and Grain Imports report.* Statutory marketing boards that have exclusive authority to purchase domestic production, sell for export, and set purchase and sales prices of commodities, are a type of state trading enterprise that is subject to GATT disciplines. The United States submitted its dispute with Canada to the WTO, alleging that WTO rules require state trading enterprises to operate solely in accordance with commercial considerations, and that the Canadian government did not require the Canadian Wheat Board to do so. The panel and the AB found that the primary discipline of the WTO regarding state trading enterprises was nondiscrimination, and that operating on the basis of commercial considerations was not an independent obligation. Instead, WTO disciplines regarding the pricing behavior of state trading enterprises use a commercial-considerations test as a possible indicator of discrimination. Although a significant degree of price discrimination is observed in the case of Canadian wheat exports, there are economic arguments why this might also be pursued by a private, profit-maximizing firm.

Commenting on the Hoekman and Trachtman paper, **Roessler** argues that the fundamental question that has been left open by the AB is what the principles of nondiscriminatory treatment covered by Art. XVII:1(a) GATT are. Roessler's answer is that it is neither necessary nor appropriate to apply this article to the denial of National Treatment through state trading operations, but that the standards set out in Articles III:2 and III:4 can and should be applied to prevent this.

The controversial *US–Gambling* report by the AB is discussed by **Irwin and Weiler**. The authors note that this report is significant mainly because of the examination of the nature of market access under Article XVI GATS, the relationship of that Article to Articles XIV and XVII GATS, and the parallels with Articles III, XI and XX GATT. Notably, the AB took the position that what on its face appeared as an internal regulatory measure, which, nonetheless, had equivalent effect to a zero quota, was captured by Article XVI GATS. A similar measure in the area of goods would have been examined under Article III GATT and would require a showing of discrimination. The facts of the case would have allowed the decision to be based on Article XVII GATS. The lion's share of the paper deals with this issue. The authors agree with this interpretation of Article XVI GATS by the AB, but are critical of its hermeneutics, suffering in their eyes from a textual fetish and a policy phobia. Some other elements in the decision are also examined critically.

Ortino, in his comment, principally criticizes the AB's decision in *US–Gambling* insofar as (i) it potentially expands the scope of the *per se* prohibition in Article XVI GATS to cover measures having an effect equivalent to an express quantitative restriction, and (ii) it reiterates the apparent confusion, created since *Korea–Beef*, on the nature of the 'balancing' exercise carried out under Article XIV GATS. Furthermore, he briefly highlights two interesting developments in *US–Gambling* on the 'burden of proof' and 'availability of alternative measures' under the least-trade-restrictive test of Article XIV GATS.

In the remaining part of the volume we discuss seven reports dealing with contingent protection instruments, the first four from the field of subsidies, and the remaining three from the field of antidumping. **Bown and Sykes** address issues that came before the AB in the *US–Softwood Lumber V* dispute, concerning an affirmative antidumping determination by the US Department of Commerce. The paper discusses both the original AB opinion in the dispute, and the later opinion reviewing the compliance panel findings. The authors focus primarily on the 'zeroing' issue in 'transaction-to-transaction' calculations of dumping. In general, they are ambivalent about the AB's approach to the zeroing issue. On the one hand, zeroing inflates dumping margins without any sound economic rationale for doing so. On the other hand, zeroing has been a standard administrative practice for many years and the Anti dumping Agreement (ADA) does not clearly prohibit it. The AB's legal analysis of the matter in T-T cases, in particular, rests on shaky premises. Bown and Sykes also consider the wisdom of addressing the zeroing issue in piecemeal fashion through what has proven to be a lengthy sequence of narrow decisions.

In her comment, **Crowley** concurs with the analysis of Bown and Sykes and offers two additional points. First, allowing zeroing in the calculation of dumping margins penalizes foreign exporting firms subject to volatile costs. Second, cost allocation within a multi-product firm should attempt to equate the real economic returns across products.

Hoekman and Howse discuss the *EC–Export Subsidies on Sugar* litigation, which implicated a large number of developing countries with divergent interests. Brazil, Thailand, and Australia alleged that the EU exports had substantially exceeded permitted levels as established by European Union commitments in the WTO. This case had major implications for both European Union sugar producers and developing countries that benefited from preferential access to the European Union market. It was also noteworthy in the use of economic arguments by the WTO dispute-settlement panel, which held that the excess sugar exports were in part a reflection of illegal *de facto* cross-subsidization rents from production that benefited from high support prices being used to cover losses associated with exports of sugar to the world market. Although in principle the economic arguments of the panel could apply to many other policy areas, in practice WTO provisions greatly limit the scope to bring similar arguments for trade in products that are not subject to explicit export subsidy reduction commitments of the type that were made for sugar and other agricultural commodities.

Conconi, in her comment, notes that the most controversial issue regarding the dispute involves the EC exports of so-called C sugar. The WTO Panel and AB found that below-cost exports of an agricultural product might represent proof of export subsidization, even in the absence of direct export subsidies, if there is close linkage between these exports and domestic support programs. In her discussion of the economic analysis of the case, she reviews the possible reasons for the production of C sugar to evaluate the validity of the cross-subsidization argument.

Sapir and Trachtman deal with the *US–Upland Cotton* litigation, which, in their view, illustrates the challenges that panels face when they are required to evaluate complex economic matters. The serious-prejudice provisions of the SCM Agreement call for an initial determination by the panel, rather than the review of national agency determinations that is called for in the countervailing-duty provisions. In the countervailing-duty context, as in the safeguards and dumping contexts, the AB, the authors note, has seemed satisfied to have panels engage in procedural review of national agency determinations, rather than substantive review. Although this position is subject to question, given the substantive requirements of WTO law, it is patently untenable in the serious-prejudice context, where there is no initial national agency determination. In these cases, requirements to determine issues such as 'causation', 'price suppression', and 'significant' must, in the authors' view, be understood as requirements that panels use the best analytical tools reasonably available to make such determinations.

Commenting upon the analysis by Sapir and Trachtman, **Vandenbussche** discusses the validity of the argument advanced by the complainants to the effect that the United States, through its subsidies, was indeed depressing world prices for cotton. In her view, the authors argue that the decision in favor of Brazil insufficiently demonstrated a causal link between price depression and US subsidies to upland cotton. The Panel and the AB, she argues, made no effort to disentangle the effects of a US subsidy from other potential causes of price depression. In line with the arguments advanced by Sapir and Trachtman in favor of the application of rigorous economic methods in the determination of *causality*, she tries to shed, by means of a graphical exposition, some additional light on how economic analysis can be used for the causation analysis.

Francois and Palmeter discuss *US–Countervailing Duty Investigation on DRAMS*. In modifying and largely reversing the Panel's decision that the US improperly levied countervailing duties on DRAMS from Korea, the AB dealt for the first time with the 'entrusts or directs' language of subparagraph (iv) of Article 1.1(a) of the *SCM Agreement* and set forth the proper methodology for deciding issues on the basis of circumstantial evidence. The AB essentially held that a finding that subsidy exists can be lawfully based on circumstantial evidence. The authors take the view that it is unavoidable that the WTO adjudicating bodies will have to rely on circumstantial evidence in similar cases, and welcome the AB's openness to such a test in this respect. Additionally, they find no serious fault with the standard of review employed in this case.

In his comment, **Prusa** notes that the analysis of the two authors focuses on the question of whether creditors were 'entrusted or directed' to make financial contributions to Hynix, the Korean company at stake in this dispute. In Prusa's account, the view of the authors is that a series of events taken together can be construed to satisfy the 'entrusted or directed' standard even though any single incident is not definitive; the old adage 'the sum of the parts is greater than the whole' could be used to summarize their argument. He does not necessarily disagree with this view, but adds that a related question is whether the intervention of the government of Korea changed the market outcome. While not addressed in the analysis of the authors, this issue is also crucial to understanding the economic impact of the alleged subsidization.

Grossman and Wauters review the WTO AB report on *US–OCTG Sunset Reviews*. This dispute is one of several that deal with sunset reviews of anti-dumping duty orders. In its ruling, the AB reasserts a rigid distinction between mandatory and discretionary law and sets a very high standard for Member challenges to laws or practices that allow for violations of WTO obligations but do not mandate such behavior. The authors argue that this ruling is unfortunate, because it diminishes scope of and incentives for 'as-such' challenges to laws and practices, which have a potentially useful role to play in the world trading system. The AB ruling also overlooks the purpose and objectives of sunset reviews – to ensure that duty orders are not extended when their removal would generate no harm to an import competing industry – by failing to impose sufficient discipline on their conduct. The authors further argue that a sunset review requires an evaluation of competitive conditions in the industry and of the reasons and incentives for dumping, in order that the investigating authority can judge whether the removal of a duty order would lead to a continuation or recurrence of dumping and injury. The AB's rulings in this and other similar cases have the effect of relieving the investigating authority of this responsibility and thereby render the sunset review process virtually meaningless.

In his comment, **Vermulst**, argues that the reason the United States is the main target of WTO challenges to its antidumping law and practice is not because it is more protectionist that other AD users, but because its system is the most transparent. Article 3 of the ADA, which regulates the requirements that a lawful demonstration of injury must contain, ought to apply equally in sunset and interim reviews. In his view, the conditions in Article 3(3)(a) ADA do not necessarily need to be applied in sunset/interim reviews. Proposals to change the underpinnings of sunset reviews in isolation of the general underpinnings of the ADA are, in his view, unlikely to succeed.

Bown and Wauters discuss *US–AD Measures on OCTG*. This paper reviews the WTO AB report on *United States–Anti-Dumping Measures on Oil Country Tubular Goods (OCTG) from Mexico* (WT/DS282/AB/R 2 November 2005). This dispute concerns the disciplines imposed by the ADA on WTO Members seeking to extend their antidumping measures beyond the original five-year period through a sunset review. Their analysis focuses on the AB's finding in this case that no causation analysis is required in sunset reviews, and addresses the AB's approach towards the legal instrument that provides for the US policy in terms of sunset reviews, the Sunset Policy Bulletin. They conclude that the ADA, as interpreted by the AB in this and other similar cases, imposes only minimal disciplines of a general nature on Members wishing to extend the antidumping measure beyond its original five-year period. They argue that the 'textual' argument relied on to support this deferential approach is weak and has resulted in undermining the practical effect of, what was considered to be, one of the major achievements of the Uruguay Round ADA: limiting the life span of an antidumping measure to five years. From an economic perspective, panels and the AB are simply debating the wrong type of questions. The prospective nature required by a sunset review analysis raises questions such as why exporters engaged in dumping in the first place, and what the conditions of the industry were so that the dumped imports caused injury. At the moment, sunset reviews seem adrift as panels and the AB fail to give guidance to Members on how to do a more economically sound and informed review.

Davey, in his comment, notes that the greater use of econometric models in the determination of whether dumping and injury are likely to recur would introduce more, desirable rigor into the sunset review process, but the inherently speculative nature of the review process ultimately precludes ever establishing an analytically satisfactory way of assessing the likelihood of recurring dumping and injury. Accordingly, in his view the rule should be that antidumping duties terminate after five years, with no possibility of extension, but with the possibility of initiation a new proceeding and reestablishing the required elements for imposing such duties.

Mavroidis and Sapir discuss *Mexico–Antidumping Measures on Rice*, which concerns the manner in which dumping margins should be calculated for exporters who have not been individually examined during the investigation process. The AB, in the authors' view, took a cautious approach seeking to limit the risk of abusing the investigation process by outlawing recourse to certain facts. It could not, however, undo the intrinsic inadequacies of the Anti-dumping Agreement, which go much deeper than the lack of clarity with respect to the treatment of unidentified exporters. It relates to whether it is countries or firms that are responsible for dumping and that should pay AD duties if they engage in injurious dumping. The authors argue that a fundamental incoherence must be removed from the AD Agreement, whereby it considers dumping a private practice on the one hand and presumes that dumping is a countrywide practice on the other. If this incoherence remains, we risk seeing many other dumping cases being brought before the WTO adjudicating bodies.

Dordi, in his comment, covers two issues: (i) the AB interpretation of the term 'known' exporters contained in article 6.10 of ADA cannot be considered either 'restrictive' or 'completely textual'; indeed, 'known' is a qualified term that has a common meaning in the procedural law of most of the countries of the international community; and (ii) companies that are located in countries where the competition is not particularly protected from abuses and where there are high import barriers potentially have more opportunity to dump products in other markets than do companies in countries where the competition is strictly regulated and where there are lower import barriers.

European Communities – Customs Classification of Frozen Boneless Chicken Cuts

HENRIK HORN

Research Institute of Industrial Economics, Stockholm, Bruegel, Brussels Centre for Economic Policy Research, London

ROBERT L. HOWSE

University of Michigan Law School, Ann Arbor

1. Background

The EC is bound in its tariff schedule not to apply a duty rate in excess of 15.4 % to 'Meat and edible meat offal, salted, in brine, dried, or smoked' (Tariff item 02.10). The complainants, Brazil and Thailand, had been exporting frozen chicken cuts treated with salt to the EC, since, respectively, 1996 and 1998. Between 1996 and 2002, EC customs points generally, although not always and everywhere, applied the bound rate in tariff item 02.10 to these imports; beginning in 2002, however, the Commission issued regulations requiring that customs authorities classify imports of meat under 02.10 only where salt has been added to the meat for the purpose of long-term preservation. The result of this regulatory action was that the exports of the claimants were reclassified as falling under tariff item 02.07, which applies to 'fresh, chilled or frozen' poultry; the bound rate under 02.07 is higher than under 02.10 (102.4 Euros per 100 kgs, an effective ad valorem rate of between 40 and 60 %). As well, products under 02.07 may face special safeguard action pursuant to the WTO Agreement on Agriculture. Because the exports of the complainants were not salted for purposes of long-term preservation, European customs authorities were thus required to apply the higher tariff rate under 02.07 to these products. The complainants argued that through its binding under 02.10, the EC was obligated to apply a duty that did not exceed 15.4 % ad valorem to their exports, *regardless of whether the salt was applied for purposes of long-term preservation*. By applying a higher rate of duty since 2002, the EC and its member-state customs authorities were, according to the complainants, in violation of Art. II:1(a) and II:1(b) GATT, which prohibit WTO Members from applying duties and charges higher than the bound rates in their schedules for the product in question.

We are grateful for very helpful discussions with Petros C. Mavroidis, Chad Bown, Tom Prusa, and Don Regan.

The disputing parties agreed that: (1) the exports in question were *not* salted for long-term preservation; (2) as explained above, the tariff rate applied to the products in question was, during the period of time that was the subject of the complaint, always higher than the bound rate under 02.10; (3) *if* the products in question did *not* fall within 02.10, the EC would not be in violation of Article II in applying the higher rate prescribed by 02.07; (4) in determining whether the products in question fell under 02.10, the EC could specify a minimum quantitative threshold in ascertaining whether the products were 'salted' (historically, in EC Regulations, the minimum threshold had been 1.2 %).

Thus, the *only* issue in this dispute, as framed by the parties, was whether or not the term 'salted' in 02.10 means, exclusively, 'salted for purposes of long-term preservation'.

The parties, the Panel, and the Appellate Body (AB) all dealt with this issue as a question of treaty interpretation: the central task was to decide the meaning of 'salted' in accordance with the canons of treaty interpretation to be found in Articles 31 and 32 of the Vienna Convention on the Law of Treaties (VCLT). Of course, the word 'salted' does not appear in any WTO treaty, and the document being interpreted here is a Harmonized System (HS) classification found in the defending member's schedule. The obligation to follow the classification practice of the HS is an obligation of WTO Members in their capacity as members of the World Customs Organization (WCO), which develops the HS. Although the Panel solicited advice from the WCO on the interpretation of 02.07 and 02.10, neither the Panel nor the AB suggested that the WTO dispute settlement organs must, as a matter of law, defer to WCO interpretations or practice with respect to HS classifications. This is consistent with earlier AB jurisprudence that considers Members' schedules as forming an integral part of the Single Undertaking: the terminology of schedules should be interpreted and applied as if one is interpreting and applying the GATT itself or any other treaty in the Single Undertaking (*EC – Lan Equipment*, Report of the AB, para. 84). The WCO Secretariat, however, took the view that it would be appropriate for the parties to resort to the WCO dispute settlement system and obtain a ruling on the meaning of 'salted' in 02.107 before having recourse to WTO procedures. The Panel concluded that there was no possibility of declining jurisdiction even temporarily under the DSU. The Panel therefore proceeded to determine whether, when read in accordance with VCLT Arts. 31 and 32, 'salted' in HS 02.10 means, exclusively, 'salted for purposes of long-term preservation'.

The Panel interpreted the norms in Arts. 31 and 32 of the VCLT as intended to be applied sequentially: thus, it began with 'ordinary meaning' in Art. 31(1), and, having found that the ordinary meaning of 'salted' did not exclusively refer to salting for long-term preservation, then proceeded to examine whether, in light of the other interpretative considerations in Art. 31 VCLT (object, purpose, and context), this was the proper meaning to attribute to tariff item 02.10. While, as discussed below, it went on to correct some specific aspects of the Panel's interpretation and application to the VCLT, the AB upheld its general approach but also noted that it is appropriate to apply the VCLT in a holistic manner and that the factual considerations in question could be taken into account either in considering 'ordinary meaning' or in considering 'context' (para. 176): here the AB was responding to a claim that the Panel had violated its own sequential methodology in going beyond the dictionary and taking into account the factual context in its determination of 'ordinary meaning'.

In what follows, we will discuss the adjudicating bodies' treatment of the burden of proof (Section 2), 'ordinary meaning of words' (Section 3), 'context' (Section 4), the WCO General Rules (Section 5), 'object and purpose' (Section 6), 'subsequent practice' (Section 7), and 'supplementary means' of treaty interpretation (Section 8). We will also discuss the choice of forum for the resolution of this dispute (Section 9). We conclude by summarizing our views concerning the extent to which the outcome of the dispute was correct (Section 10).

2. The burden of proof

According to the complainants in *EC–Chicken Cuts*, the EC violated Art. II:1(a) and II:1(b) GATT by according a less favorable treatment than that provided for in the EC schedule. A threshold question is what the complainant is required to prove in order to establish a violation of Article II based on the scheduling practices of the defendant. The Panel interprets the appropriate burden of proof as follows:

> 7.78 ... In light of the rules governing the burden of proof, it is our view that the complainants bear the burden to prove that the products at issue are, in fact, covered by the concession contained in heading 02.10 of the EC Schedule.

In our view, there is a fundamental problem with this definition of the burden of proof, and this is a point we will return to repeatedly: we believe that this is a too-low standard for a finding of a *violation*, unless 'covered by' is read as '*only* covered by'. Due to the incomplete nature of the EC schedule (as of all such schedules), it may well be the case that several of its headings can cover the product at issue. In such a case, it would be inappropriate to require of the importing country to provide the most favorable treatment, without any rationale for why this should be the default case. On the contrary, we would argue that it should *not* be viewed as a violation of the agreement if the importing country applies a tariff heading that is shown to cover the product, even if there is another heading that would also fit the product.

In our view, in order for a classification under 02.07 to amount to a *violation* of the agreement, it would have to be incorrect to classify the product at issue under 02.07. The investigation by the adjudicating bodies does not address the appropriateness of classifying under this heading however; for instance, the VCLT canons of treaty interpretation are not employed to examine this heading. The focus in the reports is instead on heading 02.10, and the conclusion is only that this heading is not *exclusively* for chicken cuts preserved through salting. A leap is thus taken from the finding that the product *is classifiable* under heading 02.10 to the conclusion that it *must not* be classified under heading 02.07. We believe that there is, in this regard, insufficient evidence for a finding of violation.

3. Ordinary meaning of words

The Panel finds no indication in the ordinary meaning of the words in heading 02.10 that the product at issue would not be covered:

> 7.151 The Panel considers that there is nothing in the range of meanings comprising the ordinary meaning of the term 'salted' that indicates that chicken to which salt has been added is not covered by the concession contained in heading 02.10 of the EC Schedule.

The AB in essence agrees with the Panel's conclusion:

> 187 ... we see no reason to disturb the Panel's conclusion concerning the ordinary meaning of the term 'salted'.

We have little objection to the conclusion as such, that the words in heading 02.10 could be read so as to include the product at issue. It is notable, however, that – although at times the issue is framed as whether the products in question are correctly classified under 02.10 *or* 02.07 – the Panel's and AB's analysis proceeds *not* by analyzing under the VCLT the 'ordinary meaning' of both 02.10 and 02.07 but rather only bringing in 02.10 as a matter of context. This approach excludes from the start the possibility that a particular product could have characteristics such that it would fall within the 'ordinary meaning' of more than one HS classification. This possibility is, however, explicitly contemplated in WCO law, which contains rules to deal with just this situation (see Section 4). The Panel notes in para. 7.238 of its report that the disputing parties agreed that these rules did not apply to the case at hand because 'the products at issue in this dispute are not prima facie classifiable under two or more headings'. This approach of only focusing on heading 02.10 is followed by the adjudicating bodies throughout their analyses.

4. The meaning of 'salted' considered in its context

In their discussion of 'context', the adjudicating bodies deal with three main issues: what constitutes the context for interpreting 'salted' in heading 02.10, the meaning of 'salted' considered in its context, and the relevance of General Rule 3 for the interpretation of the HS system. We will in this Section discuss the second issue, and in the next Section the applicability of General Rule 3.

4.1 The adjudicating bodies' findings

The Panel starts its examination of context by considering the text of the EC schedule. What it finds, and this is the pattern throughout the analysis of context, is that the text of the schedule does not provide any information, and, in particular, that it does not confirm a long-term-preservation criterion:

> 7.180 In summary, the Panel concludes that the definitions of the terms in the concession contained in heading 02.10 of the EC Schedule other than 'salted' *do not indicate any intrinsic notion that characterizes all the terms* in that concession other than that they are in a state that is not simply fresh, chilled or frozen. Nor does the Panel consider that these terms can be defined as pertaining exclusively to 'preparation' or to 'preservation' processes. In addition, the Panel does not consider that any inferences that are useful for the purposes of our interpretation of the concession contained in heading 02.10 of the EC Schedule can be drawn from the structure of Chapter 2 of the EC Schedule nor from other parts of the EC Schedule other than the fact that they do not indicate that Chapter 2, including heading 02.10, is necessarily characterized by the notion of long-term preservation. In conclusion, it is the Panel's view that an examination of these various aspects of the EC Schedule does not clarify the ordinary meaning of the term 'salted' in the concession contained in heading 02.10 of the EC Schedule. (Underlining added)

The Panel then turns to the terms and structure of the HS, the Explanatory Notes to the HS, and other parties' schedules, with similar results:

> 7.205 ... Therefore, we consider that the evolution of the terms and structure of Chapter 2 of the HS does not clarify the ordinary meaning of the concession contained in heading 02.10 of the EC Schedule. Further, it is the Panel's view that the terms and structure of the HS do not indicate that the concession contained in heading 02.10 is necessarily characterized by the notion of long-term preservation. (Underlining added)
>
> 7.223 ... we consider that the Explanatory Notes to the HS do not clarify the ordinary meaning of the term 'salted' in the concession contained in heading 02.10 of the EC Schedule. Further, it is our view that the Explanatory Notes do not indicate that that concession is necessarily characterized by the notion of long-term preservation. (Footnote omitted, underlining added)
>
> 7.244 To the extent that the terms of the relevant concessions in other WTO Members' schedules are identical to the terms of the concession contained in heading 02.10 of the EC Schedule and of the HS, we do not consider that they can assist us any further in the analysis we have undertaken thus far. (Underlining added)

The AB frames the significance of 'context' in this dispute in the following terms:

> 209. Therefore, we need to determine whether the context of the term 'salted' – or other elements of the customary rules of treaty interpretation – require or permit a reading of the term 'salted' in heading 02.10 of the EC Schedule more narrowly than the ordinary meaning of that term suggests; that is to say, that the customary rules of treaty interpretation other than 'ordinary meaning'

indicate that 'salting' under heading 02.10 contemplates exclusively the notion of 'preservation'.

The AB first examines the words in heading 02.10 that describe treatments other than salting. Even if disagreeing with the Panel's view that 'in brine' excludes preservation, the AB basically agrees with the Panel's findings that preservation is not a requirement for a product to be 'dried, in brine, and smoked':

> 212 ... We note that the dictionary meaning of the term 'to dry' is, in relevant part, 'to remove the moisture from by wiping, evaporation, draining; preserve (food, etc.) by the removal of its natural moisture'; in turn, the dictionary meaning of the term 'to smoke' is to 'dry or cure (meat, fish, etc.) by exposure to smoke'. The ordinary meanings of these terms suggest that the relevant processes can be applied to meat in various ways and degrees of intensity, thereby producing different effects on the meat, effects that may or may not place the meat in a state of 'preservation'. Nor are we persuaded by the European Communities' argument that the terms 'dried' and 'smoked', in the present context, 'concern [exclusively] means to preserve'. It is clear from the evidence on the record that, while the processes mentioned in heading 02.10 – 'salted, dried, in brine and smoked' – may include the notion of 'preservation', these processes are also used extensively to confer special characteristics on meat products. Similar reasoning may also be valid with respect to the term 'smoked'. (Footnotes omitted)

The AB then goes on to consider whether the structure of Chapter 2 of the EC Schedule and the HS support a reading of heading 02.10 as referring *exclusively* to processes of preservation.

> 217. We note that heading 02.10 does not make reference to refrigeration. By contrast, other headings of Chapter 2 – that is, headings 02.01 to 02.09 – refer to freezing and chilling. The European Communities argues that (i) this circumstance implies that refrigeration is of 'little or no importance' for heading 02.10, and that (ii) the reason for this is that these products are 'preserved' by the processes mentioned in heading 02.10. The European Communities uses this argument to support its view that heading 02.10 covers *exclusively* meats that have been 'preserved' by the processes referred to in that heading. (Footnote omitted)
>
> 218 ... In our view, whether a product has been frozen or not will not influence whether that product falls under heading 02.10 ... [But] it does not follow from the absence of refrigeration in the text of heading 02.10 that the processes referred to in heading 02.10 must *necessarily* place the meat in a state of 'preservation'. (Underlining added)

The AB also examines Chapter and Explanatory Notes to the HS, and while criticizing the Panel on certain scores basically arrives at the same overall conclusion:

> 229 ... we conclude that the Harmonized System and the relevant Chapter and Explanatory Notes thereto do not support the view that heading 02.10 is

> characterised *exclusively* by the concept of preservation. Furthermore, the term 'salted' in heading 02.10, when considered in its context, suggests that meat to which salt has been added, so that its character has been altered, will be 'salted' within the meaning of heading 02.10, even if such salting does not place such meat in a state of 'preservation'. Heading 02.10 of the Harmonized System, read in its context, suggests that it is neither limited to, nor excludes, meat that is 'prepared' by salting or that has been 'preserved' by salting. Specifically, for resolving this dispute, heading 02.10 does not contain a *requirement* that salting must, by itself, ensure 'preservation'.

As a result, the AB upholds the Panel's findings that the context of the term 'salted' in heading 02.10 does not exclusively refer to long-term preservation.

4.2 Discussion

The adjudicating bodies discuss context separately from object and purpose. First, in the discussion of context, the adjudicating bodies look at the methods of treating meat other than salting under heading 02.10 – in brine, drying, smoking – to determine whether there is a common element of long-term preservation reflected in this choice of treatments of meat. The adjudicating bodies then examine whether the EC classification principle can be implemented in a manner that is consistent with the object and purpose of the treaty.

It can be noted that the Panel and the AB fail to see any logic in the grouping of 'salted' with the other criteria that are listed in heading 02.10. For instance, the Panel states:

> 7.180 ... In conclusion, it is the Panel's view that an examination of these various aspects of the EC Schedule does not clarify the ordinary meaning of the term 'salted' in the concession contained in heading 02.10 of the EC Schedule.

We find it somewhat odd that the adjudicating bodies are content with this, having decided not to rely more heavily on advice by the WCO with regard to the classification issue. Should not their inability to detect logic to the grouping of these various kinds of treatments have impelled them to look deeper for the rationale behind the structure of the HS in this regard?

From an economic point of view, the customs classification of the product at issue should be determined in light of what the parties seek to achieve through the agreement. Such an analysis should in particular take account of the reason why the parties agreed to have different tariffs for headings 02.07 and 02.10, and how the classification affects the achievement of this purpose. Admittedly, there is no economic theory that directly deals with the principles of customs classification, at least to the best of our knowledge. But we believe that a discussion of the economic relationship between the product at issue and those falling under the two headings could still have shed some light on how to classify the chicken cuts. We are not able to undertake an analysis of the appropriate customs classification here, however, but we will just very briefly discuss some aspects that we believe would likely arise in a more thorough investigation.

In order to discuss the appropriate tariff classification of the chicken cuts, we first need to determine why the parties chose to have different tariffs under the two headings. This, in turn, requires an explanation of why the parties found it suitable to allow tariffs at all. There are, generally speaking, several reasons why an agreement may allow tariffs. For instance, for some countries tariffs may be important sources of government revenue. In the case of the EC, however, the most plausible reason seems to be that the tariffs under the two headings are meant to protect local production, and thereby indirectly the incomes and employment of certain groups of producers of competing chicken cuts. The negotiating stance of the EC suggests that the EC finds the benefit from this protection to outweigh the cost in terms of, for example, consumer welfare in the EC. Against this motive for positive tariffs on certain products stand, of course, the interests of exporters to the EC, who would prefer to compete with local EC producers without the disadvantage of tariffs. But despite the latter adverse effects, the parties agreed to allow for positive tariffs. This illustrates the more general point that it may be efficient to let an agreement feature positive tariffs on certain products, if the gain to the importing country is sufficiently large relative to the costs to the exporters.[1,2]

The issue of customs classification arises due to two fundamental circumstances. First, there is no perfect, one-to-one match between each imported product and a customs classification heading. There are probably several reasons why classification schemes such as the HS do not have such a fine distinction between products. One obvious reason is, of course, that it would be enormously costly to maintain such a system. To start with, it would require extremely elaborate product descriptions, including an uncountable number of tariff lines. Also, the negotiations would be tremendously complicated if one were to use the flexibility that such a system would permit. If for no other reasons, actual trade agreements use a much courser classification scheme.

Second, for a conflict over customs classification to arise, there needs to be a difference across tariff lines in the tariffs they stipulate (or in some other factor affecting the conditions for importation). Again, one can think of several reasons why this would be the case. It may be explained by the fact that imports under the two headings affect different domestic constituencies, and these differ in the extent to which they are harmed by the imports, or in their political clout.

1 'Efficient' is here used in the economic sense of the term, and very roughly refers to a situation where it would not be possible to reduce the tariff on chicken cuts and in return undertake some compensatory change in other tariff levels so as to make all parties to the agreement better off.

2 Note for what follows that since a negotiated agreement reflects a trade-off between exporter and importer interests, a stronger protectionist preference with regard to a certain import on part of the importing-country government (the EC, in this case) should be reflected in a higher tariff for given preferences of exporting-country governments (Brazil and Thailand). But this is not to say that the importer's (EC's) preferences solely determine the economically appropriate classification, only that they influence this.

Another reason, which we perhaps find more plausible on the basis of our admittedly very limited understanding of the factual circumstances in the dispute, is that the tariffs under both headings are meant to protect essentially the same domestic interests, but that products with the two types of characteristics pose in different ways strong competitive threats to the interests the tariffs are to protect.[3]

In the case of the product at issue in *Chicken Cuts*, we note first that it seems plausible that the cost of salting constitutes a very small proportion of total production costs, even when the salt suffices for 'long-term' preservation. Hence, such salting will not drive up exporters' costs enough to shield EC producers from competition to any considerable degree. Nor does the salting imply that the exporters have introduced a new, lower-cost production technique. If this were the case, it might have been efficient to let the exports enter under the lower tariff, despite the resulting damage to certain EC producers, since the exporters would then be able to compensate the EC for the damage, and still gain from the lower tariff treatment. There thus does not seem to be a cost-based reason for giving the salted chicken cuts a more favorable tariff treatment than the unsalted ones.

Turning to the demand side, if salt is added to improve the taste, the demand for the product would presumably be higher than it would be absent the salting. The product at issue would thus be a more severe competitive threat than the corresponding product under heading 02.07 due to the improved taste, and should, if anything, face a higher tariff in order to protect local producers.[4] This reasoning would hence suggest that to the extent the product at issue is only salted for seasoning purposes, there is a presumption that it should go under heading 02.07.

A case for a lower tariff on the product at issue than the one provided for under 02.07 would thus have to be based on it having a *dis*advantage on the demand side relative to the chicken cuts coming in under 02.07. We are not certain here about the factual aspects, but we assume that salting chicken enough so that it withstands transportation, storage, etc., will reduce the attractiveness of the product to buyers, and will thus tend to reduce the demand. If so, chicken cuts that are salted

3 The consequence of having a classification scheme that is coarser than the differentiation of products is that tariffs cannot be fully 'fine-tuned' in an agreement – the protection that the tariffs provide will, in this sense, be blunter than what the importer would prefer. As a side remark, we note that there is a parallel between the question of how to group products in a customs classification scheme and how to understand the 'likeness' notion in National Treatment (NT), in particular. First, in both instances, the question concerns how to select products that are to be given an identical policy treatment; second, both NT and a coarse-classification scheme serve to reduce contracting costs; and, third, the saving of contracting costs tend to be associated with costs in terms of misallocation of resources, since the tax/tariff structure becomes less fine-tuned to the preferences of the parties.

4 This discussion disregards the fact that a more attractive product will also have more of a value to EC consumers, which would tend to reduce the negotiated tariff. We presume that the effect pointed at in the main text dominates this consideration.

for preservation purposes would constitute less of a competitive threat to EC producers, thus providing one possible explanation of why a more favorable tariff treatment is appropriate. We can here note the statement by the EC, as summarized by the Panel, that:

> 7.310 ... [The EC] satisfied itself with significantly lower tariffs on salted products because it was aware that few products were traded on an international basis under that heading ... had it imagined that frozen chicken with added salt could have been classified under heading 02.10, it would never have set such a low tariff. (Footnote omitted)

It thus does not seem inconceivable that one could erect a plausible demand-based argument for treating chicken cuts that are salted for long-term preservation more favorably than chicken cuts that contain less salt. This would seem to fit with the difference in tariff levels between headings 02.07 and 02.10, and would thus tend to support the EC claim.

Can a similar logic be found with regard to the other characteristics under these headings – 'in brine', 'dried', and 'smoked'? Here we have to be even more speculative. But it seems unlikely that putting meat 'in brine' improves the demand for the meat, if anything the opposite. Hence, by the same logic, a lower tariff may be warranted. The 'dried' and 'smoked' attributes are more complicated. On the one hand, both these types of products have a more limited range of use, and the production also tends to be costly. Both these factors suggest that products coming under this heading pose a more limited competitive threat compared to the products that are just frozen, chilled, or fresh, thus reinforcing the picture given above. On the other hand, the processes of smoking and drying may, in some cases, increase the value of the products to consumers, seemingly in contrast to the distinction described above.

Note that the point of the discussion here is not to advocate any particular interpretation of the EC schedule – this would require a much more thorough investigation than we have been able to undertake. The point is instead to explain why we believe that when examining the appropriate customs classification of this product, the adjudicating bodies should somewhere along the line have confronted the basic questions of (i) why did the parties agree to make the tariff distinctions with regard to the product characteristics listed under the two headings?, and (ii) how should the product at issue be seen from this perspective? After all, the agreement gives a form of legal protection or sanction to the use of tariffs, and this must be due to the fact that the Members have found the use of tariffs valuable enough to explicitly agree to allow for their use. In order to determine whether the product at issue should be classified under one or the other HS heading, it would therefore be natural to consider the role the tariffs play, why they differ across headings, and how the classification in this case may help achieve this objective while taking into account exporter interests. We see little consideration of this in the present dispute.

It should also be noted that a consequence of the adjudicating bodies' failure to take into consideration what objective the higher tariff on products entering under heading 02.07 was meant to achieve, is that *the 'salted' criterion for the lower tariff treatment has been rendered essentially meaningless*: The interpretation of 'salted' endorsed by the Appellate Body would, in theory at least, compel the European authorities to provide a significantly lower rate of duty to any meat that has been treated with salt, even minimally. Consequently, an exporter who wants to compete in the frozen-chicken market only has to find a way to treat the product with salt without affecting its suitability for that market in order to circumvent the higher protection afforded by Europe to domestic industries competing in that market. We are not suggesting that we have actual evidence of such behavior by Brazilian and Thai exporters, just that the possibility for such behavior now seems to exist.

Finally, we note that the limited number of questions the Panel asks the WCO concerning customs classification practices are not very helpful for resolving the issue. This is partly due to the way the questions are formulated, and partly to the answers provided. The question that most directly concerns the principle behind the customs classification system is the following:

> What is the rationale behind the product coverage of the 4-digit heading and the 6-digit-heading levels in the Harmonized System?

The WCO responds by first giving a few details about earlier nomenclatures that affected the structure of the HS. The only information provided by the WCO that more directly answers the question is the following statement, which refers to these sources of the HS:

> Consequently, the rationale behind the product coverage in the HS was to meet the needs of those involved in international trade by including goods or groups of goods with a significant volume of international trade, taking into consideration the structure of the nomenclatures consulted. (Panel Report p. C-135, underlining added and footnote omitted)

We cannot determine the correctness of this statement. But it does seem unlikely to exhaust the issue. Also, as a marginal note, the method of including products for which there is a large volume of trade would tend to exclude from the system products with very high tariffs (and consequently little trade). Was this really what happened?

5. WCO General Rule 3

We have already alluded to the fact that there are rules in the WCO to deal with certain problems of application and interpretation of HS classifications – the 'General Rules for Interpretation of the Harmonized System'. In their discussion of context, the adjudicating bodies address the applicability of these rules in the instant dispute, and, in particular, General Rule 3, which addresses situations where goods are prima facie classifiable under two headings. The latter states in pertinent parts:

> When by application of Rule 2(b) or for any other reason, goods are, *prima facie*, classifiable under two or more headings, classification shall be effected as follows:
>
> (a) The heading which provides the most specific description shall be preferred to headings providing a more general description. However, when two or more headings each refer to part only of the materials or substances contained in mixed or composite goods or to part only of the items in a set put up for retail sale, those headings are to be regarded as equally specific in relation to those goods, even if one of them gives a more complete or precise description of the goods.
>
> ...
>
> (c) When goods cannot be classified by reference to 3(a) or 3(b), they shall be classified under the heading which occurs last in numerical order among those which equally merit consideration.

5.1 The adjudicating bodies' findings

According to the Panel, this rule is inapplicable in the instant dispute, despite the contradictory claims by the parties concerning the correct classification. The Panel here relies on the arguments of the parties:

> 7.227 With respect to General Rule 3, Brazil, Thailand and the European Communities concur that the condition for its application – namely, that the products at issue are prima facie classifiable under two or more headings – has not been fulfilled in this case. The complainants consider that the products at issue are classifiable under heading 02.10 whereas the European Communities considers that the products at issue are classifiable under heading 02.07. (Footnote omitted)

As a consequence, General Rule 3 should not be applied:

> 7.238 As regards the question of whether or not General Rule 3 applies, all the parties appear to be in agreement that a textual and contextual analysis of the relevant headings indicates that the products at issue in this dispute are not prima facie classifiable under two or more headings. Accordingly, we will proceed on the same assumption with the result that we will not apply General Rule 3....

The AB's entire treatment of General Rule 3 is the following:

> 231. We now turn to consider the General Rules for the Interpretation of the Harmonized System (the 'General Rules'). We recall that the Panel found that:
>
> ... all the parties appear to be in agreement that a textual and contextual analysis of the relevant headings indicates that the products at issue in this dispute are not prima facie classifiable under two or more headings. Accordingly, we will

> proceed on the same assumption with the result that we will not apply General Rule 3. Given our conclusion that General Rule 3 is inapplicable, we do not consider it necessary to address the various arguments that have been advanced by the parties regarding that Rule. (Footnote omitted)
>
> 232. Brazil and Thailand appeal this finding. Both argue that the Panel incorrectly found that the parties were in agreement that General Rule 3 was inapplicable in this case. Brazil also requests that the Appellate Body complete the analysis and find that the products at issue are classifiable under heading 02.10 by virtue of General Rule 3(a) or by virtue of General Rule 3(c). (Footnote omitted)
>
> 233. We note that the General Rules are, by their very name, rules for the *interpretation* of the Harmonized System. Specifically, General Rule 3 deals with the question of classification in circumstances in which goods are *prima facie* 'classifiable' under two or more headings.
>
> 234. We recall that the task of the Panel, as well as of the Appellate Body upon appeal, is to determine whether the European Communities has acted consistently with Article II:1(a) and with Article II:1(b) of the GATT 1994 with respect to the products at issue. Therefore, in our view, the primary task of the Panel, as well as of the Appellate Body, is to determine the meaning and scope of the concession contained in heading 02.10 of the EC Schedule. In our view, it is only after properly determining the meaning and scope of the tariff commitment in heading 02.10 that the question whether the products at issue are *prima facie* classifiable under two or more headings can arise. General Rule 3 is relevant in this case only for the *second* step, namely, under which heading a product is properly classified. It is therefore not necessary for us to consider, at this stage, General Rule 3. (Footnote omitted, underlining added)

Having stated this, the AB does not find it necessary to get back to this issue in its report.

5.2 Discussion

There are several aspects of the adjudicating bodies' reasoning in this context that we find puzzling.

A first difficulty we have is the fact that the Panel effectively reads into the term prima facie a requirement of a shared perception of the situation among the parties. If this was the intention behind the rule, presumably this would have been made explicit by the drafters of the HS. Also, such a reading significantly reduces the ambit of the rule, since there will presumably be relatively few instances where there is such an agreement. Moreover, it removes from the arsenal a main instrument for resolving a conflict over classification.

This is not to say that we believe that General Rule 3 provides a good way of resolving this kind of dispute, only that it seems applicable, given the situation. It is true that not all Members of the WTO are bound by the WCO treaty or are members of the World Customs Organization (WCO); however, all WTO

Members have used the HS of the WCO in tariff negotiations and the resultant schedules, which are bound under the GATT. Would it not be the common expectation of all WTO Members, therefore, that the meaning of the schedules in question be decided through the application of rules governing the HS itself and the practice of the international organization that is the guardian of the HS?[5] The Panel accepts that the HS rules and related WCO practice are relevant to resolving the dispute but for some reason refuses to provide a clear legal theory as to why they are relevant, refusing to indicate whether the HS is 'context' within the meaning of 31(2)(b) of the VCLT or rather a relevant rule of international law 'applicable between the parties' within the meaning of 31(3)(c).

Second, the dismissal by the Panel of the General Rule is, in some sense, internally consistent, even if, in our view, based on erroneous reasoning. We find the approach by the AB more peculiar, however. The AB does not exclude the applicability of the rule, but instead says that it first has to address whether the product fits under heading 02.10. On this logic, the Panel having found the products at issue indeed to be classifiable under 02.10 would have had to go on and examine whether they were also classifiable under 02.07, and if the answer were also positive, at that point the Panel would need to apply the General Rule. Oddly, although *accepting* (unlike the Panel) the possibility that the Rule may be applicable *and* upholding the Panel's finding that the products are classifiable under 02.10, the AB does *not* fault the Panel for *not* proceeding to the next logical step in ascertaining whether to apply the rule, namely considering whether the products are *also* classifiable under 02.07. We simply cannot understand how the Panel could have made a proper determination of whether to apply the rule unless it proceeded to that second step. In sum, while we agree with the AB's finding that the rule may be applicable, we see incoherence or contradiction in the AB's failure to correct the Panel for not taking all necessary steps to determine whether the conditions for applying the rule existed in the case at hand.

The AB does not explain why it does not evaluate the possibility that the product at issue is classifiable under heading 02.07. The AB does argue, in footnote 443, that the interpretation of the concept 'prima facie' is unresolved:

> We note that General Rule 3 refers to circumstances in which a product is '*prima facie*' classifiable under two or more headings. In this respect, nothing on the Panel record indicates how the term '*prima facie*' has been interpreted by the WCO's Harmonized System Committee, or the WCO itself.

But are there not sufficient indications in the dispute that the appropriate classification of the product at issue is unclear, and that therefore one need

5 In the *Oil Platforms* case, the International Court of Justice considered that, in determining whether a national security provision of a trade treaty between the US and Iran should be read in light of the general international law of the use of force, the reasonable expectations of the parties were the logical beginning point. *Case Concerning Oil Platforms* (*Islamic Republic of Iran* v. *United States of America*), merits, November 6, 2003, opinion of the Court.

consider whether, prima facie, both headings could apply? For instance, the AB continues the same footnote by providing evidence suggesting that the classification of the product at hand is an unresolved issue:

> However, according to information provided by the WCO Secretariat to the Panel, the Harmonized System Committee has not, so far, considered classification issues related to headings 02.07 and 02.10. (WCO's response to Question 8 posed by the Panel, Panel Reports, p. C-139) Furthermore, the WCO did not provide specific guidance to the Panel as to the meaning of the term 'specific', so as to determine the 'most specific description' within the meaning of General Rule 3(a) for purposes of the present dispute; according to the WCO, heading 02.07 could be considered more 'specific' due to the term 'poultry', but, at the same time, heading 02.10 could be considered more 'specific' by virtue of the term 'salted'. (Panel Reports, para. 7.235) We also note that the participants do not argue that General Rule 3(b) is applicable to the dispute at hand. (Underlining added)

Furthermore, the WCO argues in the above-quoted footnote that the classification is not self-evident, at least not as it concerns the question of the degree of specificity in the two headings. To quote the Panel report:

> 7.235 The WCO states that, for the purposes of General Rule 3(a), it could be argued that heading 02.07 of the HS provides the more 'specific' description since it refers to 'meat of poultry, frozen', whereas heading 02.10 of the HS refers to 'meat, salted', in general. However, the WCO states that it could also be argued that the reference to the specific type of meat (poultry) in heading 02.07 should not be taken into consideration since it is the processing (freezing and salting) that matters when determining the classification of the products at issue in this case, giving rise to a possibility of heading 02.10 providing a more specific description. (Footnote omitted)

But could it not be argued that if a main tie-breaker for customs classification issues – General Rule 3(a) – cannot resolve the question concerning classification, there is at least prima facie a possibility that the product could be classified under two separate headings?

This goes to a basic question of the nature of state responsibility under Article II of the GATT, where the defending Member's customs classification practices are at issue. It is arguable that where more than one possible classification is reasonable, and WCO rules and practice do not dictate the use of one or the other, a WTO Member has some margin of discretion for determining which classification to apply to a particular product. In other words, the nature of the obligation in Article II, inasmuch as it applies to customs classification practices by individual Members, might well be to classify products in a reasonable, objective, and non-discriminatory manner, consistent with WCO rules and practice. The Panel and AB approach to Article II suggests that there must be a single, correct way in which to classify every product in terms of the HS classifications and that the

Article II obligation implies that a WTO Member must follow this single, correct way. This implicit view of state responsibility – a crucial issue that is not addressed *explicitly* by either the Panel or the AB – seems at odds with the very nature of the classification problem pointed out in Section 4.2 above: namely that for transaction-cost reasons it is impossible to have a separate customs classification number for each conceivable product that countries may want to identify. Instead, classification schemes will always leave ample room for groups of different products to fall under the same classification number – the classification scheme will, in this sense, always be 'coarse'. This inevitable coarseness implies that any classification scheme will be plagued by many ambiguities in terms of whether a particular 'variant' is to be slotted into one (relatively crude or fine) classification or another.

In deciding *what* is the prima facie case that the complainant must make in a case such as this in order to discharge its burden of proof, it is necessary to take some view as to the nature of state responsibility. Our analysis of the basic nature of the problem of customs classification – the inevitable coarseness of such schemes – would suggest that, in this instance, the prima facie case must be that the EC choice *between* 02.10 and 02.07 is unreasonable, discriminatory, contrary to WCO rules and practice, or otherwise not in accord with the common intentions of the parties and/or the WTO Membership in agreeing to schedules. If General Rule 3 could be applied so as to determine the clear answer as to which of the two headings is to be applied, then arguably the EC was required to so apply the rule; thus, one way of the complainant discharging its burden of proof would be to show that a proper application of General Rule 3 would yield a choice of classification different from the one adopted by the EC.

6. Object and purpose

Having concluded that neither the ordinary meanings of words as such, nor the interpretation of these words in light of their context, supports the EC claim that salted chicken cuts have to contain enough salt to be preserved in order to qualify for the tariff treatment under heading 02.10, the Panel and the AB turn to the question of whether the 'object and purpose' of the agreement sheds light on the issue.

6.1 The adjudicating bodies' findings

According to the Panel, the object and purpose of the WTO Agreement:

> 7.320 Taken together, the relevant aspects of the WTO Agreement and the GATT 1994 indicate that concessions made by WTO Members should be interpreted so as to further the general objective of the expansion of trade in goods and the substantial reduction of tariffs ... In other words, the terms of a concession should not be interpreted in such a way that would disrupt the balance of concessions negotiated by the parties. Finally, the interpretation must ensure

the security and predictability of the reciprocal and mutually advantageous arrangements manifested in the form of concessions.

7.321 ... the question has arisen in this case as to whether the interpretation of the concession contained in heading 02.10 of the EC Schedule to include a long-term preservation criterion could undermine this objective. In this regard ... it is necessary to look exclusively at the 'objective characteristics' of the product in question when presented for classification at the border ... As regards the present case, the WCO surmises that laboratory analyses might be required to determine whether a product can be regarded as 'salted' within the meaning of heading 02.10 of the HS. (Footnote omitted)

7.322 ... despite questioning by the Panel and by Brazil, the European Communities has not provided the Panel with any clear idea of what is meant by 'long-term preservation' in practice ... [I]f a product arrives at the EC border that is salted and then frozen, (as in the case of the products at issue), the Panel questions how a customs officer at the border tasked with identifying the appropriate heading under which the product should be classified is to know whether: (a) the product has been preserved for the long-term; and (b) if so, whether the long-term preservation is the result of salting, freezing or a combination of the two. While the first question may be addressed through laboratory analyses, which the European Communities states that it conducts when necessary, it is far from clear to us how the answer to the second question will be determined. Yet, without a means to determine the answer to the second question, the customs officer will not be in a position to know whether the product in question should be classified under heading 02.10 (i.e., because the long-term preservation is attributable to the salting) or under heading 02.07 (because the long-term preservation is attributable to the freezing). (Underlining added, footnotes omitted)

The Panel concludes that the difficulty for customs officers to classify products means that the outcome is hard to predict and that this makes it violate GATT:

7.323 In the Panel's view, the lack of certainty associated with the application of the criterion of long-term preservation with respect to the concession contained in heading 02.10 of the EC Schedule runs counter to one of the objects and purposes of both the WTO Agreement and the GATT 1994, namely that the security and predictability of the reciprocal and mutually advantageous arrangements must be preserved. Therefore, the Panel concludes that an interpretation of the term 'salted' in the concession contained in heading 0.210 of the EC Schedule to include the criterion of long-term preservation could undermine the object and purpose of security and predictability, which lies at the heart of the WTO Agreement and the GATT 1994.

Turning to the AB, it notes a potentially important objection by the EC to the Panel's reasoning:

245. The European Communities contends that the Panel misrepresented the criterion of preservation, because EC Regulation 1223/2002 and EC Decision

> 2003/97/EC do not, in fact, apply a 'criterion of long-term preservation' but, instead, treat chicken cuts with a salt content of up to 3 per cent as falling under heading 02.07 rather than heading 02.10. (Footnote omitted)

The AB notes that there is nothing wrong in principle with a preservation criterion in the HS:

> 246 ... we consider that the Harmonized System does not preclude the use of a criterion of preservation, as such ... the application of such a criterion would not necessarily be in conflict with the objectives of security and predictability of the *WTO Agreement* and the GATT 1994 (including Schedules of tariff commitments). (Underlining added)

The AB recalls one of the problems the Panel found with the preservation criterion:

> 247 ... However, it was unclear to the Panel whether preservation for the long-term had to be the result of salting, or freezing, or a combination of the two. (Footnote omitted)

The AB notes that this issue is effectively resolved by the EC. But for the AB there remains a concern about the second problem, in that the EC has not explained how the separate preservation effect of salting could be determined. There is consequently uncertainty concerning the criterion that is actually applied to evaluate the preservation effect:

> 248. Although the European Communities clarifies that, for purposes of heading 02.10 of the EC Schedule, preservation has to be the result of the processes mentioned in that heading and not of the processes listed under heading 02.07 (namely, chilling, freezing), it does not explain how, in respect of frozen and salted meat, the preservation effect of the processes listed in heading 02.10 could be distinguished from the processes listed in heading 02.07. Therefore, we share the Panel's concern about the lack of certainty in the application of the preservation criterion used by the European Communities regarding the tariff commitment under heading 02.10 of the EC Schedule. (Underlining added, footnote omitted)

This uncertainty is detrimental to the object and purpose of the agreement:

> 249. In the light of these considerations, we see no reason to disturb the Panel's finding, in paragraph 7.328 of the Panel Reports, that 'the lack of certainty associated with the application of the criterion of long-term preservation with respect to the concession contained in heading 02.10 of the EC Schedule ... could undermine the object and purpose of security and predictability, which [underlie] both the WTO Agreement and the GATT 1994'.

6.2 *Discussion*

There are two aspects of the adjudicating bodies' object and purpose analysis that we would like to highlight.

The *first* issue concerns the sense in which the EC measure is found to contradict the object and purpose of the WTO Agreement. It appears as if the Panel (and the AB seems to follow the Panel in this regard) oscillates between two different interpretations of the notions of predictability and security for the object and purpose of the agreement. In its analysis under object and purpose, summarized above, the focus is on the alleged *uncertainty* of the outcome of the new customs classification procedure. However, the Panel in its concluding Section jumps to another problem involving the object and purpose of the agreement. The two final paragraphs of the Panel Report subsection 'Conclusions regarding the application of Article II of the GATT 1994 in this case', where the Panel summarizes its findings, state that:

> 7.426 It is the Panel's view that the products at issue are covered by the concession contained in heading 02.10 of the EC Schedule. Therefore, such products are entitled to treatment provided for by that concession. Since the products at issue are not being accorded such treatment, the European Communities is in violation of Article II:1(a) and Article II:1(b) of the GATT 1994.
>
> 7.427 In reaching this conclusion, the Panel recalls that a fundamental object and purpose of the WTO Agreement and the GATT 1994 is that the security and predictability of reciprocal and mutually advantageous arrangements must be preserved. In the Panel's view, <u>a Member's unilateral intention regarding the meaning to be ascribed to a concession</u> that Member has made in the context of WTO multilateral trade negotiations cannot prevail over the common intentions of all WTO Members as determined through an analysis undertaken pursuant to Articles 31 and 32 of the Vienna Convention. (Underlining added)

As can be seen here, in finding that the EC violates Article II, the Panel heavily leans on the reduced security and predictability that the measure is found to cause. Note, however, that the Panel now seems to refer to the *unilateral nature* of the EC's imposition of its interpretation of the schedule, rather than to the uncertainty as to the customs classification outcome. However, this reference to unilateralism begs the question of whether one can establish that the interpretation in question is somehow contrary to the *common* intentions of the parties. The fact that, when one applies WCO rules and practice, the EC choice of the one classification over the other does not obviously appear to be impermissible or unreasonable, indicates that while 'unilateral' in the trivial sense that all customs administration is normally 'unilateral', the EC classification decision does not violate any established common expectations or intentions of the WTO Membership or the parties to the dispute.

The *second* aspect of the finding under object and purpose that we would like to point to is the uncertainty that the adjudicating bodies are concerned with. As is clear from para. 248 of the AB report, the alleged source of the uncertainty is the difficulty in distinguishing the effect of freezing from the effect of salting on long-term preservation. What is not sufficiently explained, however, is the reason *why* this would be difficult. Is the problem that one cannot tell whether a defrosted chicken cut is salted enough for long-term preservation? Or is it that the notion of 'long-term' is left undefined? Or is there some other problem?

The determination invites several questions on this score. For instance, what if the EC had used a minimum quantitative threshold as a surrogate for the criterion of preservation? In other words, the EC might have established a new minimum salt requirement, which reflected the minimum quantity of salt that would be needed, as a general rule, in order for a product to be effectively preserved in the long term through treatment by salt. Although such a criterion might be somewhat crude – as such a level would, in any given case, likely not always perfectly reflect the exact quantity needed for preservation – it would provide a bright-line standard that supported predictability and certainty in the application of tariffs. The AB is unclear as to whether a bright-line quantitative threshold to limit the ambit of 02.10 to products salted for preservation would still violate Article II GATT inasmuch as there is no intrinsic reason to consider 02.10 as limited by the concept of preservation. In other words, the legal weight attached to the question of administrability remains unclear.

Or, to consider another modification, what if the procedure is altered such that it *always* results in the higher tariff under heading 02.07? This would presumably take care of the problem with uncertainty, since the outcome is now completely foreseeable. Would this modification mean that the measure no longer threatens the 'object and purpose' of the agreement?

In any case, we note that customs regulations are subject to the transparency requirements in Art. X GATT, which have recently been the subject of an important AB judgment (*EC–Customs Practices*). Arguably, the issue of the administrability of the 'preservation' standard is more appropriately addressed under Art. X:(3)(b) GATT, which requires that, 'Each contracting party shall administer in a uniform, impartial and reasonable manner all its laws, regulations, decisions and rulings' pertaining inter alia to customs classification.

7. Subsequent practice

In the *EC – LAN Equipment* case, the AB held, pursuant to Art. 31:(3)(b) VCLT, that subsequent practice in tariff classification by WTO Members was relevant to the interpretation of a tariff schedule but only to the extent that it revealed the *common* intention of the parties (para. 90). Thus, the subsequent practice of only one WTO Member would be of limited relevance. In *EC – Chicken Cuts*, the EC was the only importing WTO Member engaged in classifying the products in question for customs purposes. Nevertheless, the Panel found that the consistent practice of the EC in classifying the products in question under 2.10 prior to 2002 constituted relevant 'subsequent practice' establishing the common intent of the parties. The Panel based its conclusion on the notion that the acquiescence of other WTO Members established that the practice of the EC, during this period, reflected the common intentions of WTO Members. The AB saw this logic as at odds with its understanding of common intentions in *EC– LAN Equipment* and reversed the Panel:

> 259 ... To our mind, it would be difficult to establish a 'concordant, common and discernible pattern' on the basis of acts or pronouncements of one, or very few parties to a multilateral treaty, such as the *WTO Agreement*. We acknowledge, however, that, if only some WTO Members have actually traded or classified products under a given heading, this circumstance may reduce the availability of such 'acts and pronouncements' for purposes of determining the existence of 'subsequent practice' within the meaning of Article 31(3)(b).
>
> 262 ... although this dispute concerns the scope of a tariff commitment contained in the WTO Schedule specific to the European Communities, the relevant headings are common to all WTO Members.
>
> 266 ... we fail to see how the Panel's finding that it was 'reasonable to rely upon EC classification practice alone in determining whether or not there is 'subsequent practice' that 'establishes the agreement' of WTO Members within the meaning of Article 31(3)(b)' can be reconciled with these statements of the Appellate Body in *EC–Computer Equipment.* (Footnote omitted)
>
> 270. In our view, as the Panel examined only a subset of salted meat products classifiable under heading 02.10, and it did not examine classification practice with respect to alternative headings such as heading 02.07, it could not draw valid conclusions as to the existence of 'subsequent practice' establishing the agreement of the parties within the meaning of Article 31(3)(b) with respect to all salted meat products potentially covered by the tariff commitment under heading 02.10 of the EC Schedule. (Underlining added)
>
> 272 ... We, therefore, disagree with the Panel that 'subsequent practice' under Article 31(3)(b) has been established by virtue of the fact that the Panel '[had] not been provided any evidence to indicate that WTO Members protested against the EC classification practice in question from 1996–2002'. (Footnote omitted)
>
> 273 ... 'lack of reaction' should not lightly, without further inquiry into attendant circumstances of a case, be read to imply agreement with an interpretation by treaty parties that have not themselves engaged in a particular practice followed by other parties in the application of the treaty.
>
> 276. For the reasons set out above, we *reverse* the Panel's interpretation and application of the concept of 'subsequent practice' within the meaning of Article 31(3)(b) of the *Vienna Convention*; consequently, the Panel's conclusions, in paragraphs 7.289–7.290 and 7.303 of the Panel Reports, that the European Communities' practice of classifying, between 1996 and 2002, the products at issue under heading 02.10 of the EC Schedule 'amounts to subsequent practice'

within the meaning of Article 31(3)(b) of the *Vienna Convention* cannot stand. (Underlining added)

We believe the AB is correct in stating that one cannot, without very careful analysis of the entire context, come to the conclusion that silence concerning one Member's tariff classification practice constitutes assent to that practice. The product in question was imported only by the EC and exported only by complainants. It would be odd if other WTO Members, in these circumstances, were to pay any attention to the customs classification of these products. The logic of the Panel's approach is that one or a few WTO Members who have an original import or export interest in a product may establish an approach to classification that then becomes binding on other WTO Members who may have an import or export interest in the future; to avoid this outcome the other Members in question would have to speak out, even before they were aware that they had any import or export interest!

8. Supplementary means of interpretation

In the *EC – LAN Equipment* case, the AB found that Art. 32 VCLT may be relevant to interpretation of a WTO Member's schedule (para. 86). In particular, the AB referred to the possibility for a treaty interpreter, under Art. 32, to take into account 'circumstances of [the] conclusion of the treaty', which the AB understood to entail 'an examination of the historical background against which the treaty was negotiation' (para. 86). Art. 32 may be used either to confirm an interpretation of a treaty based on Art. 31 VCLT, to resolve ambiguity that remains after the use of Art. 31, or where the interpretation resulting from Art. 31 results in absurdity.

The historical elements considered by the Panel as 'circumstances of [the] conclusion of the treaty' included EC law and classification practice prior to and during the Uruguay Round negotiations. First of all, the Panel considered EC Regulation 535/94, which came into effect shortly prior to the conclusion of the EC Uruguay Round schedule. The Panel found: '[t]he effect of that Regulation ... was that if meat had been deeply and homogeneously impregnated with salt, with a minimum salt content of 1.2 % by weight, it would meet the requirements of that Regulation and would qualify as "salted" meat under heading 02.10 of the CN'. Second, the Panel had recourse to minutes of the EC Customs Code Committee, which the Panel held 'provide compelling evidence that the principle of long-term preservation was not included in the definition of "salted" in EC Regulation No. 535/94' (Paras. 7.365–370). Third, the Panel considered the *Dinter* and *Gausepohl* judgments by the European Court of Justice. The Panel concluded that these were of little or no assistance, since they focused on a different tariff classification (*Dinter*), or were ambiguous (*Gausepohl*) and superseded by Regulation 535/94 prior to the conclusion of the Uruguay Round. The Panel rejected the relevance of certain other historical materials, such as evidence of US tariff classification practice prior to the Uruguay Round. As for the Explanatory Notes to the EC customs code, the Panel assumed these to have been superseded by the Additional Notes to Regulation 535/94 prior to the conclusion of the Uruguay Round and hence not relevant.

On appeal, the EC challenged the Panel's use of historical background on a number of grounds. First of all, the EC argued that to be relevant under Art. 32 VCLT, an instrument or document must have had a direct influence on the treaty negotiators. The AB responded that this is too narrow a conception: the instrument or document may be relevant simply by virtue of illuminating what the negotiators' thinking or assumptions were at the time, without necessarily having influenced any actual positions or conduct in the negotiations. Second, the EC argued that to be considered as part of the 'circumstances of [the] conclusion of the treaty', the instrument or document must have a close temporal proximity to the conclusion of the negotiations. The AB considered that temporal proximity went to probative weight or relevance and that there was no specific time period beyond which a document or instrument would necessarily not qualify as part of the 'circumstances'. Third, the EC argued that in order for an instrument or document to be considered as part of the 'circumstances', it must be demonstrated that the negotiators had actual knowledge of that instrument or document. The AB rejected this argument, holding that where an instrument or document was publicly available to negotiators they could be deemed to have knowledge of it; however, the AB also noted that where actual knowledge could be shown to exist, probative weight or relevance might be greater. Fourth, the EC argued that the Panel erred in ignoring the classification practice of the United States prior to the Uruguay Round. The AB appeared to assume that, as a matter of law, practice of other WTO members would be relevant (and indeed this had been emphasized by the AB in *EC–LAN Equipment*), but deferred to the Panel judgment as a trier of fact that different products were at issue in the case of the United States and thus that the practice in question was not relevant to the dispute at hand. Fifth, the EC claimed that the Panel had erred in finding that the *Gauspohl* judgment had been superseded by Regulation 535/94; according to the EC, as a matter of internal Community law a Regulation could not supersede a ruling of the ECJ but only implement it. The AB found that it did not have to decide this question of internal Community law, because a proper reading of *Gauspohl* revealed that *Gauspohl* did not stand for the proposition that only meat salted for purposes of long-term preservation was 'salted' within the meaning of 2.10, and thus *Gauspohl* did not provide support for the EC position in any case.

It is our impression that the challenges of the EC with respect to the Panel's use of historical background as 'circumstances' are largely formalistic. They imply, generally speaking, that the exercise under Art. 32 is an extremely mechanical one, involving the a priori inclusion or exclusion of particular categories of instruments or documents using narrow criteria such as temporal proximity. But the AB is surely right that Art. 32, which deals with supplementary means of interpretation used at the discretion of the treaty interpreter (unlike the sources in Art. 31 that are obligatory), and does not claim even to exhaust what is a 'supplementary means', should not be read in this inflexible or rigid manner; the aim is to try and get a comprehensive and persuasive picture of the common assumptions and intentions of the negotiators. What kinds of instruments and documents are most relevant will be a matter of judgment and finesse, and depends on the issue and the circumstances, as indeed any actual historian would know.

If we were to take issue with any element of the Panel's and the AB's analysis, it would be with the overall conclusion that the instruments and documents in question confirm the interpretation that salting is not limited to salting for long-term preservation, merely because none of these documents sets out clearly or explicitly the limitation in question. For none of the instruments or documents explicitly rejects that limitation either, nor is in direct contradiction with such an implied assumption. The Panel and AB assumed that the EC must show explicit indications of the limitation that it claims on the meaning of salting and not that the complainants need to show evidence that such a limitation was *rejected*. It is as if, once the adjudicator had determined that the 'ordinary meaning' of 'salted' in light of context, object, and purpose is not restricted to salting for long-term preservation, the EC bears the burden of showing the existence of a special understanding to the contrary. This seems at odds with the AB's own notion of the application of the VCLT rules as a holistic exercise. However, in fairness to the AB, while Art. 32 can be used to *confirm* an interpretation under Art. 31, it is far from clear that Art. 32 could be used to displace an interpretation based on the use of the primary and obligatory means of interpretation in Art. 31.

9. Where should the dispute have been adjudicated?

EC – Chicken Cuts concerns conflicting claims about the correct tariff classification of a product that was not traded at the time of the conclusion of the Uruguay Round, but that subsequently was exported to the EC by firms in the complaining countries. At an abstract level, it is the result of contractual incompleteness. Products in general have a large number of different features: they come in different colors, weights, shape; they contain different materials; are produced through different production processes, etc. As we have discussed above, it would be extremely costly to write a tariff classification schedule with such a degree of precision that it would be crystal clear where each and every product should be classified. Instead, product descriptions are more or less vague – and thus incomplete – just like the trade agreement is incomplete in many other respects (such as the ambiguity it leaves concerning domestic instruments). The particular incompleteness at issue in *EC – Chicken Cuts* is the fact that the agreement does not explicitly state what tariff treatment the salted chicken cuts should receive. Instead, the parties to the agreement have to interpret imprecise concepts such as 'salted' in order to determine this.

When an agreement does not regulate every conceivable situation the parties may end up in, the parties have a degree of discretion with regard to their actions at least in some circumstances. The parties' expectations concerning the behavior of other parties will then tend to play an important role, and may importantly affect the willingness of parties to make concessions in the first place. This is where the notions of *good-* and *bad-faith* behavior obtain meaning. Interestingly, in the instant dispute, neither the Panel nor the AB refers to these notions at all, despite the fact that the measure must be said to concern events that are not fully accounted for in the agreement, perhaps being restricted by the arguments advanced by the parties. Of course, we have no knowledge of what provoked this particular dispute, and whether either side can be said to have acted in bad faith. But it is still interesting to contemplate more generally the different scenarios that may give rise to a dispute of this type.

One possibility is that there was a mutual understanding at the time of the completion of the Uruguay Round negotiations concerning the appropriate classification, but that one party subsequently opportunistically sought to exploit an ambiguity in the text to its advantage. For instance, perhaps there was an understanding among the parties that the imports of chicken cuts from Brazil and Thailand were to be classified under heading 02.07, but producers in these countries saw the possibility of adding some salt with the sole purpose of getting a more favorable tariff treatment. Or alternatively, maybe the understanding was to classify the product under heading 02.10, but the EC saw the opportunity to effectively increase the tariff on the product by adding a 'long-term preservation' criterion that was not part of the understanding. In these cases, it would be natural to view the opportunistically acting party as behaving in bad faith, undermining the cooperative spirit of the agreement. The natural forum for adjudicating such a dispute would be the DSU, albeit with the input of some expert advice from the WCO.

A second and related possibility is that the parties did not think at all about the classification of this particular type of product that is both frozen and salted, since there was no trade at the time of the completion of the Uruguay Round. It can be noted that it is established in this case that Thailand started exporting the product in 1996 and Brazil in 1998, hence in both cases after the completion of the Uruguay Round negotiations.[6] This may have been caused by market developments, such as increased demand in the EC – indeed, the complainants claim that their firms have responded to explicit requests from EC buyers – or expanded export capacities in the complaining countries. Here there is a genuine uncertainty concerning the classification, and it seems as if the WCO could have a more prominent role to play, to the extent the matter can be resolved on technical grounds. But it may also call for negotiations between the parties.

6 See WT/DS269/R, p. A-3, and WT/DS269/R, p. C-3.

A third possibility is that there was a genuine misunderstanding during the negotiations concerning the classification of the product. Maybe the complainants sincerely expected the chicken cuts to come under heading 02.10, while the EC sincerely believed that the parties shared the view that 'salted' referred to preservation. This is clearly an issue to be resolved through the DSU, and perhaps also through negotiation between the parties.

Yet another possibility is that there was a mutual understanding that each WTO Member's customs authority has the right to interpret their custom classification schedules, subject to general WTO norms such as nondiscrimination and transparency and subject to the possibility of resort to the WCO in the case of a disagreement concerning a Member's interpretation.

As is stated in the Panel report, the WCO Secretariat took the position that since the WTO claim of Brazil and Thailand entailed an underlying dispute over the meaning of HS classifications, that underlying dispute should first be brought before the WCO, pursuant to the compulsory dispute settlement clause in the WCO Convention. One interpretation of the existence of such a provision is that the WTO members bound their tariff schedules based on the understanding that each WTO Member's customs authorities have the right to interpret these schedules, subject to general WTO norms such as nondiscrimination and transparency and subject to the possibility of resort to the WCO in the case of a disagreement concerning a Member's interpretation. The parties certainly did not, in the Uruguay Round instruments related to customs matters, seek to limit or circumscribe the extent to which disputes about the meaning of HS classifications would be matters for the WCO. Customs nomenclature is a highly specialized technical vocabulary for which canons of interpretation exist in the WCO. These canons are different from those of the VCLT.

While the AB in *EC – LAN Equipment* held that 'the only rules which may be applied in interpreting the meaning of a concession are the general rules of treaty interpretation set out in the VCLT' (para. 84), the VCLT itself contemplates that some treaty terms have been given a specialized meaning by the parties, and therefore the methods in 31.1–3 of the VCLT may be preempted by an inquiry into this specialized meaning. Thus, Art. 31.4 VCLT provides: 'A special meaning shall be given to a term if it is established that the parties so intended.' Art. 31.4's 'special meaning' clearly contrasts with 'ordinary meaning', which is to be seen from the sources set out in Art. 31.1–3. In our view, the Panel and the Appellate Body ought to have considered the possibility that the WCO Convention, including its compulsory dispute settlement clause to which almost all WTO Members are parties (and certainly all parties to the dispute), indicates a common intention that the meaning attributed to HS classifications be that which has been established in the WCO.

If so, then the AB may have failed to grasp the underlying nature of the legal obligation in Art. II:(1) GATT in its relation to the WCO system. A WTO Member may have a right to apply a tariff up to the bound rate for a particular classification to a particular product, provided that product falls within the classification *as understood in the WCO system*. Thus, if the burden of proof is on the complainant to make a prima facie case, arguably Brazil and Thailand should have had to show that the interpretation by the EC of the HS classification in question was inconsistent with the specialized meaning of that classification established in the WCO.

The issue of 'fragmentation' is one of the largest challenges facing international law today – the possibility of more than one forum and/or international legal regime applying to a given problem or dispute: there are few meta-rules in international law to resolve such situations.[7] The response of the Panel to the challenge, as it emerges in this dispute, is formalistic and preemptory:

> 7.56 We understand that, once seized of a matter, Article 11 prevents a panel from abdicating its responsibility to the DSB. In other words, in the context of the present case, we lack the authority to refer the dispute before us to the WCO or to any other body.

This statement concerning the nature of the Panel's jurisdiction under the DSU may be technically or literally true,[8] but, as we have just explained, a plausible interpretation of the nature of the underlying substantive obligation of WTO Members concerning customs classification is that they are required to follow WCO practice with respect to the treatment of particular products under HS classifications of the WCO. On this view, a WTO Member would discharge its obligations under Art. II GATT if its decision to apply an HS classification to a particular product is consistent with WCO practice. In a case like this one, where no previous clear WCO ruling exists on the matter at hand, the practical consequence of this view is that, in order to make their case before the WTO Panel, the complainants will need to go first to the WCO to establish that the defendant has

7 See generally, International Law Commission (2006).

8 Pauwelyn (2005) nevertheless suggests that, 'For a panel ... to suspend its work whilst the parties go back to another legal system ... may be borderline between, on the one hand, transferring jurisdiction to another body without the agreement of the parties (something that a panel cannot do) and, on the other hand, seeking advice from an epistemically superior institution (something that ought to enhance the legitimacy of the WTO process).' 'Introductory Report on the World Trade Organization, Unity and Fragmentation in International Law', Palma Workshop, 20–21 May 2005. The implication is that, in *some* situations, where a panel's right to seek information would be frustrated if it did not suspend proceedings while another tribunal is seized of the matter, it might be legitimate for a panel to interpret its right to seek information as extending to such a suspension. In the case at hand, the Panel of course did seek advice of the WCO, but the WCO, while providing some answers to questions of the Panel, deemed the appropriate avenue for fully determining the issue as recourse to its dispute settlement mechanism. In such circumstances, along the lines Pauwelyn is suggesting, we think the Panel could reasonably have said that it cannot discharge its duty to make an objective assessment of the matter (DSU 11) unless the parties to the WTO dispute first engage the WCO dispute settlement procedures. It is arguable that the capacity to make an objective assessment is an inherent condition of a panel's jurisdiction. As Pauwelyn (2005) notes, in the MOX Plant case, the UNCLOS tribunal suspended proceedings pending a ruling by the European Court of Justice. Thus, even if the Panel is right that it has no 'authority' to refer or transfer the whole dispute to the WCO, it may have been able to suspend proceedings as a proper exercise of its jurisdiction, and indeed this might have been necessary to properly discharge its fundamental duty as a panel to make an objective assessment.

interpreted the classification in question in a manner that is impermissible in the WCO system. We emphasize that it is far from clear that the WCO would have provided a more satisfactory resolution of the dispute in substantive terms (i.e. a more efficient outcome); it would most likely have decided the matter by applying a set of mechanical rules for dealing with situations where, in principle, more than one HS classification might apply to a given product. The question is whether the adhesion of the parties to the WCO Convention and the arguably related absence of any code on customs classification in the WTO itself indicate the expectation or assumption that problems of interpretation of the HS would be dealt with in the WCO.

One kind of argument for not requiring, in effect, that the complaining Member have first gone to the WCO is that not all WTO Members are WCO Members, and thus in the case of a dispute where the complaining WTO Member is not a WCO Member, the complaining Member in question would be faced with discharging its burden of proof without the benefit of a prior WCO ruling. This would arguably result in a nonequitable or at least nonuniform application of Article II of the GATT to different WCO Members. However, as the International Law Commission Study Group has pointed out, it is an inevitable feature of 'fragmentation' that states are bound by different multilateral and bilateral treaties, overlapping in subject matter and partly but not entirely overlapping in membership. The rights and obligations of parties to agreement A may affect how agreement B applies to them; agreement B may thus inevitably have a somewhat different effect on parties to B who are not parties to A. There is no structural principle of international law that suggests the rights and obligations in agreement A should be rendered ineffective so as to make interpretation of agreement B uniform across states party to A and states nonparty to A. Indeed, there have been decisions of WTO dispute settlement organs precisely to the contrary. Thus, for example, in *EC – Poultry*, the AB held that a bilateral agreement between the EC and Brazil was relevant as a supplementary means of interpretation:

> to the extent relevant to the determination of the EC's obligations under the WTO agreements *vis-à-vis* Brazil. (§ 202, italics in the original).

This statement contains an obvious recognition of the possibility that WTO rights and obligations may apply differently *vis-à-vis* particular WTO Members depending on the meaning of other agreements between those particular Members to which the entire WTO Membership is not bound. However, since very few WTO Members are not WCO Members, the degree of asymmetry is not likely to be significant.

On the other hand, there are important respects in which requiring the complaining Member to rely on a previous WCO ruling, where that Member is a party to the WCO and its compulsory dispute settlement arrangements, risks increasing uncertainty in the meaning of WTO obligations. What if, subsequent to a WTO ruling interpreting a customs classification, a dispute based on similar facts were brought to the WCO? The WTO findings would not be binding on the WCO adjudicator as res judicata; the weight given them would depend on the WCO's view of their persuasiveness.[9] There is more than a mere possibility that the WCO might make a finding concerning the meaning of HS classifications that is inconsistent in whole or in part with the result and/or reasoning of the WTO adjudicator. Now remember that the vast majority of WCO Members are also WTO Members. In such a situation, that vast a majority would be faced with conflicting obligations: as WCO Members, they would be required to follow WCO decisions concerning the proper interpretation of the HS; as WTO Members, they would have to follow the approach to interpretation of the HS laid out by the WTO dispute settlement organs. Thus, far from contributing to uniformity and consistency, the development of a WTO case law on the principles of HS classification, largely autonomous from decisions of the WCO, is a recipe for conflict and uncertainty.

10. Conclusion

At numerous points in this paper, we have expressed serious misgivings at the overall framing of this dispute by the parties, the Panel, and the AB:

1. The definition of the burden of proof for establishing a violation is too onerous for the importing country. In a case where two headings can be argued with equal force as the appropriate classifications, we see no reason to choose the one the exporter prefers to be the correct heading.
2. The argument that this is not a customs classification case is at best only partially correct. The core of the adjudicating bodies' determination concerns appropriate interpretation of 'salted' with regard to heading 02.10, and this is, as far as we can see, a customs classification issue. For this determination, the Panel should have asked for expert opinion by the WCO.
3. We believe that the adjudicators need to reflect more deeply on the nature of the obligation in Art. II, as it relates to the interpretation of the HS in domestic customs administration and to the jurisdiction and rules of the WCO. We are not persuaded that the intent or expectation of the WTO Membership was that a correctness standard of review under the VCLT would apply to the interpretation by domestic agencies of customs schedules. It is at least as plausible, if not more, that the background assumption was that disagreements about customs administration would be settled through the compulsory dispute settlement mechanism of the WCO, to which the vast majority of WTO Members are parties. Indeed, this might go a long way to explaining why, although customs classification issues have arisen often in international trade, they have not given rise to negotiation of specialized rules or practices in the WTO itself.

9 See *Bosnia-Herzegovina* v. *Serbia*, Opinion of the Court, International Court of Justice, para. 211ff.

4. For the above reasons, we do not think that the conclusion that there was an EC violation of Art. II of the GATT could be justified on the basis of the evidence presented in this dispute.
5. This being said, we do think the actual outcome of the case might well be justified on other grounds. Quite apart from whether the WCO would find that the EC interpretation of salted was correct or not, Art. X of the GATT obliges each WTO Member to 'administer in a uniform, impartial and reasonable manner all its laws, regulations, decisions and rulings' concerning, inter alia, customs classification. An unexplained, unreasoned determination by the EC that, after years of almost all its customs offices classifying the products in question as salted, this practice is an error, and the resultant imposition of duties effectively double or even treble or more on the products in question may well not amount to a 'reasonable manner' of customs administration. Despite numerous questions asked to the EC by the Panel, and hundreds of pages of submissions in this litigation, the EC never provided a clear reasoned account of how this error was allowed to continue for years, from the perspective of what policy concerns it was an error, and how exporters were supposed to grasp, from EC practice, that even though its customs offices were routinely classifying these products erroneously, all along EC law and regulation imposed the more restrictive interpretation of when a product was to be considered 'salted'. This relates to another provision of GATT Art. X, which requires that 'Laws, regulations, judicial decisions and administrative rulings of general application, made effective by any contracting party, pertaining to the classification ... of products' be published promptly and in such a manner 'to enable governments and traders to become acquainted with them'. It is the position of the EC that the long-term preservation criterion was always part of EC law and regulation, and that its own authorities were simply erroneously applying the law. If so, it is hard to imagine from any of the materials how a trader would have become acquainted with such a requirement – the EC's own officials obviously weren't even acquainted with it. In sum, the lack of reasoned explanation by the EC of its course of conduct in the administration of customs duties in regard to these products makes it difficult to argue for a different result in this case.

To conclude, we believe that the outcome of the dispute may possibly be justified, albeit with a different legal basis than that in the dispute, but we have severe reservations concerning the legal grounds for finding a violation of Art. II on the basis of the evidence presented.

References

International Law Commission (2006), *Fragmentation of International Law: Difficulties Arising from the Diversification and Expansion of International Law*, Report of the Study Group of the International Law Commission. Finalized by Martti Koskenniemi, A/CN.4/L.682, 13 April 2006.

Pauwelyn, Joost (2005), 'Unity and Fragmentation in International Law: Introductory Report on the World Trade Organization', Palma Workshop, 20–21 May.

Comment

European Communities – Customs Classification of Frozen Boneless Chicken Cuts (DS269/DS286)

Prepared for the ALI Project on the Case Law of the WTO

NIALL MEAGHER
Senior Counsel, Advisory Centre on WTO Law (ACWL), Geneva

1. Introduction

This brief comment addresses several, but not all, of the points made in the paper by Robert Howse and Henrik Horn on the WTO Panel and Appellate Body reports in *European Communities – Customs Classification of Frozen Boneless Chicken Cuts.*[1]

The *EC–Chicken Cuts* case involved a not uncommon situation, in which a WTO Member made tariff concessions in multilateral trade negotiations and subsequently found that trade gravitated towards products benefiting from lower tariffs. The WTO Member then attempted to address the situation by changing its practice of classification of one such product to subject that product to a higher tariff. While it may be frustrating to the importing Member, as a practical matter it seems inevitable that commercial interests will always gravitate towards the lowest-cost method of trading their goods across international boundaries. In this case, the European Communities (the 'EC') departed from an established practice of classifying imported chicken cuts that had been treated with salt under a

The views expressed in this comment, as well as any errors, are those of the author alone. I would like to thank Petros Mavroidis, Henrik Horn, and The American Law Institute (ALI) for inviting me to participate in this project and to provide this comment.

1 Appellate Body Report, *European Communities – Customs Classification of Frozen Boneless Chicken Cuts*, WT/DS269/AB/R, WT/DS286/AB/R, and Corr.1, adopted 27 September 2005 (hereafter 'Appellate Body Report'), modifying Panel Report, *European Communities – Customs Classification of Frozen Boneless Chicken Cuts, Complaint by Brazil*, WT/DS269/R, adopted 27 September 2005, and Panel Report, *European Communities – Customs Classification of Frozen Boneless Chicken Cuts, Complaint by Thailand*, WT/DS286/R, adopted 27 September 2005 (the latter cited to hereafter as 'Panel Report').

lower-tariff heading (02.10, covering 'meat ... salted ...') and began to classify the increasing volume of such imports under a higher-tariff heading (02.07, covering 'fresh, chilled or frozen' poultry).

A threshold question in disputes about the tariff treatment of imports such as *EC – Chicken Cuts*, therefore, is how reviewing WTO Panels should frame the issue: in making classification decisions, are WTO Members bound to respect strictly the language of their concessions, or may they reclassify goods in order to protect their own understanding of what they intended by their concessions? It is important to approach this issue clearly: to describe the original classification of the goods as an 'error' by the importing Member, would suggest that the importing Members have broad authority to remedy such 'errors' by changing the classification of goods. On the other hand, to suggest that importing Members have limited authority to review the classification of goods in light of changing trading patterns and to prevent improper classification might undermine the mutual benefit of concessions and discourage WTO Members from continuing to make further tariff concessions.

This issue arose in the dispute in the form of determining the 'object and purpose' of the 'treaty' within the meaning of Article 31(1) of the *Vienna Convention on the Law of Treaties* (the 'Vienna Convention'), which serves as the departure point in interpreting the WTO Agreements. The EC had argued that the Panel had improperly relied on the 'expansion of trade' as an object and purpose of tariff concessions of WTO Members.[2] The Appellate Body found that the Panel had properly construed the object and purpose of the WTO Agreements generally to include 'the security and predictability of "the reciprocal and mutually advantageous arrangements directed to the substantial reduction of tariffs and other barriers to trade"'.[3] This emphasis on 'security and predictability' strikes a proper balance between the approaches described above by focusing on a strict interpretation of the text of the tariff concession itself to ensure that the importing Member's trading partners may benefit from the tariff concession in question, while still permitting importing Members to ensure that their concessions are not abused through the misclassification of goods.

2. The WTO and the WCO

I would disagree with the authors' description of this dispute as primarily one of customs classification rather than treaty interpretation. As the authors note, it is well established under WTO jurisprudence that WTO Members' schedules of tariff concessions form part of the WTO Agreements and may be the subject of WTO dispute settlement proceedings in the same manner as any provision of the so-called 'covered' agreements. Thus, the issue of the correct tariff on imports

2 Appellate Body Report, para. 242.
3 Ibid., para. 243, quoting Panel Report, para. 7.318.

of chicken cuts to the EC is as much a question of WTO law as, for example, the proper interpretation of the prohibition on export subsidies. In these circumstances, while acknowledging the broader issue of the 'fragmentation' of international law mentioned by the authors, I do not see how a WTO Panel could decline jurisdiction or formally defer its jurisdiction on this issue to the WCO dispute resolution process. Any problem of fragmentation exists not by hazard but by the choice of sovereign states to create discrete bodies to address particular issues. Any confusion between the jurisdictions of those bodies must be resolved by the sovereign states, not by the bodies themselves declining to complete the tasks assigned to them.

3. Interpretative issues

Article 31 of the Vienna Convention provides that treaties are to be interpreted in accordance with the ordinary meaning to be given to the terms of the treaty in their context and in the light of the treaty's object and purpose. Article 31.3(b) provides that together with the context of the provision, the interpreter shall take into account 'any subsequent practice in the application of the treaty which establishes the agreement of the parties regarding its interpretation'. Three aspects of the Panel's and Appellate Body's application of this interpretative approach deserve mention.

First, the authors correctly observe that the Panel framed the issue before it as whether the chicken cuts at issue were 'salted' within the meaning of, and therefore properly classifiable under, tariff heading 02.10, without separately considering whether the chicken cuts might also fall within the 'ordinary meaning' of tariff heading 02.07. By framing the issue in this manner, the Panel avoided applying WCO rules of interpretation that apply where products are prima facie classifiable under two tariff headings. While it is possible that the Panel's analysis may have been better if it had considered that the chicken cuts were prima facie classifiable under both headings, it is by no means clear that the outcome would have been any different. In any event, as the authors note, the parties presented the issue to the Panel in a manner that precluded this approach, agreeing that the chicken cuts were not prima facie classifiable under both headings and that, if they were not properly classifiable under heading 02.10, the EC was permitted to classify them under the higher-tariff heading 02.07. Absent extenuating circumstances, the Panel is constrained to follow the parties' agreement on and explanation of the issue before it.

Second, in interpreting the ordinary meaning of the term 'salted', the Panel did not content itself, as many Panels frequently do, with looking at the Oxford English Dictionary meaning of the term. The Panel stated that it was necessary to 'test the appropriateness of those dictionary definitions against the factual context in which the concession in question exists' and that the 'factual context' could include 'aspects associated with the physical characteristics of the products at issue'.[4] On appeal, the Appellate Body recalled that dictionaries are no more than a 'useful starting point' for interpretation; the ordinary meaning of a term is to be determined according to the particular circumstances of each case.[5] The Appellate Body noted that the Panel's term 'factual context' does not appear in the Vienna Convention, but stated that it did not consider that the Panel was incorrect to look at the elements it considered to be 'factual context' in trying to derive the ordinary meaning of the term 'salted'.[6] Although perhaps not perfectly articulated, the Panel's effort to look for 'ordinary' meanings in 'ordinary' sources other than the Oxford dictionary is to be commended. As the limitations of dictionary definitions become evident in future cases, it may be expected that Panels will continue to look beyond dictionaries to other, perhaps more practical, sources in identifying the 'ordinary meaning'. The Appellate Body's description of the interpretative process as a 'holistic exercise that should not be mechanically subdivided into rigid components' should facilitate this.[7]

Third, regarding the Panel's and Appellate Body's analysis of the 'subsequent practice' provision of Article 31.3(b) of the Vienna Convention, Howse and Horn suggest that the silence of other WTO Members cannot be considered as assent to that practice. I would go a little further. In the present case, the EC's practice had changed, and the issue before the Panel was, in effect, whether the former or latter practice was WTO consistent. In such circumstances, where the WTO consistency of the defending Member's practice is itself the issue, it seems difficult to rely on any aspect of that Member's practice, in itself, as evidence of the WTO consistency of either the Member's former or latter practice.

4. GATT Article X

The authors suggest that the case should properly have been argued under GATT Article X, rather than GATT Article II. GATT Article X : 3(a) provides that WTO Members shall 'administer in a uniform, impartial and reasonable manner' all of their laws and regulations affecting, inter alia, customs classification. In their view, the EC's reclassification of chicken cuts was not inconsistent with GATT Article II, but the EC's failure to explain its understanding of its concession constituted a failure to administer its laws reasonably within the meaning of Article X : 3(a).

As a practical matter, however, GATT Article X : 3(a) would not have been much use to the complainants in this case. Leaving aside the question of any bias in the EC's decisionmaking *process* (and none was alleged in the case), it is not inconsistent per se with Article X : 3(a) for the EC to review the tariff classification of imported goods or to make decisions that change the tariff classification of

4 Panel Report, para. 7.105.
5 Appellate Body Report, para. 175.
6 Ibid., para. 176.
7 Ibid.

those goods. Thus, the question of whether the EC uniformly and reasonably administered its customs laws in this case would turn on the issue of whether the EC reached a reasonable conclusion in its regulation changing the classification of chicken cuts.

This is, in other words, the same issue presented by the complainants in their claim under GATT Article II. Thus, a reviewing WTO Panel probably could not resolve a claim under Article X : 3(a) without first considering the issue presented by a claim under GATT Article II and, once it had done so, the Panel would be quite likely to exercise judicial economy with respect to the further claim under GATT Article X : 3(a). Also, from the complainant's point of view, a ruling under GATT Article II would essentially establish that the reclassification of chicken cuts was WTO-inconsistent. This would be much more valuable in terms of the EC's implementation than a ruling under GATT Article X : 3(a), which would merely establish that there was a WTO-inconsistency in the EC's decisionmaking process. Such a finding may be of no practical benefit to the exporters: on implementation, the EC would be able to continue to classify the chicken under the higher-tariff heading, but would simply have to explain its process and rationale more thoroughly.

Canada–Wheat: discrimination, non-commercial considerations, and the right to regulate through state trading enterprises

BERNARD HOEKMAN

Senior Advisor, Research Manager, International Trade Group, Development Research Group, World Bank

JOEL P. TRACHTMAN

Professor of International Law, Fletcher School of Law and Diplomacy, Tufts University

1. Introduction

In the *Canada–Wheat* case,[1] the WTO Appellate Body delimited the scope of disciplines applicable to state trading enterprises (STEs) under WTO law. The US challenged several Canadian measures. We will focus here on the Canadian Wheat Board (CWB) export regime for wheat. The *Canada–Wheat* case was brought by the US to address certain practices of the CWB.

Although Canada lost at the Panel stage on certain GATT Article III:4 grounds, Canada mounted a successful defense in connection with claims regarding the CWB's behavior as an STE at the Panel stage: the Panel found that the US had failed to establish that Canada had violated Article XVII:1(a) or (b).[2] The US appeal addressed the Panel's interpretation of subparagraph (b) of Article XVII:1, and the Panel's application of this interpretation to the CWB export regime. Canada's appeal argued that the Panel inappropriately failed to address the relationship between subparagraph (a) and subparagraph (b) of Article XVII:1, and erroneously assumed that a breach of subparagraph (b) is sufficient to establish a breach of Article XVII:1.

In this case, the Appellate Body adopted an interpretation of Article XVII:1 of GATT that limits its disciplines only to antidiscrimination. The Appellate Body declined to find broader disciplines requiring STEs to operate 'solely in accordance with commercial considerations' as an independent requirement. By doing so, the Appellate Body limited the disciplines applicable to STEs to those that would apply to government regulation of private entities. It declined to find a

1 Appellate Body Report, *Canada–Measures Relating to Exports of Wheat and Treatment of Imported Grain*, WT/DS276/AB/R, adopted 27 September 2004.

2 Panel Report, *Canada – Measures Relating to Exports of Wheat and Treatment of Imported Grain*, WT/DS276/R, adopted 27 September 2004, upheld by Appellate Body Report, WT/DS276/AB/R, paras. 6.151 and 7.4(a).

broader requirement that STEs act like private persons, and therefore preserved the possibility that states may use STEs to achieve broader public-policy goals. It found that Article XVII:1 does not impose competition-law-type obligations on STEs.

2. Background

STEs commonly take the form of statutory marketing boards. These statutory marketing boards often have exclusive authority to purchase domestic production, to sell for export, and to set purchase and sales prices. They may also capture economies of scale, reducing marketing and other transaction costs for producers (see Secretariat, WTO, 1995).

The statutory objective of the CWB is to market certain grain grown in Canada in an 'orderly manner' in interprovincial and export trade. The CWB is granted exclusive authority over the sale in export markets and for human consumption in the domestic market of wheat and barley grown in a 'designated area'. The 'designated area' includes the Canadian provinces of Manitoba, Saskatchewan, Alberta, and the Peace River area of the province of British Columbia.[3] Thus, the CWB is a monopolist for sales on the domestic and export markets, and a monopsonist for Canadian producers of wheat and barley that operate in the designated area. Exclusive control over both export and domestic sales makes the CWB a so-called 'single desk' STE.

The US asserted, inter alia, that the CWB export regime was inconsistent with Canada's obligations under Article XVII:1 of GATT 1994. The US argued that the following three elements, *in combination*, violated Article XVII:1: (a) the legal framework of the CWB, (b) Canada's provision to the CWB of exclusive and special privileges, and (c) the actions of Canada and the CWB with respect to the CWB's purchases and sales involving wheat exports.[4] That is, these three measures 'collectively' constituted the measure challenged: the 'CWB Export Regime'.

More particularly, the exclusive and special privileges at issue (referred to in item (b) above) were the following:

(i) the exclusive right to purchase and sell Western Canadian wheat for export and domestic human consumption;
(ii) the right to set, subject to government approval, the initial price payable for Western Canadian wheat destined for export or domestic human consumption;
(iii) the government guarantee of the initial payment to producers of Western Canadian wheat;

3 Canadian Notification to the Working Party on State Trading Enterprises of the WTO, G/STR/N/4/CAN.

4 Panel Report, para. 6.12.

(iv) the government guarantee of the CWB's borrowing; and
(v) government guarantees of certain CWB credit sales to foreign buyers.[5]

The US argued that the CWB Export Regime led the CWB to violate Article XVII:1(a) and (b) of GATT. The US challenged the CWB Export Regime as a whole, rather than any individual element.[6] This was understood by the Panel as a '*per se*' challenge to the CWB Export Regime, rather than a challenge to a particular action.[7]

The US claim rested on four broad assertions. First, the privileges enjoyed by the CWB gave it more flexibility with respect to pricing and other sales terms than a commercial actor. This included the ability to pay wheat producers prices below the market price. Second, this flexibility allowed the CWB to offer non-commercial sales terms, denying commercial firms an opportunity to compete. Third, the structure of the CWB induced it to maximize sales, or revenues, rather than profits. Fourth, the Canadian government did not take steps to cause the CWB to comply with Article XVII:1.[8]

The substance of the US claim was that 'the CWB statute does not require the CWB to sell its wheat for export in accordance with commercial considerations, and the CWB maintains the secrecy of its transaction-specific sales practices. Moreover ... the exclusive and special privileges enjoyed by the CWB detach the CWB from the economic considerations that would govern the conduct of commercial actors engaged in the purchase and sale of wheat.'[9] Thus, the main concern of the US was structural: the issue was a perception that the CWB is structured in a way that ensures that it will not act, or at least does not ensure that it will act, 'solely in accordance with commercial considerations'.

The WTO proceeding discussed in this paper is only a part of a larger conflict between Canada and the US over wheat. In a series of domestic investigations, US authorities determined that Canadian wheat was being subsidized and dumped in the US, and was therefore subject to countervailing duties and anti-dumping duties. However, certain of these determinations were appealed to a NAFTA Chapter 19 Panel, which overturned the findings.[10] Thus, the attack under Article XVII might have been viewed as a less attractive alternative compared to these other previously frustrated routes of attack.

5 Panel Report, para. 6.15. See Alberta Agriculture, Food and Rural Development,Canadian Wheat Board Government Guarantees for a description of the three guarantees. Available at http://www.choicematters.gov.ab.ca.

6 Panel Report, para. 6.26.

7 Panel Report, para. 6.28.

8 Panel Report, paras. 6.110–6.114.

9 First Written Submission of the United States of America, *Canada–Measures Relating to Exports of Wheat and Treatment of Imported Grain*, WT/DS276, 1 August 2003, para. 20.

10 NAFTA Article 1904 Panel Review, *In the Matter of Hard Red Spring Wheat from Canada*, No. USA-CDA-2003-1904-06 (7 June 2005; 12 December 2005).

3. State trading enterprises and WTO rules

STEs are used by governments as instruments of regulation. They may be used to achieve a variety of public-policy goals in industrial policy, including in relation to the control of imports and exports. As tools of state intervention in the market, STEs may distort competition, and may be inconsistent with liberalization. But, of course, this alone does not make them inconsistent with WTO law or policy.

However, it is possible that STEs may be used to circumvent certain WTO commitments with respect to market access and subsidies.[11] They might do so in a number of ways. First, they could circumvent the MFN principle of GATT Article I by discriminating among trading partners in their decisions regarding purchase and sale. Second, they could circumvent the national-treatment principle of GATT Article III by discriminating between domestic and imported goods in their decisions regarding purchases. Third, if they hold exclusive import privileges, they could effectively restrict quantities of imports, inconsistently with the principles of Article XI of GATT. Fourth, they might exercise exclusive import rights to sell domestically at mark-ups that operate similarly to tariffs, but that exceed bound tariffs. Fifth, STEs may use their purchases and sales to subsidize sellers or buyers (Hoekman and Low, 1998). Much of the possibility for circumvention of WTO commitments is based on the possibility that STE decision making may be opaque, rendering it difficult to determine whether they discriminate or confer subsidies (Hoekman and Low, 1998; see also Petersmann, 1998). It is often difficult to evaluate whether their prices are subsidized (see Horlick and Mowry, 1998).

During the GATT period, prior to 1995, STEs did not play a major role in trade negotiations, largely because the main sectors and countries in which STEs are active – agriculture, services, and centrally planned economies – were effectively excluded from GATT disciplines (Hoekman and Low, 1998). STEs declined in importance with the growth of the Washington Consensus, and related moves toward reduced state intervention in the economy. In agriculture, for example, the New Zealand Dairy Board and the Australian Wheat Board have been transformed into grower cooperatives that do not receive government support (Young, 2005), while many of the marketing boards that were used by developing-country governments to set producer prices and control exports have been dismantled.

The Uruguay Round did not produce additional substantive regulation of STEs. The US has advocated additional disciplines on STEs, including prohibitions on monopoly rights of STEs (USDA, 2002). Specifically, the US proposed the following disciplines:

1. Members shall not restrict the right of any interested entity to export, or to purchase for export, agricultural products.

11 The Appellate Body has termed Article XVII:1(a) an 'anti-circumvention' provision. Appellate Body Report, para. 85.

2. No special financing privileges, including government grants, loans, loan guarantees, or underwriting of operational costs, shall be granted to state trading enterprises that export for sale, directly or indirectly, a significant share of the respective Member's total exports of an agricultural product.
3. Any Member that establishes, or maintains, for agricultural products, an export state trading enterprise shall give notice in writing, at least annually, to the Committee on Agriculture, of relevant information, including: initial and subsequent acquisition costs incurred and export prices of products exported or sold for export by such enterprises on a transaction-specific basis. Any Member may request the Member maintaining an export state trading enterprise for agriculture to provide specific information concerning all operations relevant to the export of agricultural products, as described above.

The US's greatest concern has been the CWB, which competes with US firms in world wheat markets, as well as in the US (Abbott and Young, 2003). However, with the entry of China into the WTO, and the expected entry of Russia, there is clearly a more general interest to ensure that STEs are not used to undercut market access and subsidization commitments.

4. Economic dimensions

The conflict that gave rise to the present case essentially revolves around competition for third markets, as both countries are major producers of wheat and large net exporters. Whereas Canada uses the CWB as the conduit for its exports of wheat, the US relies on a small number of large private firms to market wheat on export markets. Prior to the Uruguay Round (1995), US producers could benefit from export subsidies – through the US Export Enhancement Program. One result of the Uruguay Round was to impose disciplines on export-subsidy policies. A corollary was that US and other producers in countries that had benefited from export subsidies perceived an 'unfair' asymmetry to have emerged: they had become subject to disciplines, whereas countries with state trading agencies might be able to continue to price discriminate across markets and effectively subsidize exports.

From an economic perspective the relevant questions are whether (i) STEs such as the CWB do indeed engage in price discrimination on export markets; and (ii) this is a reflection of de facto export subsidization made possible by the way the CWB is structured and operates.[12]

12 That is, the observed discrimination would not also be pursued by a profit-maximizing private firm. Note that the focus in this paper is on exporting STEs, not importing STEs. In practice, STEs in net importers may circumvent negotiated market-access commitments through their behavior. This became more important post-Uruguay Round due to the shift to tariffication of agricultural protection and the use of tariff-rate quotas (TRQs) to guarantee minimum access to highly protected markets. These TRQs require management (allocation mechanisms), something that may be done by STEs. Article XVII arguably is primarily focused on this type of issue: a complement to other GATT articles that aim to preclude use of alternative instruments to restrict access more than what has been negotiated through tariff bindings. While the US did contest import-related issues, it did not appeal any of the Panel findings in this area.

A legal issue that arises insofar as the CWB can be argued to engage in subsidization of exports is to what extent such behavior is (can be) disciplined through other WTO provisions, e.g. the Agreement on Agriculture disciplines. Article XVII WTO does not deal with de jure subsidization – this is (must be) addressed through export-subsidy disciplines. However, if STE behavior results in de facto subsidization *because* of discriminatory pricing behavior and exploitation of market power, Article XVII may be violated. While other WTO provisions apply, and might be violated by the same behavior, Article XVII may provide a more effective means by which to discipline this behavior. Furthermore, to the extent that the economic 'subsidization' would not qualify as legal 'subsidization' because it involves a benefit being required to be provided by private Canadian producers to the CWB, rather than a benefit being provided by government, no WTO subsidies disciplines would apply.

Thus, the reason for the US concern with the structure of the CWB in this case seems to have been the risk of implicit subsidization in the economic sense if not in the WTO legal sense. Single-desk status potentially gives the CWB the economic power to price discriminate or to cross-subsidize between domestic and foreign markets. However, such price discrimination may reflect market factors (demand conditions in different markets) and differences in product composition (quality) as well as the monopolist-cum-monopsonist status of the CWB.

The CWB engages in a number of practices that may allow it to reduce prices on export markets below what competitors can charge in the absence of export subsidies. One of these is a two-part payment system under which farmers obtain only partial payment for their crops when delivered to the CWB. This first payment is determined by a minimum price for farmers, guaranteed by the government. It is supplemented by a final payment once output has been sold on export markets, and selling expenses, overheads, etc. have been netted out. The CWB also engages in price pooling: domestic producers are paid the average price (net of costs) obtained for a specific quality/variety of wheat and barley on the domestic and all export markets.

The combination of price pooling and two-part payment scheme may result in the CWB being able to price below competitors by credibly lowering the costs of the output that is exported (i.e., low initial payments could be used as a credible precommitment device in an export-competition game) and/or through cross-subsidization by 'pricing to market' – insofar as this entails losses on some export markets, this can be compensated by higher prices on other markets. The two-part pricing scheme may in effect imply that the CWB is being given a short-term 'loan' by Canadian farmers, as they must accept the minimum, initial, average price offered by the CWB. In addition, the CWB benefits from government guarantees of both its debt and certain credits it may grant its foreign buyers.[13]

13 In principle, government loan guarantees and credits that are conditional on exports would be covered by the Agreement on Agriculture and the SCM Agreement.

As a result of its exclusivity rights, the CWB can engage in a variety of strategies. Which strategy it will pursue will depend on the underlying objectives it has been assigned. As a government entity, the objective of the CWB is not necessarily profit maximization. Indeed, a rationale for the creation and operation of STEs generally includes equity as well as efficiency objectives. In the field of agriculture, STEs can serve important public-policy purposes, such as price support or stabilization, internalization of externalities (quality and associated reputational benefits for the country as a whole), and income redistribution. Thus, in addition to exploitation of national-market power by aggregating the supplies of many small farmers (economies of scale, etc.), STEs often act to redistribute income towards – or, more frequently, away from – farmers. The latter objective has often been important in developing countries, where governments seek to use low producer prices as a means of transferring resources to consumers of food in urban areas or to support investments elsewhere in the economy.

Knowing what the underlying national objectives are is clearly important from the perspective of national welfare and the evaluation/design of policy. However, what the objectives are is not always relevant from a WTO perspective, as its focus may be only on the question whether the trade impacts of a policy result in discrimination that goes beyond what a country may impose given its commitments in the WTO. As a result, WTO rules in this area, as in others, may result in incentives for countries to use less efficient instruments to pursue a given objective. In the case of STEs, for example, if the underlying objective is to raise exports, explicit export subsidies may be the more efficient (and transparent) instrument. For example, simple economic theory suggests that for a given target increase in domestic production, the use of export subsidies will generate lower welfare costs for the imposing country than an STE that uses price pooling as a way of raising average prices for farmers (see Alston and Gray, 2000).[14]

Canada is a major wheat exporter. Thus, it has some market power on the world market. In this connection, it is important to recognize that Canadian wheat is a differentiated product. For a given type of wheat, it is of more uniform and of higher average quality than US wheat. In part, this is because of the operation of the CWB, which sets minimum standards and specifies the type of seeds that may be used for a given quality/type of wheat or barley that is to be procured and exported.

The empirical literature on the global wheat market suggests that this may be best characterized as a quantity-setting oligopoly. In the case of barley, price

14 Important questions for domestic policy and assessing the costs and benefits of alternative instruments are the size of the excess burden of taxation needed to finance export subsidies and administrative costs (transfer efficiency), the incidence of the 'tax' that is used to generate a given transfer to farmers – taxpayers in the case of export subsidies, consumers in the case of STEs – whether the STE is being used as a mechanism to ensure that a greater share of profits accrue to farmers instead of middlemen/traders (the concentration ratio of wholesalers/distributors in the US is over 75 % for example), etc. In this paper, we abstract from these types of domestic-policy questions.

setting does not appear to be supported by the data – STEs and other suppliers do not have market leadership and can be characterized as engaging in Cournot competition. In the case of wheat, the CWB does engage in price discrimination, but the evidence suggests much, if not most, of this is due to the fact that there are significant quality differences among types of wheat exported to different markets.[15] Moreover, research suggests that the CWB does not set initial prices to farmers optimally from a profit maximization/rent shifting perspective. Prices paid to farmers are 'too high': producers receive a higher average price than they should if the CWB was seeking to maximize profits. This suggests either that strategic motivations do not drive pricing decisions, that regulation and other oversight of the CWB ensure that interests of farmers dominate, or that because of the nature of the differentiated products it makes more sense to focus on measures to improve quality and exploit quality differences (Lavoie, 2005 and Dong, Marsh, and Stiegert, 2006).[16] In practice, it appears that the CWB obtains a premium price for many of its exports, rather than selling output at 'subsidized' levels, reflecting the higher quality/differentiated nature of its exports (Lavoie, 2005 and Sumner and Boltuck, 2001).

As discussed further below, what matters from the perspective of the WTO (Article XVII) is whether any observed price discrimination across foreign markets or between domestic and foreign markets would also be pursued by a private firm (such as a cooperative of farmers). Independent of the specific features of the CWB – such as price pooling – the evidence of extensive product differentiation in the wheat market suggests that private firms would also pursue price-discrimination strategies in markets where they have (some) pricing power. That, in turn, suggests that in practice it is difficult to establish a private 'commercial' counter-factual situation where discrimination would not be optimal.

5. Analyzing the disciplines of Article XVII

Article XVII:1 of GATT applies to STEs. Article XVII:1 provides as follows:

> 1.*[17] (*a*) Each contracting party undertakes that if it establishes or maintains a State enterprise, wherever located, or grants to any enterprise, formally or in

15 See Lavoie, 2005, and Dong, Marsh, and Stiegert, 2006, for recent empirical analyses of the operation of the CWB in wheat and barley markets, respectively. These papers also contain extensive references to the economic literature on STEs in general and the CWB in particular.

16 Note that insofar as average total prices paid to Canadian producers are not suppressed so as to maximize the profits of the CWB, this may have the effect of increasing total output, enhancing competition on world markets. The same outcome may result from price pooling (paying farmers the average price obtained across all markets).

17 Asterisks refer to 'ad notes' that form part of the GATT. For example, and as relevant to this case, the ad note to Article XVII:1 provides, inter alia, that 'The charging by a state enterprise of different prices for its sales of a product in different markets is not precluded by the provisions of this Article, provided that such different prices are charged for commercial reasons, to meet conditions of supply and demand in export markets.'

effect, exclusive or special privileges,* such enterprise shall, in its purchases or sales involving either imports or exports, act in a manner consistent with the general principles of non-discriminatory treatment prescribed in this Agreement for governmental measures affecting imports or exports by private traders.

(*b*) The provisions of subparagraph (*a*) of this paragraph shall be understood to require that such enterprises shall, having due regard to the other provisions of this Agreement, make any such purchases or sales solely in accordance with commercial considerations,* including price, quality, availability, marketability, transportation and other conditions of purchase or sale, and shall afford the enterprises of the other contracting parties adequate opportunity, in accordance with customary business practice, to compete for participation in such purchases or sales.

5.1 Scope of application of Article XVII:1

GATT does not define STEs. The Uruguay Round Understanding on the Interpretation of Article XVII of the General Agreement on Tariffs and Trade (the 'Understanding') provides a working definition for STEs, to be used to determine the scope of the obligation of notification specified in the Understanding:

> Governmental and non-governmental enterprises, including marketing boards, which have been granted exclusive or special rights or privileges, including statutory or constitutional powers, in the exercise of which they influence through their purchases or sales the level or direction of imports or exports.

Importantly, the essence of this definition is, first, that there are exclusive or special privileges, and, second, that in the exercise of these powers, the STE influences through purchases or sales the level or direction of imports or exports.

However, the definition contained in the Understanding is narrower than the scope of application of Article XVII:1. The Appellate Body cited the Panel's statement that 'Like the parties, the Panel uses the term "STE" or "state trading enterprise" to refer to both types of enterprises covered by Article XVII:1, i.e., State enterprises or enterprises that have formally or in effect been granted exclusive or special privileges.'[18]

In the present case, there was no dispute as to whether the CWB is an STE, as Canada had notified the CWB as an STE.[19]

5.2 Discrimination and commercial considerations

In the *Canada–Wheat* case, Canada argued that the Panel erred 'in not considering the "proper" relationship between subparagraphs (a) and (b) of Article XVII:1 of the GATT 1994 and in proceeding to examine the consistency of the CWB Export

18 Appellate Body Report, para. 114, citing Panel Report, para. 6.33.

19 Panel Report, para. 6.108. See Working Party on State Trading Enterprises, New and Full Notification [by Canada] Pursuant to Article XVII:4(A) of the GATT and Paragraph 1 of the Understanding on the Interpretation of Article XVII, G/STR/N/4/CAN, 5 November 2002.

Regime with Article XVII:1(b) without first having found a breach of Article XVII:1(a).'[20] According to Canada, because the Panel made this error, it also erred by failing to make a finding of discriminatory conduct under subparagraph (a) before examining the 'commerciality' of the CWB Export Regime under subparagraph (b).

The United States's appeal related to 'the Panel's *interpretation of subparagraph (b)* of Article XVII:1; to the Panel's *application* of this interpretation *to the CWB Export Regime*; and to the Panel's ultimate finding that the United States had not established any inconsistency with the principles of subparagraphs (a) or (b) of Article XVII:1 of the GATT 1994.'[21] The US sought a finding of broad disciplines on the behavior of STEs, including their competitive behavior. The US argued that Article XVII:1(b) establishes an independent obligation for STEs to base their decisions on commercial considerations. The US argued that subparagraphs (a) and (b) contain 'multiple, distinct obligations'.[22]

The Appellate Body began its consideration of Article XVII:1 by examining the relationship between subparagraphs (a) and (b): between references to a finding of discrimination and a finding of failure to purchase and sell 'solely in accordance with commercial considerations'.

The US argued that its position was supported by statements of the Panel in *Korea–Various Measures on Beef*, suggesting that the obligations expressed in subparagraphs (a) and (b) are independent:

> A conclusion that the principle of non-discrimination was violated would suffice to prove a violation of Article XVII; similarly, a conclusion that a decision to purchase or buy was not based on 'commercial considerations', would also suffice to show a violation of Article XVII.[23]

Canada, on the other hand, argued that the above statement by the Panel in the *Korea–Various Measures on Beef* case was not necessary to the Panel's decision. Moreover, the Panel in *Korea–Various Measures on Beef* expressly endorsed the views of the Panel in *Canada–FIRA*, which read subparagraphs (a) and (b) as one obligation.[24] The Panel in *Canada–FIRA* stated that '[t]he fact that sub-paragraph (b) does not establish a separate general obligation to allow enterprises to act in accordance with commercial considerations, but merely defines the obligations set out in the preceding sub-paragraph, is made clear through the introductory words.'[25]

20 Appellate Body Report, para. 76.

21 Appellate Body Report, para. 77 (emphasis in original) (citation omitted).

22 U.S. Appellee's Submission, para. 5.

23 *Korea – Measures Affecting Imports of Fresh, Chilled and Frozen Beef*, WT/DS161,169/R, 31 July 2000, para. 757.

24 Panel Report, para. 6.56.

25 Report of the Panel, *Canada – Administration of the Foreign Investment Review Act*, adopted 7 February 1984, para. 5.16, L/5504, 30S/140.

In accord with the Panel in *Canada–FIRA*, the Panel in *Korea–Various Measures on Beef* stated that the scope of paragraph (b) defines the obligations in paragraph (a): evidence as to whether the STE action is based on commercial considerations is to be used to assess discrimination.[26] This would seem to confirm the Canadian argument, and the Appellate Body found that it was 'not clear that the panel in *Korea–Various Measures on Beef* intended [the language quoted above] to have the meaning the United States seeks to ascribe to it'.[27] Indeed, there is much language in the *Korea–Various Measures on Beef* decision to support the Canadian position.

The Appellate Body found that the 'shall be understood' language in subparagraph (b), referring to subparagraph (a), means that subparagraph (b) is dependent upon, and an explanation of, subparagraph (a).[28] Here the Appellate Body followed the reasoning of the Panel in the *Canada–FIRA* case.[29] Subparagraph (b) clarifies the general obligation of nondiscrimination provided in subparagraph (a). Subparagraph (b) does not establish requirements independent of subparagraph (a).[30]

Therefore, in future cases under Article XVII:1, a Panel will need to begin its analysis with an evaluation of the application of subparagraph (a). 'It appears to us that these [the subparagraph (b)] types of differential treatment would be the most likely to occur in practice and, therefore, that most if not all cases under Article XVII:1 will involve an analysis of both subparagraphs (a) and (b).'[31] Canada argued that a Panel must first find discrimination under subparagraph (a) before it can go on to make findings under subparagraph (b), and that subparagraph (b) does not create independent obligations.[32] Rather, '[i]n Canada's view, what subparagraph (b) does is to interpret and temper the obligation under subparagraph (a)'.[33]

While the Appellate Body did not find that a full analysis under subparagraph (a) is required before proceeding to subparagraph (b), it found that a Panel must at least identify the differential treatment alleged to be discriminatory under subparagraph (a) before performing its analysis under subparagraph (b).[34] The Appellate Body found that an evaluation of whether discrimination is based on commercial considerations within the meaning of subparagraph (b) might depend on the type of discrimination identified under subparagraph (a).[35] The Appellate

26 Panel Report on *Korea – Various Measures on Beef*, para. 755.
27 Appellate Body Report, para. 103.
28 Appellate Body Report, paras. 89–91; 100.
29 *Canada – Administration of the Foreign Investment Review Act*, L504, adopted 7 February 1984, 30S/140.
30 Appellate Body Report, para. 100.
31 Appellate Body Report, para. 99.
32 Panel Report, para. 6.54.
33 Ibid.
34 Appellate Body Report, paras. 111–112.
35 Appellate Body Report, para. 110.

Body stated that '[s]ubparagraph (b) sets forth two specific conditions with which an STE must comply if allegedly discriminatory conduct falling, prima facie, within the scope of subparagraph (a) is to be found consistent with Article XVII:1'.[36] Thus, as suggested by Canada, subparagraph (b) can serve to 'temper' or limit the scope of subparagraph (a): not all discrimination within the meaning of subparagraph (a) violates Article XVII:1.

The Panel in *Korea–Various Measures on Beef* had said that the variables in subparagraph (b) are to be used to assess whether the national measure is discriminatory.[37] The Appellate Body in the present case stated that it did not decide whether a Panel may find a violation of subparagraph (a) alone, without considering subparagraph (b).[38]

The Panel had reserved on its analysis of subparagraph (a), subject to its determination under subparagraph (b). Under these circumstances, the Appellate Body found that the Panel's inquiry under subparagraph (b) was made in the context of an inquiry into alleged discriminatory practices, and therefore the Panel did not misapply these two provisions by focusing its analysis on subparagraph (b).[39] That is, given that the Panel found no non-commercial sales within the meaning of subparagraph (b), and the US did not establish an independent claim of discrimination under subparagraph (a), there was no error.

The logic advanced by the Appellate Body is not ineluctable. The 'shall be understood' language could equally be understood to *deem* failure to 'make purchases or sales solely in accordance with commercial considerations' to constitute 'discrimination' under subparagraph (a), reversing the order of analysis. The US alleged pursuant to Article XVII:1 that Canada engaged in discrimination *by virtue of its alleged non-commercial* sales.[40] Indeed, the US argued that 'on the facts of this case, the alleged discriminatory sales behaviour by the CWB is a necessary result of the CWB not making sales solely in accordance with commercial considerations'.[41]

Furthermore, all discrimination in the sense of subparagraph (a) (in the WTO sense) would be expected to involve decisions based on non-commercial considerations. Discrimination in the WTO sense involves government (policy) measures that distinguish between goods in a way that a private person, absent the policy, would not. Discrimination in this context is the use of impermissible considerations in choosing suppliers or customers:[42] commercial considerations are always permissible under WTO law. Moreover, in practice it will frequently be difficult, if not impossible, to objectively determine whether or not a specific

36 Ibid.
37 *Korea–Various Measures on Beef*, para. 757.
38 Appellate Body Report, at para. 106, note 115.
39 Appellate Body Report, paras. 119–123.
40 Appellate Body Report, para. 118.
41 Panel Report, para. 6.58.
42 See Panel Report, para. 6.88.

transaction is based on commercial considerations, as pricing and allocation decisions tend to be multidimensional and may reflect factors/strategies that are not known or observable to outsiders.

Thus, it seems logically impossible for subparagraph (b) to narrow the scope of subparagraph (a). Although the Appellate Body suggests that measures that comply with the *two* prongs of subparagraph (b) – commercial considerations and opportunities to enterprises of other WTO members – might escape the disciplines of subparagraph (a),[43] this understanding seems to lack textual support, and it is difficult to see how it would apply.

5.3 *Commercial considerations*

The US argued that '[w]here an export STE has been granted special and exclusive privileges which permit it to operate without the normal market constraints faced by a commercial actor, that STE could make use of its privileges to gain market share in particular markets, but such behaviour would not be commercial'.[44] Under this reading, the prohibition of non-commercial considerations could have a scope that goes beyond discrimination: it would not necessarily be discriminatory to seek to maximize market share, but it would, according to the US, be 'non-commercial'. However, there seems little reason to believe that a requirement of commercial considerations excludes a goal of increasing market share.[45]

The Appellate Body confirmed the Panel's understanding of the term 'commercial considerations':

> The Panel began its analysis by considering the meaning of the term 'commercial considerations' in subparagraph (b) and found that this term should be understood as meaning 'considerations pertaining to commerce and trade, or considerations which involve regarding purchases or sales 'as mere matters of business'.' The Panel also determined that the requirement that STEs act solely in accordance with such considerations 'must imply that they should seek to purchase or sell on terms which are economically advantageous for themselves and/or their owners, members, beneficiaries, etc.' Thus, the Panel interpreted the term 'commercial considerations' as encompassing a range of different considerations that are defined in any given case by the type of 'business' involved (purchases or sales), and by the economic considerations that motivate actors engaged in business in the relevant market(s).[46]

Thus, there is no *a priori* reason to exclude concerns for market share, as opposed to profits.

43 Appellate Body Report, para. 110.

44 Panel Report, para. 6.74.

45 The types of actions taken to gain market share would be likely to involve price discrimination among export markets. However, the ad note to Article XVII stipulates that price discrimination is permitted, so long as it is motivated by commercial considerations.

46 Appellate Body Report, para. 140, 144 (citations omitted).

The Appellate Body's understanding of the relationship between subparagraphs (a) and (b) informed its interpretation of subparagraph (b). Subparagraph (b) does not address all failures to act in a commercial manner, but only those related to discrimination. The Appellate Body pointed out that 'Article XVII:1 imposes an obligation on Members not to use STEs in order to discriminate in ways that would be prohibited if undertaken directly by Members'.[47]

5.4 *Competition and STE behavior*

The central question addressed in this case by the Appellate Body was whether the nondiscriminatory-treatment prong of (a) is independent of the commercial considerations prong of subparagraph (b). The US argued that these were independent, several obligations, either of which could be the basis for a successful attack. The Appellate Body concluded that subparagraph (b) clarifies the scope of the non-discrimination obligation in subparagraph (a). According to the Appellate Body, the types of discrimination listed in subparagraph (b) are the most likely, but do not exhaust the category of measures that might violate subparagraph (a).[48] Therefore, Panels must begin by analyzing subparagraph (a), and will usually, but not always, also have to evaluate subparagraph (b).[49]

The Appellate Body stated that '[t]he disciplines of Article XVII:1 are aimed at preventing certain types of discriminatory behaviour. We see no basis for interpreting that provision as imposing comprehensive competition-law-type obligations on STEs, as the United States would have us do.'[50] Thus, subparagraph (b) does not establish separate requirements independent of subparagraph (a).[51] The Appellate Body quoted approvingly the *Canada–FIRA* Panel report to the effect that subparagraph (b) does not establish a separate obligation to act in accordance with commercial considerations.[52]

Importantly, Article XVII is therefore not a broad-ranging requirement that STEs emulate private-sector behavior. Rather, STEs may engage in actions that are not commercially motivated – that reflect public-policy objectives – so long as the implementation of that public policy is not discriminatory. In other words, STEs may act as agents of public policy, so long as they comply with the non-discrimination requirements of Article XVII. The Panel articulated this concept: 'Finally, the United States' argument that STEs must act like "commercial actors" tends to overlook the fact that STEs are not necessarily used only for commercial purposes. STEs may also be established or maintained to carry out governmental

47 Appellate Body Report, para. 98.
48 Appellate Body Report, para. 99.
49 Appellate Body Report, para. 109.
50 Appellate Body Report, para. 145.
51 Appellate Body Report, para. 100.
52 Appellate Body Report, para. 104. See *Canada – Administration of the Foreign Investment Review Act*, L504, adopted 7 February 1984, 30S/140, para. 5.16.

policies or programmes (e.g., policies related to food security, policies aimed at reducing alcohol consumption, policies to achieve price stabilization, etc.).'[53]

The US also argued that the second clause of subparagraph (b) of Article XVII: 1 – requiring STEs to 'afford the enterprises of other Members adequate opportunity ... to compete for participation in such purchases or sales' – requires that adequate opportunities be afforded to enterprises that wished to sell *in competition* with the STE.[54] However, the Appellate Body found that the term 'such purchases or sales' refers back to subparagraph (a), which addresses purchases and sales by the STE, not by competing enterprises. Thus, the requisite adequate opportunity is to be a purchaser or seller counterpart to the STE, not to be a competitor to the STE.[55]

The Appellate Body's understanding has important substantive ramifications. There is no independent obligation of decisionmaking in accordance with commercial considerations. Subparagraph (b) is neither a source of independent obligations, nor a basis for finding a deemed violation of subparagraph (a). Paragraph 145 of the Appellate Body report is worth quoting in full:

> At the same time, our interpretation of the relationship between subparagraphs (a) and (b) of Article XVII:1 necessarily implies that the scope of the inquiry to be undertaken under subparagraph (b) must be governed by the principles of subparagraph (a). In other words, a panel inquiring whether an STE has acted solely in accordance with commercial considerations must undertake this inquiry with respect to the market(s) in which the STE is alleged to be engaging in discriminatory conduct. Subparagraph (b) does not give panels a mandate to engage in a broader inquiry into whether, in the abstract, STEs are acting 'commercially'. The disciplines of Article XVII:1 are aimed at preventing certain types of discriminatory behaviour. We see no basis for interpreting that provision as imposing comprehensive competition-law-type obligations on STEs, as the United States would have us do. (citation omitted)

The US argument in this case can be linked to the broader argument regarding the role of competition policy in international trade. In a sense, a single-desk STE is similar to a private domestic monopolist (see McCorriston and MacLaren, 2002). A private domestic monopolist would have the *power* to price discriminate and to cross-subsidize, but would lack the *interest* that a STE might have in providing a net subsidy. So, assuming for a moment that the extent of STE net subsidization could be identified and addressed through WTO subsidies law, the other concerns are similar.

In the debate regarding competition policy at the WTO, proponents argue that states have incentives to externalize anticompetitive effects on one another through lax enforcement of competition law when the adverse effects occur abroad (see

53 Panel Report, para. 6.96 (citation omitted).
54 Appellate Body Report, para. 152.
55 Appellate Body Report, para. 157.

Guzman, 2001 and 2004). The STE context is more direct. States are not simply failing to have or enforce competition law; they are directly establishing monopolies. Indeed, Sir Leon Brittan has opined as follows:

> I should at this point raise a related issue concerning state trading, in other words, where a government has a special right to a designated corporation to import or export or to distribute certain goods ... I think that, if we are to look at international competition rules seriously, the time is ripe to consider whether this antiquated form of monopoly trading can be phased out altogether (1997).

That said, there is an important difference between the domain of competition policy, especially if defined in US terms as antitrust law and enforcement, and STEs. The latter are mandated by governments, as are any other entities with exclusive rights and privileges. In practice, competition law often does not apply to the domestic actions of government-supported or mandated entities because their actions reflect government policy. The implication is that this is a debate that must extend to what falls under Article 86 of the EC Treaty (formerly Article 90 of the Treaty of Rome): exclusive rights and State monopolies. Finally, it is worth noting that certain types of government policies – including STEs – may be appropriate *responses* to the exercise of market power by large multinational corporations in particular fields. 'The assumption of a competitive alternative inevitably leads to the conclusion that elimination of STEs would lead to improved market performance' (see Paddock, 1998). In addition to questions regarding the assumption of perfect competition, it should also be borne in mind that STEs may maximize total producer surplus rather than profits (McCorriston and MacLaren, 2002).

5.5 Article XVII and Article III

There has been some dispute as to whether Article XVII:1 includes a prohibition of discrimination in the national-treatment sense (the Article III sense), in addition to a prohibition of discrimination in the MFN sense (Petersmann, 1998). The Panel in *Canada–FIRA* suggested in dictum that it did not.[56] In the *Korea–Various Measures on Beef* decision, the Panel held that the principles referenced in Article XVII:1(a) include at least the provisions of Articles I and III of GATT.[57] In the instant case, the Panel did not consider what types of discrimination are covered by

56 It 'saw great force in Canada's argument that only the most-favoured-nation and not the national treatment obligations fall within the scope of the general principles referred to in Article XVII:1(a)'. *Canada – Administration of the Foreign Investment Review Act*, adopted 7 February 1984, BISD 30S/140, 163, para. 5.16.

57 *Panel Report on Korea – Various Measures on Beef*, para. 753, citing Panel Report on *Canada – Import, Distribution and Sale of Alcoholic Drinks by Canadian Provincial Marketing Agencies*, adopted 18 February 1992, BISD 39S/27 (EC), para. 4.26; Panel Report on *Canada – Import, Distribution and Sale of Alcoholic Drinks by Canadian Provincial Marketing Agencies*, adopted 18 February 1992, BISD 39S/27 (US), para. 5.15, stating that 'This interpretation was confirmed *a contrario* by the wording of Article III: 8(a).'

the reference to 'principles of non-discriminatory treatment' in Article XVII:1(a). Nor was the Appellate Body requested to address this issue.[58]

There are different views regarding whether Article III itself is separately applicable to STEs (see Davey, 1998). If Article III applies to STE behavior, is every violation of the antidiscrimination requirement of Article XVII:1 also a violation of Article III? It appears not. Article III:4 speaks of 'laws, regulations or requirements affecting ... internal sale, offering for sale, purchase, transportation, distribution or use.' So there may be a loophole for purchase or sale decisions, although it may be possible to read this language broadly enough to include STE purchasing requirements.

On the other hand, Article III:8(a) excludes from coverage government procurement for its own use, and by *a contrario* reasoning seems to leave included in other provisions of Article III government procurement and resale for commercial use.[59] But this argument must encounter an *expressio unius* argument based on the Ad Note to Articles XI, XII, XIII, XIV, and XVIII, which specifically states that these Articles include restrictions made effective through STEs.[60] Its failure to include Article III supports an argument that Article III does not cover acts of STEs. However, in *Canada – Import, Distribution and Sale of Alcoholic Drinks by Canadian Provincial Marketing Agencies*, the 1992 Panel found certain STE practices to violate Article III.[61]

Furthermore, there may be a question as to whether STE purchase or sale decisions are 'measures' of the relevant member state. Is the STE an organ of the relevant member state for purposes of responsibility under WTO law, or an independent legal entity? This is an issue of the scope of state responsibility for STEs. In the context of Article XVII, the Panel in the instant case stated that 'under Article XVII:1(a), non-conforming conduct by a Member's STE engages that Member's responsibility under international law, even in the absence of intervention of the Member itself, as would be necessary under Article XVII:1(c).'[62] But does a violation of Article III by a STE violate the member state's obligations thereunder? Perhaps it is best to say that if Article III governs STE behavior, then the member state has an obligation to ensure compliance. This would appear to be the result under Article XVI:4 of the WTO Charter.

On the other hand, there is some question whether the disciplines of Article XVII are subsumed by other provisions of GATT, including Article III. 'It is

58 Appellate Body Report, para. 88.

59 *Canada – Import, Distribution and Sale of Alcoholic Drinks by Canadian Provincial Marketing Agencies*, L6304, adopted 22 March 1988, 35S/27, 90, para. 4.26.

60 Canada made this argument in *Canada – Import, Distribution and Sale of Alcoholic Drinks by Canadian Provincial Marketing Agencies*, L6304, adopted 22 March 1988, 35S/27, 90, para. 4.26 (although it did not rule on the Article III claim, the Panel 'saw great force to' the opposing argument).

61 *Canada – Import, Distribution and Sale of Alcoholic Drinks by Canadian Provincial Marketing Agencies*, adopted 18 February 1992, BISD 39S/27, 80–82, paras. 5.17–5.22.

62 Panel Report, para. 6.43.

noteworthy that in the past, no GATT or WTO dispute settlement report has established a violation of Article XVII. The claims of GATT-inconsistent discrimination were always decided in favour of the complainants directly on the basis of Articles I, III, and XI rather than on Article XVII' (Petersmann, 1998).[63]

6. Commercial considerations and the right to regulate

The Appellate Body's holding seems to leave significant policy space in Article XVII:1(b). Member states that use STEs to implement development policy, or industrial policy, are protected from the application of the commercial considerations requirement of Article XVII:1(b), provided that their action is not discriminatory within the meaning of Article XVII:1(a).

This was important to a number of WTO Member States. The Appellate Body noted that:

> Canada, Australia, China, and the European Communities all disagree with the United States' reasoning. Essentially, they argue that accepting the United States' view of Article XVII:1(b) would force STEs to refrain from using *any* of the special rights or privileges that they may enjoy and, thereby, put them at a competitive *disadvantage* as compared to private enterprises, which can and do exercise any and all market power they can muster. These participants argue that any such interpretation would be inconsistent with the explicit recognition, in Article XVII:1, that Members are entitled to establish and maintain STEs and to grant them exclusive or special privileges.[64]

7. Discrimination under Article XVII:1(a)

Note that subparagraph (b) of Article XVII:1 deals with *non-commercial considerations*, which may or may not be associated with discrimination. Above, we have discussed the relationship between 'non-discrimination' under subparagraph (a) and 'commercial considerations' under subparagraph (b). This relationship depends, in part, on the meaning of 'discrimination' in Article XVII:1(a) (discussed below). On the other hand, as suggested above, while not all cases of non-commercial considerations involve discrimination, all cases of discrimination (in the WTO sense[65]) involve non-commercial considerations in the sense of subparagraph (b). After all, the WTO is concerned with discrimination because of the effects of discrimination on competition. Competition, by definition, involves the free play of the kinds of commercial considerations listed in subparagraph (b).

63 Since Petersmann wrote, a Panel in *Korea – Measures Affecting Imports of Fresh, Chilled and Frozen Beef*, WT/DS161,169/R, Appellate Body Report adopted 2001, found a violation of Article XVII.

64 Appellate Body Report, para. 147.

65 Excluding differential pricing, pursuant to the ad note to Article XVII:1.

If discrimination requires differential treatment of imported and domestic products – as would seem to be suggested by 'non-discriminatory treatment prescribed in this Agreement for governmental measures affecting imports or exports by private traders' – then there will be cases in which subparagraph (a) is narrower than subparagraph (b). That is, there will be cases where the application of noncommercial considerations has no international differential or discriminatory intent or impact. We do not yet know how future Panels, and the Appellate Body, will define discrimination under Article XVII:1(a). The reference in Article XVII:1(a) is to 'general principles of non-discriminatory treatment prescribed in this Agreement for governmental measures affecting imports or exports by private traders'.

In connection with Article III jurisprudence of de facto discrimination, a significant question arises whether national treatment is violated simply by differential treatment of like products, where likeness is determined based largely on a competitive relationship, or whether, on the other hand, national treatment is violated where regulatory categories appear to have been established with the aim of affecting the competitive position of imported products, and with that effect (see Hudec, 1998 and Porges and Trachtman, 2003). It may be that Article XVII jurisprudence will need to develop a doctrine by which to distinguish between STE measures that have been established with a similar aim and effect of discrimination, on the one hand, and STE measures that carry out a good-faith, albeit noncommercial, industrial policy.

Does the *Canada–Wheat* opinion require a different understanding of discrimination under Article XVII:1(a) from that which exists under Articles I, III, XIII, etc.? To the extent that there is a difference, it would seem to be inconsistent with the express intent of Article XVII:1(a), which respects the *principles of non-discrimination* reflected in those provisions. As noted above, there is some question as to which principles of non-discrimination are included.

To the extent that STEs are used for development-promotion purposes, it may be that Article XVII inhibits some of the behaviors that might be desirable. Does a distinction motivated by considerations of economic-development policy constitute discrimination in the Article XVII:1(a) sense? The Appellate Body in *Canada–Wheat* specifically referred to its decision in *EC–Tariff Preferences*, suggesting that 'discrimination' 'can accommodate both drawing distinctions *per se*, and drawing distinctions *on an improper basis*'.[66] While the Appellate Body was not called upon to determine which meaning prevails within Article XVII:1(a), it leaves room for a future interpretation that allows for distinctions on a proper development-policy or industrial-policy basis. Of course, STEs and similar entities that would be subject to Article XVII are just one instrument that governments may want to use to pursue development objectives. More generally, development policies may be justified under Article XVIII GATT, raising potential

66 Appellate Body Report, para. 87.

questions concerning the consistency of any interpretations of Article XVII and Article XVIII and the Enabling Clause.

8. What are the implications for STE-based economic policy?

The Appellate Body decision in *Canada–Wheat*, declining to impose a stricter requirement on STE behavior beyond non-discrimination, leaves a great deal of regulatory freedom for states using STEs as instruments of economic policy. If the Appellate Body had accepted the US argument that Article XVII:1(b) goes beyond discrimination to impose a general requirement of commercial behavior (decision making in accordance with commercial considerations), it would have been incumbent upon the Appellate Body also to identify some limits to this requirement. For example, a different interpretative approach might have found a requirement of commercial behavior, but tempered it by a least-trade-restrictive-alternative test. This would have been an act of construction, as Article XVII does not use language of this type. But it would have been practically necessary in order to allow STEs to be useful from a policy standpoint.

The Appellate Body decision does not require that STE behavior be commercial, or even efficient, but maintains the requirement that STE behavior must be non-discriminatory – that it not impose adverse effects on other states through discrimination. The definition of discrimination may pose some difficulty, but if the focus is on aim and effects, application of Article XVII will address the intentional distortions, leaving unintentional distortions in place. This seems a reasonable balance between the right to trade and the right to regulate.

Of course, if the Appellate Body had agreed with the US that there is an independent obligation to act solely in accordance with commercial considerations, it would have introduced a procrustean requirement that STEs act as though they were not STEs. The Appellate Body would have inappropriately caused the WTO to take sides in connection with the choice between different types of organization of the economy of member states.[67]

Notwithstanding the resolution of this case, it is not clear that the CWB will continue to operate in its current configuration. Some Canadian farm groups are of the view that abolishing the monopoly marketing and purchasing rights of the CWB would be beneficial to them. Forces for reform include the government of Alberta, which has commissioned a study on how the monopoly might be phased out. While pressure from trading partners may have played a role in focusing attention on the efficiency and equity performance of the CWB, what is more important appears to have been perceptions that the performance of the CWB can be improved upon, and the experience of New Zealand and Australia in moving towards a private sector/cooperative model of export marketing.[68]

67 See Cottier and Mavroidis, 1998, warning against such intervention.

68 See Marketing Choice – The Way Forward, October 25, 2006. Available at http://www.agr.gc.ca/cb/ip/pdf/final_251006_e.pdf.

References

Abbott, Philip C. and Linda M. Young (2003), 'Export Competition Issues in the Doha Round', Paper presented at the International Conference: Agricultural Policy Reform and the WTO: Where Are We Heading?, 23–26 June 2003, available at http://www2.montana.edu/lmyoung/pdf-files/Abbott%20and%20Young.pdf.

Alston, Julian M. and Richard S. Gray (2000), State Trading versus Export Subsidies: The Case of Canadian Wheat, *Journal of Agricultural and Resource Economics*, **25**(1): 51–67.

Brittan, Leon (1997), 'Competition Policy and the Trading System: Toward International Rules in the WTO', Speech presented to the Institute for International Economics, Washington, DC, November 1997.

Cottier, Thomas and Petros C. Mavroidis (1998), 'Conclusions: The Reach of International Trade Law', in Thomas Cottier and Petros C. Mavroidis (eds), *State Trading in the Twenty-First Century*, Ann Arbor, Michigan: University of Michigan Press, pp. 395–408.

Davey, William J. (1998), 'Article XVII GATT: An Overview', in Thomas Cottier and Petros C. Mavroidis (eds), *State Trading in the Twenty-First Century*, Ann Arbor, Michigan: University of Michigan Press, pp. 17–36.

Dong, Fengxia, Thomas Marsh, and Kyle Stiegert (2006), 'State Trading Enterprises in a Differentiated Product Environment: The Case of Global Malting Barley Markets', *American Journal of Agricultural Economics*, **88**(1): 90–103.

Guzman, Andrew T. (2001), 'Antitrust and International Regulatory Federalism', *New York University Law Review*, **76**: 1142–1163.

Guzman, Andrew T. (2004), 'The Case for International Antitrust', *Berkeley Journal of International Law*, **22**: 355–374.

Hoekman, Bernard M. and Patrick Low (1998), 'State Trading: Rule Making Alternatives for Entities with Exclusive Rights', in Thomas Cottier and Petros C. Mavroidis (eds), *State Trading in the Twenty-First Century*, Ann Arbor, Michigan: University of Michigan Press, pp. 327–344.

Horlick, Gary N. and Kristin Heim Mowry (1998), 'The Treatment of Activities of State Trading Enterprises under the WTO Subsidies Rules', in Thomas Cottier and Petros C. Mavroidis (eds), *State Trading in the Twenty-First Century*, Ann Arbor, Michigan: University of Michigan Press, pp. 97–114.

Hudec, Robert E. (1998), 'GATT/WTO Constraints on National Regulation: Requiem for an "Aim and Effects" Test', *International Lawyer*, **32**: 619–649.

Lavoie, Nathalie (2005), 'Price Discrimination in the Context of Vertical Differentiation: An Application to Canadian Wheat Exports', *American Journal of Agricultural Economics*, **87**(4): 835–854.

Marketing Choice – The Way Forward, 25 October 2006, available at http://www.agr.gc.ca/cb/ip/pdf/final_251006_e.pdf.

McCorriston, Steve and Donald MacLaren (2002), 'Perspectives on the State Trading Issue in the WTO Negotiations', *European Review of Agricultural Economics*, **29**(1): 131–154.

Paddock, Brian (1998), 'State Trading and International Trade Negotiations', Agriculture and Agri-Food Canada, December 1998, available at http://dsp-psd.communication.gc.ca/Collection/A22-184-1998E.pdf.

Petersmann, Ernst-Ulrich (1998), 'GATT Law on State Trading Enterprises: Critical Evaluation of Article XVII and Proposals for Reform', in Thomas Cottier and Petros C. Mavroidis (eds), *State Trading in the Twenty-First Century*, Ann Arbor, Michigan: University of Michigan Press, pp. 71–96.

Porges, Amelia and Joel P. Trachtman (2003), 'Robert Hudec and Domestic Regulation: The Resurrection of "Aim and Effects"', *Journal of World Trade*, **37**(4): 783–799.

Secretariat of the World Trade Organization (1995), *Operations of State Trading Enterprises as They Relate to International Trade*, G/STR/2 (26 October, 1995).

Sumner, Dan and Richard Boltuck (2001), 'Anatomy of the Global Wheat Market, and the Role of the Canadian Wheat Board', Report prepared for the Canadian Wheat Board, Winnipeg.

United States Department of Agriculture (USDA) (2002), 'US Proposal for Global Agricultural Trade Reform', Foreign Agricultural Service (FAS), Washington, DC, September 2002, available at http://www.fas.usda.gov/itp/wto/actual.htm.

Young, Linda M. (2005), 'Export Competition Disciplines in the Doha Round', International Agricultural Trade Research Consortium, Trade Policy Issues Paper No. 3.

Annex

Article XVII

State Trading Enterprises

1.* (*a*) Each contracting party undertakes that if it establishes or maintains a State enterprise, wherever located, or grants to any enterprise, formally or in effect, exclusive or special privileges,* such enterprise shall, in its purchases or sales involving either imports or exports, act in a manner consistent with the general principles of non-discriminatory treatment prescribed in this Agreement for governmental measures affecting imports or exports by private traders.

(*b*) The provisions of subparagraph (*a*) of this paragraph shall be understood to require that such enterprises shall, having due regard to the other provisions of this Agreement, make any such purchases or sales solely in accordance with commercial considerations,* including price, quality, availability, marketability, transportation and other conditions of purchase or sale, and shall afford the enterprises of the other contracting parties adequate opportunity, in accordance with customary business practice, to compete for participation in such purchases or sales.

Relevant ad notes, included in the treaty, follow:

Paragraph 1

The operations of Marketing Boards, which are established by contracting parties and are engaged in purchasing or selling, are subject to the provisions of subparagraphs (*a*) and (*b*).

The activities of Marketing Boards which are established by contracting parties and which do not purchase or sell but lay down regulations covering private trade are governed by the relevant Articles of this Agreement.

The charging by a state enterprise of different prices for its sales of a product in different markets is not precluded by the provisions of this Article, provided that such different prices are charged for commercial reasons, to meet conditions of supply and demand in export markets.

Paragraph 1(a)

Governmental measures imposed to insure standards of quality and efficiency in the operation of external trade, or privileges granted for the exploitation of national natural resources but which do not empower the government to exercise control over the trading activities of the enterprise in question, do not constitute 'exclusive or special privileges'.

Comment

Canada–Wheat: discrimination, non-commercial considerations, and the right to regulate through state trading enterprises

Prepared for the ALI Project on the Case Law of the WTO

FRIEDER ROESSLER

Executive Director, Advisory Centre on WTO Law (ACWL)

Paragraph (a) of Article XVII: 1 of the GATT provides that state trading enterprises shall, in their purchases or sales involving imports or exports, act in a manner 'consistent with the general principles of non-discriminatory treatment' prescribed by the GATT for government measures affecting imports or exports by private traders. According to paragraph (b) of Article XVII: 1, paragraph (a) shall be understood to mean that state trading enterprises shall make their purchases or sales involving imports or exports 'solely in accordance with commercial considerations'.

In *Canada – Wheat Exports and Grain Imports*, the Appellate Body made clear that paragraph (b) does not establish an independent obligation to ensure that state trading enterprises act solely in accordance with commercial considerations; it merely defines the obligation set out in paragraph (a). The Appellate Body thereby endorsed the finding of the GATT Panel on *Canada – FIRA*, which had ruled in 1984 that 'the commercial considerations criterion becomes relevant only after it has been determined that the governmental action at issue falls within the scope of the general principles of nondiscriminatory treatment prescribed by the General Agreement'. The ruling of the Appellate Body confirms that the Members of the WTO may use state trading enterprises to pursue noncommercial policy objectives provided they act consistently with GATT's general principles of nondiscriminatory treatment. The fundamental question that has been left

The views expressed in this comment are those of the author.

open by the Appellate Body is: what are the principles of nondiscriminatory treatment covered by paragraph (a)? It is undisputed that they include the principles set out in the most-favored-nation (MFN) clause of Article I and other MFN-type provisions in the GATT (such as Articles V: 5 and IX: 1). However, does it also apply to the principles set out in the national-treatment provisions of Article III?

Hoekman and Trachtman discuss the issue in their paper but provide no definitive answer. I would like to offer some additional observations on this point.

An enterprise under the control of the government that has been accorded the exclusive right to import or export or other privileges not enjoyed by other potential importers or exporters can be used for the same purposes as tariffs, quotas, variable levies, and other instruments regulating the trade of enterprises independent of the government. For instance, if the government creates a monopoly for the import of sugar and instructs that monopoly to resell imported sugar with a mark-up of 100 %, it effectively levies an import tariff on sugar; if it instructs the monopoly not to resell imported sugar below a fixed price, it effectively imposes a variable levy; if it instructs it to import only a limited amount of sugar, it effectively establishes an import quota for sugar.

The drafters of the GATT established a system of rules that permit the use of state trading as an instrument of trade policy and attempted to ensure that state trading operations are not used to circumvent the provisions governing the application of tariffs, quotas, variable levies, and other measures regulating the trade of enterprises independent of the government. Article II: 4 provides that an import monopoly for a product subject to a tariff binding may not operate to afford protection in excess of the protection that can be provided consistently with the tariff binding. A note to Articles XI–XIV and XVIII states that the terms 'import restrictions' and 'export restrictions' used in these Articles cover also restrictions made effective through state trading operations. A note to Article 4 of the Agreement on Agriculture provides that variable import levies and other nontariff measures maintained through state trading enterprises on agricultural products are prohibited. All these provisions are intended to capture state trading operations that do not constitute tariffs, quotas, or variable levies but have *effects equivalent* to such trade-policy instruments.

In the case of the MFN clause, the drafters adopted, for good reasons, a different approach. The MFN clause requires, in respect of customs duties and other related matters, the extension of any advantage to any product originating in any country to like products from all Members. A note extending the application of Article I to state trading operations with effects equivalent to the denial of MFN treatment would not have made sense. A state trading enterprise could not operate if it were not permitted to take actions that have the effect of denying an advantage granted to products of one country to like products of other origins. It must, for instance, be allowed to purchase products from one country and deny that advantage to products from other countries.

For these reasons, state trading enterprises had to be permitted to make distinctions between goods of different origins on the basis of criteria consistent with the basic objectives of the MFN clause. The function of Article XVII: 1 is to provide that permission and to define those criteria. If a Member applies the same customs duty to like products from all other Members, private importers will make their choice among products of different origins in accordance with commercial considerations. Article XVII: 1 ensures that state trading enterprises do the same. Articles I: 1 and XVII: 1 achieve the same objective with different standards of nondiscriminatory treatment: the former with the requirement not to make any distinctions between like products of different origins, the latter with the requirement to make such distinctions solely on the basis of defined criteria.

The national-treatment provisions of Articles III: 2 and III: 4 – unlike the provisions governing tariff, quotas, and variable levies – are sufficiently broadly worded to capture the denial of national treatment to imported products through state trading operations. They cover all internal charges levied, directly or indirectly, on imported products and hence also charges levied through state trading operations. And they cover all requirements affecting the internal sale of imported products and hence also requirements imposed through state trading operations. If the drafters of the GATT had been of the view that Articles III: 2 and III: 4 do not apply to state trading operations, they would have added a note to these provisions extending them to state trading operations with effects equivalent to national-treatment violations. The absence of such a note confirms that they meant these provisions to apply to the denial of national treatment by any means, including state trading operations.

The national-treatment provisions have consistently been interpreted to require Members to accord conditions of competition to imported products no less favorable than those accorded to domestic products. It makes sense that this standard would also apply to internal requirements imposed through state trading operations. All GATT Panels that examined claims of denial of national treatment through state trading operations have addressed those claims under Article III rather than XVII. Unlike the MFN principle, therefore, the national-treatment principle does not need to be redefined for state trading operations, and there is consequently no reason to give Article XVII: 1 that function. If one were to apply Articles III: 2 and III: 4 solely to denials of national treatment through measures affecting private traders and Article XVII: 1 to denials of national treatment through state trading operations, one would make a distinction without a rationale.

My answer to the question left open by Hoekman and Trachtman is for these reasons that it would be neither necessary nor appropriate to apply Article XVII: 1(a) to the denial of national treatment through state trading operations. This does not mean that state trading operations can be used to violate the national-treatment principle. The standards set out in Articles III: 2 and III: 4 can and should be applied to prevent this.

Measures Affecting the Cross-Border Supply of Gambling and Betting Services (DS 285)

DOUGLAS A. IRWIN
Dartmouth College
JOSEPH WEILER
New York University

Abstract: The controversial gambling decision of the Appellate Body is mostly important because of examination of the nature of Access under Article XVI GATS, the relationship of that Article to Articles XIV and XVII GATS, and the parallels with Articles III, XI, and XX GATT. Notably, the Appellate Body took the position that an apparant internal regulatory measure, which, nonetheless, had equivalent effect to a zero quota, violated Article XVI GATS. A similar measure in the area of goods would have been examined under Article III GATT and require a showing of discrimination. The facts of the case would have allowed the decision to be based on Article XVII GATS. Most of this paper deals with this issue. We agree with this interpretation of Article XVI by the Appellate Body but are critical of its hermeneutics, suffering from a textual fetish and a policy phobia. Some other elements in the decision are also examined critically.

In the *US–Gambling* dispute, Antigua and Barbuda (Antigua) challenged a number of provisions of United States Federal and State law, notably the Wire Act, the Travel Act, and the Illegal Gambling Business Act,[1] which, according to Antigua, amounted to an effective ban on Internet gambling. This, it was alleged, effectively shut out Antiguan service providers in a sector in relation to which the United States had, in its Schedule, given a commitment namely 'recreational, cultural, and sporting services' in violation of, notably, Article XVI GATS.

The United States denied that it had made such a commitment, and argued that even if it had given such a commitment, the internal measures in question were origin neutral and of a regulatory nature and therefore did not violate its access commitments under Article XVI. It further argued that the measures in question were in furtherance of policies designed to protect 'public morals and public order' and were thus permitted under the General Exceptions ex Article XIV GATS. The United States maintained at all times that it did not discriminate between domestic- and foreign-service providers in enforcing the prohibition on Internet gambling.

1 18 U.S.C 1084; 18 U.S.C 1952; 18 U.S.C. 1955.

In November 2004, the WTO Panel[2] ruled that the United States had made a specific commitment to open its market to gambling services and that on their face these measures did violate Article XVI. The Panel further held that they could have been justified under Article XIV but failed to satisfy some of the conditions, notably necessity of said Article by failure to engage in consultation.

The Appellate Body, in its April 2005 Report,[3] largely affirmed the Panel's main findings, sometimes with alternative reasoning. Importantly, it rejected the Panel's finding on necessity ex Article XIV but held that the US failed under the chapeau of said Article since in certain instances within the US, notably horseracing, Internet and other remote forms of gambling were allowed.

The resulting dispute rulings, both of the Panel (as modified by the Appellate Body) and of the Appellate Body itself, were adopted by the Dispute Settlement Body. At the DSB meeting of 19 May 2005, the United States stated its intention to implement the DSB's recommendations and indicated that it would need a reasonable period of time to do so. As Antigua and the United States failed to agree on a reasonable time period for implementation in accordance with Article 21.3(b) of the DSU, on 6 June 2005 Antigua requested that the reasonable period of time be determined through binding arbitration pursuant to Article 21.3(c) of the DSU. On 19 August 2005, the Arbitrator circulated his Award to the Members, determining that the reasonable period of time for implementation was 11 months and 2 weeks from 20 April 2005, expiring on 3 April 2006.[4] In an interesting twist, the United States then took the view that in fact the Appellate Body had not found that it was in violation but that it simply failed to 'prove' the necessity of its otherwise justified measures and thus had to do nothing in order to bring itself into compliance other than surmount that burden of proof. This argument was rejected by a 'Compliance Panel' established at the request of Antigua.[5] The Panel Reported on 30 March 2007.[6] The United States decided not to appeal that decision but also announced that it would be withdrawing its commitment in this sector.[7] The saga continues. In the language of the Report to the DSB:

> On 21 June 2007, Antigua and Barbuda requested authorization from the DSB, pursuant to Article 22.2 of the DSU, to suspend the application to the United States of concessions and related obligations of Antigua and Barbuda under the GATS and the TRIPS Agreement. On 23 July 2007, the United States (i) objected to the level of suspension of concessions and obligations proposed by Antigua

2 WT/DS285/R, 10 November 2004.

3 WT/DS285/AB/R, 7 April 2005.

4 Arbitration under Article 21.3(c) of the Understanding on Rules and Procedures Governing the Settlement of Disputes, Award of the Arbitrator Claus-Dieter Ehlermann, WT/DS285/13, 19 August 2005; provided to the Chairman of the DSB, WT/DS285/14, 23 August 2005.

5 Recourse to Article 21.5 of the DSU by Antigua and Barbuda, Request for the Establishment of a Panel, WT/DS285/18, 7 July 2006.

6 WT/DS285/RW, 30 March 2007.

7 See, e.g., http://worldtradelaw.typepad.com/ielpblog/2007/05/developments_in.html or http://www.ntra.com/content.aspx?type=pr&id=25606.

and Barbuda and (ii) claimed that Antigua and Barbuda's proposal does not follow the principles and procedures set forth in Article 22.3 of the DSU. At its meeting on 24 July 2007, the DSB agreed that the matter referred to by the United States be referred to arbitration.[8]

The Gambling case has far-reaching implications. The case was the first to deal with the Internet and e-commerce, and only the second case dealing with the GATS. Gambling is a heavily regulated activity in many countries, and these regulations often restrict the geographic domain of where gambling can take place (e.g., legal casinos in specified locations). There are two threats to these regulations. First, the Internet threatens to erode this geographic element of domestic regulation by giving consumers easy access to gambling opportunities offered by providers away from their own home.[9] Second, the GATS may pose an obstacle to the use of domestic regulations to restrict Internet gambling. In the case of the United States, both of these factors were part of the impetus for the passage of the Unlawful Internet Gambling Enforcement Act (UIGEA) in October 2006. As regards the GATS, the case highlights areas where it would seem that the legal disciplines for the liberalization of services have a greater margin of uncertainty compared to the parallel discipline for goods under the GATT. Tariff classification is not without its difficulties, but these seem at times lesser than the interpretation of service commitments. Likewise, as we shall see, the relationship between Articles XI, III, and XX GATT also appears more determinate than that between parallel Articles XVI, XVII, and XIV.

To help our reader, we provide in edited form an annex with a synopsis of the case as developed by the DSB itself, the issues on appeal, and the conclusions and finding of the AB.

The background to the Appellate Body decision: some economic and political issues

The economic issues are only tangentially related to the main stakes in the Gambling case, but we will discuss them first because it provides the background for some of the legal interpretation to follow.

While there is a gambling industry in the United States – indeed, one with gross revenues of nearly $80 billion in 2003 – most of it arises from highly regulated commercial casinos, Native American casinos, and State lotteries (Kearney, 2005). However, the present case did not concern the legality of gambling, but the restrictions on the long-distance provision of gambling services. At issue in the

8 http://www.wto.org/english/tratop_e/dispu_e/cases_e/ds285_e.htm.

9 See Wilson (2003). Indeed, although on-line gambling is generally illegal in the country, the United States is the home to more gambling websites than any other country (in terms of registered domain names) that serve as forwarding sites to serve customers in other countries.

dispute was the ability of Internet sites located in Antigua to accept bets from customers located in the United States.[10]

The ban on Internet gambling does not appear on its face to be designed as a disguised trade restriction to protect domestic interests because the US prohibitions in the Wire Act of 1961 predate the Internet by decades, i.e. US policy has been longstanding on the issue. The regulation of gambling is a State and Federal issue in the United States. Several States ban Internet gambling altogether, and several Federal laws restrict the use of the technology associated with Internet gambling. The relevant Federal laws were the Wire Act, the Travel Act, and the Illegal Gambling Business Act. The Wire Act of 1961 'prohibits the knowing use of any "wire communication facility" to transmit bets or wagers, use of information assisting betting or wagering on a sports event or contest, or any communication which entitles the recipient to receive money or credit resulting from betting or wagering'.[11]

The nature of the US commitment

The first major issue before the Panel was whether these State and Federal restrictions on Internet gambling violate US commitments under Article XVI of the GATS, which prohibit certain quantitative restrictions on market access. This raised the highly contested issue of what specific commitments the United States had agreed to in its GATS schedule. The US commitment is ambiguous because there is no line in the GATS schedule that explicitly mentions gambling and certainly not Internet gambling.

Antigua held that the United States did not indicate any restrictions on market access in its schedule of GATS commitments. The United States had indicated 'none' in terms of the limitations on market access under the heading of 'Other Recreational Services (except sporting)'. Antigua argued that 'other recreational services' covered gambling and that gambling was not 'sporting' in part on the basis of a document distributed by the GATT Secretariat during the Uruguay Round. The 1993 Services Sectoral Classification List, which in turn made reference to the United Nations' Provisional Central Product Classification, has two subcategories under 'Sporting and Recreational Services': 'Sporting Services' and 'Other Recreational Services'. The sub-subcategory 'Gambling and Betting Services' falls under the latter subcategory, i.e. not under

10 The dispute was initiated at the instigation of Jay Cohen, as US national and founder of World Sport Exchange, who had been sentenced to jail for selling gambling services to US citizens from Antigua. He convinced the Antigua authorities to bring a case against the United States in the WTO, raising the issue of the privatization of dispute settlement. It is, of course, quite common that powerful corporate interests are behind WTO disputes.

11 18 USC 1084. It is unclear whether the Wire Act prohibits non-sports gambling, but the Department of Justice has interpreted it to cover all forms of gambling. As a result, any online gambling businesses located in the United States risks prosecution under the Wire Act.

sporting services but under other recreational services. Although the document's classification scheme was a reference point only, and was not a legal and binding classification system, to the extent that this was used to frame most countries'

GATS commitments, this classification could be interpreted as implying that the United States had not made a commitment on sporting services but had made a commitment on gambling and betting services. Antigua argued that the United States made a full commitment for the cross-border supply of gambling and betting services.

The United States insisted that the classification list was never meant to bind Members to the definitions and that the list could not control the interpretation of the US schedule. Other countries had put gambling services in various sections (entertainment services, tourist services, etc.) of their GATS commitment schedule, and there was no single place where such a commitment was recognized. Thus, gambling and betting services could fall under 'sporting services', which had been excluded from the US commitment.

The problem, of course, is that the precise US commitment is ambiguous because there is no explicit commitment statement; the US schedule is silent on the issue of gambling, so the question turns on which category of services gambling is believed to fall under. Both the Panel and the Appellate Body sided with Antigua in holding that gambling and betting services were covered by the GATS schedule of the United States and decided this issue by referring to the relevant schedule of US services commitments with respect to 'other recreational services (except sporting)'. The Appellate Body agreed that the US commitment did not exclude gambling services by the exclusion of 'sporting'.

The Panel recognized that the failure to exclude gambling may have been an oversight by US negotiators at the Uruguay Round, noting (7.3):

> the United States may well have inadvertently undertaken specific commitments on gambling and betting services. However, it is not for the Panel to second-guess the intentions of the United States at the time the commitment was scheduled. Rather, our role is to interpret and apply the GATS in light of the facts and evidence before us.

Indeed, given the predominant jurisdiction of the US States in gambling matters and the existing State restrictions, it would have been odd for US negotiators to have signed on to a commitment to open markets in gambling services, although these were negotiated before the Internet had begun to flourish.

Even though it was found to have made a GATS commitment to provide market access in gambling services and that several of its measures denied such access, the United States could (and did) invoke the 'General Exceptions' Article XIV of the GATS to justify its actions. Article XIV reads:

> Subject to the requirement that such measures are not applied in a manner which would constitute a means of arbitrary or unjustifiable discrimination between

> countries where like conditions prevail, or a disguised restriction on trade in services, nothing in this Agreement shall be construed to prevent the adoption or enforcement by any Member of measures:
>
> (a) necessary to protect public morals or to maintain public order;
>
> ...
>
> (c) necessary to secure compliance with laws or regulations which are not inconsistent with the provisions of this Agreement including those relating to:
>
> (i) the prevention of deceptive and fraudulent practices or to deal with the effects of a default on services contracts.

This was the first WTO Panel to consider a dispute that involved these provisions in the GATS.

The United States argued that the restrictions on Internet gambling were necessary to prevent minors, who are generally forbidden from gambling, from accessing gambling websites and to prevent money laundering by organized crime. The gambling industry has always had a disreputable aspect to it and economists have identified some of the negative externalities associated with sites that have legal gambling, particularly in terms of crime and other community costs (Grinols and Mustard, 2006). In terms of the public-welfare justification for the Internet ban, the costs of Internet gambling, in particular, have not been as well documented, but the Panel and Appellate Body had little difficulty accepting the public-morals exception claimed by the United States.

The Panel set forth a two-part test to determine if this provision was met. As it stated (6.455):

> in determining whether a challenged measure is provisionally justified under that Article, the Member invoking that provision must demonstrate two elements, namely:
>
> (a) the measure must be one designed to 'protect public morals' or to 'maintain public order'; and
> (b) the measure for which justification is claimed must be 'necessary' to protect public morals or to maintain public order.

The Panel decided affirmatively with respect to (a). They agreed with the United States that issues related to public order and morals – such as fraud, underage gambling, and organized crime – were specifically related to the remote provision of gambling services that justified the regulations.

However, Antigua maintained that it could have addressed the US concerns if the United States had been willing to consult or negotiate an agreeable outcome. Because the United States refused to consult or negotiate, the Panel decided that the US laws were not 'necessary' to enforce the Article XIV(a) exception. As they explained (6.533, 6.534):

> while the United States has legitimate specific concerns with respect to money laundering, fraud, health and underage gambling that are specific to the remote

> supply of gambling and betting services, which suggests that the measures in question are 'necessary' within the meaning of Article XIV(a), the United States has declined Antigua's invitation to engage in bilateral and/or multilateral consultations and/or negotiations to determine whether there is a way of addressing its concerns in a WTO-consistent manner.
>
> ... given the circumstance of this case and for the reasons explained above ... the United States, before imposing a WTO inconsistent measure, was obliged to explore these options in a good faith manner with a view to exhausting WTO-consistent alternatives, even if it considered that the measures in question were 'indispensable'.

Thus, the Panel (6.526) stated:

> The United States' obligation to consult with Antigua before and while imposing its prohibition on the cross-border supply of gambling and betting services derives from the fact that it has undertaken a specific market access commitment for mode 1 ... In rejecting Antigua's invitation to engage in bilateral or multilateral consultations and/or negotiations, the United States failed to pursue in good faith a course of action that could have been used by it to explore the possibility of finding a reasonably available WTO-consistent alternative.

The Panel also found that the United States had not satisfied the conditions required by the chapeau of Article XIV, which reads: 'Subject to the requirement that such measures are not applied in a manner which would constitute a means of arbitrary or unjustifiable discrimination between countries where like conditions prevail, or a disguised restriction on trade in services, nothing in this Agreement shall be construed to prevent the adoption or enforcement by any Member of measures.' The Panel noted that: 'The chapeau requires that the measures in question are not *applied* in a manner that would constitute a means of arbitrary or unjustifiable discrimination between countries where like conditions prevail, or a disguised restriction on trade in services.'

The Panel found that the United States acted inconsistently with the chapeau in negotiating with some Members but not others and also selectively enforcing the Internet ban against domestic suppliers. In particular, the Internet Horseracing Act permits the remote supply of gambling and betting services for horse races. The Panel (6.607) found that the United States failed to show 'that it applies its prohibition on the remote supply of these services in a consistent manner as between those supplied domestically and those that are supplied from other members'.

The Appellate Body overruled the Panel's finding on Consultation as well as its ruling that inconclusive evidence of differential enforcement was evidence of discrimination in violation of the chapeau, but upheld the finding of discrimination (369) 'solely to the possibility that the [Interstate Horseracing Act] exempts only *domestic* suppliers of remote betting services for horse racing from the prohibitions in the Wire Act'.

The Panel and Appellate Body regarded the Interstate Horseracing Act as inconsistent because it allows Internet gambling on horseracing, but foreign websites are not authorized to participate. This would seem to put the United States in the awkward position of either allowing all Internet gambling or repealing the IHA, neither of which would have been attractive to Congress.[12] Indeed, the IHA is subject to dispute. The Justice Department has taken the position that the 1961 Wire Act overrides the IHA, even though the IHA is a more recent statute, because neither statute expressly exempts IHA transactions from the Wire Act. The domestic horseracing industry strongly disagrees. The UIGEA of 2006 is carefully drafted to maintain the status quo regarding horseracing, preserving the ability of the Executive Branch and the horseracing industry to litigate the proper interpretation of these two statutes; the text of the bill states: 'It is the sense of Congress that this Act does not change which activities related to horse racing may or may not be allowed under Federal law.' Congress does not intend that the new enforcement tools be used against transactions that are apparently legal under IHA, but the Department of Justice could still attempt to prosecute a horseracing transaction under the Wire Act and test their interpretation in court.

Regardless of the decisions specifically related to this case, the ban on Internet gambling raises several interesting economic issues having to do with its enforcement and the regulation of information markets in general.

Given the open-access nature of the Internet, the United States faces significant jurisdictional and enforcement obstacles to maintaining a ban on the gambling of domestic citizens using offshore Internet sites (Clarke and Dempsey, 2001). As noted, the States, and not the Federal government, have a major authority to determine which activities are legal or not. The determination of which activities are legal or illegal often involves fine distinctions between specific actions. For example, in most States playing games on the Internet (poker, etc.) is not illegal, but the betting on those games is illegal. Because foreign-based gambling websites cannot be shut down, the enforcement approach has been to stop the financial-transactions payments. In 2001, major credit-card companies (Visa, Mastercard)

12 Congress passed the Interstate Horseracing Act (IHA) of 1978 to regulate interstate wagering on horseracing and to prevent States from interfering with the gambling policies of other States, thus affirming that States have primary responsibility for regulating gambling within their borders. In 2000, Congress amended the IHA to clarify that Internet technology could be used in the transmission of interstate off-track wagers, noting that the statute only regulates 'a legal wager placed or accepted in one State with respect to the outcome of a horserace taking place in another State ... where lawful in each State involved, placed or transmitted by an individual in one State via telephone or other electronic media and accepted by an off-track betting system in the same or another State' (15 U.S.C. 3002(3)). Therefore, a wager on a horserace that violates any State law is not permitted under the IHA.

and banks began refusing to make transactions with Internet gambling sites, but it is quite likely that these restrictions could be evaded through third parties, although this may impose a substantial cost on those attempting to gamble.[13]

A final issue is the broader regulation of information markets. Information markets allow trading in contracts that yield a payment based on the outcome of an uncertain future event. These markets allow trading in contracts on candidates in political elections (such as the Iowa electronic markets), futures contracts in terms of a firm's sales, commodities prices, etc. In some instances, the distinction between trades on these information markets and gambling is not at all clearcut. For example, does the trading of commodity futures constitute 'gambling' or is it something that serves a useful economic purpose by hedging risks? How about the trading of oil-price futures when it is not oil that will actually be traded, but rather payments based on the realization of one's expectations of the future price of oil? What about payments related to the outcome of a presidential election? In some of these cases, there may be a fine line between 'gambling' and those that elicit information that is useful for firms or traders.

Although the Commodities Futures Trading Commission has some regulatory authority in this area, the current regulatory structure is dominated by State and Federal laws that regulate Internet trading. Hahn and Tetlock (2006) propose that there be Federal laws that allow the Commodities Futures Trading Commission to establish an 'economic purpose' test to allow information-market contracts that provide financial hedging opportunities or information that improves economic decision making.

13 Indeed, the Unlawful Internet Gambling Enforcement Act of 2006 is an enforcement measure that does not explicitly ban Internet gambling. The Federal government does not have the jurisdiction to ban within-State Internet gambling, a determination that is reserved for the States. But the legislation seeks to prohibit the 'acceptance of any financial instrument for unlawful internet gambling', where it is up to the States to determine what constitutes 'unlawful' Internet gambling. The law attempts to restrict the mechanisms linked to the funding of such gambling, such as by shutting down the use of electronic funds transfers involved in unlawful gambling.

Sec. 5363. Prohibition on acceptance of any financial instrument for unlawful internet gambling:

No person engaged in the business of betting or wagering may knowingly accept, in connection with the participation of another person in unlawful Internet gambling –

(1) credit, or the proceeds of credit, extended to or on behalf of such other person (including credit extended through the use of a credit card);
(2) an electronic fund transfer, or funds transmitted by or through a money transmitting business, or the proceeds of an electronic fund transfer or money transmitting service, from or on behalf of such other person;
(3) any check, draft, or similar instrument which is drawn by or on behalf of such other person and is drawn on or payable at or through any financial institution; or
(4) the proceeds of any other form of financial transaction, as the Secretary and the Board of Governors of the Federal Reserve System may jointly prescribe by regulation, which involves a financial institution as a payor or financial intermediary on behalf of or for the benefit of such other person.

Clearly, even in the absence of the WTO case, US regulatory authorities would face an abundance of challenges in trying to limit Internet gambling because of the nature of the technology and the difficulties of enforcement.

The Appellate Body Report – some critical reflections

Doctrinally, given that this Report is only the second AB Report on the GATS and the first to deal directly with 'cyberspace and trade' it may be thought to be of significant importance in a field that no doubt will yield future disputes and will be mined with that future prospect in mind. However, given the conceptual and linguistic proximity of certain provisions of the GATT and the GATS, notably Articles XX and XIV respectively, the doctrinal significance of some aspects of the case are not limited to Services and Cyberspace.

Beyond doctrine, we consider it as an example a self-identity tension in the self understanding of the Appellate Body. On the one hand, it is a demonstration of a more mature and self-assured Appellate Body, consolidating a richer and more nuanced voice in the application of the DSU and understanding its role as not only determining appeals but also as largely in charge of a delicate and difficult dispute-settlement process. Thus, the Report is attentive to the structural asymmetries between the *ad hoc* Panels and the permanent Appellate Body and far more sensitive to the importance of a constructive relationship within these two columns of the 'judicial' dispute-settlement system.[14] In the judicial approach, the Report is more laconic and incremental, matter of fact (as well as 'matter of law') rather than 'formulaic'[15] and didactic. The Appellate Body in this Report is notable in its willingness to leave things 'to another day',[16] to resist the temptation of 'completing the analysis', and thus, on occasion dramatically, making the Parties responsible for the outcome of cases. It struck down, *a titre juste* in our view, review of a large number of US State measures on the grounds that Antigua had not in its Statement of Claim and pleadings discharged the relatively low threshold of making a prima facie case of violation – a case that could have easily been made on the basis of data within the briefs themselves. Likewise, in addressing the requirement of necessity in relation to Article XIV GATS, the implicit rebuke was not, as often in the past, to the Panel but to deficient lawyering. The judicial quality of WTO dispute settlement ultimately will depend on each element in the process – parties, Panels, and the AB itself – operating at a high level and with a clear understanding of their respective, oftentimes nonfungible roles. Gambling in this respect is another illustration of an AB that understands its role to be the husbanding of the system itself and not just the settlement of a specific dispute.

14 See generally Voon (2006).
15 The arresting analysis of Nagel in Nagel (1985) should be obligatory reading for all judges.
16 E.g., Recital 256.

On the other hand, and in relation to the most fraught legal issue in the case, the Appellate Body reverts to its almost obsessive reliance on, as we shall seek to show, rather flimsy textualism and, at times, equally flimsy contextualism as the mainstay of its hermeneutics.

We do not propose to examine all aspects of the Appellate Body Report but instead to focus on a series of issues that, in our view, merit critical discussion.

1. *Violation of a WTO obligation by cumulative measures*

The first issue on appeal, seemingly trivial, was the question whether the Panel erred in finding that the 'total prohibition' on the cross-border supply of gambling and betting services alleged by Antigua was neither capable of constituting an autonomous measure that can be challenged in and of itself, nor identified as a measure in Antigua's request for the establishment of a panel.

The Appellate Body's analysis proceeds as follows. It draws a sharp distinction between measures and their 'effects.' (Recital 123): '[T]he "measure" must be the *source* of the alleged impairment, which is in turn the *effect* resulting from the existence or operation of the "measure"' (Recital 121 – emphasis in original). And, 'if the "total prohibition" were a measure, a complaining party could fulfil its obligation to identify the "specific measure at issue", pursuant to Article 6.2 of the DSU, merely by explicitly mentioning the "prohibition". Yet, without knowing the precise source of the "prohibition", a responding party would not be in a position to prepare adequately its defence, particularly where, as here, it is alleged that numerous Federal and State laws underlie the "total prohibition"' (Recital 125).

It then concludes:

> Therefore, we conclude that, without demonstrating the source of the prohibition, a complaining party may not challenge a 'total prohibition' as a 'measure', *per se* ... Accordingly, we *uphold* the Panel's finding ... that 'the alleged "total prohibition" on the cross-border supply of gambling and betting services describes the alleged effect of an imprecisely defined list of legislative provisions and other instruments and cannot constitute a single and autonomous "measure" that can be challenged in and of itself'. (Recital 126).

There is more doctrinal and policy significance to this holding than might meet the eyes. Clearly, it would seem that a single formal measure prohibiting or having the effect of so prohibiting cross-border supply of service would be caught: the measure and its effect would be one. But what if this were not the case?

The Panel holding is ambivalent: Does it turn on the fact that the list of legislative provisions and other instruments were imprecisely defined? Or because the total prohibition was the alleged 'effect' of such of that list? In other words, if the list was precisely rather than imprecisely defined, would the 'total prohibition' effect (if proven, of course) constitute a single and autonomous 'measure' that could be challenged in and of itself. This does not seem to be the case – since after all the Panel went ahead and constructed a very precise list of Federal and State measures, and yet it still did not consent to regard the potential total-prohibition effect of that precise list as constituting a challengeable measure.

There is a different ambiguity in the analysis of the Appellate Body. In the first part of its analysis (reproduced above), it would seem that if the total prohibition is the cumulative *effect* of several measures it cannot, in and of itself, be considered a challengeable measure. In its 'conclusion' it seems to change tack for here it states: 'Without demonstrating the source of the prohibition [etc.].' Does this not suggest that as long as the complaining party demonstrated the source creating an effect, such effect could be considered the measure to be challenged? But immediately afterwards the AB goes on to endorse the holding of the Panel, which suggests otherwise.

Why is this hair splitting of consequence? As Members become legally acculturated to WTO and GATT disciplines, they are much more careful not to adopt egregious border or other measures. The interesting case is, thus, a series of measures, each of which, in and of itself, does not amount to a full prohibition (or to understand the full significance of the point, each of which does not amount to a violation of a distinct GATT or GATS obligation) and which may include also 'soft' measures such as in *Semiconductors*[17] but the cumulative effect of which, and only the cumulative effect of which, would bring about the impairment that the AB speaks of, an impairment that amounts to a violation of a specific obligation.[18]

We would like to suggest tentatively that even an 'effect' that violates an obligation can constitute a measure as long as, faithful to the formulation of the AB itself, the source of such an effect in other measures (which alone may not be violative) is demonstrated.

2. *The role of lawyers and panels in establishing and discharging the duty of making a prima facie case*

The AB struck down the Panel holding that Antigua had made a prima facie case in relation to the eight State measures. Indeed, prima facie, it would seem that the Panel process was curious:

> 151. In our view, certain general statements made by Antigua in its second written submission were insufficient to permit the Panel to proceed on the basis that Antigua had established a *prima facie* case regarding the eight State laws identified by the Panel. For example, Antigua's second written submission contains a general discussion of State gambling laws, with footnote citations to, *inter alia*, a report by the United States General Accounting Office and a law review article.[173] The law review article contains a discussion of State regulation of gambling, with reference, primarily in footnotes, to the laws of several States, including California, Hawaii, Illinois, Louisiana, and South Dakota. As we understand it, the Panel followed this trail of footnote references, and then

17 Japan–Trade in Semiconductors, Panel Report of 24 March 1988. See: Porges, (1989).
18 We are not alluding here to nullification and impairment issues.

compared the statutes cited in the footnotes of that law review article with Antigua's panel request to determine whether Antigua had identified provisions of those statutes and, thereby, to ascertain which State law Antigua intended to include as part of its claim. [174] This led the Panel to conclude that certain laws of Louisiana and South Dakota were challenged by Antigua under Article XVI.

152. The Panel engaged in a similar multi-step analysis in seeking to discern some connection between the laws of Massachusetts, New Jersey, New York, and Utah, and Antigua's references in its written submissions and various exhibits.[175] Yet we are unable to detect *any* connection, however tenuous, between the relevant laws of Colorado and Minnesota, on the one hand, and the allegation of inconsistency with Article XVI: 2, on the other hand. Although Antigua did submit these laws in its exhibits, we see no arguments in any submissions that would have clearly informed the Panel and the United States how those two laws would form part of Antigua's claims under Article XVI: 2(a) and XVI: 2(c). It follows that, without providing a stronger link between the particular State law being challenged and the obligation alleged to have been infringed, Antigua failed to make a *prima facie* case with respect to any of these eight State laws. (Footnotes omitted)

By contrast, the AB upheld the Panel in finding that Antigua had made a prima facie case in relation to the three Federal laws in question. But the AB reasoning is worth noting, and in particular Recital 148:

147. We begin our examination of the challenged measures with the three Federal laws, namely, the Wire Act, the Travel Act, and the IGBA. We observe that Antigua submitted the texts of these statutes and explained its understanding of them. In support of its argument that the three Federal statutes prohibited certain kinds of cross-border supply of gambling services, Antigua submitted to the Panel a report by the United States General Accounting Office on internet gambling, and a letter from a Deputy Assistant Attorney General of the Department of Justice informing an industry association of broadcasters that internet gambling violates the three Federal statutes. (footnotes omitted)

148. In addition, as we noted above, Antigua, in its second written submission, alleged the '[f]ederal laws' prohibiting cross-border supply to be inconsistent with Article XVI. The United States argues that Antigua never 'specifically alleged' the inconsistency of the three specific Federal statutes with Article XVI. Although, Antigua did not expressly mention these statutes by name when alleging inconsistency with Article XVI, we are of the view that, in the context of Antigua's previous statement clearly identifying these three statutes and the Panel's subsequent questioning on these particular measures, the reference to '[f]ederal laws' clearly covered the Wire Act, the Travel Act, and the IGBA. As a result, in our view, Antigua's arguments and evidence were sufficient to identify the Wire Act, the Travel Act, and the IGBA, and to make a *prima facie* case of their inconsistency with sub-paragraphs (a) and (c) of Article XVI: 2. (footnotes omitted)

It is the intervention of the Panel's 'subsequent questioning' that merits attention. Is it not the case that had the Panel not 'subsequently intervened' the Federal measure prima facie case in relation to Article XVI would be weaker, perhaps inexistent? And is it not the case that had the Panel engaged in a bit of 'subsequent questioning' in relation to the State measures rather than follow the trail of footnotes, the nexus between the State measures and Article XVI would be equally clear?

Now, of course there is a difference between Panel questioning to which both parties may respond and the Panel *proprio muto* going on its own trail and drawing its own conclusions that were not informed by the adversarial process, but should the burden of making a prima facie case depend on the inclination of the Panel to engage in 'subsequent questioning'? Consistent with the overall approach in this Report should the AB not have inquired whether, absent the questions and response of the Panel, the prima facie case also in relation to the Federal laws was in fact discharged by the Party?

Our purpose in raising this issue is not to nitpick; it actually raises two important and interrelated issues of process. In abstract, it raises the issue whether, in the interest of, say, ensuring equality of arms (and especially in a case in which a developing country is unsupported by rich multinationals) the Panel may 'complete the analysis' as it seemed to do in relation to the Federal laws and which the AB seemed to endorse. Or should such Panel 'activism' be considered as a violation of Article 11 DSU? And it also raises the question whether this question of principle should be influenced by the measure of substantive lacunae found, in say, the Statement of claim. The State of the art today is such, and this is confirmed also in this case itself, that the *prima facie* raff is very low. For the Panel to step in could be thought of not only as harmless error, but maybe a positive duty in the interest of justice. Both the question of inconsistency (State Measure – no subsequent questioning; Federal measure – subsequent questioning) and the role of the Panel in such a case remain unresolved. This, by contrast is not the situation in the latter parts of the Report where the AB highlighted Antigua's failure to discharge the alternative-measure burden under the 'necessary' requirement of Article XIV.[19]

3. *The USA commitment and its violation ex Article XVI: measures having an effect equivalent to quantitative restrictions*

These, in some respects, are the two principal planks on which the case rests. As regards the question of United States commitment, we do not find that we share some of the criticism leveled against the AB on its interpretative methodology. In fact, the decision and reasoning on this issue seem to us a useful correction of the unsatisfying LAN decision.[20] In that case, the AB correctly stipulated, as it does

19 Recitals 266 et seq.

20 WTO Appellate Body Report, European Communities – Customs Classification of Certain Computer Equipment, AB-1998-2, WT/DS62, 67, 68/AB/R (98-2271).

here, that a Schedule is to be interpreted as part of an agreement with both parties in mind as to its meaning. In LAN, the Panel failed to do so, relying instead on 'legitimate expectations' but, it is submitted, for unpersuasive reasons it concluded that the Panel's failure resulted in proof that the EU interpretation of the Schedule in that case was more persuasive than its adversary. In Gambling, the AB actually engages in an analysis which indicates that Antigua's interpretation had more hermeneutic pull than that of the US – notably in text leading to Recital 203. By contrast, on the issue of Article XVI we do not dispute the result but find the hermeneutics wanting. Potentially one of the most far-reaching legal implications of the Decision in Gambling concerns the application of Article XVI to origin-neutral measures that on their face do not apply directly to the provision of services by outside providers and may appear to be simply part of the regulatory matrix of a Member that have implications for the provision of services.

The US Wire Act[21] provides, inter alia:

> Whoever being engaged in the business of betting or wagering knowingly uses a wire communication facility for the transmission in interstate or foreign commerce of bets or wagers ... shall be fined ... or imprisoned not more than two years, or both.

The Panel had found that this US statute prohibited the use of at least one or potentially several means of delivery included in Mode 1 of services covered by Article XVI GATS, and that, critically, the Statute constituted a 'zero quota' for one or more or all of those means of delivery[22] that were part of the US commitment in its schedule and thus amounted to a violation of Article XVI: (2)(a) and (b).

The Travel Act[23] and the Illegal Gambling Business Act[24] are drafted in equally origin-neutral language and were both interpreted by the Panel to amount to a similar 'zero quota'.

The United States argued, inter alia, in its Appeal that Article XVI: (2)(a) and (c), correctly interpreted, did not apply to the type of measures exemplified by the Wire Act, the Travel Act, and the Illegal Gambling Act.

On this issue, the AB confirmed both the Panel's interpretation of the GATS provisions and their application to the US Statute.

Market access: 'Preliminary Matters'[25] or a 'Gaping Hole?'

On the issue as to whether, in principle, Article XVI can apply to origin-neutral internal measures that may have the effect of producing a zero quota on the

21 Section 1084(a) of Title 18 of the US Code.
22 Panel Report 6.363.
23 Section 1952(a) and (b) of Title 18 of the US Code.
24 Section 1955 (a) and (b) of Title 18 of the US Code.
25 This is the title the AB gives its treatment of partial access – see Recitals 218 et seq.

provision of services, we find ourselves in agreement with the controversial position[26] adopted by the Panel and the Appellate Body for reasons that we shall later explain. It is, however, far from certain whether the measures challenged in Gambling fall into this category. It is far from certain because of a failure to deal with an indispensable step in the legal reasoning, a step necessary before one may arrive at the conclusion that an origin-neutral regulatory measure having a 'zero effect' does in fact and in law violate Article XVI. Even if one takes the view, as did the Panel and the Appellate Body, that in principle such measures may violate Article XVI, there is a serious issue if such is the case if the effects of the measure are felt only 'on part of a scheduled sector' or if the measure in question restricts only one means of delivery covered by Mode 1, leaving others unaffected.

Imagine, for example, a hypothetical commitment to 'Internet gambling and betting services' by the US. Imagine further a hypothetical US Statute applicable both to domestic and foreign Internet gambling service providers that banned, for reasons of consumer protection, the placing of Internet bets and especially the paying for such bets without automatic encryption of consumer credit-card information by the service provider. Or an internal measure which required that the provider use software that was able to verify the age of Internet gamblers so as to ensure against gambling by minors, or even more challenging, prohibited Internet gambling through wireless access (because of the unknown health effect of extensive WiFi) but which allowed it over Internet wires. A nondomestic provider offering 'non encrypted Internet gambling' or 'unrestricted gambling' or using wireless services, could argue that such provisions amount to a 'zero quota' on his means of delivery or his segment of the market and were thus violative of Article XVI. The only redress of the United States in such a case would be to defend such measures as an exception provided by Article XIV. The Panel Decision seems to support such an interpretation.

One could also take the view that, even assuming the Commitment in the schedule covered Internet gambling, such (hypothetical) measures did not amount to a limitation contemplated by Article XVI. On this view, there is no violation of Article XVI since Internet gambling remains open to service providers as per the commitment, and what one has is simply origin-neutral legitimate regulation of the Internet pursuant to public policy. On this view, there is no 'zero quota' of the relevant service market, which is Internet gambling in its totality. The measures do not 'zero quota' the provision of services thus understood, even if they might shut out the market to a provider who refused to use encryption or use software that could be used to verify the age of gamblers if the law so required or insisted on using WiFi. On this view, provided the United States did not violate the distinctly separate obligation of National

26 Ortino (2006); Mavroidis (2007).

Treatment ex Article XVII,[27] there would be no violation of the GATS and no need for a justification ex Article XIV.

It would seem evident that this very issue would not only be germane but indispensable in the resolution of the actual Gambling case. Even having found, the continuous and consistent protestations of the United States notwithstanding, that Gambling was covered by the Commitment, it would surely be necessary to consider whether the banning of one form of gambling services, namely Internet gambling, could in itself, according to the first view outlined above and as the Panel found, amount to a 'zero quota' on a covered commitment, or whether, in line with the second view, it was simply an origin-neutral internal regulation of the gambling sector pursuant to certain public-policy considerations, no different than, say, a prohibition of gambling on Sundays, or a prohibition of Gambling by Minors, which would still allow nondomestic providers to supply gambling services in the US and on the same conditions as domestic providers, just as, say, US providers provide gambling services in Macao but are subject to the various regulatory regimes of the local government.

And yet, as indicated above, this issue – both the question of principle, as well as its application to the factual circumstances of the case – remains unresolved even after the appeal.

This curious outcome is the result of what appears to be a serious error of 'lawyering' by the United States, who raised the point and then abandoned it, combined with a legally puzzling willingness of the Appellate Body to acquiesce in such an omission and to move to a decision, somehow papering over the need to resolve it, without, however, confirming the legal construct of the Panel on this point.

In its notice of Appeal, the US raised the issue by appearing to challenge:

> The Panel's finding that a WTO Member does not respect its GATS market access obligations under Article XVI: (2) if it limits market access to any part of a scheduled sector or subsector, or if it restricts any means of delivery under mode 1 with respect to a committed sector.[28]

27 On the actual facts of the Gambling case, because the United States legal regime discriminated in favor of a variety of domestic providers, there probably was a violation of Article XVII. Since the Panel found and the Appellate Body affirmed a violation of Article XVI, it was not necessary to address directly Article XVII, and the issue of discrimination only became relevant in the context of Article XIV, where, indeed, it was fatal to the attempted justification of the measures found to have violated Article XVI. In relation to Horserace Gambling the 'Compliance Panel' found, inter alia, that '[s]ome of the suppliers and industry associations also confirm that they operate under the IHA. Most of these suppliers State that they accept wagers placed in other States.[27] These suppliers are substantial and even prominent businesses with, collectively, thousands of employees and apparently tens of thousands of clients, paying taxes or generating revenue for government owners, having traded openly for up to 30 years and in some cases even operating television channels. Three are publicly listed corporations making filings with the United States Securities and Exchange Commission or subsidiaries of such corporations' (Recital 6.115; footnotes omitted).

28 Quoted from AB decision Recital 219, which refers to US Notice of Appeal, para. 3(c).

The findings in question, from Recitals 6.287 and 6.290 of the Panel were that:

(i) as regards a particular service, a Member that has made an unlimited market access commitment under mode 1 commits itself not to maintain measures that prohibit the use of one, several or all means of delivery of that service; and (ii) a Member that has made a market access commitment in a sector or subsector has committed itself in respect of *all* services that fall within the relevant sector or subsector.[29]

At this point, it is worth quoting from the AB Report *in extensu*:

> The United States did not, however, adduce any arguments in support of such a challenge in its appellant's submission. Nor did the United States expressly refer to, or request us to reverse, any paragraph of the Panel Report in which the 'finding' referred to in the above excerpt is found. Accordingly, we understand that the United States does *not* challenge separately the Panel's findings as regards restrictions on the supply of *part of a sector*, or as regards restrictions on *part of a mode of supply* (that is, on one or more means of supplying a given service). In response to questioning at the oral hearing, the United States confirmed that its appeal focuses on the Panel's interpretation of sub-paragraphs (a) and (c) of Article XVI: (2), and we shall limit our examination accordingly.[30]

It is inexplicable why the United States would have flagged in their notice of appeal this issue of doctrinal and conceptual principle and then abandon it in their argument. On this point in the Appeal, they seem to concentrate almost entirely on questions related to the form of the restriction – arguing essentially that their measures are not 'in the form of numerical quotas' or 'numerical units in the form of quotas' as required by the language of Article XVI: (2)(a) and (c) respectively, but seeming to cede that if it were to be found that their measure was 'numerical', then it would in fact constitute a violation of Article XVI. They do not, having initially raised the issue, argue that even if the measures could, if in fact they amount to a zero quota, be covered by Article XVI; this is not the case here since the sector of gambling remains open, and the measures, whilst certainly affecting certain possible modes of gambling, do not amount to a zero quota of the committed service in its totality.

Formally, if the US *de facto* abandoned this ground for appeal, the Appellate Body could so 'limit its examination'. The Appellate Body, so adept at 'completing the analysis' even when it applies to factual questions, which are typically outside its proper province, was happy to leave this gaping hole in this construction of Article XVI: (2). Its entire analysis, showing that measures having an effect to zero quotas are covered by Article XVI: (2)(a) and (c), is premised on the measures in question in fact constituting a zero quota. But this would depend on

29 The Quote is from the AB Report, footnote 262.
30 Recital 220, emphasis in the original but footnotes omitted.

the manner in which one construes the issue just left open. And yet, while explicitly refusing to endorse the Panel's construction of this issue, it nevertheless proceeds as if it has. It is often a commendable feature of courts and tribunals – a sign of jurists' prudence – to avoid deciding moot points or issues not sufficiently argued before them. But in this case, since its eventual finding depends on this issue, the Appellate Body should, it is respectfully submitted, have 'completed the legal analysis', prodding both parties to brief it adequately on the issue. Further questioning is a device not open only to the Panels.

The decision of the Appellate Body: textual fetishism and policy phobia

In turning to examine the remaining issue of Market Access ex Article XVI: (2), we will henceforth assume that the measures in question did in fact have the effect of a 'zero quota' – even if this finding would depend on a legal premise that the Appellate Body left unanswered.

Article XVI: (2) provides:

> 2. In sectors where market-access commitments are undertaken, the measures which a Member shall not maintain or adopt either on the basis of a regional subdivision or on the basis of its entire territory, unless otherwise specified in its Schedule, are defined as:
>
> (a) limitations on the number of service suppliers whether in the form of quotas, monopolies, exclusive service suppliers or the requirements of economic needs test;
>
> ...
>
> (c) limitations on the total number of service operations or on the total quantity of service output expressed in terms of designated numerical units in the form of quotas or the requirement of an economic needs test.

The prohibitions contained in the US Acts do not seem to be in the form of numerical quotas or expressed in terms of designated numerical units in the form of quotas even if they do have the effect of a zero quota. This is not just a lexical or textual issue. After all, as we are reminded *ad tedium* in case after case, Article 31 of the VCLT provides:

> A treaty shall be interpreted in good faith in accordance with the ordinary meaning to be given to the terms of the treaty in their context and in the light of its object and purpose.

As noted by the International Law Commission (ILC) – the original drafter of Article 31 of the Vienna Convention – in its commentary to that provision:

> The Commission, by heading the article 'General Rule of Interpretation' in the singular and by underlining the connexion between paragraphs 1 and 2 and again between paragraph 3 and the two previous paragraphs, intended to indicate that

> the application of the means of interpretation in the article would be a single combined operation. All the various elements, as they were present in any given case, would be thrown into the crucible and their interaction would give the legally relevant interpretation. Thus [Article 31] is entitled 'General *rule* of interpretation' in the singular, not 'General *rules*' in the plural, because the Commission desired to emphasize that the process of interpretation is a unity and that the provisions of the article form a single, closely integrated rule.[31]

It has become obvious over the years, and *Gambling* is but the latest instance, that the Appellate Body has difficulties in treating the provisions of Article 31 of the Vienna Convention on Treaty Interpretation as a single, closely integrated rule. It privileges the textual and the contextual (the 'ordinary meaning' of terms[32]) and grudgingly and sparingly analyzes the teleological, as if engaging in serious object and purpose analysis (other than a perfunctory textual citation of phrases from this or that preamble) which is somehow itself a supplementary means of interpretation. A rather typical statement of the Appellate Body illustrates this 'hierarchical' approach to the elements of Article 31:

> Article 31 of the *Vienna Convention* provides that the words of the treaty form the foundation for the interpretive process: 'interpretation must be based above all upon the text of the treaty ... [t]he provisions of the treaty are to be given their ordinary meaning in their context. The object and purpose of the treaty *are also* to be taken into account in determining the meaning of its provisions'.[33] (emphasis added)

At issue in the Gambling dispute is not simply a lexical conflict between the text of the United States measures and the text of Article XVI: (2)(a) and (c). There is also a deep-seated policy tension.

31 Yearbook of the ILC, 1966, Vol. II, pp. 219–220.

32 The Panel in Section 301 Case explained: 'Text, context and object-and-purpose correspond to well established textual, systemic and teleological methodologies of treaty interpretation, all of which typically come into play when interpreting complex provisions in multilateral treaties. For pragmatic reasons the normal usage ... is to start the interpretation from the ordinary meaning of the "raw" text of the relevant treaty provisions and then seek to construe it in its context and in the light of the treaty's object and purpose. However, the elements referred to in Article 31 – text, context and object-and-purpose as well as good faith – are to be viewed as one holistic rule of interpretation rather than a sequence of separate tests to be applied in a hierarchical order. Context and object-and-purpose may often appear simply to confirm an interpretation seemingly derived from the "raw" text. In reality it is always some context, even if unstated, that determines which meaning is to be taken as "ordinary" and frequently it is impossible to give meaning, even "ordinary meaning", without looking also at object-and-purpose.' United States: Sections 301–310 of the Trade Act of 1974, Panel Decision WT/DS152/R at Recital 7.22.

33 Appellate Body report on *Japan – Taxes on Alcoholic Beverages* ('*Japan – Alcoholic Beverages*'), WT/DS8/AB/R, adopted 1 November 1996, pp. 11–12. Also notable is the understanding of the Appellate Body that the object and purpose in question are limited to those of the Treaty as a whole as if excluding the object and purpose of the provisions under interpretation. Although Article 31 refers to 'its' (the treaty's) object and purpose, this is so simply because it so agrees with the subject of the entire sentence. Other international tribunals and, notably the World Court have not limited object and purpose analysis only to that which can be culled from the Preamble of the instrument as a whole'.

The lexical argumentation is fully ventilated. The United States, armed with that great legal authority, the *New Shorter Oxford English Dictionary*, explains that numerical actually pertains to numbers. The Panel, in looking at XVI: (2)(c) for example, resorts to the Spanish and French texts. The French version reads, 'limitations concernant le nombre total d'opérations de services ou la quantité totale de services produits, exprimées en unités numériques déterminées, sous forme de contingents ou de l'exigence d'un examen des besoins économiques'; and the Spanish version reads, 'limitaciones al número total de operaciones de servicios o a la cuantía total de la producción de servicios, expresadas en unidades numéricas designadas, en forma de contingentes o mediante la exigencia de una prueba de necesidades económicas'.

Since, in both these texts, there is a comma before the words 'in the form of quotas', the Panel concluded that numerical units and form of quotas were two separate ways in which a Member might violate its obligations, and that the US measures, while not expressed in numerical units, were in a form of a quota.

The Appellate Body, for its part, destabilizes both these arguments and reaches the conclusion that all three languages are grammatically ambiguous. After an exhaustive and sophisticated analysis, they come to the conclusion that the text in (c) does not preclude its application to a measure that produces a zero quota. They reach the same result in relation to the text in XVI: (2)(a).[34] This allows them to turn to supplementary means. In relation to (a) they turn to the 1993 Scheduling Guidelines and find an example pertaining to Article XVI: (2), namely: 'nationality requirements for suppliers of services (equivalent to zero quota)'.[35] For the Appellate Body, this is dispositive: 'This example confirms the view that measures equivalent to a zero quota fall within the scope of Article XVI: 2(a).'[36] Also in relation to (c), they resort to the same Scheduling guidelines. In this case, the example they come up with is '[r]estrictions on broadcasting time available for foreign films'.[37] The Appellate Body then reasons:

> The strict interpretation of Article XVI: 2(c) advanced by the United States would imply that only limitations that contain an express reference to numbered units could fall within the scope of that provision. Under such an interpretation, subparagraph (c) could not cover, for example, a limitation expressed as a percentage or described using words such as 'a majority.' It is neither necessary nor appropriate for us to draw, in the abstract, the line between quantitative and qualitative measures, and we do not do so here. Yet we are satisfied that a prohibition on the supply of services in respect of which a full market access commitment has been undertaken is a quantitative limitation on the supply of such services.[38]

34 See Recitals 247 and 236 respectively.
35 Recital 237, citing p. 6 of the Scheduling Guidelines.
36 Recital 237.
37 Recital 249, citing the Guidelines on p. 6.
38 Recital 250.

What is remarkable in this display of hermeneutics is the near total absence of any teleological analysis. The resort to context, or to supplementary means of interpretation, is simply so as to find another source of what the Appellate Body believes is clearer lexical support. Not only does it not seem even to follow its rather reductionist view of teleology cited above – 'The object and purpose of the treaty are also to be taken into account in determining the meaning of its provisions'[39] – it seems positively to avoid such analysis.

In relation to Article XVI: (2)(c), the Appellate Body, when resorting to supplementary means refers not only to the Scheduling Guidelines but to a Statement of a Co-Chairman of the negotiations. There follows the reasoning of the Appellate Body in full.

The market access obligations set forth in Article XVI were intended to be obligations in respect of *quantitative*, or 'quantitative-type', measures. The difficulties faced by the negotiating parties concerned not *whether* Article XVI covered quantitative measures – for it was clear that it did – but rather how to 'know where the line should be drawn between quantitative and qualitative measures'.[40]

The meaning of the Co-Chair statements seems fairly obvious: The drafters of Article XVI: (2) had to grapple with and draft a text that, on the one hand, would prohibit quantitative measures that would contradict a Member's commitment, negotiated and freely given, to allow market access to nondomestic-services providers as expressed in its schedule, and, on the other hand, would still allow qualitative measures – which may indeed have a limiting impact on the provision of services but which, nonetheless, must be permitted as an expression of the regulatory freedom that all Members continue to enjoy.

Resolving that tension is one of the principal objectives of Article XVI: (2). All textual and contextual exegesis, as the Vienna Convention on the Law of Treaties instructs, has to be done *in the light* of such object and purpose. It is also clear why, since the words chosen by the drafters were so chosen in order to serve an object and purpose the drafters had in mind. Even, in the more limiting language of the Appellate Body this object and purpose, as articulated by the Co Chairman is '*also to be taken into account* in determining the meaning of [the] provisions'.

And yet, as seen above, the Appellate Body not only avoids any discussion of the policy underlying the provision it is interpreting. It valorizes such avoidance: 'It is neither necessary nor appropriate for us to draw, in the abstract, the line between quantitative and qualitative measures, and we do not do so here.'[41] Then, with no more, they simply state that 'a prohibition on the supply of services in respect of

39 Appellate Body report on *Japan – Taxes on Alcoholic Beverages* (*Japan–Alcoholic Beverages*), WT/DS8/AB/R, adopted 1 November 1996, pp. 11–12.

40 Recital 248, citing 'Statement by the Co-Chairman at the meeting of 17–27 September 1991', MTN.GNS/45 Para. 16 (footnotes omitted).

41 Recital 250.

which a full market access commitment has been undertaken is a quantitative limitation on the supply of such services'.[42]

The textual and contextual analysis of the Appellate Body is important and necessary, but they take it one step too far. It allows the Appellate Body, in the first place, to demonstrate the textual ambiguity of Article XVI: (2), which, in turn, permits them to turn to Supplementary Means ex Article 32 of the VCLT. The few textual snippets or examples found from the trawling of these 'Supplementary Means' are important in demonstrating that the interpretation adopted by the Panel and confirmed by the Appellate Body cannot be excluded. But to suggest that these snippets (which not even the parties to the dispute let alone the Panel considered fundamental) may, on their own, resolve the textual ambiguity, without any attempt to locate the problem and its solution in the light of object and purpose, is, ironically, not the hermeneutics indicated by the ordinary meaning of the terms of the Vienna Convention on the Law of Treaties and leaves this fundamental interpretation of Article XVI GATS on the flimsiest of lexical grounds.

We find a similar 'escape from policy' in the Appellate Body's analysis of XVI: (2)(a).

Here, too, the Appellate Body acknowledges that an important policy consideration undergirds the issue.

In Recital 223, they first cite the holding of the Panel:

> In interpreting sub-paragraph (a) of Article XVI: 2, the Panel determined that:
>
> [a prohibition on one, several or all means of delivery cross-border] is a 'limitation on the number of service suppliers in the form of numerical quotas' within the meaning of Article XVI: 2(a) because it totally prevents the use by service suppliers of one, several or all means of delivery that are included in mode 1.

In Recital 224, they then turn to the American appeal from this holding:

> The United States submits that this interpretation ignores the text of sub-paragraph (a), in particular the meaning of 'form' and 'numerical quotas', and erroneously includes within the scope of Article XVI: 2(a) measures that have the *effect* of limiting the number of service suppliers or output to zero. Although the Panel opined that any other result would be 'absurd', the United States stresses the opposite – that a contrary result would be consistent with the balance between liberalization and the right to regulate that is reflected in the GATS.

We note that the American submission, even as very briefly summarized by the Appellate Body, reads the textual and contextual argument in the light of the general policy consideration – the need for that balance between liberalization and the right to regulate.

And yet, in the following 15 Recitals of its Decision – from Recital 224 until its conclusion where it upholds verbatim the Panel's holding, the Appellate Body

42 Ibid.

focuses entirely and almost exclusively on the textual and contextual. The one perfunctory reference to object and purpose is limited to a reference to the Preamble of the GATS as a whole (rather than to an engagement with the underlying purpose of the provision under scrutiny) and even there, quite exquisitely, the Appellate Body's appeal to object and purpose is to explain why such do not readily assist in interpreting the provision.[43] In sum, the policy behind the text of the provision is not used either to provide the light under which the textual analysis is to take place as instructed by the VCLT nor are object and purpose more than minimally taken into account as the Appellate Body itself indicates should be the case.

One can only speculate about the motivation of this peculiar brand of hermeneutics developed by the Appellate Body and demonstrated so clearly in this case that repeatedly plays lip service to the VCLT while ignoring its holistic and integrative approach to text, context, and purpose.

Our impression is that it is driven by an understandable and laudable concern by the Appellate Body for the legitimacy of its decisions and its very own position in the institutional matrix of the WTO. It appears to be based on the belief that a very strong textual grounding of its decision is the key for such legitimacy, since such grounding, more than any other, links judicial outcomes to the real intention of the Parties and makes them, and their Treaty, rather than the Appellate Body, their mere mouthpiece of the law, masters of, and responsible for, the content of WTO legal obligations.

In this way, it palpably draws a sharp distinction between, for example, the legal path the European Union has taken under the tutelage of the European Court of Justice (which has championed a strong teleological hermeneutics) and, appropriately, the very different legal path that it, the Appellate Body, is charting for the WTO – despite the fact that both judicial bodies often find themselves interpreting very similarly drafted material provisions.

Even on this issue, we agree with what appears to be the underlying ethos of the Appellate Body and distance ourselves expressly from that school of thought that would like to see a 'constitutionalization' of the WTO and so forth.[44]

And yet we doubt if, in the long run, this overreliance on textualism and 'textual-contextualism'[45] to the exclusion or near exclusion of object and purpose is, indeed, the path to legitimacy. Exaggerated textualism is as undermining as is exaggerated teleology since, among many other concerns, at a profound level it severs the legitimating nexus between the law as the handmaiden of its social, political, and economic goals. One measure of legitimate judicial decisionmaking is reflected in the attitude of losing parties. Over-textualized decisions deracinated

43 Recital 235.

44 See Weiler and Trachtman (1997).

45 By which we mean the use of the contextual method by the Appellate Body simply as a means to find additional sources, the *wording* of which supports their interpretation. This is much in evidence in this case, too. See, e.g., Recital 233.

from the policy objectives of the law leave the loser with the impression of having 'lost on a technicality'. When, increasingly, as in this case and others,[46] the textual and contextual arguments that turn out to be dispositive are such that *neither* party to the dispute, nor the Panel, nor even the WTO secretariat,[47] considered fundamental, the Appellate Body's textual fetish and policy phobia has the paradoxical effect of rendering it not the mouthpiece of the law but quite the opposite, its oracle.

There is one additional cost the system is paying for this approach. Inevitably, lawyers take their hermeneutic cues from the judicial organ before which they appear and hope to win cases. The 'battle of the dictionaries', which so frequently characterizes arguments before the AB, and the palpable tilting in the respective weight given to the various elements of Article 31 VCLT are evidence to a worrying and impoverishing shift of legal discourse in the universe of actual WTO dispute settlement.

It is important to emphasize that we are not making these points polemically or argumentatively. We are not engaged in a would-be appeal against this interpretation of Article XVI by the Appellate Body; indeed, we agree (with some reserves and limitation) with the substance of the legal interpretation. But we note the discrepancy between the remarkable conceptual and pragmatic significance of the decision – which paradoxically brings it closer to EC thinking – and its flimsy hermeneutic basis. Caught between its textual fetish and its policy phobia, the Appellate Body ends up undermining the very legitimacy it so assiduously courts.

Balancing open markets and regulatory autonomy: some policy considerations

It is possible to cull some of the essential policy considerations from within the decision of the Appellate Body itself. As already noted, the Co Chair of the Drafting Meeting considering Article XVI regarded the Article as attempting to draw some kind of line between 'quantitative and qualitative' measures – the first forbidden, the latter permitted. In the American submission, this translated into a 'balance between liberalization and the right to regulate', which are reflected in the GATS. Let us first try and tease out the tension that informs these two statements.

In paragraph 6.332 of its Report, the Panel reasoned that:

> To hold that only restrictions explicitly couched in numerical terms fall within Article XVI: 2(a) would produce absurd results. It would, for example, allow a law that explicitly provides that 'all foreign services are prohibited' to escape the application of Article XVI, because it is not expressed in numerical terms.

46 Cf., e.g., the LAN decision.
47 The views of which weigh heavily in the Panel decisions.

We agree, but it is partly the textual absurdity of the example that produces the absurd result and does not capture the American argument at its strongest. We do not think that even the US would regard a measure that explicitly said all foreign services are prohibited as not coming within the ambit of the prohibition on Market Access expressed in Article XVI.

To capture the dilemma, we should consider, in the first place, a measure that is origin neutral, applies equally to domestic and foreign services, and is not, on its face, about market access as such but has an impact on the provision of services.

Imagine, say, a commitment in the Advertising Sector enabling the providers of foreign advertising services to enter the domestic market. Imagine then that the State that took such a commitment passed an origin-neutral law that forbade Billboard advertising in the interest of preserving the natural beauty of the environment as is now common in many countries. Imagine an agency whose specialty is that particular mode of providing advertising. It (and its domestic counterpart) would be faced with a measure having an effect equivalent to a zero quota. With a moment's thought, one can see that there would be literally an innumerable number of regulatory provisions of the State enacted pursuant to various public policies that would have such an effect on service providers, domestic and foreign: prohibition on television advertising of tobacco or alcohol products; prohibitions dictated by considerations of public morality such as the use and abuse of sexuality in advertising, the duration of advertising spots in any single hour of broadcasting, etc. In fact, almost any regulatory regime can translate into some quantitative numerical impact on the provision of services, and in cases where the regulation is not as to the commercial arrangement of the provision of the service[48] but go to the provision of service itself[49] will amount to some form of 'zero quota' on a service provider whose business is limited to that which the regulation prohibits.

In part, this goes to the issue of limitations on market access in respect of part of a committed sector and limitations on one or more means of cross-border delivery for a committed service on which, as mentioned above, the Appellate Body expressly withheld judgment. But it does end up upholding the Panel finding in relation to Article XVI: (2)(a) that:

> [a prohibition on one, several or all means of delivery cross-border] is a 'limitation on the number of service suppliers in the form of numerical quotas' within the meaning of Article XVI: 2(a) because it totally prevents the use by service suppliers of one, several or all means of delivery that are included in mode 1.

48 Such as opening hours, labor-protection laws, etc.

49 E.g., no TV advertising of alcohol or tobacco.

And that, in relation to Article XVI: (2)(c):

that a measure prohibiting the supply of certain services where specific commitments have been undertaken is a limitation:

> ... within the meaning of Article XVI: 2(c) because it totally prevents the services operations and/or service output through one or more or all means of delivery that are included in mode 1. In other words, such a ban results in a 'zero quota' on one or more or all means of delivery include[d] in mode 1.[50]

Indeed, in its analysis, the Appellate Body seems to go even further than the Panel. The Panel is careful to insist that its ruling is limited to situations where the internal measure can be shown *totally* to prevent the provision of services. The Appellate Body uses language which seems to suggest that any internal prohibition which has a quantitative impact on the supply of services will be caught by Article XVI: (2)(c):

> The strict interpretation of Article XVI: 2(c) advanced by the United States would imply that only limitations that contain an express reference to numbered units could fall within the scope of that provision. Under such an interpretation, subparagraph (c) could not cover, for example, a limitation expressed as a percentage or described using words such as '*a majority*'. It is neither necessary nor appropriate for us to draw, in the abstract, the line between quantitative and qualitative measures, and we do not do so here. Yet we are satisfied that a prohibition on the supply of services in respect of which a full market access commitment has been undertaken is a *quantitative limitation* on the supply of such services.[51] (emphasis added)

Be this as it may, under either construct this result seems to us no less absurd than the examples used by the Panel and the Appellate Body. Is it really conceivable that this is the balance between quantitative and qualitative the Members had in mind in drafting Article XVI: (2). Were the Members committing themselves that any origin-neutral internal regulation that takes the form of some prohibition of the manner in which services are offered and that as a result has a quantitative impact, or even any such measure that has a zero effect on any slice of the service in question, becomes a violation of their market-access commitment, and as such is challengeable and places on them the burden to justify under Article XIV? Would not, in this type of case, the appropriate locus for legal scrutiny be Article XVII on national treatment?

The US position is, in our view, equally untenable though not because of the potential of textual circumvention and abuse that, characteristically, the Panel and the Appellate Body employ.[52] The opening up of the services sector

50 Recitals 239 and 252 respectively.

51 Recital 250.

52 The Appellate Body is troubled that, under the American approach, Article XVI: (2)(c) could not cover 'a limitation expressed as a percentage or described using words such as "a majority"'. Ibid. The Panel on Article XVI: (2)(a): The American approach 'would ... allow a law that explicitly provides that

to foreign providers is not just, or always, or often, the result of noble self-interest. It is just as often, or more often, the result of tough negotiations and complex bargains struck. Now imagine a Member, such as the US, with a huge and lucrative gambling sector that decides, as part of such a complex bargain, to make an unrestricted commitment in its schedule in respect of foreign providers of gambling services. Imagine further that after some time a new administration is elected and for moral and other noncommercial reasons imposes a blanket prohibition on all gambling services, regardless of the national origin of the provider. It is not on its face an access measure, since the provision of that service internally is denied. It is really an internal regulation, part of the criminal law, but it has of course the effect of denying market access to all providers of gambling services.

The problem of the US position in Gambling is not linked to whether, in its verbal expression, such a prohibition uses numericals or otherwise as the Panel seems to think. The problem is that according to the American rationale, however drafted, since this is an internal regulatory measure, which simply has the effect of shutting out the supply of services by foreign providers, it should not in their view, as such, be caught by Article XVI: (2). This, too, seems to us a position that it would be difficult to square with the intended balance between the quantitative and qualitative in the drafting of Article XVI.

Though the Appellate Body says it is neither necessary nor appropriate to draw, in the abstract, a line between quantitative and qualitative measures and claims not to have done so. But, of course, it cannot avoid the legal and policy implications of its rulings simply by refusing to articulate the implicit assumptions and reasoning that undergird them. It may not have consciously drawn a line and thus leave those who must be guided by its decisions in the dark. But, in fact, its ruling and its reasoning, such as it is, may be understood or misunderstood as suggesting a line which tilts the balance away from the qualitative towards the quantitative, away from regulatory autonomy and towards WTO oversight over a rather wide array of internal, origin-neutral regulation in the services area.

If this becomes the common understanding of the import of this decision, right or wrong, one undesirable impact it might produce is a chilling effect on the willingness of Members to make commitments and/or to circumscribe such commitments as they do eventually make.

In what follows, we want to offer some consideration how one might think in a principled manner about the tension between the liberalization and regulatory autonomy in Article XVI: (2) and even, as is surely appropriate and necessary at

"all foreign services are prohibited"'. It is only in the textualist 'Alice in Wonderland', which WTO dispute settlement sometimes resembles, that a Panel or the Appellate Body could believe that a Member would institute a total ban on foreign services and believe that it could get away with it, or even argue that it could get away with it, because it framed such a ban by a clever use of language that avoided numerals. However, if this hermeneutic trend continues, we might eventually find ourselves all turning into legal Mad Hatters.

least for serious academic writing, attempt to draw a line between the quantitative and the qualitative. We are aware that we are placing our necks squarely on the chopping block. We are also aware that there will be no shortage of executioners. But our hope is that, by doing so, we will be starting a conversation that eventually will lead to a closing of the two major gaps left open by the decision of the Appellate Body in Gambling.

Drawing the line – a 'comparative' look at the GATT and the EU

The question is whether an internal regulatory measure that quantitatively affects the marketplace applies not only to services but also to goods. And the policy tensions and balancing while not identical are not unsimilar. Let us follow in the footsteps of the Appellate Body and look, too, at any illumination that can be achieved from the GATT.[53]

The GATT has an analogous structure to Articles XVI and XVII. Article XI GATT plays in relation to goods the function that *grosso modo* Article XVI plays in relation to GATS. It is different in that it already makes the commitment to quantitatively unimpeded access that under the GATS is voluntary. But it is similar in that it attempts, additionally, to describe the conditions under which such access would be compromised.

Article III of the GATT is the counterpart of Article XVII of the GATS. It constitutes the discipline that governs the tax and regulatory regime applied within a State's marketplace. There is a duty not to treat the imported goods in a manner so as to afford protection to domestic production and an analogous duty in respect of 'imported' (foreign) services and service providers.

There is, however, a similar category of measures in relation to which it is not clear whether they are meant to be covered by Article XI or Article III. Imagine a State measure, addressed in equal manner to domestic and imported producers and products, which said that one may not market in the State an automobile that did not have side airbags. The effect of this measure would, of course, exclude from the marketplace any imported vehicle that did not have side airbags. As such, it could be argued that it violates Article XI – the market-access Article in the GATT and hence be illegal. Alternatively, it could be argued that this is not a market-access measure at all, but an origin-neutral internal regulatory measure that applies equally to domestic and imported products and, as such, is covered only by the discipline of Article III.

In the GATT, the issue to date has been resolved by the Agreement itself. Ad note III provides that origin-neutral regulatory measures, not specifically directed at imports, are covered by Article III (national treatment) and not by Article XI (Quantitative Restrictions).

53 Recital 233.

> Ad Article III
>
> Any internal tax or other internal charge, or any law, regulation or requirement of the kind referred to in paragraph 1 which applies to an imported product and to the like domestic product and is collected or enforced in the case of the imported product at the time or point of importation, is nevertheless to be regarded as an internal tax or other internal charge, or a law, regulation or requirement of the kind referred to in paragraph 1, and is accordingly subject to the provisions of Article III.

We can only speculate about the policy behind this. It could be argued that to hold otherwise would become a wholesale assault on the regulatory autonomy and sovereignty of a Member if each and every internal regulation that was origin neutral and simply defined regulation of the internal marketplace, and that happened to affect imports as well, would be considered as a violation of Article XI, which prohibited quantitative restrictions and would require the State to justify itself before the WTO. As argued above, almost every safety regulation, every labeling requirement, every health measure relating to products would, of course, affect imported products and become per se a violation of the market-access provision Article XI – even if it was applied in equal measure to domestic products.

It could, however, be motivated by quite the opposite policy consideration. In the early days of the GATT, most extant quantitative restrictions were grandfathered and Article XI was read as *de facto* applicable only to new Quantitative Restrictions. If one were to take the view that internal regulations that had an equivalent effect to border quantitative restrictions were to be considered as covered by Article XI and then apply to all of those the Grandfathering provisions applied to extant Quotas, the GATT would have been gutted. Ad note III thus ensured that all these measures that, in fact, did have an effect equivalent to a quantitative restriction would, at least, be scrutinized under Article III.

The US position in the Gambling dispute would have the GATS adopt a position analogous to the GATT and hold that internal measures, even those that totally exclude a service and amount to measures having an effect equivalent to a zero quota, should not be considered under Article XVI just as in the GATT they are not considered under Article XI. Why, it could be argued, would the Members even contemplate changing the settled logic of the GATT in its extension to services through the GATS? It would seem on this view odd if the GATS, unlike the GATT, were to be interpreted so that any origin-neutral internal measure that applies on its face equally to domestic services and foreign services and that had the effect of quantitatively limiting such services (both domestic and foreign) were to be construed as a violation of Article XVI, thereby opening the State to a suit by another Member and requiring justification by reference to the General Exceptions of the GATS before the WTO Dispute Settlement organs, all this in contrast with settled practice in the area of goods under the GATT.

There are however textual, contextual, and policy considerations that may counter that argument. First, is the inconvenience that this question in the GATT was settled by the Members in the Agreement itself by the inclusion of the explicit Ad Note III. Reasoning *a contrario* one could argue that the failure to include an analogous provision in the GATS cannot be attributed to forgetfulness and represents a deliberate choice that Ad Note III should not apply to GATS.

There could seem to be at least two policy considerations that may have informed such a choice. First, unlike Article XI GATT, which not only defines the circumstances under which access is to be deemed to have been denied, but also contains the material commitment that outlaws all quotas, Article XVI is only structural. A Member is not obliged to make any commitments in relation to services. Further, when it makes such commitments it can restrict them in any way it wishes (e.g., gambling, with the exception of Internet gambling). Thus, the Members have great autonomy to decide the extent of their market access in the way they draft their commitments. But once given, they should be held strictly to their bargains.

Second, in relation to goods, unlike services, the WTO took two giant steps in the form of the SPS and TBT Agreements towards a regime that does, in fact and law, allow one Member to sue another in respect of measures that are origin neutral and nondiscriminatory. Thus, to allow a challenge under Article XVI: (2) to restrictions on services that are origin neutral and nondiscriminatory would not seem to depart so much from the GATT, Ad Note III notwithstanding, in which so many cases of goods will come under the new SPS and TBT regime. In other words, since in the GATT, under SPS and TBT the Members already accepted that in vast areas nondiscriminatory measures could be challenged as inimical to trade liberalization, it did not seem such a radical decision not to include the equivalent of Ad Note III in the GATS.

It would, thus, seem that one cannot simply borrow the practice of GATT regime in relation to nonborder origin-neutral internal measures that have an effect equivalent to quantitative restrictions and apply it to Article XVI: (2) GATS. The arguments go in either way. One cannot avoid a choice based on some normative policy choice.

In this respect, the practice of the EC, at all times to be treated with caution given the very different telos of that Organization and the equally different economy of its founding Treaties, may be instructive in considering such a normative policy choice.

Famously in its Dassonville canonical statement, in the field of free movement of goods, the European Court ruled back in 1974, in the early days of the Common Marketplace that:

> *All trading rules enacted by Member States which are capable of hindering, directly or indirectly, actually or potentially, intra-Community trade are to be considered as measures having an effect equivalent to quantitative restrictions.*[54]

54 Case C-8/74, *Procureur du Roi* v. *Benoît* and *Gustave Dassonville* [1974] ECR 837, 852 (Recital 5).

The result of this ruling as eventually interpreted and applied in the EC was to make any internal rule, even origin-neutral rules not directed as such at trade, which had any quantitative impact on imports by placing on them any burden, a prima facie violation of the EC market-access provisions of the Treaties and requiring justification under the respective general-exceptions doctrine. This would be the impact if we were to give a similar meaning to the statement of the Appellate Body in Recital 250 of Gambling.[55]

About 20 years later, in the equally famous *Keck* decision, the European Court revisited this doctrine and clawed it back considerably:

> *contrary to what has previously been decided, the application to products from other Member States of national provisions restricting or prohibiting certain selling arrangements is not such as to hinder directly or indirectly, actually or potentially, trade between Member States within the meaning of the Dassonville judgment (case 8/74 [1974] ECR 837), so long as those provisions apply to all relevant traders operating within the national territory and so long as they affect in the same manner, in law and in fact, the marketing of domestic products and of those from other Member States.*[56]

The Court itself, uncharacteristically, addresses in Recital 14 of its decision the rationale:

> *In view of the increasing tendency of traders to invoke Article 30 of the Treaty as a means of challenging any rules whose effect is to limit their commercial freedom even where such rules are not aimed at products from other Member States, the Court considers it necessary to re-examine and clarify its case-law on this matter.*[57]

Oceans of ink powder and forests of trees have been respectively consumed and decimated in trying to articulate the precise conditions under which *Keck* applies. We would argue for the understanding contained in the decision itself and fairly consistently applied in subsequent case law, namely that a State measure that has

55 The strict interpretation of Article XVI: 2(c) advanced by the United States would imply that only limitations that contain an express reference to numbered units could fall within the scope of that provision. Under such an interpretation, sub-paragraph (c) could not cover, for example, a limitation expressed as a percentage or described using words such as 'a majority'. It is neither necessary nor appropriate for us to draw, in the abstract, the line between quantitative and qualitative measures, and we do not do so here. Yet we are satisfied that a prohibition on the supply of services in respect of which a full market access commitment has been undertaken is a quantitative limitation on the supply of such services.

56 Joined Cases C-267/91 and C-268/91, *Criminal Proceedings against Bernard Keck and Daniel Mithouard*, [1993] ECR-I, 6097, Recital 16. The court thus concludes in Recital 17: 'Provided that those conditions are fulfilled, the application of such rules to the sale of products from another Member State meeting the requirements laid down by that State is not by nature such as to prevent their access to the market or to impede access any more than it impedes the access of domestic products. Such rules therefore fall outside the scope of Article 30 of the Treaty.'

57 Joined Cases C-267/91 and C-268/91, *Criminal Proceedings against Bernard Keck and Daniel Mithouard*, [1993] ECR-I, 6097, Recital 14.

a quantitative effect will be caught by the Market Access provision only when the effect in question is such as totally to exclude the product from the marketplace. In addition, State measures will be scrutinized if they are discriminatory and protectionist.

> *Provided that those conditions are fulfilled, the application of such rules to the sale of products from another Member State meeting the requirements laid down by that State is not by nature* ***such as to prevent their access to the market*** *or to impede access any more than it impedes the access of domestic products. Such rules therefore fall outside the scope of Article 30 of the Treaty.*[58] (Emphasis added)

We believe this balance is promising also in the context of the WTO, both GATT and GATS.

On the one hand, once you allow products or services of another Member access to your market, such goods and services are to be welcome and treated no less favorably than domestic competitors (ex Article III GATT; Article XVII GATS). For their part, such goods or services should accept to be bound on an equal footing as their domestic competitors by the variety of sociopolitical, economic, and cultural choices of their host country, as reflected in its legal and regulatory regime. If the law and practice is to mandate – for example, that for social reasons, employees may not be made to work more than 38 hours a week or that there are mandatory opening and closing hours of businesses – a foreign importer of goods cannot complain that such amounts to a restriction on the access granted him, even though such regulation limits the amount of goods he may sell, any more than he could complain about the rate of income tax, or the law of contract that might have similar effects on the volume of his sales. Likewise in the area of services, if a provider of cinematographic entertainment, or television transmission, is told that he may not allow children into certain types of movies or that certain types of transmissions may only take place at certain late hours of the night, he may not complain, absent discrimination, that this amounts to a restriction on his ability to provide services. This is the market they have gained access to. The Member has promised access, but has not promised that Membership of the WTO will force it to change the social and cultural norms that are also reflected in its marketplace or even submit such to WTO approval. As the Appellate Body has explained more than once, even in the area of SPS and TBT, which put in place a discipline that may be violated without a show of discrimination or protectionism, a State is not required to lower its standards of risk or other sociocultural norms.[59]

On the other hand, under the same logic, when the effect of the internal regulation, even if not discriminatory, is actually to exclude totally a product or service

58 Recital 17 Keck.

59 See, e.g., *Japan – Measures Affecting Agricultural Products*, adopted by Dispute Settlement Body, 19 March 1999, WT/DS76/R and WT/DS/AB/R.

lawfully traded in the market of your partner, then the Access provisions such as Article XVI GATS should be triggered.[60] Note that we are speaking not of any negative quantitative effect that an internal measure might have, but an actual and full denial of access.

In support of this construction, we would want to offer the following considerations. First, an internal measure that totally excludes a good (or a service) that indeed has the effect equivalent to a zero quota, seems to be consistent with the purpose of such articles more than an internal measure that does not bar access but simply sets regulatory conditions for such even if they have some quantitative impact (you sell less).

Second, it should be remembered that bringing such measures under the canopy of Article XVI does not mean that the State has to abandon them but simply to justify them. One way of thinking of such is, as indicated above, as submission to WTO approval. A different and perhaps more convincing and appealing way is to think of this construct as being part of a 'Duty of Comity' towards one's trading partners. After all, if a product or a service is perfectly legal and acceptable in its place of origin, it may seem arbitrary to exclude such from the marketplace in the importing state. It may also seem offensive sending a signal that the 'exporting' country might care less about the welfare of its own market. An explanation as a matter of legalized comity would not be alien to the legal world of international trade.[61]

Thirdly, one of the benefits of an open-trading system is not only the efficiency gains but also the richness consumers in the importer market are exposed to through the introduction of new or different products and services. If a product or service is allowed, but simply subject to the regulatory requirements of the local market it is one thing. If they are actually excluded, it could be in the interest of domestic consumers to allow a challenge to such exclusions that, after all, might be motivated by Special Interests rather than the collective good. The Gambling dispute itself may illustrate this point. The 'Compliance Panel' found, inter alia, the existence in the USA of:

> substantial and even prominent businesses with, collectively, thousands of employees and apparently tens of thousands of clients, paying taxes or generating revenue for government owners, having traded openly for up to 30 years and in some cases even operating television channels ... The evidence regarding

60 In principle, under this theory also, Article XI GATT should be triggered, but that is expressly prohibited by the specially inserted Ad Note III.

61 See, for example, Article 2.5 of the TBT Agreement: 2.5: 'A Member preparing, adopting or applying a technical regulation which may have a significant effect on trade of other Members shall, upon the request of another Member, explain the justification for that technical regulation in terms of the provisions of paragraphs 2 to 4. Whenever a technical regulation is prepared, adopted or applied for one of the legitimate objectives explicitly mentioned in paragraph 2, and is in accordance with relevant international standards, it shall be rebuttably presumed not to create an unnecessary obstacle to international trade.'

> these suppliers demonstrates the existence of a flourishing remote account wagering industry on horse racing in the United States operating in ostensible legality.[62]

Finally, such a distinction finds some textual support, too. The nature of numericals is their quantifiable precision. A domestic regulation that has an impact on the quantity of the goods sold or services offered, as would be the case with most internal regulatory regimes, would not be caught by the balance we are suggesting here on this ground, too: it has a quantitative effect but is not in the nature of a quota with its numerical precision. By contrast, the zero quota is of such a nature and thus to be caught.[63]

The application of this to the market in goods is easier than to the market in services.[64] If the good in question is allowed on to the marketplace, even if under a variety of conditions, it should neither be caught nor justified, provided it is not subjected to a protectionist regime. As we have seen, it is much more difficult to have such a clean determination in the market of services. In the example used above, is the exclusion of billboard advertising a zero-quota on billboard-advertising providers or is it an internal regulation of the broader advertising industry?

A starting point in considering this issue, from which we would not wish at this point to go further, would be to suggest that if the internal regulation has the effect of totally gutting a service commitment, it would be an easy case in which Article XVI would be triggered. But it could not be the only case: in Gambling, the commitment was for entertainment under which so many disparate services may be included, that a total gutting principle would be too restrictive. On the other hand, the Panel's construct, which includes one, several, or all means of delivery, etc., might be too broad. The American measure was a zero quota only if one construed Internet gambling as a stand-alone service, rather than as a means, such as billboard advertising, of providing gambling services. Would a ban, within Internet gambling, on say, the guessing game of Kino because of its long odds, be a regulation of Internet gambling or a zero quota on Kino?

The provisions for impairment and nullification always beckon as an 'easy' solution for difficult cases, but to resort to that difficult device as the systemic answer to this systemic question is not an alluring prospect.

Without resolving this issue, one cannot reach a safe conclusion on the Application of Article XVI: (2). This is of little comfort to the United States in this case, since they would, in any event, be caught under Article XVII for violation of the National Treatment provisions.

62 Compliance Panel 6.115 and 6.116.

63 (And we would also include, though very exceptional in reality, other quantitatively precise regulations, such as 'the Majority' example offered by the Appellate Body: Majority is of such a precise nature: more than 50%.)

64 Cf. Pauwelyn (2006).

4. *Article XIV – due process*

This case is notable by the aggressiveness of the Parties in accusing the Panel, albeit not in so many words, of judicial impropriety.[65] For the most part, the AB has deflected such criticism. But, in this instance, it would be interesting to adopt a dynamic approach to the decision where the focus of our enquiry is not simply the propriety – legal or otherwise – of the decision but the impact it might have on the litigation strategies of parties in the future.

Antigua claimed that the US raised its defense ex Article XIV only in its second written submissions and that this fact compromised its ability to mount an effective response and, worse still, because of this tardiness and the consequent deficiency in the adversarial process, the Panel's 'ability to assess that defence' was hampered and, more gravely, that this resulted in 'the Panel's making the defence for the United States' (Recital 275).

The AB rejected the due-process charge of Antigua by stating that (a) Antigua 'was apparently aware that the United States might argue that its measures satisfy the requirements of Article XIV' (Recital 276); (b) that it raised no objection at the time of the proceedings (ibid.); and that (c) it did have an opportunity to respond adequately to the US submission, albeit at a late stage (ibid.).

This might not be taking due process all that seriously. In its First Written Submission, there is an indication that Antigua may have anticipated the use of Article XIV by the US – which in fact did not turn out to be the case either in the first US written or oral submissions. Antigua thus dropped the issue in its second written submissions only to discover that the US had raised them in its own second written submission. So, as the AB points out: 'Both parties discussed issues relating to Article XIV in their opening statements at the second substantive panel meeting' (Recital 274). In some respects, Article XIV was germane to the outcome of the case. This is rather unsatisfactory both in terms of due process and in terms of the benefit that the adversarial process is meant to yield. It is particularly poignant since part of the Article XIV holding turned on Antigua's failure to discharge its Least Restrictive Measures burden. Maybe this was a situation where the Panel should have exercised its powers under Article 12.2 of the DSU to allow for additional time to respond and perhaps even for additional submissions.

But beyond this point, one may wonder if, as a result of this part of the Ruling, perverse litigational strategies might develop. For example, Antigua was 'penalized' because in its first submission it briefly hypothesized about the possibility of an Article XIV defense. Should Members be discouraged from doing so? Should Members be encouraged to save some very material defenses

65 'The United States contends that the Panel's interpretation of Article ... XVI: 2(c) would "unreasonably and absurdly" deprive Members of much of their right to regulate services' Recital 26 of AB Report. See, too, Recital 12 '"egregious" nature of the Panel's approach.'

to the Second Submission phases as a means of limiting the ability of their adversary to respond effectively? And should one encourage strategies of 'appeal protest' of parties before Panels so as not to be estopped later before the AB?

5. *Article XIV 'relative importance' and the doctrine of 'vital interests'*

Gambling leaves one crucial issue for both GATT and GATS, tantalizingly ambiguous in relation to the usage of Articles XX GATT and Article XIV GATS. *Korea–Beef* features prominently in the decision as the yardstick for exception analysis. Interestingly, although the AB talks about the factors that are to be 'weighed and balanced' and the 'relative importance', it omits from its analysis explicit reference to the most controversial aspect of *Korea–Beef*. In that decision, it was clear that the necessity of a measure of enforcement, for example, was dependent on the 'vitality' of the interest protected. A question of life and death would justify a more exigent measure. Mere fairness of commercial transactions and consumer information would not justify such exigent measures. In effect, the Appellate Body was lucidly and overtly (perhaps inadvertently) spelling out what was noticeable in other contexts, namely that Members did not have full freedom to set their own acceptable level of risk in relation to the policy claimed under Articles XX GATT and XIV GATS. Enforcement, after all, impacts the level of risk that will be tolerable. If the separation of imported beef and domestic beef were to touch on life and death, the AB would have accepted a much more stringent enforcement mechanism. But since it affected less 'vital' interests, Korea was to satisfy itself with a regime that would allow a greater degree of violation of its policy.

In Recital 308 of Gambling, the AB ironically cites *Korea–Beef* for the more orthodox position, namely that a Member has a 'right to achieve its desired level of protection with respect to the objective[s] pursued under [Articles XX and XIV]'. How is this to be read? A retreat from the doctrine of Vital Interests or a mere retreat from the lucidity of *Korea–Beef* to the camouflage and fiction of Member autonomy in setting in all circumstances its own standards?

6. *(Insert heading as for 1–5)*

Finally, in our view, the AB has been wise in clarifying, once and for all, that the so-called duty of consultation is not an automatic requirement of Article XIV and XX as some have been wont to suggest in the wake of *Turtle–Shrimp* and *Gasoline* and that the burden of advancing actual LRMs rests on the defending party.[66]

66 See Akbar, 'The 'Necessary' Connection Between the Duty to Negotiate and Least Restrictive Measures Analysis: The Gambling Dispute Reconsidered', Jean Monnet Working Papers 03/2007.

References

Clarke, Roger and Gillian Dempsey (2001), 'The Feasibility of Regulating Gambling on the Internet', *Managerial and Decision Economics*, **22**: 125–132.

Grinols, Earl L. and David B. Mustard (2006), 'Casinos, Crime, and Community Costs', *The Review of Economics and Statistics*, **88**: 28–45.

Hahn, Robert W. and Paul C. Tetlock (2006), 'A New Approach for Regulating Information Markets', *Journal of Regulatory Economics*, **29**: 265–281.

Mavroidis, Petros (2007), 'Highway XVI Re-Visited: The Road from Non-Discrimination to Market Access in GATS', *World Trade Review*, **6**(1): 1–23.

Kearney, Melissa S. (2005), 'The Economic Winners and Losers of Legalized Gambling', *National Tax Journal*, **58**: 281–302.

Robert F. Nagel (1985), 'The Formulaic Constitution', *Michigan Law Review*, **84**: 165–212.

Ortino, Federico (2006), 'Treaty Interpretation and the WTO Appellate Body Report in *US–Gambling*: A Critique', *Journal of International Economic Law*, **9**: 117–148.

Pauwelyn, Joost (2006), 'Rien ne Va Plus? Distinguishing Domestic Regulation from Market Access in GATT and GATS', *World Trade Review*, **4**: 131–170.

Porges, Amelia (1989), 'Japan – Trade in Semi-Conductors, No. L/6309, *The American Journal of International Law*, **83**(2): 388–394.

Voon, Tania (2006), 'To Uphold, Modify or Reverse? How the WTO Appellate Body Treats Panel Reports', *The Journal of World Investment and Trade*, **7**: 507.

Weiler, J. H. H. and Joel P. Trachtman (1997), 'European Constitutionalism and Its Discontents', *Northwestern Journal of International Law and Business*, 354.

Wilson, Mark (2003), 'Chips, Bits, and the Law: An Economic Geography of Internet Gambling', *Environment and Planning A*, **35**: 1245–1260.

Wunsch-Vincent, Sacha (2006), 'The Internet, Cross-Border Trade in Services, and the GATS: Lessons from *US–Gambling*', *World Trade Review*, **5**: 319–355.

Annex 1 – DSB summary of the case

On 21 March 2003, Antigua and Barbuda requested consultations with the US regarding measures applied by central, regional and local authorities in the US which affect the cross-border supply of gambling and betting services. Antigua and Barbuda considered that the cumulative impact of the US measures is to prevent the supply of gambling and betting services from another WTO Member to the United States on a cross-border basis.

According to Antigua and Barbuda, the measures at issue may be inconsistent with the US obligations under the GATS, and in particular Articles II, VI, VIII, XI, XVI and XVII thereof, and the US Schedule of Specific Commitments annexed to the GATS.

On 12 June 2003, Antigua and Barbuda requested the establishment of a panel. At its meeting on 24 June 2003, the DSB deferred the establishment of a panel. Further to a second request by Antigua and Barbuda, the DSB established a panel at its meeting on 21 July 2003. Canada, the EC, Mexico and Chinese Taipei reserved their third-party rights. On 23 July 2003, Japan reserved its third-party rights.

On 15 August 2003, Antigua and Barbuda requested the Director-General to compose the panel. On 25 August 2003, the Director-General composed the panel. On 29 January 2004, the Chairman of the Panel informed the DSB that it would not be possible for the Panel to complete its work in six months because various factors had had an impact on the Panel's timetable, such as a party's request for preliminary rulings, the intervention of the holiday season, the heavy agenda of the panelists as well as the complexity of the legal and factual questions which had been raised. The Panel hoped to complete its work by the end of April 2004.

In the context of the negotiations for a mutually agreed solution to the present dispute, the parties requested the Panel to suspend the panel proceedings, in accordance with Article 12.12 of the DSU, until 23 August 2004. On 25 June 2004, the Panel has agreed to this request. The parties subsequently requested a continuation of the suspension until 4 October 2004, and the Panel agreed to the request on 18 August 2004. The parties requested a continuation of the suspension until 16 November 2004, and the Panel agreed to the request on 8 October 2004. On 5 November 2004 Antigua, requested the resumption of the panel proceedings to the Panel and the United States did not object to this request. The Panel has therefore agreed to resume the panel proceedings as from 8 November 2004.

On 10 November 2004, the report of the Panel was circulated to Members. The Panel found that:

- The GATS Schedule of the United States has been interpreted to include specific commitments for gambling and betting services under the sub-sector entitled 'Other Recreational Services (except sporting)';
- Three US Federal laws (the Wire Act, the Travel Act and the Illegal Gambling Business Act) and the provisions of four US State laws (those of Louisiana,

Massachusetts, South Dakota and Utah) on their face, prohibit one, several or all means of delivery included in mode 1 of GATS (i.e. cross-border supply), contrary to the United States' specific market access commitments for gambling and betting services for mode 1. Therefore, the United States failed to accord services and service suppliers of Antigua treatment no less favourable than that provided for under the terms, limitations and conditions agreed and specified in the US Schedule, contrary to Article XVI: 1 and Article XVI: 2 of the GATS (i.e. concerning market access);

- Antigua failed to demonstrate that the measures at issue are inconsistent with Articles VI: 1 and VI: 3 of the GATS (i.e. concerning domestic regulation);
- The United States was not able to invoke successfully the GATS exceptions provisions. In this regard, the United States was not able to demonstrate that the Wire Act, the Travel Act and the Illegal Gambling Business Act are 'necessary' under Articles XIV(a) and XIV(c) of the GATS (i.e. 'exceptions' provisions, including for public morals) and are consistent with the requirements of the chapeau of Article XIV of the GATS;
- The Panel decided to exercise judicial economy with respect to Antigua's claims under Articles XI (i.e. concerning payments and transfers) and XVII (i.e. concerning national treatment) of the GATS.

On 7 January 2005, United States notified its intention to appeal certain issues of law and legal interpretations developed by the Panel. On 19 January 2005, Antigua and Barbuda notified its intention to appeal certain issues of law and legal interpretations developed by the Panel.

On 8 March 2005, the Chairman of the Appellate Body informed the DSB that the Appellate Body would not be able to circulate its Report within the 60-day period due to the time required for completion and translation of the Report, and that it estimated it would be circulated to WTO Members no later than 7 April 2005.

On 7 April 2005, the report of the Appellate Body was circulated. The Appellate Body:

- upheld the Panel's finding that an alleged 'total prohibition' on the cross-border supply of gambling and betting services cannot, in and of itself, constitute a 'measure' subject to dispute settlement under the GATS;
- found that the Panel should not have ruled on claims advanced by Antigua with respect to eight State laws of the United States, as to which Antigua had not made a prima facie case of inconsistency with the GATS;
- upheld the Panel's finding, albeit for different reasons, that the United States' Schedule includes a commitment to grant full market access in gambling and betting services. In particular, in the course of its interpretation of the United States' Schedule, the Appellate Body disagreed with the Panel's designation of two documents – referred to as W/120 and the 1993 Scheduling Guidelines – as 'context' for the interpretation of Members' Schedules, finding instead that they constitute 'preparatory work';

- upheld the Panel's finding that the United States acts inconsistently with Article XVI: 1 and sub-paragraphs (a) and (c) of Article XVI: 2 by maintaining certain limitations on market access not specified in its Schedule; and
- reversed the Panel's finding that the United States had not shown that the three Federal statutes are 'necessary to protect public morals or to maintain public order', within the meaning of Article XIV(a); found that the United States' measures are justified under Article XIV(a) of the GATS as measures 'necessary to protect public morals or to maintain public order'; and upheld, albeit on a narrower ground, the Panel's finding that the United States had failed to show that these measures satisfy the conditions of the chapeau of Article XIV.

At its meeting of 20 April 2005, the DSB adopted the Appellate Body report and the Panel report, as modified by the Appellate Body report.

Implementation Status of Adopted Reports

At the DSB meeting of 19 May 2005, the United States stated its intention to implement the DSB's recommendations and indicated that it would need a reasonable period of time to do so. As the Antigua and Barbuda and the United States had failed to agree on a reasonable time period for implementation in accordance with Article 21.3(b) of the DSU, on 6 June 2005, Antigua and Barbuda requested that the reasonable period of time be determined through binding arbitration pursuant to Article 21.3(c) of the DSU. On 30 June 2005, pursuant to the request from Antigua and Barbuda, the Director-General appointed Dr. Claus-Dieter Ehlermann to act as arbitrator under Article 21.3(c) of the DSU. On 19 August 2005, the Arbitrator circulated his Award to the Members, determining that the reasonable period of time for implementation was 11 months and 2 weeks from 20 April 2005, expiring on 3 April 2006.

On 24 May 2006, the parties informed the DSB that, given the disagreement as to the existence or consistency of measures taken by the United States to comply with the recommendations and rulings of the DSB, they had agreed on certain procedures under Articles 21 and 22 of the DSU.

On 8 June 2006, Antigua and Barbuda requested consultations under Article 21.5 of the DSU. On 6 July 2006, Antigua and Barbuda requested the establishment of an Article 21.5 panel. At its meeting on 19 July 2006, the DSB referred the matter to the original panel, if possible. On 16 August 2006, the Panel was composed.

For details of the Article 21.5 panel, see above.

On 21 June 2007, Antigua and Barbuda requested authorization from the DSB, pursuant to Article 22.2 of the DSU, to suspend the application to the United States of concessions and related obligations of Antigua and Barbuda under the GATS and the TRIPS Agreement. On 23 July 2007, the United States (i) objected to the level of suspension of concessions and obligations proposed by Antigua and Barbuda and (ii) claimed that Antigua and Barbuda's proposal does not follow the principles and procedures set forth in Article 22.3 of the DSU. At its meeting on 24 July 2007, the DSB agreed that the matter referred to by the United States be referred to arbitration.

Annex 2: Summary of Main Legal Issues, as prepared by the Secretariat of the WTO

http://www.wto.org/english/tratop_e/dispu_e/cases_e/1pagesum_e/ds285sum_e.pdf

US – GAMBLING[1] (DS285)

1. MEASURE AND SERVICES AT ISSUE

- Measure at issue: Various US measures relating to gambling and betting services, including Federal laws such as the 'Wire Act', the 'Travel Act' and the 'Illegal Gambling Business Act' ('IGBA').
- Services at issue: Cross-border supply of gambling and betting services.

2. SUMMARY OF KEY PANEL/AB FINDINGS[2]

- Scope of GATS commitments: The Appellate Body upheld, based on modified reasoning, the Panel's finding that the US GATS Schedule included specific commitments on gambling and betting services. Resorting to 'document W/120' and the '1993 Scheduling Guidelines'[3] as 'supplementary means of interpretation' under Art. 32 of the VCLT, rather than context (Art. 31), the Appellate Body concluded that the entry, 'other recreational services (except sporting)', in the US Schedule must be interpreted as including 'gambling and betting services' within its scope.
- GATS Art. XVI: 1 and 2 (market access commitment): The Appellate Body upheld the Panel's finding that the United States acted inconsistently with Art. XVI: 1 and 2, as the US Federal laws at issue, by prohibiting the cross-border supply of gambling and betting services where specific commitments had been undertaken, amounted to a 'zero quota' that fell within the scope of, and was prohibited by, Art. XVI: 2(a) and (c). However, it reversed a similar finding by the Panel on State laws because it considered that Antigua and Barbuda ('Antigua') had failed to make a prima facie case with respect to these State laws.
- GATS Art. XIV(a) (public morals defence): The Appellate Body upheld the Panel's finding that the US measures were designed 'to protect public morals or to maintain public order' within the meaning of Article XIV(a), but reversed the Panel's finding that the United States had not shown that its measures were 'necessary' to do so because the Panel had erred in considering consultations with Antigua to constitute a 'reasonably available'

1 *United States – Measures Affecting the Cross-Border Supply of Gambling and Betting Services.*

2 Other issues addressed: confidentiality of panel proceedings; terms of reference; the relevance of statements by a party to the DSB; measure at issue (total prohibition); practice as a measure; establishment of a prima facie case; late submission of a defence (DSU Art. 11); burden of proof.

3 'W/120', entitled 'Services Sectoral Classification List', was circulated by the GATT Secretariat in 1991. It contains a list of relevant service 'sectors and subsectors', along with 'corresponding CPC' numbers – from the UN Provisional Product Classification – for each subsector. The '1993 Scheduling Guidelines' were set out in an 'Explanatory Note' issued by the Secretariat in 1993.

alternative measure. The Appellate Body found that the measures were 'necessary': The United States had made a prima facie case showing of 'necessity' and Antigua had failed to identify any other alternative measures that might be 'reasonably available'. With respect to the Article XIV(c) defence, the Appellate Body reversed the Panel due to its erroneous 'necessity' analysis and declined to make its own findings on the issue.

The Appellate Body modified the Panel's finding with respect to the chapeau of Article XIV. The Appellate Body reversed the Panel's finding that the measures did not meet the requirements of the chapeau because the United States had discriminated in the enforcement of those measures. However, the Appellate Body upheld the second ground upon which the Panel based its finding, namely that in the light of the Interstate Horseracing Act (which appeared to authorize domestic operators to engage in the remote supply of certain betting services), the United States had not demonstrated that its prohibitions on remote gambling applied to both foreign and domestic service suppliers, i.e. in a manner that did not constitute 'arbitrary and unjustifiable discrimination' within the meaning of the chapeau.

Comment

United States – Measures Affecting the Cross-Border Supply of Gambling and Betting Services

Prepared for the ALI Project on the Case Law of the WTO

FEDERICO ORTINO
Lecturer in International Economic Law, Kings College, London

My remarks will focus mainly on the following two issues: (a) the scope of the per se prohibition in Article XVI GATS and (b) the nature of the balancing exercise carried out under Article XIV GATS.[1] I will also add two brief points on the 'burden of proof' and 'availability of alternative measures' under the least-trade-restrictive test of Article XIV GATS.

1. Scope of Article XVI GATS

The Appellate Body's apparent reading of Article XVI GATS to cover measures having an effect equivalent to an express quantitative restriction raises certain fundamental issues regarding the balance struck by the GATS between liberalizing trade in services and recognizing a Member's right to regulate the provision of services. While the reach of the Appellate Body's reading of Article XVI GATS is not altogether clear, the *Gambling* decision may be compared with the 1974 landmark decision by the European Court of Justice in *Dassonville*, which expanded the scope of the prohibition under Article 28 of the Treaty of Rome to 'all trading rules enacted by Member States which are capable of hindering, directly or indirectly, actually or potentially, intra-community trade'. First of all, I would argue that this is not the most plausible reading of Article XVI GATS. Secondly, I am not certain of the advantages of such a broad interpretation of Article XVI.

1 I have raised several criticisms towards the way the Appellate Body has reached its conclusion with regard to the scope of Article XVI GATS in 'Treaty Interpretation and the WTO Appellate Body Report in US – Gambling: A Critique', JIEL (2006).

On the first point, I would argue that the rationale behind Article XVI GATS appears to lie in the presumed absence of a legitimate public policy justifying the measures listed under Article XVI. In light of the rigid discipline to which these measures are subject (per se prohibition, rather than 'reasonableness' or 'non-discrimination'), it is indeed plausible that, in the minds of the treaty drafters, the underlying rationale of Article XVI is a presumption that the measures listed in subparagraph (2)(a)–(f) generally lack any legitimate policy justification (in much the same way as quotas and other restrictions on the importation of goods).[2] Accordingly, in the ideal world envisioned by the drafters of the GATS,[3] the measures listed therein should be in principle prohibited. Nonetheless, since such a presumption is based on a general value judgment (which may not be applicable in all circumstances), the drafters provided for the possibility that the market-access limitations of Article XVI may, in exceptional circumstances, be justified through recourse to Article XIV GATS. In other words, the above presumption is a rebuttable one.

The dividing line between what is per se prohibited by Article XVI and what is subjected to nondiscrimination and reasonableness standards may be fine, but it is there! While it is conceivable that the drafters of the GATS viewed formal 'quotas' as domestic measures that could not be permitted under WTO law since they lacked a legitimate policy justification, it is unconceivable that they also included within such a category of 'incriminated' measures any domestic regulation that has simply an effect equivalent to a quota (i.e., restricting access to national markets). Banning (online) gambling, like imposing an entry exam for lawyers or a minimum-capital requirement for banks, undeniably pursues legitimate policy objectives. It seems to follow that, even if these types of measures potentially restrict market access, they should not be subjected to the rigid approach (per se prohibition) of Article XVI.

Consider, for example, the case of a license requirement imposed by State A on the opening of a new restaurant in its territory. If the granting of the license in question depends on a pre-established quota ('only 5 restaurants may operate in the relevant area') or is based on an economic-needs test ('new restaurant licenses

2 This presumption may also stem from the perception that quantitative restrictions have a discriminatory or protectionist tendency since, by limiting how many suppliers operate within a specific market, they are bound to constitute protection to existing domestic operators (sub-paragraph (f) of Article XVI:(2) seems to confirm this view). However, this is not always true, especially with regard to new service fields or products and to developing countries. In these circumstances, Article XVI GATS could even be perceived as a pro-competitive instrument, insofar as it prohibits national governments to protect, not just domestic, but any incumbent service supplier.

3 As previously noted, (similar to tariffs) Article XVI market-access limitations are not prohibited immediately because it would not be economically and thus politically feasible to do so. For example, protection of a specific infant-service industry might be achieved through one of the quantitative measures listed in Article XVI. However, in the ideal world designed by the GATS, these types of justification are only temporary, and thus market-access restrictions are subject to the progressive liberalization 'commitments' in Article XIX GATS.

shall be granted only in the case of unsatisfied customers' demand'), then that requirement falls within the scope of application of Article XVI and is per se prohibited (as long as State A has entered a market-access commitment). On the other hand, if the granting of the restaurant license depends on the quality of the service supplied or on the ability of the supplier to supply the service, the measure falls outside the scope of Article XVI (and is potentially subjected to the disciplines of Articles XVII and VI). The difference between the two cases lies on the criteria employed in determining whether or not the license should be granted: while a simple numerical criterion or an economic-needs test is presumed to constitute illegitimate grounds upon which to base a limitation on market access, the quality of the service supplied or the ability of the supplier to supply the specific service are deemed to constitute legitimate regulatory policies.[4]

Shortly on the second point: are there any advantages of the broad interpretation of Article XVI? Clearly, a broad reading of Article XVI (such as the one rendered by the Appellate Body in *Gambling*) would expand the liberalizing scope of GATS at least for the sectors that Members have already committed to in their schedules. However, such a broad reading may also have the likely effect that, in future negotiations under the GATS, Members would be very reluctant to commit to the 'Market Access' disciplines of Article XVI making that provision 'dead letter'. In this regard, it would be interesting to assess whether the decision in *Gambling* has had already some effect in some of the recent accession negotiations.

2. Balancing under Article XIV GATS?

Since the Appellate Body Report in *Korea–Beef*, there appears to be a contradiction in the approach to the 'necessity test' under the general exception provisions of Articles XX GATT and XIV GATS. *Gambling* simply confirms this apparent contradiction. In the Appellate Body's view, a determination of whether a measure is 'necessary' within the context of Article XX GATT or Article XIV GATS involves in every case a process of *weighing and balancing* a series of factors that prominently include 'the contribution made by the compliance measure to the enforcement of the law or regulation at issue, the importance of the common interests or values protected by that law or regulation, and the accompanying impact of the law or regulation on imports or exports'.[5] At the same time, the

4 There is also empirical evidence that a measure, which has been found to violate a per se prohibition type of discipline (such as Article II or Article XI GATT), has never been found to be justified on the basis of one of the legitimate public-policy objectives listed in the general-exception provision (Article XX GATT). The only case where Article XX GATT was successfully employed to justify a violation of Article XI was *US – Shrimp 21.5*. However, the measure at issue in that dispute was the border arm of an internal regulation and thus should have been reviewed on the basis of Article III rather than Article XI GATT. For a fuller discussion of the issue see Ortino, *Basic Legal Instruments for the Liberalisation of Trade: A Comparative Analysis of EC and WTO Law* (Oxford: Hart 2004) at 220–221.

5 Appellate Body Report on *Korea–Beef*, para. 164.

Appellate Body firmly recognizes that WTO Members have the right to determine for themselves the level of protection.[6] Is the necessity test a 'cost/benefit' or 'proportionality *stricto sensu*' test, as the former language may seem to suggest, or more simply a 'cost/effectiveness' or 'least-trade-restrictive' test, as the latter sentence implies?

I believe that the 'weighing and balancing' test advanced by the Appellate Body in *Korea–Beef* and applied in *Gambling* should not be equated to what in EC law terminology is the test of 'proportionality *stricto sensu*', according to which the Court of Justice balances the national interest in pursuing a legitimate public policy against the Community interest in ensuring the free movement of goods and services. On the basis of this test, for example, it would be possible to strike down a national measure even if it is found to be 'necessary' to pursue a legitimate aim like environmental protection, on the basis that, on balance, the measure's negative effects on trade are *disproportionate* to its benefits on the environment.

This apparent contradictory language with regard to the meaning of the term 'necessary' within the general exceptions in the GATT and GATS clearly evidences the struggle in which the Appellate Body finds itself in attempting to deal with two diverging needs: 'flexible application' and 'legal certainty'. If the Appellate Body recognizes the inescapable and indispensable flexibility in applying concepts such as the 'necessity' requirement, it also tries to provide the elements upon which to base a 'necessity' determination. Although in doing so the Appellate Body did put forward certain new elements, it seems that this general approach does not differ substantially from the least-trade-restrictive test as enunciated in the famous *Section 337* GATT Panel Report. The several factors included in the weighing and balancing process in *Korea–Beef* are all to be employed in order to determine whether there exists an alternative measure that (1) is less restrictive than that found to violate one of the obligations of the GATT and (2) may equally protect the relevant public policy pursued by the Member.[7]

It should be stressed that even the necessity test understood as a least-trade-restrictive test may involve some form of 'balancing'. For example, determining what is the 'appropriate level of protection' (pursued by the regulating Member) is not a scientific exercise, and it grants judicial organs a certain margin of appreciation (determining Korea's relevant level of consumer protection in *Korea–Beef* was a key, and somewhat, controversial issue). Similarly, deciding whether a less trade-restrictive alternative achieves the same level of protection (as well as deciding whether an alternative is less restrictive) involves a certain margin of appreciation. Clearly this would not be 'balancing' of the same kind as that

6 Appellate Body Report on *Korea–Beef*, para. 176.

7 I would submit that the Appellate Body's reference to the *extent* of the *restrictive effects* on international commerce produced by the GATT-inconsistent compliance measure should not be regarded as introducing this type of 'weighing and balancing', but simply as the necessary limb in the determination of the existence of a *less-restrictive* measure that may equally secure compliance with the relevant 'laws and regulations'.

characterizing cost–benefit balancing; rather it is a form of balancing that cannot be avoided even in applying 'necessity' and 'less trade-restrictive' tests. This is what the Appellate Body was trying to grapple with in *Korea–Beef*: this could explain the reference to 'a range of degrees of necessity', the so-called 'continuum', as well as the reference to the 'trade costs' and 'contribution to the realization of the end pursued'. Also, the reference to the importance of the values protected by the regulating Member (the first criterion mentioned by the Appellate Body in *Korea–Beef*) may also be simply an attempt by the AB to come to face with an unavoidable factor at play in applying the 'necessity test' (rather than as part of a cost–benefit balancing). The importance of the public-policy goal will affect the above-mentioned 'balancing', which the judicial organs need to carry out within the 'least-trade-restrictive' test.

3. Burden of proof and availability of measures

The Appellate Body application of the 'necessity test' in *Gambling* did have two new features: one dealing with the burden of proof and one with the availability of alternative measures.

First, the Appellate Body emphasizes that it is for the defending party to make a prima facie case that its measure is 'necessary' by putting forward evidence and arguments in respect of the relevant factors to be weighted and balanced. The focus here is on the measures under review. If the defending party is successful in making a prima facie case of necessity, then it is for the complaining party to raise WTO-consistent alternative measures (capable of achieving the same level of protection) that the responding party should have taken. The focus here is on the alternative measures.[8]

Second, the Appellate Body recognizes expressly in *Gambling* that a purely 'theoretical alternative' is not enough to rebut a prima facie case of necessity; for example, if 'the responding Member is not capable of taking it, or where the measure imposes ... prohibitive costs or substantial technical difficulties'.[9] This statement allows WTO dispute settlement panels some flexibility in determining the existence of alternative measures reasonably available when the defending Member is, for example, a developing country.

8 *Gambling*, para. 309.
9 *Gambling*, para. 308.

The Zeroing Issue: a critical analysis of Softwood V

CHAD P. BOWN

Department of Economics and International Business School, MS 021, Brandeis University, PO Box 549110, Waltham, MA, 02454-9110 USA
Email: cbown@brandeis.edu

ALAN O. SYKES

Stanford Law School, Stanford, CA

Abstract: This paper addresses the issues that came before the Appellate Body in the Softwood V dispute, concerning an affirmative antidumping determination by the US Department of Commerce. The paper addresses both the original Appellate Body opinion in the dispute, and the later opinion reviewing the compliance panel findings. We focus primarily on the 'zeroing' issue in 'transaction-to-transaction (T–T)' calculations of dumping, and briefly on two other cost-allocation issues. In general, we are ambivalent about the Appellate Body's approach to the zeroing issue. On the one hand, zeroing inflates dumping margins without any sound economic rationale for doing so. On the other hand, zeroing has been a standard administrative practice for many years and the ADA does not clearly prohibit it. The Appellate Body's legal analysis of the matter in T–T cases, in particular, rests on shaky premises. We also consider the wisdom of addressing the zeroing issue in piecemeal fashion through what has proven to be a lengthy sequence of narrow decisions.

1. Introduction

The softwood-lumber dispute between the United States and Canada has been one of the longest-running trade disputes in history, producing extensive litigation in the United States, the NAFTA, and the WTO, spanning questions of subsidization, dumping, and injury. For the moment at least, the dispute appears to have been settled by the entry into force of the Softwood Lumber Agreement between the two disputants, under which Canada has agreed to impose a tiered system of export taxes, quantitative controls, and export licenses on its softwood-lumber exports.[1] The particular dimension of the dispute on which we focus is

Thanks to Meredith Crowley, Edwin Vermulst, Petros Mavroidis, Joel Trachtman, David Palmeter, and ALI conference participants in Geneva for useful comments on an earlier draft. All remaining errors are our own.

1 See Notification of Mutually Agreed Solution, WT/DS264/29 G/L/566/Add.1 G/ADP/D42/2, November 16, 2006 (covering all outstanding WTO softwood disputes: DS236, DS247, DS257, DS264, DS277, and DS311).

the complaint brought to the WTO by Canada in 2002 concerning an affirmative antidumping duty determination by the United States Department of Commerce (Commerce). This case is commonly termed 'Softwood V'; the WTO decisions in Softwood I–IV and Softwood VI address other aspects of the broader softwood–lumber dispute.

In Softwood V, Canada challenged numerous aspects of the dumping determination by Commerce as being inconsistent with the Antidumping Agreement (ADA), including the decision to initiate the investigation, the like-product determination, and various adjustments to the dumping calculations that Commerce made or refused to make.[2] The aspect of Canada's case that became central before the Appellate Body, however, was the practice of 'zeroing' by Commerce in the calculation of dumping margins, a practice that we explain below. Canada's original complaint challenged the practice of zeroing in 'weighted average to weighted average' (W–W) calculations of antidumping duties. After Canada prevailed on this challenge before the panel[3] and the Appellate Body,[4] Commerce purported to comply with the ruling by shifting its method of calculation to the 'transaction-to-transaction' (T–T) method, again employing the practice of zeroing. Canada challenged the resulting determination before an Article 21.5 compliance panel, where the United States prevailed.[5] The Appellate Body reversed the panel, and held that zeroing was also impermissible in T–T calculations, at least in the context of original investigations.[6]

Softwood V is neither the first nor the last WTO dispute in which zeroing has been a central issue. The Appellate Body has now addressed zeroing in four other opinions,[7] with perhaps still more to come. Further challenges to US zeroing practices are pending in cases brought by Mexico, Ecuador, and Thailand. In addition, the Appellate Body has not yet addressed the use of zeroing in the 'weighted-average-to-transaction' (W–T) method of calculating dumping

2 See *United States – Final Dumping Determination on Softwood Lumber from Canada*, WT/DS264/R, April 13, 2004 (hereafter Panel Report).

3 Ibid.

4 See *United States – Final Dumping Determination on Softwood Lumber from Canada*, Report of the Panel, WT/DS264/AB/R, August 11, 2004 (hereafter AB Report).

5 See *United States – Final Dumping Determination on Softwood Lumber from Canada*, Recourse to Article 21.5 of the DSU by Canada, WT/DS264/RW, April 3, 2006 (hereafter Compliance Panel Report).

6 *United States – Final Dumping Determination on Softwood Lumber from Canada*, Recourse to Article 21.5 of the DSU by Canada, WT/DS264/AB/RW, August 11, 2006 (hereafter Compliance AB Report).

7 See *European Communities – Anti-Dumping Duties on Imports of Cotton-Type Bed Linen from India*, WT/DS141/AB/R, March 1, 2001; *United States – Sunset Review of Antidumping Duties on Corrosion-Resistant Carbon Steel Flat Products from Japan*, WT/DS244/AB/R, December 15, 2003; *United States – Laws Regulations and Methodology for Calculating Dumping Margins ('Zeroing')*, WT/DS294/AB/R, April 18, 2006; *United States – Measures Relating to Zeroing and Sunset Reviews*, WT/DS322/AB/R, January 9, 2007.

margins, which is permitted under certain special and imprecisely defined circumstances.

The focus of this paper will be on the zeroing issue, and on the broader question whether the Appellate Body's incremental approach to the practice of zeroing is procedurally desirable from a legal and economic standpoint. In brief, we are ambivalent about the Appellate Body's approach to the zeroing issue. On the one hand, zeroing inflates dumping margins without any sound economic rationale for doing so. On the other hand, zeroing has been a standard administrative practice for many years and the ADA does not clearly prohibit it. The Appellate Body's legal analysis of the matter in T–T cases, in particular, rests on shaky premises. We also discuss the wisdom of addressing the zeroing issue in piecemeal fashion through what has proven to be a lengthy series of narrow decisions.

In addition to the discussion of zeroing, we touch briefly on two cost-allocation issues that came before the Appellate Body in Softwood V. In both instances, the underlying practices by Commerce are questionable from an economic standpoint.

2. Factual and legal issues and their disposition

The practice of zeroing and its effects

Dumping occurs when export transactions occur at prices below 'normal' or 'fair' value, which is in turn computed with reference to home-market prices, third-country prices, or estimated costs of production, depending on the circumstances. Roughly speaking, a 'dumping margin' measures the extent to which export prices fall below the selected benchmark for normal value. Exporters typically have multiple transactions with the importing country that is investigating dumping, however, and hence dumping margins in practice are almost invariably based on some 'average' amount of dumping. In computing this average, the investigating authority can treat transactions for which the export price is above normal value as 'negative dumping', so that the amount by which export prices exceed normal value in some transactions will offset the amount by which export prices fall below normal value in others, thereby lowering the average amount of dumping. The zeroing method of calculation treats all instances of 'negative dumping' as zero dumping, however, so that only the transactions in which the export price is below normal value 'count' in computing the numerator for purposes of averaging. The inevitable effect is to increase the computed average and thus also to increase any resulting antidumping duties.

To illustrate zeroing, suppose that the normal value for all export transactions is established to be 100. Three export transactions occur at prices of 90, 100, and 110. The first of these transactions is 'dumped' because $90 < 100$. The other two are not. Nevertheless, the average price for the export transactions is 100, exactly equal to normal value. Without zeroing, the magnitude of dumping for the three transactions would be computed as 10, 0, and -10, so that the average amount of dumping across the three transactions would be zero $\{[10+0+(-10)]/3\}$ and no antidumping duty could be imposed. With zeroing, by contrast, the transaction with the 'negative' dumping is treated as a transaction with zero dumping, and the 'average' amount of dumping is found to be 3 and 1/3 {[10+0+0]/3}.

The technique of zeroing can be employed regardless of the exact method of calculating the magnitude of dumping. To explain how, we begin with Article 2.4.2 of the ADA:

> Subject to the provisions governing fair comparison in paragraph 4, the existence of margins of dumping during the investigation phase shall normally be established on the basis of a comparison of a weighted average normal value with a weighted average of prices of all comparable export transactions or by a comparison of normal value and export prices on a transaction-to-transaction basis. A normal value established on a weighted average basis may be compared to prices of individual export transactions if the authorities find a pattern of export prices which differ significantly among different purchasers, regions or time periods, and if an explanation is provided as to why such differences cannot be taken into account appropriately by the use of a weighted average-to-weighted average or transaction-to-transaction comparison.

Thus, as noted in the introduction, three methods of calculation are authorized 'during the investigation phase'.[8] The calculation shall 'normally' be W–W or T–T, with W–T allowed only under special circumstances. Those circumstances seemingly relate to cases of narrowly targeted dumping that is concentrated on particular 'purchasers, regions or time periods', but to date the W–T method has apparently been little used and no case involving zeroing with the W–T method has come before the Appellate Body.

In a W–W case, one might suppose that zeroing cannot occur because the dumping margin is based on a comparison between normal value and average rather than individual export prices. In fact, however, W–W cases often involve comparisons across several product categories, which are then aggregated to produce the average dumping margin. Zeroing can then occur if 'negative' dumping in one or more product-category comparisons is zeroed when computing the aggregate average. For example, suppose that widgets come in two models, A and B. The normal value for model A is 50, while the average export price is 60. For model B, the normal value is 80 and the average export price is 70. Thus, model B is dumped and model A is not. The dumping margin for all widgets will be computed using the amount of dumping for model A and the amount for model B, weighted by the sales of each model, and divided by the total sales of both models. Zeroing treats the amount of dumping for model A as zero, while a calculation without zeroing will treat it as −10. The resulting 'average' is plainly

8 This language hints at another set of issues: namely, whether different rules apply at other points in the process such as periodic reviews, sunset reviews, and new-shipper reviews. These issues have been raised in some of the other zeroing cases to come before the Appellate Body, but we will not address them here.

higher with zeroing. Because the effect of zeroing in a W–W case results from zeroing the results for particular subcategories or 'models' of the broader product under investigation, it is sometimes termed 'model zeroing'.

The operation of zeroing in T–T cases is more transparent. The investigating authority will compare the prices of individual export transactions to 'comparable' transactions in the home country or a third country, or perhaps to cost of production. Whenever the individual export transaction price is above the benchmark for normal value, the amount of dumping is said to be zero rather than negative. Again, the inevitable effect is to raise the 'average' amount of dumping. When zeroing is used in a T–T case it is sometimes termed 'simple zeroing'.[9]

Zeroing in Softwood V: the initial phase

In its original softwood-lumber investigation, Commerce investigated the six largest Canadian exporters and determined individual dumping margins for them. Smaller Canadian exporters received an 'all others' margin based on a weighted average of the margins for the six investigated companies. Export prices were based on a weighted average of transaction prices for each company within several product categories. Normal value was based on a weighted average of home-market-transaction prices for each product category, although for each company Commerce disregarded a number of lower priced home-market sales that were deemed to be below cost of production. The case was thus a W–W investigation, and in computing the average amount of dumping for the covered softwood products as a whole, Commerce employed zeroing.[10]

Before the softwood-lumber investigation was initiated by Commerce in April 2001, the Appellate Body had already held in *EC–Bed Linen* that the EC's practice of zeroing, in investigations using the W–W method, violated Article 2.4.2 of the ADA. *EC–Bed Linen* is discussed and analyzed in Janow and Staiger (2003). Predictably, therefore, Canada included a challenge to zeroing in the softwood case and brought a claim under Article 2.4.2 of the ADA that was largely identical to the one that had prevailed in *EC–Bed Linen*.

Before the panel and the Appellate Body, Canada focused on the language in Article 2.4.2 requiring that W–W comparisons encompass 'all comparable export transactions'. Zeroing, in Canada's view, effectively excluded some comparable export transactions from the comparison.

The United States argued that the obligation to use 'all comparable export transactions' simply meant that all export transactions involving comparable goods must be used in the calculation, and that it had fulfilled this obligation

9 The effect of zeroing on a W–T calculation is also obvious and might be termed simple zeroing. Whenever the individual-export-transaction price is above the weighted average that is used as the basis for normal value, zeroing treats the amount of dumping as zero rather than negative and the average amount of dumping across all export transactions will increase.

10 Additional details of the calculations may be found in Commerce's preliminary and final dumping determinations, 66 Fed. Reg. 56062 (November 6, 2001) and 67 Fed. Reg. 15539 (April 2, 2002).

when it decomposed softwood lumber into subgroups of comparable products and used all of the export transactions for each subgroup in its analysis. Each subgroup had its own 'margin of dumping' based on the W–W comparisons. And once it computed dumping margins for each subgroup in accordance with the text, argued the United States, the ADA provided no further guidance as to how those dumping margins were to be aggregated to obtain an overall average margin for softwood products. Because the text was silent on the method of aggregation, zeroing was not precluded in the US view. The United States also pointed to the ADA standard of review under Article 17.6, which requires that if the ADA has more than one permissible interpretation, decisions by national authorities should be upheld if they rest on one of the permissible interpretations. Finally, the United States insisted that its interpretation of the ADA was confirmed by its negotiating history.

Not surprisingly, in light of the Appellate Body decision in *Bed Linen*, the panel sided with Canada. On appeal, the Appellate Body affirmed the panel. It framed the legal issue as follows: Under the view of the United States, 'dumping' can occur and 'margins of dumping' can be computed for subgroups of a product under investigation. Once 'all comparable export transactions' have been taken into account at the subgroup level, the obligation in Article 2.4.2 is met. Under Canada's view, 'dumping' can only occur for a product as a whole, and the 'margin of dumping' can only be determined for a product as a whole. When the single 'margin of dumping' is computed on the basis of zeroing, some of the 'comparable export transactions' are effectively disregarded.

After laying out the alternative views, the Appellate Body reaffirmed its conclusions in *Bed Linen*. It pointed to the text of GATT Article VI and to Article 2.1 of the ADA, both of which define dumping as a situation in which 'products' are sold below normal value. From this language, the Appellate Body inferred that 'dumping' only exists for a 'product as a whole', not for subgroups of a product. Likewise, dumping margins only exist for a 'product as a whole'. The text of Article 2.4.2 thus requires that 'all comparable export transactions' be used to compute the final dumping margin for the product as a whole, not just in the computations for product subgroups. Because the Appellate Body considered the text of Article 2.4.2 to be clear on the matter, the standard of review in Article 17.6 had no applicability – there was only one 'permissible interpretation' of Article 2.4.2. Likewise, the negotiating history and context of Article 2.4.2 had no relevance because the text was clear.

Zeroing in Softwood V: the compliance phase

Commerce responded to the Appellate Body ruling by recalculating the dumping margins for the Canadian producers. Rather than using a W–W method without zeroing, however, it shifted to a T–T method and employed zeroing once again.

Canada took the position that zeroing is impermissible in a T–T calculation, and brought the matter to a compliance panel under Article 21.5 of the DSU again under ADA Article 2.4.2, and also Article 2.4, which states in pertinent part that '[a] fair comparison shall be made between the export price and the normal value'. The panel rejected Canada's claim under the ADA, however, noting that the Appellate Body rulings in *Bed Linen* and Softwood V were expressly limited to W–W cases. Furthermore, in both decisions the Appellate Body had relied on the phrase 'all comparable export transactions' in the text of Article 2.4.2, which is linked to the W–W method of computation only – no similar language appears in the text with regard to the T–T method of computation. The panel also found that a general prohibition of zeroing in the ADA would lead to some other anomalies, such as a mathematical equivalence between W–W and W–T calculations.

The Appellate Body reversed. It concluded that, in a 'comparison of normal value and export prices on a transaction-to-transaction basis', the use of the plural 'export prices' in the first sentence of Article 2.4.2 'suggests that all of the results of the transaction-specific comparisons should be included in the aggregation'.[11] The absence of the phrase 'all comparable export transactions' in reference to the T–T method was of no significance in the view of the Appellate Body. That phrase was simply intended to require that when investigating authorities break a product into subgroups for purposes of a W–W calculation, they must ensure that transactions are 'comparable' and that all of the relevant transactions are included.[12] The Appellate Body was also of the view that to allow zeroing under one method of calculation but not another would mean that the results of the two methods would be 'systematically different', an anomalous situation given that both methods are intended to measure dumping.[13] As for the suggestion that a complete prohibition on zeroing would render the W–W and W–T methods mathematically equivalent and thus deprive the W–T method of any utility, the Appellate Body noted, inter alia, that it was not ruling on zeroing in a W–T calculation, and that in any case the details of such a calculation were unclear because no such calculation had been made. The Appellate Body also rejected various other arguments put forward by the panel to bolster its position.

Other issues and their disposition

Two other issues came before the Appellate Body in its original review of the case. Both arose from the calculation of the Canadian producers' 'cost of production' by Commerce, an exercise that served as the basis for excluding below-cost home-market transactions from the normal-value calculation.

First, for the producer Abitibi, Commerce insisted that its financial expenses be allocated among its various product lines (only some of which were covered by the softwood-lumber investigation) using the 'cost of goods sold' (COGS) method.

11 Compliance AB Report, ¶88.
12 Ibid. ¶91.
13 Ibid. ¶93.

This method would allocate Abitibi's total financial expenses to softwood-lumber production based on the proportion of softwood-lumber production in Abitibi's total cost of goods sold. Abitibi instead wished to use an allocation method based on the proportion of its capital assets devoted to softwood production (which, presumably, would have resulted in a smaller allocation of financial expenses and thus a lower cost of production). Its rationale for the alternative method was that softwood production required proportionally fewer capital assets than other production activities within the company, and thus its proper share of capital-financing costs was lower than the COGS method suggested.

Commerce rejected Abitibi's request. It stated that the COGS method was its standard practice for the allocation of financial expenses. Further, it argued that if capital expenses were higher for lines of production other than softwood products, that difference would be accounted for in the calculation through the depreciation rate – less interest expense would be allocated to softwood production to the degree that financial statements showed less capital depreciation in softwood production.[14]

Canada challenged this determination, but the panel ruled for the United States. The Appellate Body reversed the panel's legal conclusions. It focused on the text of Article 2.2.1.1, which provides in pertinent part that '[a]uthorities shall consider all available evidence on the proper allocation of costs'. The Appellate Body held that the term 'consider' imposes a substantive obligation on investigating authorities that goes beyond simply receiving evidence and reciting that it has been 'considered'. Rather, in appropriate circumstances, authorities may be obligated to compare allocation methods and evaluate their merits. The panel had held that Article 2.2.1.1 'does not require that investigating authorities compare various allocation methodologies', and thus had interpreted the text incorrectly. Having held that the panel applied the wrong legal standard, however, the Appellate Body did not complete the factual analysis as to whether Commerce had complied with Article 2.2.1.1.[15]

The second issue concerned the calculation of by-product revenues for the producer Tembec. The production of the softwood-lumber products under investigation yields wood chips as a by-product, which are used by the pulp and paper industry. The revenue from the sale of wood chips reduces the effective cost of production for softwood-lumber products. In calculating the appropriate cost offset for Tembec, Commerce used its internal-transfer prices for sales between its wholly owned sawmill and pulp-mill divisions. For another Canadian producer (West Fraser) that made sales to affiliated companies, however, Commerce had disregarded the stated prices as being not at 'arm's-length' and substituted market prices instead. Tembec urged Commerce to do the same for its interdivisional transactions, but Commerce refused. The panel upheld Commerce on this issue,

14 AB Report ¶121.
15 Ibid. ¶¶125–145.

finding that the two companies were not similarly situated and that Commerce had not departed from its normal practices in the case.

On appeal, the Appellate Body accepted arguendo Canada's legal claim that Commerce had an obligation to treat producers in even-handed fashion, and that it had to act consistently across cases and thus adhere to its standard practices without good reason to depart from them. But the Appellate Body further determined that the panel had made *factual* findings against Canada on these points, and saw no reason to interfere with those factual determinations on appeal.[16]

3. Analysis

Zeroing

An economic perspective on zeroing

To begin our discussion of zeroing, it is perhaps useful to consider the rationale for zeroing that is put forward by its US proponents. They analogize dumping to speeding in a motor vehicle. When a motorist is caught speeding by a police officer, what matters is that the motorist is exceeding the speed limit at the time. There is no inquiry into the question of whether the motorist obeyed the speed limit on average, and no offset for speeding if the motorist was going below the speed limit at an earlier time. Zeroing is analytically equivalent in the view of its proponents – firms that dump should not enjoy any offset for the occasions on which they price above normal value.

Is this analogy apt? An economic perspective on accident law suggests that 'negligence' in general represents a failure to take cost-effective measures to reduce risks to others created by an actor's activities. Speed limits represent a legislative substitute for case-by-case inquiry into the costs and benefits of driving speed. Excessive speed is subject to sanction irrespective of prior behavior because the legislature has determined that each act of speeding creates an unacceptable level of risk.

Does each 'dumped' sale of a product create a similarly unacceptable risk of economic harm that deserves sanction, regardless of the pricing behavior of the firm in other transactions? To answer this question, one must embrace a theory of why dumping is worrisome in the first instance. But modern economic learning has difficulty explaining why dumping should be subject to sanction at all.

Price-discrimination dumping is a natural response by firms with market power facing separate markets with different elasticities of demand. It may also result quite naturally from volatile market conditions and exchange-rate fluctuations. 'Below cost' dumping, with 'cost' understood not as marginal or variable cost but as total cost including an allocation of capital and overhead costs, is common in many industries where cost and demand conditions fluctuate. Firms in a

16 Ibid. ¶¶159–180.

competitive industry will tend to break-even against average total cost in the 'long run', but in the 'short run' will often see prices that vary above or below average total cost. Consequently, most instances of dumping are perfectly normal and benign manifestations of ordinary market conditions. These points are hardly original to us, but have been made by other commentators too numerous to warrant citation.

Defenders of antidumping rules most commonly suggest that the rationale for them lies with concerns about monopolization, and that dumping is akin to what antitrust scholars term predatory pricing. Although it is true that national antidumping laws were originally pitched as an important supplement to antitrust policy, they have never been so in practice. A sensible anti-predation policy would utilize structural filters, examining only concentrated industries where a danger of monopolization is plausible. Yet, antidumping duties are routinely used in unconcentrated industries where monopolization concerns are fanciful. Likewise, a sensible anti-predation policy would make a serious effort to ascertain whether low prices are an attempt to drive out competitors rather than a normal market phenomenon. There would be no presumption against price discrimination, and any cost-based floors would be linked to marginal or variable costs rather than fully allocated costs. Modern antidumping laws lack these characteristics. Finally, for nations with sensible antitrust laws, even narrowly tailored antidumping laws aimed at predation would seem superfluous.

For these reasons, it is impossible to argue that antidumping law is a sensible component of antitrust policy. Indeed, Sykes (1998) argues that the antitrust rationale for antidumping laws was pretense from the very outset, and that such laws were understood by their early proponents to be a disguised form of protectionism for troubled industries.

If the overwhelming weight of economic commentary is correct, individual transactions at 'dumped' prices are generally of no concern whatsoever. They are simply not analogous to dangerous behaviors such as speeding that are properly subject to sanction. As a corollary, any policy or practice that reduces the incidence or magnitude of antidumping duties in the global economy might be deemed desirable. To the degree that a prohibition of zeroing reduces antidumping duties, such prohibitions may seem quite welcome from an economic standpoint.

This proposition is subject to a potentially important caveat. Although economic commentators are almost uniformly critical of antidumping law as a normative matter, economic analysis has made considerably less progress on the positive issue of why antidumping law is so survivable in the global trading system. If antidumping duties are indeed silly from a policy standpoint, why have trading nations not agreed to abolish them (just as they have been abolished internally in the United States and European Union)? One must entertain the possibility that they serve some useful political function. If so, perhaps the availability of antidumping remedies has some other salutary effect, such as the facilitation of trade concessions that might not otherwise be made (an explanation often given for safeguard measures). And should this be the case, one can no longer say with confidence that any Appellate Body ruling that lessens the use or magnitude of antidumping duties is economically desirable.

More generally, if one views the ADA as part of a sophisticated contract among WTO members that promotes their mutual political interests when melded with the rest of the WTO bargain, one cannot be sanguine about any Appellate Body decision that does violence to the objectives of the ADA. From this perspective, the economic soundness of the Appellate Body rulings against zeroing in Softwood V and in other cases turns closely on the question of whether the rulings are sound as a legal matter. To that question we now turn.

The legality of zeroing

In Softwood V and its other rulings on zeroing, the Appellate Body has held fast to its conventional emphasis on textualism, paying relatively little heed to the negotiating history of the text. We understand this practice, as well as the principle that inferences from an often-murky negotiating history should not be permitted to override clear textual mandates. Nevertheless, we have some quarrels with the analysis of the Appellate Body in Softwood V that are perhaps best motivated by placing the issue in some historical context.

The practice of zeroing is not some arcane and technical practice that went unnoticed before the ADA. To the contrary, numerous commentators had written about zeroing and the arguably pernicious effect that it has on dumping margins.[17] Many of these same commentators had also written about other 'biases' in antidumping calculations. A common criticism was that investigating authorities (especially Commerce) routinely used W–T methods to calculate dumping margins. This method of calculating margins tends to produce findings of dumping as a matter of course when coupled with zeroing. In particular, imagine comparing a volatile time series to a moving average of itself. Some data points will be below the moving average and some above. If the moving average is used as normal value, and individual data points below average are 'dumping', then the W–T method (coupled with zeroing) will find dumping even if the time series that is the basis for normal value is *identical* to the time series of export prices!

Such issues were plainly known to the negotiators of the ADA. And on the use of the W–T method, the negotiators produced a text that curtailed it greatly. Under Article 2.4.2, margin calculations shall 'normally' be W–W or T–T, with the W–T method reserved for special cases of dumping targeted at particular 'purchasers, regions or time periods'.

17 See, e.g., the collection of papers in Boltuck and Litan (1991), particularly the papers by Palmeter and by Boltuck, Francois, and Kaplan.

Thus, when the negotiators reached agreement on the elimination or curtailment of one of the well-known 'biases' in antidumping calculations, they were quite capable of embodying that agreement in the treaty text. Yet, in stark contrast to the express curtailment of W–T methods by the ADA, there are no references anywhere in the ADA to the practice of zeroing. The United States argued, and we have some sympathy for this position, that this lack of attention to zeroing means that the negotiators reached no consensus on this issue, at least in so far as zeroing might be used in W–W or T–T calculations.

A possible counterargument is that the negotiators did not clearly separate the issue of zeroing from the effects of the W–T method and instead conflated the two. Indeed, the 'bias' inherent in W–T calculations evaporates without zeroing. One might thus conjecture that when the negotiators curtailed the use of W–T methods, they believed that they had also addressed the issue of zeroing. The difficulty with this argument is that zeroing also has a clear effect on W–W (with product subgroups) and T–T calculations as well. Were the negotiators simply oblivious to this fact? Or was the lack of attention to zeroing in these other calculation methods a manifestation of their inability to achieve agreement? We do not know the answers to these questions.

Against this backdrop, we turn to the Appellate Body's textual analysis, and its conclusion that the text unambiguously prohibits zeroing in both W–W and T–T cases. We agree that the text might be interpreted as prohibiting zeroing through general references to 'all comparable export transactions' and 'fair comparisons'. Yet it is difficult for us to accept that a prohibition on zeroing is the only possible reading of the text, and some of the Appellate Body's reasoning is troubling. For example, there can be no dispute that in both *Bed Linen* and the original Softwood V opinion, the Appellate Body placed great weight on the phrase 'all comparable export transactions' in holding that zeroing is prohibited under the W–W method. Yet, when the T–T method came before it in the compliance proceeding, the Appellate Body gave the back of the hand to the absence of this phrase in Article 2.4.2 in its reference to the T–T method. It insisted that the phrase 'all comparable export transactions' simply calls for comparability and comprehensiveness when product subgroups are used in a W–W calculation, and is not the basis for the prohibition on zeroing. This interpretation of the phrase 'all comparable export transactions', of course, was advanced by the United States in the original proceeding in support of its argument that the ADA did not prohibit zeroing in W–W cases! And if the phrase 'all comparable export transactions' is not about zeroing, as the Appellate Body suggests in its Softwood V compliance decision, then the textual basis for a prohibition on zeroing seems questionable indeed. The phrase 'fair comparison' in Article 2.4 simply begs the question of what is fair. And it seems quite a stretch to suggest that the use of the plural 'export prices' in the reference to the T–T method is enough to preclude zeroing.

Ultimately, the Appellate Body itself must fall back on nontextual arguments from policy, such as its claim that the drafters of the ADA would not have created an agreement under which W–W and T–T calculations yield 'systematically different' results because only one method allows zeroing. Even if the premise here is correct, it is equally compatible with the proposition that zeroing is acceptable in *both* W–W and T–T cases, as the United States maintained in Softwood V.

As a legal matter, therefore, we have considerable sympathy for the proposition that the text of the ADA is at least ambiguous regarding the use of zeroing in W–W and T–T calculations. In the face of that ambiguity, the United States had a strong argument that the deferential standard of review under Article 17.6 should be invoked.

Incrementalism in Appellate Body decisionmaking

In this section, we analyze how the Appellate Body has confronted the issue of 'zeroing' more broadly in the cases that have come before it (and may yet come before it). Its strategy has been to decide each case narrowly, and generally to disclaim any intent to rule on the question of zeroing as it may arise in other contexts. The result has been a long sequence of cases brought by numerous complainants to address zeroing in various settings – in W–W cases, in T–T cases, and perhaps someday in W–T cases – in the context of original investigations, periodic reviews, sunset reviews, and new-shipper reviews. This approach to decision making we term 'incrementalism'. Our objective is to assess the costs and benefits of incrementalism as one approach in the range of potential law-making strategies that the Appellate Body could adopt.

Incrementalism is, in a sense, one extreme of the distribution, where the other extreme might be for the Appellate Body to adopt a more comprehensive approach to zeroing at the onset of the issue in *EC–Bed Linen*. As a thought exercise, we examine the tradeoffs of a narrow, incrementalist approach when compared to a stark alternative – suppose the Appellate Body in *EC–Bed Linen* had undertaken to address the issue of zeroing comprehensively in all three methods of calculation as employed at all possible stages of the antidumping law process. It might, in theory at least, have announced an intention to address the issue comprehensively, sought briefs from all interested parties on all of the relevant issues, and then decided all of them once and for all at the outset.

In engaging in this thought experiment, we are putting to the side the obvious constraints of the DSU and the limitations on the scope of a proceeding contained in the terms of reference to a panel. Accordingly, we do not mean to suggest that the Appellate Body necessarily has the legal authority to proceed in fully comprehensive fashion under current WTO law. We do note, however, that even within existing constraints the Appellate Body has some leeway to foreshadow decisions on other issues through dicta and through legal analysis that has inevitable logical implications for issues that may arise in future disputes. Thus, if one were to conclude that a more comprehensive approach to decisionmaking were desirable, the Appellate Body has some significant leeway to move in that direction.

Some advantages of incrementalism

A complete economic treatment of the choice between incremental and comprehensive approaches to decisionmaking would require a formal theoretical model, and we will not undertake to construct one here. We nevertheless sketch the basic set of assumptions needed to examine the tradeoffs involved, and we explore their implications informally. First, the analysis must contemplate multiple periods to allow for the possibility of sequential decisionmaking by judges.[18] Furthermore, the analysis must assume that judges face uncertainty when making their decisions as to the correct interpretation of the law, and that there are costs associated with errors in judicial rulings. In other words, rulings that are legally correct are also 'efficient'. It is also natural to assume that there is a negative relationship between the *narrowness* of the issue before the judge and the amount of uncertainty the judge faces – i.e., the more narrow the issue, the smaller the uncertainty and the more likely the judge makes a correct ruling, other things being equal. Lastly, it is natural to assume that the likelihood of error in any context can be reduced if the decisionmaker acquires more information (legal briefs, facts, etc.) and if the decisionmaker spends more time on the decision. Both of these options, however, are costly.

With these assumptions, a clear benefit to incrementalism as a law-making strategy in the judicial process is that it is parsimonious in the information required to decide cases holding constant the probability of error. Likewise, holding constant the amount of 'information' available to the decisionmaker and the time spent in deciding the case, incrementalism is less likely to result in error.

An additional benefit to incrementalism may arise if we extend the analysis to assume judges also have personal *biases* – i.e., personal preferences that differ from what is legally correct – which may further cause decisions to deviate from correct rulings.[19] This is arguably an important consideration in the zeroing cases that are a subset of WTO litigation over the politically charged issue of antidumping. In line with this assumption, one could imagine a scenario in which Appellate Body members hold a personal bias either against antidumping measures (predisposed to complainants challenging another country's use of antidumping policy) because of its protectionist nature and lack of grounding in any economics or, alternatively, in favor of antidumping measures (predisposed to respondents being challenged) as a policy of fairness that governments require to maintain their political ability to engage in the WTO at all. A potential benefit of incrementalism as a lawmaking rule in this context is that it leads to rulings that are limited in

18 The models developed by Gennaioli and Shleifer (2007a, b) are built on similar foundational assumptions, though their analysis is structured to examine the efficiency properties of different judicial lawmaking rules from the incrementalist rule under discussion here. We discuss the insight of these models and relevance for incrementalism in more detail below.

19 This assumption is common to the Gennaioli and Shleifer (2007a, b) models, which assume that judges hold personal 'biases' that deviate away from efficient rulings in favor of different types of disputants, and these biases vary across the population of judges.

scope. Over time, if various biases in incremental rulings tend to 'cancel out', the potential for deviation from efficiency is lessened.[20]

A final institutional benefit to incrementalism may be that it is more likely to allow the Appellate Body to avoid being accused of engaging in 'judicial activism'. In the context of the WTO and the political trade-offs that it confronts in maintaining legitimacy in the eyes of its members, a perceived virtue to incrementalism is thus 'judicial restraint'.

If we were to stop here, incrementalism would seem an obviously superior approach to decisionmaking. But it remains to consider some items on the other side of the ledger.

Incrementalism and resource costs of litigation

One cost of incrementalism relates to the resource costs of litigation, as these can be substantial in the WTO system. In this context, there are at least two sets of costs to examine – the costs to the potential litigants themselves, as well as the resource costs to the WTO institution.

The first costs are the resources expended by the litigants involved in the additional cases that need to be litigated to fully flesh out the relevant law. A first-order concern is that resolving a legal issue incrementally, as opposed to all at once, can lead to increased use of litigant resources if there are substantial fixed costs to the litigants associated with each new dispute. For example, a fixed cost arises if the litigants in the subsequent cases are different from the litigants in the first case, as the legal team in each subsequent case will also need to relearn the issues critical to the first ruling. A fixed cost may also exist even if the litigants are the same, given the longevity of DSU litigation and that there is likely to be turnover within a legal team (likely to be within a government agency) for a number of reasons, including ongoing changes in governments associated with elections, and so forth.[21]

In addition to the potential inefficient use of resources, the existence of substantial litigation costs may also create uneven patterns in the utilization of the

20 This relates to some extent to the analysis provided in Gennaioli and Shleifer (2007a, b), who consider two period models in which a judge in the first period makes a legal decision that establishes a precedent. In the second period, the authors examine equilibria under two different assumptions on legal rulemaking. In Gennaioli and Shleifer (2007a), the authors focus on a second-period legal rule of 'distinguishing', in which a second ruling can modify an existing precedent by introducing an additional dimension along which to interpret facts. In Gennaioli and Shleifer (2007b), the authors focus on a second-period legal rule of 'overruling', not by introducing another dimension along which to rule, but by merely allowing a new judge to change the first ruling. Their results are that the lawmaking strategy of distinguishing has beneficial evolutionary properties (even in the presence of biased judges), while the strategy of overruling leads to unstable legal rules that rarely converge to efficiency. We conjecture that the lawmaking rule of incrementalism may have similar efficiency-enhancing evolutionary properties to a rule of distinguishing.

21 The fixed costs may be especially pronounced in the context of WTO litigation, which frequently involves public–private partnerships between industry, private lawyers, and government lawyers and representatives. For a discussion, see Shaffer (2003).

dispute-resolution system that can adversely affect efficient evolution of the law. For example, economic research provides empirical evidence suggesting high litigation costs contribute to explaining why poor countries are noticeably absent from formal participation in DSU litigation.[22] While such research has thus far focused on the 'missing parties' (i.e., poor countries) involved in potential disputes, an additional concern is that 'missing issues' will fail to be resolved because litigation costs will prevent certain issues from coming forward for a legal opinion. Under an incrementalist approach to something like zeroing, one could imagine an iterative scenario in which the most 'economically important' zeroing issue (e.g., say, W–W in antidumping investigations) was brought forward first, followed by the second-most economically important, followed by the third, etc. The concern is that, if litigation costs are substantially high, the 12th (least economically important), 11th, 10th, ... issues may end up not getting legally resolved. What if the potential resource costs to litigation are so high that no one ever challenges zeroing using, say, the W–W method in a new-shipper review? The implication is a resulting inefficient and/or incomplete law. On the other hand, with a more comprehensive approach to decisionmaking, it is possible that legal issues that are nevertheless 'economically small' would also receive attention from jurists. In the presence of high resource costs of litigation, a comprehensive approach can be seen as creating a positive externality in that it clarifies the legality of (economically smaller) issues that would otherwise go unresolved under the incrementalist approach.

A second resource cost of incrementalism falls on the Dispute Settlement Body and the WTO institution itself. From an institutional perspective, there may be substantial fixed costs of establishing a panel, and thus there are economies of scale to litigating as many issues as possible within the context of the single panel. Grossman and Sykes (2006) have already provided an expansive discussion of this issue in the context of the consolidation of claims in a proceeding, and we will not repeat them here.

Incrementalism and resource costs of industry adjustment

In the context of the zeroing issue in particular, the incrementalist approach also creates costs for any industries or countries affected by what will ultimately be ruled to be a WTO-inconsistent use of zeroing in antidumping proceedings. A failure to clarify at the stage of *EC–Bed Linen* which zeroing methods were WTO-inconsistent meant that a number of imported products in the US (and other countries that use zeroing) continued to face illegal protectionist measures – either antidumping measures that would not have been imposed but for the zeroing methodology, or measures with levels biased upward relative to what they would

22 See, for example, the discussion in Bown and Hoekman (2005), as well as the empirical evidence found in studies such as Bown (2005a, b). For our purposes, the concern is that the costs of litigation may make it economically irrational for a country to pursue a case even if there is a legal reason to do so.

be in the absence of the ability to use zeroing.[23] The resulting costs are by and large familiar.

First, the import protection associated with an illegal antidumping measure leads to the standard welfare-economic costs – consumers pay higher prices than they would otherwise have to, and the economy suffers from deadweight (efficiency) welfare losses relative to an outcome in which the measure is removed. These economic losses remain until the incrementalist approach ultimately eliminates each instance in which zeroing is ruled WTO-inconsistent and there is compliance.

Second, there are additional dynamic considerations in the face of a prolonged period of protection while the zeroing issue is incrementally being resolved. Of foremost concern is how the incrementalist nature of the approach affects the adjustment incentives of the industry currently benefiting from the (eventually) WTO-inconsistent protection. By prolonging the state of protection, the result may be a possibility of excess profits and an incentive for entry. If the market has no substantial entry barriers (*vis-à-vis* domestic resources, i.e. foreign entry cannot occur by assumption because of the protection), new investment may come into the industry to take advantage of the excess profit opportunity.[24] Thus, the incrementalist approach can retard efficient industry adjustment (resource exit) by creating incentives for new investment.

In sum, incrementalism is a double-edged sword. It has clear advantages, but is not obviously the most efficient approach to adjudication in all circumstances. Other things being equal, incrementalism is less advantageous when the decisionmaker can anticipate that future disputes will arise over issues closely related to those in the dispute at hand, and when the decisionmaker has the ability to solicit briefs and arguments from interested parties on such issues. The WTO zeroing litigation poses a scenario that perhaps fits these conditions, although we are reluctant to weigh in too heavily on that proposition. If our suspicion is correct, however, one cannot but wonder whether the incremental approach to zeroing has led to unnecessary delay and litigation in the resolution of the issues associated with zeroing, and whether the attendant costs might have been averted or at least diminished had the Appellate Body taken a more aggressive approach to resolving the issues early in the process.

23 For this discussion, we rule out the possibility that antidumping authorities would find alternative WTO-inconsistent techniques resulting in the same bias; furthermore we rule out any issues of compliance.

24 While not within the context of antidumping, this phenomenon of industry churning while being heavily protected has been documented for the US textile industry in the empirical results of Levinsohn and Petropoulos (2001). The US steel industry is another example of a sector that has seen substantial investment from new entrants (mini-mills) that has contributed to within-industry churning and displacement of historical plants and workers, despite substantial protectionist measures being in place. Bown and McCulloch (2005) provide a discussion of antidumping as an 'anti-adjustment' policy more broadly.

Competing methods of overhead cost allocation

A narrow issue in the dispute relates to how Commerce allocated the Canadian firm Abitibi's interest expenditure via its 'cost of goods sold' (COGS) method. Before turning to the practical difficulties in capital-cost construction in this particular dispute, it is important to identify the purpose of this accounting exercise from the perspective of economics: the goal is to construct a capital-cost measure that most closely reflects the opportunity cost of the capital input.[25] The issue of how to appropriately construct proxies for capital costs in this context raises a number of questions.

The Abitibi issue involves the further question of how to construct appropriate measures when the entity is a conglomerate (multi-product) firm, and the firm's various products are differentially capital-intensive so that the average capital expense per dollar in sales is not necessarily representative of the capital expense per dollar in sales of the particular product under investigation. Under such a scenario, the economic question is what is the best proxy for the conglomerate firm's capital costs for the products subject to the antidumping investigation. A first suggestion is the following neutrality benchmark: we would not want a stand-alone softwood firm that is identical to the softwood division of a conglomerate to have different estimated capital costs. The practical question is then how can the conglomerate firm's capital allocation be done to ensure that consistency?

Commerce's utilization of the COGS method to allocate capital expenditures based on the share of cost of goods sold would only get this allocation correct by coincidence.[26] In this particular case, it is not likely to allocate capital expenditures correctly when the conglomerate has substantially different capital intensities for its investigated versus non-investigated product lines. It seems to us that if the conglomerate's other products are relatively more capital intensive than softwood lumber (as Abitibi asserted) then the COGS method will overestimate the capital costs of the softwood-lumber line and serve to inflate the construction of overall costs and thereby the size of the dumping margin (relative to an otherwise identical, but stand-alone softwood-lumber firm).

25 This issue raises a broader question of whether financial statement information is useful to proxy for opportunity costs at all. Insight from research in corporate finance suggests that the answer to this question is no, and that to construct accurate, market-based measures requires a model-based estimate that would also allow for the influence of risk and return. Of course, this problem infuses all of antidumping law, which is based on accounting costs rather than economic costs.

26 Let $COGS_i$ be cost of goods sold and R_i be the cost of capital (interest) for the conglomerate with products $i \in I$. Then the COGS method for calculating the cost of capital for lumber is based on the following formula: $R_{Lumber} = (\sum_{i \in I} R_i)\left(\frac{COGS_{Lumber}}{\sum_{i \in I} COGS_i}\right)$, which is simply to allocate total capital costs (interest) to the share of cost of goods sold associated with lumber sales. Nothing in the formula relates interest expended on lumber to how much capital is used in lumber production relative to production of other goods in the conglomerate.

Commerce asserted that this problem is not significant because if there is less capital used in softwood, it will show less depreciation expense, and that will result in a lower constructed cost for softwood. Without knowing more about exact accounting requirements and practices in this particular dispute, it is difficult to know whether Commerce is correct. First, what if the conglomerate only reports consolidated information on depreciation, so that depreciation expenses also cannot be allocated across different product lines? Second, even if depreciation expenses are reported for a particular product line associated with a distinct division, will those accurately reflect differences in capital intensity? To the extent that mandated depreciation rates differ according to the year of the capital expenditure and/or capital expenditures differ within the divisions over time, we have little confidence that the depreciation calculation will accurately reflect capital costs. We are also led to wonder whether these accounting methods will introduce biases according to whether the firm is financed with debt or equity.

Abitibi proposed an alternative method for allocating interest expense based on the relative amount of capital assets used by the various lines of production within the corporate group. Such an alternative methodology could lead to additional sources of concern. For example, a conglomerate firm may have an internal structure where one corporate division takes on the role of holding and leasing out capital assets to all of the other producing subsidiaries. If this were to be the case, the balance sheet of the producing subsidiary would also not reflect the value of the capital and the income statement would not reflect the depreciation on that capital, but instead some sort of lease payment that might or might not approximate opportunity costs.

Hence, there are potential problems with both the Commerce and Abitibi proposals, and we do not have sufficient information to say which method is better. And although an alternative method might be to use capital costs from a stand-alone softwood-products firm as a benchmark for the costs of a conglomerate such as Abitibi, finding a comparable firm might be exceedingly difficult.

Transfer-pricing and the cost of production

This section provides an economic analysis of one of the by-product revenue issues in Softwood V. As background, the Canadian firm Tembec faced much higher (10.21% vs. 2.18%) final margins in the dumping determination than a competing Canadian firm, West Fraser. One of the contributing factors was Commerce's construction of the estimates of the revenue each firm received from its sale of wood chips, a 'by-product' in the production of softwood lumber. Wood chips have value as an input in downstream pulp and/or paper production. The key distinction between the two firms that is of interest to our analysis relates to how Commerce differentially treated within-firm (non-arm's-length) transactions of wood chips.[27] For the case of West Fraser, Commerce treated the data on its internal-transfer price of wood chips as unrepresentative of their true value and instead used the price of its wood-chip sales made in arm's-length transactions to determine the total value of combined wood-chip sales made to affiliated and unaffiliated parties. In contrast, Commerce used Tembec's internal (within-firm) price for wood-chip sales to construct the value of by-product revenue. Since Commerce used the income from sales of by-product wood chips as an offset to each firm's costs of producing softwood lumber, Tembec's low transfer price for the within-firm sales contributed to it receiving a higher dumping margin. The Panel concluded that Commerce's determination did not violate the ADA, and the Appellate Body upheld the Panel's findings.

Canada's appeal on this issue raises the question of how to account appropriately for costs when there are concerns about reported data within a firm because of the potential manipulation of transfer prices. The issue highlights the importance of using the economic concept of opportunity cost to measure costs when calculating dumping, and the practical difficulty in doing so.

The economic literature suggests many potential reasons why firms set internal prices (for non-arm's-length transactions) that deviate substantially from the opportunity costs of the resources involved. One possibility is that the tax law has created incentives for firms to report 'artificially' low (or high) prices for a non-arm's-length transaction of wood chips from a lumber mill to a pulp mill. For example, a firm may have an incentive to underprice (overprice) the value of the transaction on its internal books if there are higher (lower) federal or provincial tax rates on income earned due to woodchip sales relative to income earned from timber sales.[28]

Yet another reason for transfer-price manipulation is suggested by the softwood dispute itself. Suppose a firm like Tembec properly anticipated that it would face a future antidumping investigation and dumping-margin calculation. If Commerce has signaled a likelihood of relying on reported internal prices, the firm would have a clear incentive to over-report the internal price of wood chips, ceteris paribus, as this serves to reduce the constructed cost measure and decrease the dumping margin on the investigated product.

If reported internal prices are potentially unreliable measures of the opportunity costs of by-products, what is a better proxy in practice? If the firm under

27 To clarify, we will not address the question of whether Commerce properly classified the firm's sales as non-arm's-length or arm's-length transactions, as we do not have enough information to do so. Nevertheless, as will become clear below, such an issue is not important for the point that we make regarding the necessity of evaluating the value of the wood chips based on their opportunity costs.

28 The industrial organization literature suggests other possibilities. For example, firms may use internal-transfer prices to create incentives for employees to overcome what economists refer to as a principal-agent problem. Such internal contracts may contain prices manipulated to induce optimal employee effort when there are monitoring costs or uncertainty generated by unobservable employee characteristics (e.g., 'skill').

investigation makes sales at arm's length to unaffiliated buyers, the prices in those sales will typically be a good indicator of opportunity costs.[29] This is what we understand Commerce to have done with respect to West Fraser, and it is difficult to object to it. The harder question is why Commerce did not do the same for Tembec. If, indeed, Tembec's internal prices were in fact much the same as its prices to unaffiliated companies, of course, there can be little objection to the use of the internal prices. But it is obvious from the challenge brought by Canada that Tembec's internal prices were for some reason materially lower than the market-price benchmark. Commerce's unwillingness to shift to a market benchmark under these circumstances is suspect. Indeed, one infers that Commerce seems to choose between market prices and internal prices according to which choice yields the highest dumping margin. Even if such an approach is 'standard practice' for Commerce, it strikes us as quite illegitimate.

The legal distinction that the panel drew (and the Appellate Body accepted) between Tembec and West Fraser also rings hollow. At Tembec, all divisions involved in the by-product transaction were wholly owned. At West Fraser, by contrast, the by-product sales were between companies that were merely 'affiliated'. If anything, there is more reason to distrust internal-transfer prices in the case of Tembec than in the case of West Fraser, so that the use of a market benchmark for West Fraser but not Tembec seems indefensible. The mere fact that the two companies were 'differently situated' does not, in our view, provide an economically rational basis for the disparate treatment.

4. Conclusion

For the reasons developed above, we question the Appellate Body's approach to the zeroing issue in Softwood V. Although any decision that tends to reduce antidumping duties has some appeal from an economic standpoint, the legal foundation for the Appellate Body's ruling is somewhat dubious, doubly so in the face of the standard of review applicable under the ADA. The danger of such decisions is that they will undermine confidence in the Appellate Review process and make it more difficult for WTO members in the future to reach agreement on contentious issues. We also wonder whether the Appellate Body might have done more to ward off the extensive litigation over zeroing through more comprehensive decisions earlier in the process, although we are mindful of some offsetting

29 Another place to look for a proxy might be an arm's-length (market) transaction between two firms unrelated to the producer under investigation and to use this transaction price to value internal (within-firm) sales of the by-product by the firm being investigated. A simple caveat to such an approach is that even an arm's-length transaction may fail to reflect opportunity costs if there are other substantial imperfections in this market. For example, if the arm's-length transaction takes place in the presence of market power – i.e., the lumber mill selling the pulp is a monopolist or the paper mill purchasing it is monopsonist – the revealed market price may also not be a good proxy for the opportunity cost of the wood chips. Likewise, it may be difficult to determine whether the market conditions facing the two unrelated firms are comparable to those facing the firm under investigation.

considerations. Finally, with respect to the cost-allocation practices of Commerce that were at issue in the appeal, we find both of those practices to be questionable.

References

Boltuck, Richard and Robert E. Litan (eds.) (1991), *Down in the Dumps*, Washington, DC: The Brookings Institution Press.

Bown, Chad P. (2005a), 'Trade Remedies and World Trade Organization Dispute Settlement: Why Are So Few Challenged?', *Journal of Legal Studies*, **34**: 515–555.

Bown, Chad P. (2005b), 'Participation in WTO Dispute Settlement: Complainants, Interested Parties and Free Riders', *World Bank Economic Review*, **19**: 287–310.

Bown, Chad P. and Bernard M. Hoekman (2005), 'WTO Dispute Settlement and the Missing Developing Country Cases: Engaging the Private Sector', *Journal of International Economic Law*, **8**: 861–890.

Bown, Chad P. and Rachel McCulloch (2005), 'US Trade Policy and the Adjustment Process', *IMF Staff Papers*, **52**: 107–128.

Dam, Kenneth W. (1970), *The GATT: Law and International Economic Organization*, Chicago, IL: University of Chicago Press.

Gennaioli, Nicola and Andrei Shleifer (2007a), 'The Evolution of Common Law', *Journal of Political Economy*, **115**: 43–68.

Gennaioli, Nicola and Andrei Shleifer (2007b), 'Overruling and the Instability of Law', *Journal of Comparative Economics*, **35**: 309–328.

Grossman, Gene M. and Alan O. Sykes (2006), 'European Communities – Anti-Dumping Duties on Imports of Cotton-Type Bed Linen from India: Recourse to Article 21.5 of the DSU by India', in Petros C. Mavroidis and Henrik Horn (eds), *The WTO Case Law of 2003*, Cambridge: Cambridge University Press.

Janow, Merit E. and Robert W. Staiger (2003), 'European Communities – Anti-Dumping Duties on Imports of Cotton-Type Bed Linen from India', in Petros C. Mavroidis and Henrik Horn (eds), *The WTO Case Law of 2001*, Cambridge: Cambridge University Press.

Levinsohn, James and Wendy Petropoulos (2001), 'Creative Destruction or Just Plain Destruction?: The US Textile and Apparel Industries Since 1972', *NBER Working Paper 8348.*

Shaffer, Gregory C. (2003), *Defending Interests: Public–Private Partnerships in WTO Litigation*, Washington, DC: The Brookings Institution Press.

Sykes, Alan O. 1998. Antidumping and Antitrust: What Problems Does Each Address?, in Robert Lawrence (ed.), *Brookings Trade Forum 1998*, Washington, DC: The Brookings Institution Press.

Comment

United States – Final Dumping Determination on Softwood Lumber from Canada: Recourse to Article 21.5 of the DSU by Canada (Softwood V)

Prepared for the ALI Project on the Case Law of the WTO

MEREDITH A. CROWLEY*

Federal Reserve Bank of Chicago, 230 S. LaSalle St., Chicago, IL 60604
Email: mcrowley@frbchi.org

This comment summarizes and critiques the analysis of the Softwood V case by Chad P. Bown and Alan O. Sykes. It concurs with their analysis and offers two additional points. First, allowing zeroing in the calculation of dumping margins penalizes foreign exporting firms subject to volatile costs. Second, cost allocation within a multiproduct firm should attempt to equate the real economic returns across products.

Bown and Sykes provide a thorough analysis of the issues raised in the softwood-lumber dispute between the United States and Canada. In this dispute, Canada objected to several of the practices employed by the Commerce Department in calculating dumping margins. Two general substantive questions were at issue. First, how should a government body investigating an allegation of dumping aggregate information from different transactions and different products into a single dumping margin? Second, if an investigating body must construct a cost of production in order to establish a 'normal value', how should this be done in the presence of cross-product subsidization within a firm?

Three specific practices were challenged. First, Canada objected to the use of 'zeroing' in which ostensibly fair-priced transactions are omitted from the weighted-average calculation of a dumping margin. Second, Canada objected to the method the Commerce Department employed to allocate financial expenses

The opinions expressed in this paper are those of the author and do not necessarily reflect those of the Federal Reserve Bank of Chicago or the Federal Reserve System.

across different product lines within the firm, Abitibi. Lastly, Canada objected to the Commerce Department's use of an internal-transfer price for calculating one Canadian firm's by-product revenue and using an arm's-length-transaction price for calculating by-product revenue for a second firm.

In terms of the legal analysis, Bown and Sykes provide a compelling argument that the text of the Uruguay Round Agreements is vague with no clear statement that zeroing is permitted and no clear statement that it is prohibited. They note that a methodology known as 'weighted average to transaction' that was in use at the time of the Uruguay Round negotiations is clearly discouraged by the text as its use is only permitted in exceptional circumstances. Because this methodology was historically plagued by 'zeroing', Bown and Sykes interpret the text's preference for the two other methodologies, 'weighted average to weighted average' and 'transaction to transaction' as evidence that the Uruguay Round negotiators wished to discourage the use of zeroing in dumping-margin calculations.

However, in the absence of a specific textual prohibition on zeroing under the 'weighted average to weighted average' and 'transaction to transaction' methods, Bown and Sykes find the Appellate Body's rulings questionable. Given the vagueness of the text, they argue that the US's position should have been given deference under the Antidumping Agreement's standard of review.

Regarding their economic analysis of zeroing, Bown and Sykes make an extremely insightful observation. If a government body conducting an investigation into alleged dumping were to compare a time series of prices of a product and a moving average of the same prices, the zeroing methodology would always generate a positive dumping margin, *even though the prices are identical.*

This note extends this insight from Bown and Sykes to argue that an economic analysis of zeroing suggests that, if the WTO allows zeroing, it is essentially allowing governments to impose a tax on foreign firms that operate in a volatile economic environment. A large economics literature examines the efficiency of antidumping policy. I abstract from the efficiency issues inherent in antidumping policy and ask: if we push a rule to permit zeroing to its extreme, what does this imply about the underlying causes of dumping in a world where zeroing defines the dumping margin?

Consider the following stylized example. Suppose a German firm produces widgets that it sells domestically and exports to the United States. Further suppose that the US dollar/euro exchange rate is volatile, but, for simplicity, assume that it can only take on three possible values, each with equal probability (0.8$/euro, 1$/euro, or 1.2$/euro). On average, the dollar/euro exchange rate is thus 1$/euro. It costs the German firm 0.9 euros to make a widget. In the European market, the German firm charges 1 euro per widget, earning a 10 euro-cent profit on each sale. If the German firm charges $1 in the US market regardless of the value of the exchange rate on the day the sale takes place (a strategy known as pricing-to-market), what are the implications of a rule to allow for zeroing by the US government in an antidumping investigation?

If the US government uses the German market price as 'normal value' in the dumping-margin calculation, the mathematically defined weighted average of the dumping margin is zero. On one-third of days, the dumping margin is zero because the US price and German price are identical. On one-third of days, there is a negative dumping margin with the US price 20 cents higher than the German price. Only on the final one-third of days is the German firm dumping with the US price 20 cents lower than the German price. However, under the zeroing rule, by ignoring transactions with zero and negative dumping margins, the US would impose an antidumping duty of 6 cents on every imported unit! Even though the firm is not dumping in the traditional sense of systematically price undercutting in the US market (in fact it is systematically charging the same price in both markets), it will be subject to an antidumping duty under the zeroing rule.

What happens if the US government uses German costs to construct a 'normal value' for the dumping-margin calculation? On days when the exchange rate is 1$/euro, the German firm will earn a profit of 10 cents on each sale in the US (a negative margin of 10 cents). On days when the exchange rate is 0.8$/euro, the German firm will earn an even larger profit of 28 cents on each sale. Only on days when the euro is a relatively strong 1.2$/euro will the German firm suffer a loss of 8 cents on each US sale. Weighting all sales under the zeroing rule implies an antidumping duty of 2.6 cents per widget. However, when we calculate the mathematically defined weighted-average dumping margin, it is a negative 10 cents, reflecting that the firm's average profits on its US sales are 10 cents per unit!

What does this example suggest about the role of zeroing in a volatile economic environment? Firms face uncertainty over their costs from a variety of sources. Exchange rates are highly volatile, notoriously impossible to forecast, and an important area of strategic concern for firms that wish to export. A strategy of setting a foreign-market-currency price that adjusts slowly to movements in the exchange rate seems to be a sensible business practice for two reasons. First, from a logistical standpoint, it would be almost impossible for an exporter to adjust its sales price every day (or even every minute) in response to small exchange-rate movements. Second, both final-goods consumers and intermediate-input purchasers prefer to have some stability in the prices they face. If a foreign firm were to price each and every transaction to the exchange rate of the moment, consumers would almost certainly shift their purchases to domestic sources that didn't insert this added risk.

This suggests that the zeroing rule transforms antidumping policy from a policy intended to prevent systematic price undercutting to one that simply imposes an additional tax on foreign firms because they operate in a volatile economic environment, and the firm cannot feasibly adjust its output price at the same rate at which the exchange rate moves.

The example presented here emphasizes the role of the exchange rate because it is an important cost variable for exporting firms, but the volatile costs confronting firms are not limited to the exchange rate. Energy costs and the costs of petroleum-derived inputs are highly volatile. If a firm that is heavily reliant on inputs with volatile prices is subject to an antidumping investigation in which its costs of production are used in constructing a dumping margin, then the firm could be found guilty of dumping under the zeroing rule even when its foreign-market sales generate profits over a broader time horizon of months, quarters, or years.

From an economic perspective, it seems inconceivable that the Uruguay Round Agreements, whose preamble emphasizes the beneficial role of 'mutually advantageous agreements directed to the substantial reduction of tariffs and other barriers to trade', intended to create, in the form of an antidumping duty that embraces zeroing, a new volatility tax. In a pragmatic sense, volatile exchange rates present a barrier to trade because many firms that would otherwise export are unable to bear exchange-rate risk. To argue that the zeroing rule should be allowed and, thus, to leave firms saddled with not only exchange-rate risk, but also a tax on this risk, seems logically inconsistent at best and a very bad public policy at worst.

Turning to the issues of cross-subsidization within the firm, the text of the Agreement on Antidumping offers little guidance to a national authority. Bown and Sykes conclude that in this environment of little textual guidance, the panel and Appellate Body's decision to side with the US's methodology in the question of cost allocation was reasonable. With regard to the question of transfer pricing, little can be added to Bown and Sykes's point that the correct price to use in constructing a measure of costs is the price that best reflects the real economic value of the product being sold. In most cases, this will be an arm's-length-transaction price. The panel and Appellate finding that it was reasonable for the US to use an internal-transfer price for one Canadian firm and to use an arm's-length-transaction price for a second firm seems questionable.

With regard to the question of how best to allocate financing costs, the following point can be added to those raised by Bown and Sykes. In the long run, a multi-product firm should be equalizing the expected real economic returns across different products. If it is not, then it is wasting resources on unprofitable activities. Economic theory teaches that in the long run, only firms that maximize their profits can survive. However, fluctuations in demand, the costs of inputs, and risk adjustments to financing costs could lead to differences in real economic returns across products in short time periods. Thus, even if a government established rules in which cost allocation was subject to a strict requirement that firms equate real economic returns across products, it would not necessarily be feasible or a good public policy.

To assess the basic arguments put forth by the US and Canada, one can examine their arguments in the context of a production function. Economists use production functions to quantify the 'total factor productivity' (TFP) of firms or of different activities within firms. TFP can be viewed as a rough proxy for real economic returns and, thus, one sensible approach to allocating costs across products within a firm would be to allocate costs so as to equate TFP across products. In Softwood V, the US argued that the correct method of allocating financing costs would be to assume that financing costs are proportional to revenues for all products. In contrast, Canada argued that the correct method would be to assume that financing costs are proportional to capital. Both the US and Canadian methods impose restrictions on the firm's production function that are unsupported by any empirical evidence and could even imply that the firm is systematically earning a lower return on one product versus another. In brief, neither leads us closer to what we really want: a method for allocating costs so that real returns are equalized across products.

To summarize the point about cost allocation, economic theory suggests that cost allocation within a firm should be done in a way to equate economic returns across products. However, even in the abstract, there are many legitimate reasons for a firm's behavior to deviate from this. Thus, while the best method should pay heed to this, it is not obvious that it would be appropriate in all circumstances.

In conclusion, I concur with Bown and Sykes's analysis of zeroing. I add to their economic analysis the point that when dumping-margin calculations employ zeroing, antidumping duties are taxes on volatility. With regard to the economics of the problem of cost allocation, I suggest that any methodology should seek to allocate costs so as to equate real economic returns. Finally, Bown and Sykes's analysis of the transfer-price question is perfectly on the mark.

EC–Sugar

BERNARD HOEKMAN
World Bank and CEPR
ROBERT HOWSE
University of Michigan

Introduction

In the early 1970s, the EC was a net importer of sugar, buying some 2.5 million tonnes on the world market. As a result of high intervention prices for sugar – averaging more than double the world price since the mid 1980s, and rising to a multiple of four in 2000 – production expanded so much that the EC became a net exporter. In the late 1990s and early 2000s, the EC's net exports of sugar were in the range of four to five million tonnes. EC policies resulted in the EC becoming a major player on world markets: in 2005, it was the second largest exporter in the world (after Brazil), accounting for 12% of world exports. At the same time, the EC was also the world's fourth largest importer, an idiosyncrasy that reflected the preferential access granted to African, Caribbean, and Pacific (ACP) countries under the ACP Sugar Protocol.

In the Uruguay Round, the EC scheduled export subsidy commitments for sugar of €499 million and 1.2735 million tonnes. In *EC–Sugar*, Australia, Brazil, and Thailand argued that the EC provided export subsidies in excess of its WTO export-subsidy commitment levels for sugar, in part through *de facto* cross-subsidization of exports as a result of guaranteeing high annual intervention (support) prices for a given quantity of EC sugar, and in part as the result of re-exporting an amount of sugar equivalent to what the EC imported from ACP countries on a preferential basis. The EC argued that re-exports of ACP sugar were covered by its export subsidy commitments through a footnote in its schedule, and that the acceptance of the inclusion of this footnote by WTO Members implied that its schedule effectively altered its obligations under the Agreement on Agriculture (AoA). The EC also held that, because WTO Members had not previously raised objections to exports of so-called 'C sugar' as being subsidized, the complainants were not acting in good faith and were estopped from invoking dispute proceedings.[1]

We are grateful to Paola Conconi and participants at the American Law Institute meeting for helpful comments on an earlier draft. The views expressed are personal and should not be attributed to the World Bank.

1 The principle of estoppel is defined in Section 2 below.

We address each of these dimensions of the case in this paper. We start in Section 1 with a brief description of EC policy and some of its likely effects. Section 2 provides an economic and legal analysis of the cross-subsidization argument brought by the complainants. Section 3 turns to the consistency of the EC measures with the EC's WTO obligations, as well as the estoppel defense argument of the EC. Section 4 discusses the finding of the Appellate Body (AB) that the Panel erred in its invocation of the principle of judicial economy to not address claims that aspects of the WTO Agreement on Subsidies and Countervailing Measures (SCM) had been violated. Section 5 presents concluding remarks.

1. EC sugar policy

Subsidies play a major role in the EC sugar industry.[2] In 1999–2001, the value of gross receipts of sugar producers in the EC was more than double the value of their output measured at world prices: the producer nominal assistance coefficient was 2.1. In this period, total OECD support for sugar was equivalent to about half of global exports ($6.35bn compared to $11.6bn), similar in value to the total exports of sugar of all developing countries ($6.5bn). The EC accounted for 43 % of the $6.35bn in OECD support for sugar. Much of this support was provided through very high border protection – around 90 % for the EC.

The EC policy regime for sugar complements high intervention or support prices for sugar with production quotas. These are of two types: so-called quota A and quota B. The sum of A and B quotas determines the maximum amount of sugar that may be sold in the EC market in a given year. All excess production must be exported – if not, producers are penalized.[3] Production of A and B sugar benefits from the high intervention price in the EC. Excess production by an EC producer over and above its A+B quotas does not benefit from the high intervention/support price. In EC-speak, such excess output is called C sugar. Note that there is no physical difference between these various categories of sugar; there is one world price for sugar, be it A, B, or C sugar.

The producer price for A sugar is greater than the producer price received for B sugar. Both are less than the basic intervention or support price as a result of a levy that is used to finance the export subsidies needed to sell excess production on the world market. Thus, producer prices of A and B sugar are endogenous; they are a function of how much of B is exported if the sum of A+B quotas exceeds total EC consumption at the (fixed) intervention price for sugar. The levy on A sugar is 2 %, i.e. the producer price received is 2 % below the 'basic' support price confronting buyers. In the case of B output, the levy varies, ranging up to a maximum of 37.5 %.[4]

2 Figures in this paragraph are from Mitchell (2005).

3 However, there is some allowance for carry forward – up to 20 % of a firm's A+B quota per year.

4 The producer price of A sugar would be equal to that of B sugar if there were no exports of B sugar.

Figure 1.

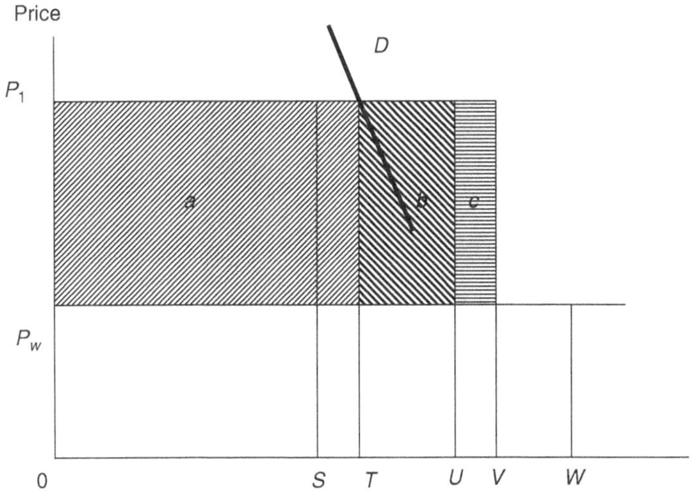

Source: Fransden, Jensen, Yu, and Walter-Jorgenson, 2003.

In addition to (part of) the B quota, the EC also exports an amount of sugar that is equal to what it imports from ACP countries under its preferential access program (the Cotonou Convention). The total EC import commitment *vis-à-vis* the ACP is some 1.3 million tonnes, although in some years this has been expanded under a special (additional) preference program. As a result, the maximum amount imported from the ACP has ranged up to 1.6 million tonnes. Given that EC production exceeds consumption at the intervention price, in effect all the ACP sugar is 're-sold' on the world market. Thus, the effects of the ACP sugar protocol imports on the EC market are 'sterilized' by exporting the amount imported.[5] As the ACP sugar is bought at the intervention price, the export sales incur a significant loss, which is absorbed by the EC budget (taxpayers). These costs are clearly export subsidies, and are recognized as such by the Panel and the EC.

The resulting EC-wide market for sugar is illustrated in Figure 1. Of some 18–20 million tonnes of sugar produced per year in the EC, some 15% is exported. In 2001, the EC exported 4.1 million tonnes: the quantity represented by line segment *TW* in Figure 1. However, the EC had only scheduled 1.2735 million metric tonnes of sugar (line segment *TU* in Figure 1) as being eligible for export subsidies.[6] The excess exports of 2.8 million tonnes were comprised of 1.3 million

5 The extent to which this is actually a physical re-export of the cane sugar imported, or constitutes exports of beet sugar is unknown. Some 98.5% of total EC output is from sugar beet, whereas ACP sugar imports are derived from sugar cane. If sugar is sugar, i.e. is a homogenous product, it does not matter. In this paper, we assume that sugar is homogenous.

6 The value of these subsidies was capped in the EC's WTO commitments at €499 million.

Figure 2.

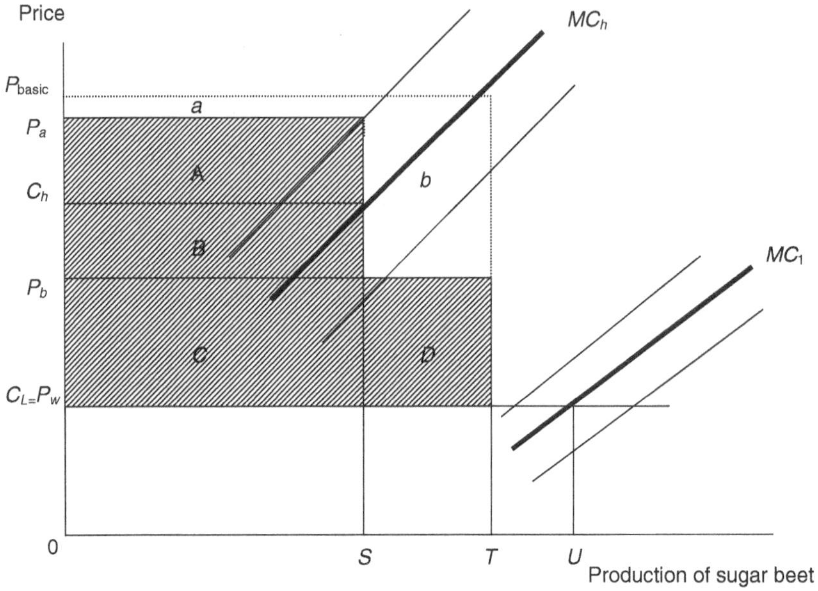

Source: Fransden, Jensen, Yu, and Walter-Jorgenson, 2003.

metric tonnes of ACP sugar (line segment *UV*) and 1.5 million tonnes of C sugar (line segment VW). Thus, EC exports consist of B-quota sugar (benefiting from scheduled export subsidies financed by the levy on EC quota production) plus the (equivalent of) ACP sugar imports (also benefiting from a direct export subsidy, financed by the EC budget) plus C production. Only the latter does not benefit from direct export subsidies.

Two groups finance the sugar scheme: EC consumers of sugar, who pay two to four times the world price for sugar, and EC taxpayers (in order to re-export ACP sugar). The rest of the world, non-ACP producers that do not benefit from preferential access and confront lower world prices as a result of EC subsidization of exports of sugar, incur losses as a result of the policy. Two groups gain from the policy: EC and ACP producers. As illustrated in Figure 2, the rents EC producers obtain are determined by the high producer prices in the EC: P_a for A quota (2 % less than the support price), and P_b for B-quota sugar (up to 37.5 % less than the basic price, illustrated by area '*b*' in Figure 2). The magnitude of the rents depends on the cost functions of producers: the more efficient the producer, the greater the rents. This also applies to ACP sugar protocol countries that have export quotas into the EC market. Low-cost producers – for simplicity, say those that can sell at the world price and cover their costs – will get a rent equal to the shaded area in Figure 2: areas $A+B+C$ as a result of the A sugar quota for which they get P_a; area D as a result of the B quota (for which they get P_b).

A high-cost producer – with marginal cost schedule MC_h in Figure 2 – will only obtain a rent equal to area A.[7]

A key question in the dispute revolved around what producers do with the rents; in particular, whether they use them to cross-subsidize production and exports of C sugar. A second major issue in the case concerned the total volume of exports of sugar, which the complainants argued exceeded the EC's schedule of export subsidy commitments. The following two sections discuss these two dimensions of the dispute.

2. Cross-subsidization of C sugar – legal and economic analysis

Article 9.1(c) of the AoA defines export subsidies subject to reduction commitments as including:

> [P]ayments on the export of an agricultural product that are financed by virtue of governmental action, whether or not a charge on the public account is involved, including payments that are financed from the proceeds of a levy imposed on the agricultural product concerned or on an agricultural product from which the exported product is derived[.]

The Panel found that the measures complained of fell within this provision, because: (1) Producers of C sugar were able to purchase C sugar beet at below cost; (2) the EC required C sugar to be exported; (3) the below-cost sales were financed through sales of A and B sugar at above-market prices, which were determined at least in part by EC regulations. It is clear that the legal theory here is one of cross-subsidization: above-normal profits from the sale of one product subsidize the export of another. The Panel argued that the sugar regime in the EC resulted in cross-subsidization of all EC sugar output, including C production that does not benefit from direct subsidies on export and is sold at world prices. The basic argument of the Panel is that rents on A and B quota sugar can be used to cover below-cost sales of C output. While in general such a cross-subsidy need not be an export subsidy, under EC policy, if C production is *not* exported (or used under the carry-forward provision), it is subject to high financial penalties – thus there is a clear incentive to export C sugar.

From an economic perspective, a key question is why farmers would produce C sugar given that it does not benefit from direct support (is sold at the world price). One possibility is fixed costs of production (scale economies): more output lowers average unit costs, perhaps by enough to make total production profitable if it goes beyond the level of A and B output levels. Another possibility is that some EC producers may be efficient and able to sell at the world price without incurring losses. A third possibility is uncertainty – farmers may plant more than is needed to

7 This description abstracts from various factors that will determine the incidence of any rents. In practice, the rents will be shared with importers/distributors in the case of ACP producers, and with processors/refiners in the case of EC producers.

Figure 3. Positive profits at B, cross-subsidization to Q^* ($P^* > AVC^*$)

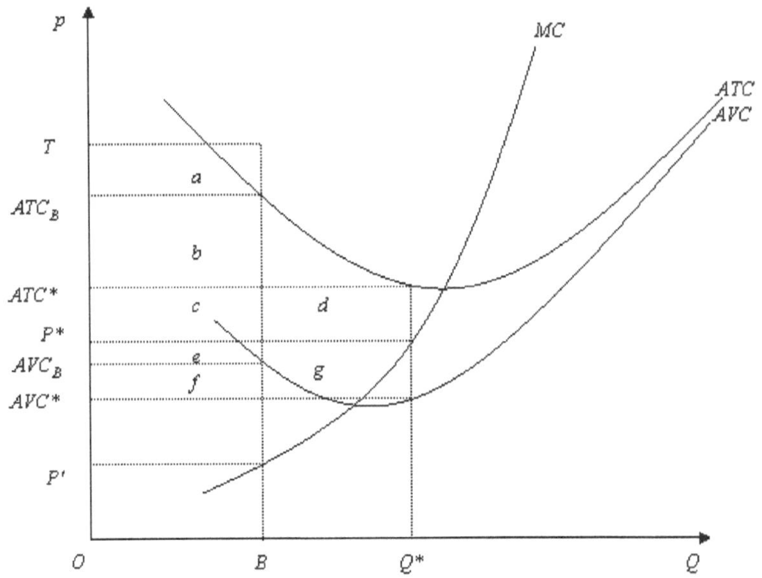

generate the A+B level of output as a form of insurance: to make sure that they will be able to meet long-term contracts they have with refiners. As these are very profitable, overplanting ensures that if harvests are bad, farmers will still be able to fully satisfy their contracts, and thus capture all of the rents they can make on quota sugar. If harvests are good, however, there will be excess production – i.e., C sugar.

If the world price for C sugar is such that the resulting total average cost of production falls because of scale economies – i.e., there are fixed costs/fixed factors – the rents derived from quota (A and B) production can be used to cross-subsidize C production and enhance profits. Given a level of output B, defined as the maximum amount on which firms can get the high support price (more generally the share of output on which producers get a subsidy/rent), as long as the world price exceeds the marginal costs of producing this level of output, farmers will have an incentive to produce more. They will produce up to the point where marginal revenue (determined by the world price) equals marginal cost of production. This optimal level of output will exceed the quota level of sales. In general, De Gorter, Just, and Kropp (2008) show that cross-subsidization is possible for a variety of permutations of production costs, world price levels and support prices implied by a quota level B. A number of possible situations where cross-subsidization can occur are illustrated in Figures 3–6. These include situations where firms make losses at the quota level of output and situations where the world price is less than the average variable costs of production.[8]

8 We are grateful to Harry de Gorter (Cornell University) for sharing these graphs.

Figure 4. Positive profits at *B*, possible cross-subsidization to Q^* ($P^* < AVC^*$)

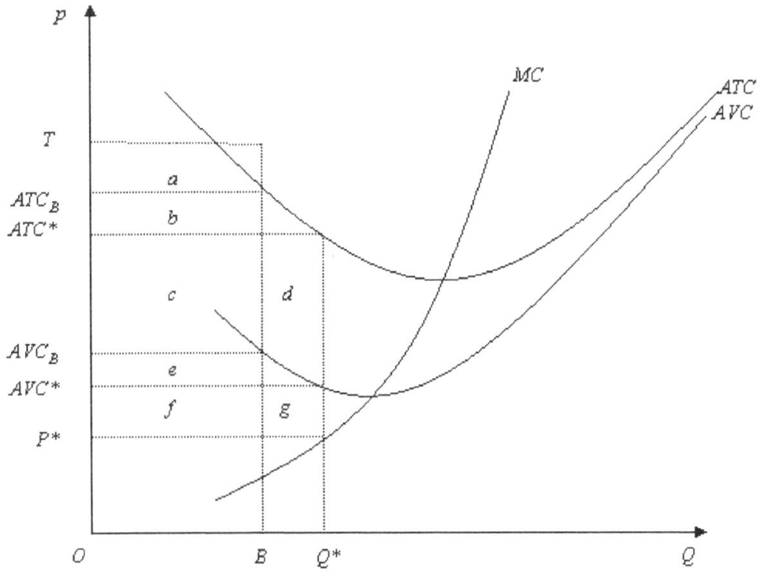

Figure 5. Negative profits at *B*, possible cross-subsidization to Q^* ($P^* > AVC^*$)

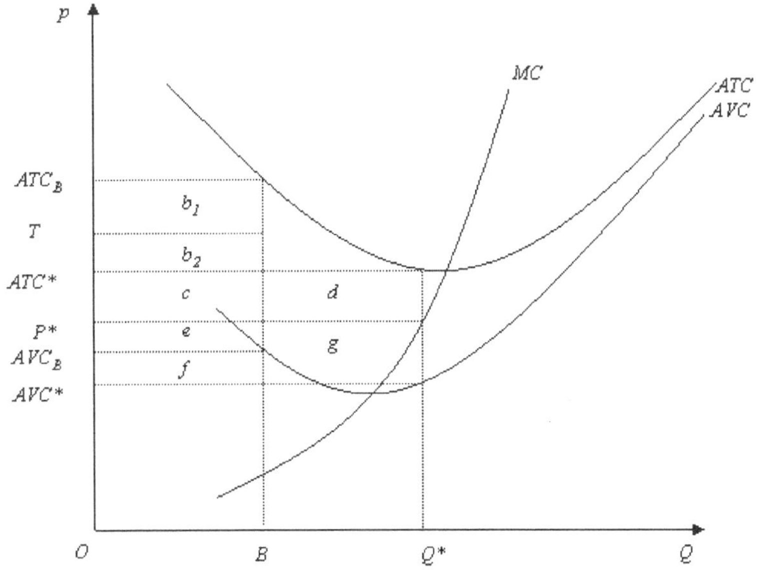

Figure 6. Negative profits at *B*, possible cross-subsidization to Q^* ($P^* < AVC^*$)

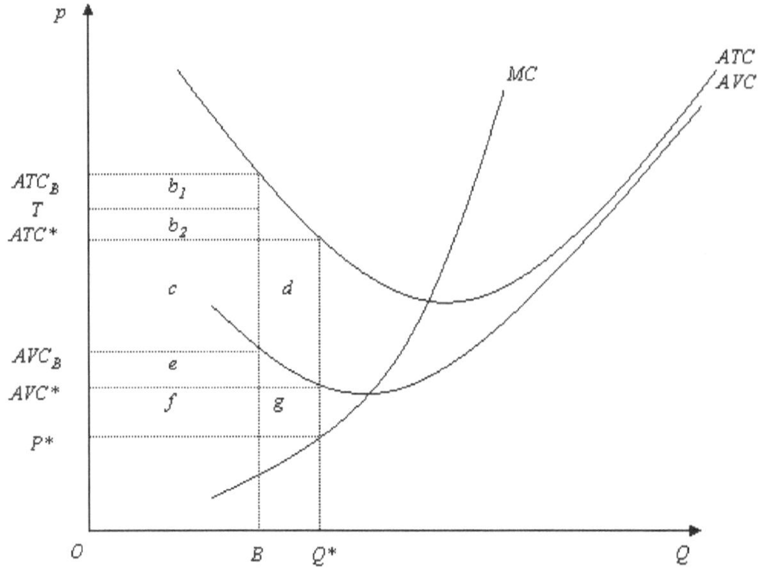

De Gorter, Just, and Kropp (2008) note that, even if marginal-output decisions are determined by the world price, not the quota (support) price, the existence of the rents on quota sugar may deter exit and thus result in output that is too high. There may also be firms that would be unprofitable producing at quota (support) level B but that become profitable by increasing their output at the margin because of the support that is offered for output up to level B (see also Figures 3–6). Thus, total output is likely to exceed what would be observed under free trade because there are producers in the market only because of the subsidy.

Only if there are producers that can cover their marginal costs at the world price without subsidies is there no cross-subsidization. In such cases, the EC policy will simply be a redistributive one: firms are allowed to capture rents, but they would be in the market anyway. A problem in assessing the validity of this possibility is that there is little information on costs of production, so it is not known to what extent there are such firms in the EC. However, the likeliest presumption is that there will only be few such producers in the EC.

Turning to the insurance motive possibility for C production and exports, if there is rational overproduction to deal with uncertainty *ex ante*, Gohin and Bureau (2006) show that the cross-subsidy conclusion still applies: the EC quota/support system acts as a cross-subsidy in such situations because the likelihood of 'overproduction' is a positive function of the difference between the EC intervention and the world price. However, they also point out that the carry-forward provisions of the sugar regime attenuate the incentive to overproduce, as they allow for quota rights to be transferred to the next year.

If a more long-run view is taken, the cross-subsidization argument based on fixed costs becomes less compelling. Producers should adjust production factors so that these are optimal for producing at level B. Gohin and Bureau (2006) argue that, as the EC regime has been in place for decades, such adjustments should have been made in the past. Moreover, they note that it is not clear that there actually are significant scale economies in beet production (fixed costs), although the possibility of such costs and long-lived assets is more likely for processors/refiners. These considerations make the De Gorter *et al.* finding that cross-subsidization is not limited to instances where world prices are less than average total costs of production more important in bolstering the economic argument for cross subsidization. Of particular importance here is the exit-deterring influence of policies that result in *de facto* cross-subsidization of exports.

Thus, it is indeed possible, based on the known facts, that cross-subsidization would be an effect of the EC regime. However, it is also conceptually possible that sugar producers could decide to do otherwise with the above-normal profits from A and B sales than subsidize sales of C beet.[9] As a matter of law then, is the requirement of governmental action satisfied if the governmental conduct in question will not *necessarily* induce the subsidization complained of? We are inclined to answer in the affirmative and thus to support the findings of the Panel and the Appellate Body. Art. 9.1(c) requires only that 'payments on the export of an agricultural product' be '*financed by virtue of governmental action*' (emphasis added). In other words, all that is necessary is for the government to have done *something* 'by virtue of which' the payments are financially enabled; it is not required to show that the government has *mandated or caused the payments to be actually made*, much less that the governmental action *itself* is in the form of a 'payment', however so defined. Thus, *whether* or not such payments are made might still be at the discretion of nongovernmental actors; *if* they are made, and it is governmental action that results in the financial *capacity* to make them, they are covered by 9.1(c). It was not in dispute that the high prices for A and B sugar and sugar beet were a consequence, in part, if not large part, of the EC regulatory regime. The question then becomes, as a matter of proof, what the complainant must show in order to establish that below-cost sales of C beet were enabled by the profits generated through these high prices. Should there be a rebuttable presumption, based on standard economic axioms, that, absent above-normal profits on one product, it is simply not viable to sell another product at below-cost? This would leave it for the defendant to explain how, despite the standard economic axioms, in the particular case at hand, the firm would have been able to finance the below-cost sales in the absence of the above-normal profits due to

9 We stress that while it is certainly conceptually possible for producers not to use A + B rents to subsidize C production, and that this justifies the legal analysis that follows, the practical relevance of the argument for the case at hand is limited as it is premised on alternative uses of these excess profits/rents not generating higher returns, be it through investment or consumption.

government-influenced or government-determined above-market prices for other products. Certainly, the EC does not seem to have offered a very clear explanation of how the behavior in question with respect to C might have occurred anyhow in the absence of above-normal A and B profits.

Commentary

A concern may be raised that, in opening the door to 'cross-subsidization' claims, the Appellate Body has considerably expanded the scope for Members to challenge subsidies in WTO law, as well, arguably, to legally countervail them. It is our view that in fact there will be limited scope for such claims outside the context of 9.1(c) of the AoA. The SCM Agreement requires that, for a measure to be considered a subsidy, there must be a 'financial contribution *by* government' (emphasis added), not merely that a payment (by anyone) be financially enabled 'by virtue of governmental action'. The AoA is clearly addressed to dealing with the pervasive distortion of competition in agricultural markets through the combined and interactive effects of a wide variety of government policies: levies, export subsidies, quotas and price support mechanisms. It is thus understandable that 'cross-subsidization' would be disciplined by such a comprehensive agreement. The SCM Agreement is more limited, on the other hand: unlike the case with the EC's own internal law on state aids, the WTO rules on subsidies exist in the absence of agreement among WTO Members on antitrust or anticompetition law principles; indeed whether such principles should be part of the WTO system at all is intensely controversial. The definition of 'financial contribution' in the SCM Agreement makes clear that there is only a very narrow range of circumstances where a 'financial contribution' by government would exist by virtue of payments through a nongovernmental entity: SCM 1 provides that a financial contribution exists where 'government makes payments to a funding mechanism, or entrusts or directs a private body to carry out one or more of the type of functions illustrated in (i) to (iii)'. These functions are: direct payments or transfers, forgoing revenue otherwise due, and provision of goods and services other than general infrastructure and purchase of goods.

In the case of provision of goods and services, a benefit is deemed to be conferred only if these are provided at below-market prices. Merely enabling a private entity to provide goods or services at below market prices would seem to fall short of 'entrusting' or 'directing' such an entity to do so. In the *US–Export Restraint* case, Canada challenged provisions of US countervailing duty law and regulation that included export restraints as among the kinds of countervailable subsidies. The context of this complaint was the longstanding dispute between Canada and the US over softwood lumber; US producers wanted export restraints on Canadian logs to be treated as subsidies to Canadian lumber producers, on the grounds that the effect of these restraints was to increase supply and reduce the price of such logs in the Canadian market, thereby reducing the input costs of Canadian lumber producers. Unlike in *EC–Sugar*, in this case the government was altering the conditions of the market such as effectively to *compel*, and not merely to enable, sales at lower prices. Nevertheless, the Panel held:

> Government entrustment or direction is very different from the situation in which the government intervenes in the market in some way, which may or may not have a particular result simply based on the given factual circumstances and the exercise of free choice by the actors in that market. Indeed, governments intervene in markets in various ways, and with various policy or profit objectives, and these interventions might have various results, including results that are not intended by, or that are even undesirable for, the government.' (para. 8.31)

According to the Panel, there must be an explicit act of delegation or command to the private body to engage in the conduct in question for a situation of entrustment or direction to exist. In our view, this interpretation of 'financial contribution' provides very limited opportunities for making 'cross-subsidization' arguments under the SCM Agreement.

At the same time, cross-subsidization must not be confused with the issue of 'pass-through' subsidies, that is the question of whether by providing an actual financial contribution in respect of one product, a government confers a benefit and creates a subsidy on another. Thus, again in the softwood lumber dispute, most of the measures besides the export restraints that were the basis for US agency findings of subsidization, conferred a financial contribution with respect to the production of logs, not lumber (fees for the harvesting of timber at arguably below-market rates). The claim was that by subsidizing the production of logs, the government was reducing the price of the crucial input in the production of lumber and thereby conferring a 'benefit' or competitive advantage on Canadian lumber producers. The approach of the Appellate Body to situations where a financial contribution is conferred on one industry but the benefit and thus the subsidy is with respect to another is as follows:

> The phrase 'subsid[ies] bestowed ... *indirectly*', as used in Article VI:3, implies that financial contributions by the government to the production of *inputs* used in manufacturing products subject to an investigation are not, in principle, excluded from the amount of subsidies that may be through the imposition of countervailing duties on the *processed product*. Where the producer of the input is not the same entity as the producer of the processed product, it cannot be presumed, however, that the subsidy bestowed on the input passes through to the processed product. In such case, it is necessary to analyze to what extent subsidies on inputs may be included in the determination of the total amount of subsidies bestowed upon processed products. For it is only the subsidies determined to have been granted upon the *processed products* that may be offset by levying countervailing duties on those products. In our view, it would not be possible to determine whether countervailing duties levied on the processed product are *in excess* of the amount of the total subsidy accruing to that product, without establishing whether, and in what amount, subsidies bestowed on the producer of the input flowed through, downstream, to the producer of the product processed from that

> input. Because Article VI:3 permits *offsetting*, through countervailing duties, no more than the 'subsidy determined to have been granted ... directly or indirectly, on the manufacture [or] production ... of such *product*', it follows that Members must not impose duties to offset an amount of the input subsidy that has *not* passed through to the countervailed processed products. It is only the amount by which an indirect subsidy granted to producers of inputs flows through to the processed product, together with the amount of subsidy bestowed directly on producers of the processed product, that may be offset through the imposition of countervailing duties. (paras. 140–141)

3. Consistency of the measures complained of with the EC's schedule under the Agreement on Agriculture

Interpretation of Footnote 1 of the EC's schedule

The EC argued that, even if the measures complained of constituted export subsidies within the meaning of the Agreement on Agriculture, the payments in question fell within the ceilings to which the EC had bound itself in its schedule pursuant to the AoA. The AoA requires WTO Members to make commitments to reduce export subsidies on agricultural products (Article 9.1). Article 3.3 provides that, if an export subsidy is not listed in the Member's schedule, it may not be granted. Article 9.2(b)(iv) of the AoA stipulates that a Member's budgetary outlays for export subsidies and the quantities benefiting from such subsidies, at the conclusion of the implementation period shall be no greater than 64 % and 79 % of the 1986–1990 base period levels, respectively. For developing country Members these percentages shall be 76 % and 86 %, respectively. Thus, if a WTO Member wishes to continue to grant an export subsidy, (1) it must be scheduled; (2) it must be subject to reduction commitments; and (3) these commitments must be such that the percentage reductions in budgetary outlays and quantities specified in 9.2(b)(iv) of the AoA are achieved by the end of the implementation period.

The EC did in fact schedule reduction commitments with respect to subsidized exports on sugar. These are contained in Section II, Part IV of the EC Schedule and are summarized by the Appellate Body as follows:

> (i) the 'base quantity level' (the average of the quantity of subsidized exports of sugar during the base period 1986–1990) was 1,612,000 tonnes, and this quantity level would be progressively reduced to 1,273,500 tonnes in the year 2000 as the 'final quantity commitment level' for sugar; and (ii) the 'base outlay level' (the average of the budgetary outlay on subsidized exports of sugar during the base period 1986–1990) was €779.9 million, and this budgetary outlay level would be progressively reduced to €499.1 million in the year 2000 as the 'final [budgetary] outlay commitment level' for sugar. (para. 159)

The EC did not contest that, if the payments complained were found to constitute export subsidies, by virtue of these payments the EC would have failed to meet the reduction commitments to which it was bound in the above-noted provisions of its Schedule. However, the EC claimed that, by virtue of Footnote 1 to its Schedule, the total ceiling it had bound itself to achieve, in quantity terms, was not 1,273,500 tonnes, but this amount plus a maximum of an additional 1.6 million tonnes. The EC essentially argued that the purpose of Footnote 1 was to allow it to meet its commitments in the body of its schedule while continuing to subsidize exports of sugar of ACP and Indian origin up to 1.6 million tonnes.

Footnote 1 reads as follows: 'Does not include exports of sugar of ACP and Indian origin on which the Community is not making any reduction commitments. The average of export in the period 1986 to 1990 amounted to 1,6 mio t.' The EC version of the meaning of this footnote depended on a certain interpretation of both the first and the second sentence. The AB considered each of these interpretations in turn. In the case of the first sentence, the EC claimed that its intent was not to exclude 'exports of sugar of ACP and Indian origin' as such from reduction commitments, but only the quantities of exports *equivalent* to such exports from its scheduled ceiling for reduction commitments, thereby in effect raising the total ceiling by that amount. The EC advanced this interpretation, one assumes, because it was aware that under the AoA there was no basis for excluding a specific subset of export subsidies from reduction commitments.

The basis the EC gave for its nonliteral reading of the first sentence was the negotiating history of the Uruguay Round. As summarized by the AB, the EC's claim was that 'it was well known to all parties at the time of conclusion of the WTO Agreement that the EC did not grant export refunds only on the re-export of sugar originally of ACP/Indian origin, but granted export refunds for a quantity equivalent to such exports'(para. 176). The EC referred to two documents from the *travaux* to support its assertion. The first was a March 1992 letter to the negotiating parties in which the EC stated that it 'ha[d] not included the volume of sugar *corresponding* to its imports of sugar from ACP countries' (emphasis added). The second was an Australian memorandum dated 31 January 1994 that described Footnote 1 as covering 'direct export restitutions (corresponding to [the European Communities'] imports of sugar from ACP countries and India)'.

The AB rejected the EC's interpretation, stating:

> Like the Panel, we are not persuaded by these arguments, which rely on the presumed knowledge of other Members of the World Trade Organization (the 'WTO') on the export subsidy practices of the European Communities with respect to ACP/India sugar. We note that the Complaining Parties have rebutted the interpretations put forward by the European Communities on the terms, context, and negotiating history of Footnote 1. We also wish to note that the European Communities was unable to clarify at the oral hearing, why, having written the aforementioned letter in March 1992, it did not consider it necessary to use that same language in Footnote 1 in the December 1993 text, or to use language that plainly shows that the exports referred to were those equivalent in

> volume to the sugar that was imported from ACP countries and India. In any event, we are of the view that the European Communities' submissions do not alter the plain meaning of the first sentence of Footnote 1, so as to make it cover the exports of sugar equivalent in volume to the European Communities' imports of sugar from ACP countries and India. (para. 180)

With respect to the second sentence of the footnote, the EC claimed that the statement 'The average of export in the period 1986 to 1990 amounted to 1,6 mio t' amounted to a legal undertaking that the total amount of sugar exempted from the reduction commitments in the body of the EC's schedule would not exceed 1.6 million tonnes. In effect, the EC was saying that this was a cap or limitation that satisfied the requirement of the AoA that all export subsidies be included in overall reduction commitments in Members' schedules.

The AB rejected this interpretation, stating:

> The fact that the second sentence makes a specific reference to the average of such exports in the base period does not necessarily lead to an inference that there is a commitment in the sentence to 'limit' the quantity of subsidization to that level, particularly when the first sentence says that the European Communities is not making 'any reduction commitments'. Nor does the practice of the European Communities providing subsidies on exports equivalent to its actual imports from ACP countries and India lead to an inference that that practice flows from a commitment contained in the second sentence of Footnote 1.
>
> Lastly, we see merit in the Panel's reference to the notification practice of the European Communities to the WTO Committee on Agriculture to conclude that this practice does not support the interpretation advanced by the European Communities. If Footnote 1 does contain a commitment on the part of the European Communities with respect to the export subsidies provided by it on exports of sugar equivalent in volume to its actual imports from ACP countries and India or 1.6 million tonnes (albeit such a commitment is only a 'limitation' commitment and not a 'reduction' commitment), we fail to see why the European Communities did not notify the WTO Committee on Agriculture of the status of its compliance with that commitment throughout the period of implementation of the *Agreement on Agriculture*. The fact that the European Communities did not do so undermines its interpretation of the second sentence of Footnote 1. (paras. 186–187)

Commentary

In our view, the AB's rejection of the EC's 'everybody knows' reading of Footnote 1 is a correct approach to treaty interpretation under the Vienna Convention on the Law of Treaties (VCLT) and is also desirable from the perspective of fundamental systemic concerns in the WTO legal system, namely internal and external transparency. The VCLT Article 32 permits recourse to the negotiating history only 'in order to confirm the meaning resulting from the application of article 31, or to determine the meaning when the interpretation according to article 31: (a) leaves the meaning ambiguous or obscure; or (b) leads to a result which is manifestly absurd or unreasonable'. There is nothing 'ambiguous or obscure' in the language 'does not include exports of ACP/India Sugar on which the community is not making any reduction commitments'. The words plainly say that the EC is not making any reduction commitments *on* these particular exports.

The question of whether the plain meaning leads to a result that is 'absurd or unreasonable' is somewhat more difficult. It is arguable that the plain meaning is 'absurd or unreasonable' as it would lead to the result that the EC would have made a scheduling that violates the unqualified obligation in AoA 9.1 to schedule reduction commitments on export subsidies *and* in AoA 3.3 not to grant any subsidy that has not been scheduled. The fact is, however, that even if one reads the second sentence as containing a legally binding commitment to limit the quantity subsidized to 1.6 million tonnes, the nonliteral meaning urged by the EC would not save it from the result of noncompliance with the AoA, since a *limitation* to this amount could not be construed, and indeed the EC was not urging it to be construed, as a commitment to *reduction* of the amount by the percentage and in the time frame required by the AoA.

In sum, if what is 'absurd or unreasonable' in the result of the literal interpretation of the first sentence of the footnote is that it would entail a scheduling by the EC contrary to the AoA, that result could not be avoided through recourse to the negotiating history in the manner suggested by the EC. Thus, under Article 32 of the VCLT, there was no basis for the EC to demand that the AB rely on the negotiating history.

As for the AB's rejection of the view that the second sentence of the Footnote contains a binding legal commitment to limit – albeit not reduce – subsidization to 1.6 million tonnes, the AB's view that a mere statement of the practice of a state party cannot without some further wording be understood as binding in international law is broadly consistent with general international law doctrine. To establish an obligation of customary international law, not only is evidence of state practice required but proof of intent to follow the practice as a matter of international legal obligation (opinio juris). Perhaps even more relevant is the law as it relates to binding unilateral declarations of states. As the adopted panel in the *US – S. 301* case noted, a statement by a state should not be taken to give rise to a legal obligation unless strict conditions are met, including a manifest intent to be bound by the statement (*US – S. 301 of the Tariff Act*, para. 7.118 and accompanying footnote). In this respect, we note that the AB adverted to a significant piece of evidence indicating that the EC had not intended to be bound, namely that the EC had not notified the WTO Agriculture Committee of its compliance with this purported commitment, as it was required to do under the AoA.

More generally, the EC's contention that its Schedule should be interpreted based on insider knowledge of the trade negotiator community about the history of its export subsidization practices is at odds with policies of internal and external transparency that are important to the legitimacy of the WTO. Such knowledge is obviously available only to a limited group of persons and is not documented in any public transparent venue.[10] At most, those negotiating parties most intimately engaged in negotiations with the EC over export subsidies would have become aware of the practices in question (even assuming that they could infer from awareness of the practices the particular interpretation of the legal commitments in question urged by the EC). Scheduled commitments indicate the terms and conditions on which economic actors may compete in the global marketplace with the scheduling Member; it is important for advancing the goals of the trading system that such terms and conditions be accessible to economic actors and to all interested constituencies, for that matter, and that they be secure and legally predictable (see *US – S. 301 of the Tariff Act* on the importance of security and predictability to advancing the goals of the WTO system).

Consistency of the EC reduction commitments with the EC's obligations under the Agreement on Agriculture

Having determined that the ordinary meaning of Footnote 1 to the EC schedule was that the EC was purporting to exempt export subsidies on ACP/India sugar from reduction commitments altogether, it is hardly surprising that the AB would then go on to determine that this exemption was inconsistent with the AoA.

First of all, the AB held that reduction commitments must be scheduled both in terms of budgetary outlays for export subsidies and the quantities benefiting from such subsidies; thus, even if the AB had been able to agree with the meaning of Footnote 1 advanced by the EC, Footnote 1 would still have run afoul of the AoA by failing to mention any limitation or reduction of budgetary outlays, instead referring exclusively to quantities.

The EC argued that there was no specific provision of the AoA that required scheduling both in terms of budgetary outlays and quantities subsidized. However, the AB relied on the nature of the underlying obligation to make reduction commitments as set forth in AoA 3.3, which reads as follows:

> Subject to the provisions of paragraphs 2(b) and 4 of Article 9, a Member shall not provide export subsidies listed in paragraph 1 of Article 9 in respect of the agricultural products or groups of products specified in Section II of Part IV of its Schedule in excess of the budgetary outlay and quantity commitment levels specified therein and shall not provide such subsidies in respect of any agricultural product not specified in that Section of its Schedule.

10 In *US–Shrimp*, the Appellate Body held that the 'sprit' of transparency, as reflected in the obligations in Article X of the GATT, should inform interpretation of other WTO provisions, especially where a WTO Member is claiming 'exception.' (paras. 182–183). While the 'letter' of Article X applies to domestic regulations and their administration, and the schedule is an international legal instrument, the schedule provides the basis on which economic actors from other WTO Members can form expectations concerning the terms and conditions of competition with the scheduling Member; therefore the 'spirit' of Article X is definitely engaged where a Member schedules so as to express in a nontransparent manner a limitation or exception to what would normally be expected to be its liberalization obligations.

Concerning the implications of this obligation, the AB suggested:

> In our view, the use of the conjunctive 'and', and the corresponding use of the word 'levels' in the plural, suggest that the drafters of the Agreement intended that both types of commitments must be specified in a Member's Schedule in respect of any export subsidy listed in Article 9.1. Had the drafters intended that a Member could specify one or the other of the two forms of commitments, they would have chosen the disjunctive 'or' and correspondingly used the word 'level' in the singular. Given the choice, Members would choose only one or the other type of commitment, but not both, so as to minimize their obligations. Therefore, it appears to us that the drafters intended to ensure that export subsidy commitments are specified in Members' Schedules in terms of both budgetary outlay and quantity commitments, by using the word 'and' as well as the word 'levels' in the text of Article 3.3. (para. 193)

The AB further noted:

> We find contextual support for the above interpretation in Article 9.2(b)(iv) of the *Agreement on Agriculture*, which provides that Member's budgetary outlays for export subsidies and the quantities benefiting from such subsidies, at the conclusion of the implementation period, are no greater than 64 per cent and 79 per cent of the 1986–1990 base period levels, respectively. For developing country Members these percentages shall be 76 and 86 per cent, respectively. This provision prescribes the export subsidy commitment levels to be reached at the conclusion of the implementation period (and to be maintained thereafter), and those commitment levels are expressed in terms of both budgetary outlays and quantities. We do not see how a Member could comply with Article 9.2(b)(iv), or for that matter Article 9.2(a), without having specified its export subsidy commitments in terms of both budgetary outlays and quantities. We also consider it significant that both Article 9.2(b)(iii) and Article 9.2(b)(iv) use the expression 'budgetary outlays for export subsidies and the quantities *benefiting from such subsidies*'. (emphasis added) This shows the drafters' recognition of the need to address the budgetary outlays and quantities together. (para. 194)

More fundamentally, however, the AB went on to affirm the obvious respect in which Footnote 1 was inconsistent with the substantive obligations of the Agreement on Agriculture: Art 9.1 simply does not provide any 'carve out' or safe haven for particular subsidies in respect of the obligation to make reduction commitments. The AB noted:

> The chapeau of Article 9.1 says that the subsidies listed in that Article 'are subject to reduction commitments under this Agreement'. The export subsidies given to ACP/India equivalent sugar, which admittedly fall within the ambit of Article 9.1(a), are therefore subject to reduction commitments. Furthermore, as noted by the Panel, the provisions of Article 9.2(b)(iv) apply to Members that take advantage of the flexibility provisions of Article 9.2(b). Article 9.2(b)(iv) specifies the reduction levels to be achieved at the conclusion of the implementation period with respect to both budgetary outlays and quantities. The provisions of

> Article 9.2(b)(iv) lend contextual support to the view that export subsidies listed in Article 9.1 are subject to reduction commitments. We further note that Article 9.2(a)(i) and (ii) also make it clear that both budgetary outlay and quantity commitments specified in a Member's Schedule for each year of the implementation period are 'reduction' commitments. It follows that the export subsidies provided to ACP/India equivalent sugar are subject to reduction commitments in terms of Article 9.1 of the *Agreement on Agriculture*. (para. 206)

Finally, the AB addressed an argument of the ACP countries, third parties in the litigation, that in certain circumstances the AoA permits limitations of export subsidies in lieu of reduction commitments (this argument of course assumes the validity of the EC reading of Footnote 1, namely that this footnote articulates a legally binding limitation on export subsidies, if not a literal reduction commitment; since the AB had already rejected such a reading of Footnote 1, its remarks on the ACP argument are, strictly speaking, obiter dicta). The AB opined:

> The ACP Countries[11] have argued that 'limiting subsidization', without reducing budgetary outlays or quantity, is permissible under Article 3.1 of the *Agreement on Agriculture*, which says that '[t]he domestic support and export subsidy commitments in Part IV of each Member's Schedule constitute commitments *limiting subsidization*' (emphasis added). According to the ACP Countries, 'the basic obligations of the Agreement with respect to a scheduled product such as sugar are found in Articles 3.3 and 8. These paramount provisions are framed around and are directly linked to *what is specified* by the respective member *limiting subsidization* in the sense of requirements in Article 3.1 of the Agreement.' In response to questioning at the oral hearing, the ACP Countries also emphasized that Article 3.1 permits 'limiting' subsidization, and only what is specified in a Member's Schedule governs its obligation with respect to subsidization.
>
> We are not persuaded by this argument. We do not see Article 3.1 as permitting a Member to limit subsidization to whatever commitment it chooses to specify in its Schedule without regard to Members' obligations under the *Agreement on Agriculture*. Rather, with respect to export subsidy commitments, we see Article 3.1 as requiring a Member to limit its subsidization to the budgetary outlay and quantity reduction commitments specified in its Schedule in accordance with the provisions of the *Agreement on Agriculture*. This is also clear from the provisions of Article 9.2(a) of the Agreement, which requires adherence by a Member in each year of the implementation period to the budgetary outlay and quantity 'reduction commitments', as specified in the Member's Schedule. (paras. 208–209)

Commentary

The AoA clearly requires WTO Members to achieve the *result* of reduction commitments both in terms of budgetary outlay and quantity of exports

11 The third-participant ACP countries in this appeal are: Barbados, Belize, Côte d'Ivoire, Fiji, Guyana, Jamaica, Kenya, Madagascar, Malawi, Mauritius, St. Kitts & Nevis, Swaziland, Tanzania, and Trinidad & Tobago.

subsidies: inferring from this obviously intended result the requirement that schedules be structured in those terms is, however, not a self-evident interpretive move. One reading of the *Chile–Price Band* and *Argentina–Footwear* AB Reports is that, absent an explicit textual requirement, a Member should be able to express and apply its liberalization commitments as it pleases, provided that it achieves the result of operating within the ceilings that it is legally bound to conform to. In these cases, the defending WTO Members had used formulas or methodologies for determining tariffs in customs administration that deviated from the ad valorem or specific methods used for scheduling; the approach of the AB in these cases was to determine whether, regardless of the formula or methodology used, the *result* was the possibility of protection being imposed in excess of the underlying legal obligation not to exceed the scheduled ad valorem MFN-bound tariff rate. From this perspective, arguably it would not be necessary to require that both budgetary outlay and quantity be scheduled, as long as within the specified time period EC policies were adjusted so as to ensure the required reductions in both *actually occurred*.

Did the AB therefore take an unjustified interpretative leap in reading in a requirement that schedules specify both budgetary outlay and quantity? We think not. In *Chile–Price Band* and *Argentina–Footwear*, there was an objective benchmark already in the defending Member's schedule against which it was possible to assess whether the obligation of result had been met, namely a tariff ceiling expressed in ad valorem terms. In the case of export subsidies under the AoA, determining whether the underlying obligation of result has been met, i.e. whether a certain percentage reduction in both budgetary outlay and quantity has been achieved, is *impossible* unless the Member in question specifies at a minimum the base outlays and quantities against which the percentage reductions can be measured over the specified time period. The fact is that transparency and specificity in scheduling and reporting are essential to legal security in a regime such as this, where Members are required to improve market access through the adjustment of labyrinthine and often opaque (in design and/or administration) domestic policy schemes.

In any event, we see the other interpretations of the AoA made by the AB in this part of its report as straightforward and logical, and not meriting specific commentary. Certainly, we agree with the AB that the use of the word 'limiting' does not necessarily imply that, in the absence of operative language, the AoA entertains the possibility of Members discharging their obligations under 9.1 through limits *other than*, or not including, the manifestly required reduction commitments.

Can a WTO Member limit or reduce its obligations under the AoA through scheduling?

The EC argued that, even if Footnote 1 was inconsistent with the AoA, by the acceptance of its schedule in the Uruguay Round negotiations, the EC had effectively altered its obligations under the AoA, or that the schedule somehow had an equal legal status to the AoA itself such that the obligations of the EC under the AoA should be read such that they were consistent with the rights reserved under the schedule. The AB rejected this argument. It observed:

> Article 8 of the *Agreement on Agriculture*, entitled 'Export Competition Commitments', reads: Each Member undertakes not to provide export subsidies otherwise than in conformity with this Agreement and with the commitments as specified in that Member's Schedule. It is clear from the plain wording of Article 8 that Members are prohibited from providing export subsidies otherwise than in conformity with the *Agreement on Agriculture* and the commitments as specified in their Schedules. Thus, compliance with both is obligatory. As compliance with the provisions of the *Agreement on Agriculture* is obligatory, it is clear that the commitments specified in a Member's Schedule must be in conformity with the provisions of the Agreement. Only then would the export subsidies be in compliance with the requirements of Article 8. (paras. 215–216)

The EC had argued that the notion that scheduling cannot be used to limit or qualify obligations under a WTO treaty was derived in an unwarranted manner from the ruling in an old GATT case, coincidentally also concerning sugar. Thus, according to the EC, the panel in that case had depended on specific language in the GATT that addressed the possibility of qualifying obligations that were specific to the GATT regime, and the reasoning in question could not be transferred mutatis mutandis to the interpretation of the AoA.

The AB disagreed with the EC, finding that the panel had articulated a more general jurisprudential notion:

> The GATT panel in *US – Sugar* did not rely solely on the language of Article II:1(b) of the GATT 1947 in making its ruling, as the European Communities suggests. Instead, the panel's reasoning was that, in the absence of a specific provision that would entitle Members to depart from their obligations under the GATT 1947, Members were not entitled to do so. Thus, the GATT panel in *US – Sugar* concluded: Article II:1(b) does not permit contracting parties to qualify their obligations under other provisions of the General Agreement and that the provisions in the United States GATT Schedule of Concessions can consequently not justify the maintenance of quantitative restrictions ... inconsistent with the application of Article XI:1. Similarly, in this case, we find no provision under the *Agreement on Agriculture* that authorizes Members to depart, in their Schedules, from their obligations under that Agreement. Indeed, as we have noted, Article 8 requires that, in providing export subsidies, Members must comply with the provisions of both the *Agreement on Agriculture* and the export subsidy commitments specified in their Schedules. This is possible only if the commitments in the Schedules are in conformity with the provisions of the *Agreement on Agriculture*. Thus, we see no basis for the European Communities' assertion that it could depart from the obligations under the *Agreement on Agriculture* through the claimed commitment provided in Footnote 1. (paras. 219–220)

Finally, the AB rejected the EC argument that its schedule was equal in hierarchy of legal norms with the AoA itself and thus that the obligations of the AoA should be interpreted in a manner consistent with the schedule. The AB noted:

> that Article 21 of the *Agreement on Agriculture* provides that: '[t]he provisions of [the] GATT 1994 and of other Multilateral Trade Agreements in Annex 1A to the WTO Agreement shall apply subject to the provisions of this Agreement.' In other words, Members explicitly recognized that there may be conflicts between the *Agreement on Agriculture* and the GATT 1994, and explicitly provided, through Article 21, that the *Agreement on Agriculture* would prevail to the extent of such conflicts. Similarly, the *General interpretative note to Annex 1A* to the *WTO Agreement* states that, '[i]n the event of conflict between a provision of the [GATT 1994] and a provision of another agreement in Annex 1A ..., the provision of the other agreement shall prevail to the extent of the conflict.' The *Agreement on Agriculture* is contained in Annex 1A to the *WTO Agreement*.

The AB then observed:

> As a separate matter, we note that the European Communities asserts that Footnote 1 was 'negotiated' with its partners in the Uruguay Round negotiations and that it has been 'respected'. Accordingly, Footnote 1 forms part of the treaty ratified by the WTO Members. Similarly, the ACP Countries allege that Footnote 1 'was negotiated and agreed upon' or acquiesced in by the Complaining Parties before the end of the Uruguay Round. The Panel found, however, that '[t]he evidence and submissions produced by all parties show that the Complainants did not agree to any European Communities' deviations from the *Agreement on Agriculture*. The Panel concluded that 'participants in the Uruguay Round and WTO Members did not agree to the European Communities' inclusion of Footnote 1 as an agreed departure from the European Communities' basic obligations under the *Agreement on Agriculture*.' Accordingly, we see no basis in the Panel Reports for the contention of the European Communities and the ACP Countries that the Complaining Parties or the WTO Members negotiated or agreed to Footnote 1 as a departure from the European Communities' obligations under the *Agreement on Agriculture*

Commentary

According to Article 19 of the VCLT, 'a State may, when signing, ratifying, accepting, approving or acceding to a treaty, formulate a reservation unless: (a) the reservation is prohibited by the treaty; (b) the treaty provides that only specified reservations, which do not include the reservation in question, may be made; or (c) in cases not falling under subparagraphs (a) and (b), the reservation is incompatible with the object and purpose of the treaty'. The findings of the *US–Sugar* Panel did not apparently take into account this provision of the VCLT and indeed seem to be inconsistent with it, in as much as the Panel declared an opposite default rule, namely that no reservations are permitted from a treaty unless the text explicitly allows them. Nevertheless, the default rule of the *US–Sugar* Panel has now been incorporated into the WTO system as a default rule, by virtue of the WTO Agreement Article XVI:5, which provides that 'Reservations in respect of any of the provisions of the Multilateral Trade Agreements may only be made to the extent provided for in those Agreements'. By virtue of VCLT 19(b), this lex specialis must prevail.

Moreover, the WTO Agreement elaborates a very specific detailed procedure that must be followed where a WTO obligation is to be waived for a particular WTO Member (Article IX:3–5). Even if it existed as the EC claimed, acquiescence or casual agreement among negotiators to Footnote 1 as a departure from the obligations of the AoA could hardly substitute for the waiver procedure outlined in Article IX of the WTO Agreement, and which is in any event only available in 'exceptional circumstances'. Finally, there is an issue as to whether Article 41 of the VCLT, which deals with modifications of treaties that change obligations only between certain parties, would apply to a situation where *all* of the parties to a multilateral treaty modify the obligations of *a single party* towards all of them (the situation of waiver). However, in any case, Article 41 on its terms defers to any limitations or procedures in the treaty itself concerning such modifications, and this brings us back to the lex specialis of waivers in Article IX of the WTO Agreement.

The above analysis clearly supports the result of the AB ruling. We find it odd, however, in terms of the hierarchy of sources of law in the WTO system, that the AB would rely on a GATT panel ruling rather than on the provisions of the WTO Agreement, the foundational charter of the WTO legal system.

Estoppel and good faith

The EC claimed that the Complaining Parties acted inconsistently with Article 3.10 of the DSU and the principle of good faith by exercising their rights under the DSU in an 'unreasonable' and 'abusive manner' by 'seeking to exploit what would be, at most, an excusable scheduling error in order to secure a manifestly unfair advantage', and further that they were estopped from bringing DSU proceedings because they, along with all the other participants in the Uruguay Round negotiations, had given the EC to understand that they did not consider C sugar to benefit from export subsidies; here, the EC pointed to the nonreaction of Uruguay Round participants when the EC failed to include C sugar in its base levels. The Panel found that this mere nonreaction was insufficient to establish the kind of representation upon which an estoppel might be based[12] and that there was no

12 Estoppel refers to the notion that some kinds of representations and conduct are such that the party responsible for them may be precluded from repudiating them, meaning often that the party in question may have legal responsibility for the reliance of other parties on the representations and conduct. Brownlie (2003), following Bowett, has suggested three conditions that must be fulfilled to establish an estoppel: '(1) a statement of fact that is clear and unambiguous; (2) this statement must be voluntary, unconditional, and authorized; and (3) there must be reliance in good faith upon the statement either to the detriment of the party so relying on the statement or to the advantage of the party making the statement.' In the

direct evidence of an actual shared understanding by Uruguay Round participants concerning C sugar. But the Panel also expressed serious doubts as to whether the principle of estoppel was applicable to WTO disputes.

In addressing the issue of estoppel, the Appellate Body echoed the uncertainty of the Panel as to the applicability of the principle of estoppel to WTO dispute-settlement proceedings. The AB opined:

> The principle of estoppel has never been applied by the Appellate Body. Moreover, the notion of estoppel, as advanced by the European Communities, would appear to inhibit the ability of WTO Members to initiate a WTO dispute settlement proceeding. We see little in the DSU that explicitly limits the rights of WTO Members to bring an action; WTO Members must exercise their 'judgement as to whether action under these procedures would be fruitful', by virtue of Article 3.7 of the DSU, and they must engage in dispute settlement procedures in good faith, by virtue of Article 3.10 of the DSU. This latter obligation covers, in our view, the entire spectrum of dispute settlement, from the point of initiation of a case through implementation. Thus, even assuming *arguendo* that the principle of estoppel could apply in the WTO, its application would fall within these narrow parameters set out in the DSU. (para. 311)

The AB went on, however, to make no finding of law concerning the applicability of estoppel in WTO proceedings; it held that even assuming applicability along the lines that the EC was arguing, the Panel had determined that the EC had not proven the facts necessary to establish an estoppel.

Commentary

The AB's approach here is incoherent. It is impossible to establish what facts would be needed to prove an estoppel without examining the nature and scope of the principle itself, as circumscribed or limited (if at all) by the WTO treaty texts. For example, if acquiescence or silence can be a basis for estoppel, it is far from clear that the findings of the Panel concerning the lack of proof of explicit statements or representations or the lack of proof of a 'shared understanding' would be enough to reject a claim of estoppel.

The legal authorities are divided as to whether estoppel includes acquiescence upon which a state may reasonably rely or whether estoppel and acquiescence are separate equitable grounds for refusing a legal claim.[13] In the *Guatemala–Cement* case, the panel contrasted estoppel with a situation of 'acquiescence', which meant 'silence in the face of events that call for a reaction of some sort'(para. 8.23). In the *Temple of Preah Vihear* case, the International Court of Justice found that Thailand,

Argentina – Poultry case, Argentina unsuccessfully invoked this definition of estoppel to argue that by commencing proceedings in MERCOSUR in relation to the same dispute (on antidumping duties), Brazil was estopped from bringing a further action in the WTO; while finding that the conditions stated by Brownlie had not been met in that case, the Panel seemed open to the view that this definition could be an adequate statement of the definition of estoppel as a general principle of law.

13 See Sinclair (1995, p. 110).

in not objecting to a map filed as an annex to an agreement with Cambodia, could not claim that it had sovereignty over a temple that was drawn on the map as within Cambodian territory. The ICJ also noted that in the 50 years or more since the map was filed, Thailand's subsequent conduct was consistent with the view that the temple was within Cambodian jurisdiction.[14] In his separate opinion in the case, Judge Fitzmaurice appeared to take the view that acquiescence could be understood as one basis for estoppel rather than a separate legal principle:

> The principle of preclusion is the nearest equivalent in the field of international law to the common-law rule of estoppel, though perhaps not applied under such strict limiting conditions (and it is certainly applied as a rule of substance and not merely as one of evidence or procedure). It is quite distinct theoretically from the notion of acquiescence. But acquiescence can operate as a preclusion or estoppel in certain cases, for instance where silence, on an occasion where there was a duty or need to speak or act, implies agreement, or a waiver of rights, and can be regarded as a representation to that effect.

Victor Rodríguez Cedeño, Special Rapporteur to the International Law Commission, noted in 2005 that in the *Preah Vihear* case, 'in the reasoning of the Court the elements of estoppel and acquiescence are combined'.[15]

The correct way for the AB to proceed in considering the EC's estoppel claim was to begin by considering first the nature and scope of estoppel as a general principle of international law, and, secondly, whether the provisions of the WTO treaties have altered or narrowed its applicability in the WTO. Only then could the AB properly conclude that the facts, as determined by the Panel, did not support a valid claim of estoppel.

In the passage cited above, *without* first considering the nature and scope of estoppel as a general principle, the AB nevertheless suggests, in *dicta*, that its application is somehow narrowed by the terms of the DSU. The notion seems to be that DSU 3.7 and 3.10 somehow replace and circumscribe the broader concept of equity in general international law.

It is true that 3.10 *expresses* one element of equity, namely 'good faith'. It is unclear why this should lead to the conclusion that 3.10 thereby narrows or limits the application of *other* principles of international law based on equity, such as estoppel. In the *Shrimp–Turtle* case, the AB had held that 'The chapeau of Article XX is, in fact, but one expression of the principle of good faith. This principle, at once a general principle of law and a general principle of international law, controls the exercise of rights by states' (para. 158). Notably, the AB did not conclude that by expressing one aspect of the principle of good faith in the chapeau, the WTO Membership had limited or replaced good faith as a general principle of international law with a narrower treaty obligation; on the contrary,

14 *Case concerning the Temple of Preah Vihear, Merits, Judgment of 15 June 1962: I.C.J. Reports 1962*, p. 32.

15 International Law Commission (2005, para. 161).

the AB stated that its responsibility was to 'interpret the language of the chapeau, *seeking additional interpretative guidance, as appropriate, from the general principles of international law*'(para. 158; emphasis added). Even earlier, in *the EC–Meat Hormones* Report, para. 124, the AB had found, although reflected in a specific provision in the SPS Agreement (5.7, which allows preliminary measures in the absence of sufficient scientific evidence), was not *exhausted* by 5.7; it could thus affect the application of other provisions of the SPS.

It is difficult to reconcile the approach taken to estoppel in *EC–Sugar* with that taken to good faith in *US–Shrimp*. Perhaps it is significant that the EC was invoking estoppel as a bar to legal proceedings in *EC–Sugar*. We do agree with the AB to the extent that it is saying that the invocation of general principles of international law as a bar to adjudicative jurisdiction can be problematic in a legal system such as the WTO where the bases for jurisdiction of the dispute-settlement organs are set out explicitly by treaty, and provide virtually no discretion to panels to decline to adjudicate a dispute on broad equitable considerations. However, the AB never clearly distinguishes the issue of the general applicability of the principle of estoppel in the WTO with the issue of whether estoppel can function as a jurisdictional bar (which is what the EC appeared to be arguing). Indeed, quite apart from the WTO context, it is far from clear that estoppel as a *general principle of international law* can or should be understood as a bar to jurisdiction rather than to the advancement of a specific legal claim.

As for the AB's treatment of the EC claim concerning 'good faith', it rather summarily upheld the Panel's rejection of that claim. This is not surprising, for the same considerations that were rejected as a foundation for the estoppel claim were the basis, it seems, for the (partly separate or additional) claim of a violation of 'good faith'.

4. Judicial economy

In WTO dispute settlement, a situation often arises where a complainant makes claims under a variety of provisions in a covered agreement or under several covered agreements. Often, if the adjudicator finds a violation of one or more provisions of an agreement, they will not go on to consider the other claims, including those under a different covered agreement. This practice is known as judicial economy. The rationale behind judicial economy is that a finding of violation under one provision or one agreement is adequate to 'resolve' the dispute, in that it is sufficient to give rise to the remedy that the complainant is seeking, usually withdrawal of the measures complained of, or their modification in such a way as to permit the market access or the competitive conditions that are the complainant's underlying objectives. The Panel in *EC–Sugar*, having found that the EC payments complained of were in violation of the AoA, did not go on to consider the complainants' claims that provisions of the SCM Agreement had also been violated. This use of judicial economy raised a serious legal issue on appeal, however, because the SCM Agreement contains a remedy for illegal export subsidization that would not be provided by the DSU in the case of violations of the AoA. This special remedy is provided for in SCM 4.7: 'If the measure in question is found to be a prohibited subsidy, the panel shall recommend that the subsidizing Member withdraw the subsidy without delay. In this regard, the panel shall specify in its recommendation the time-period within which the measure must be withdrawn.'

In rejecting the Panel's use of judicial economy as a legal error the AB held:

> In this case, the Panel's findings under Articles 3 and 8 of the *Agreement on Agriculture* were not sufficient to 'fully resolve' the dispute. This is because, in declining to rule on the Complaining Parties' claims under Article 3 of the *SCM Agreement*, the Panel precluded the possibility of a remedy being made available to the Complaining Parties, pursuant to Article 4.7 of the *SCM Agreement*, in the event of the Panel finding in favour of the Complaining Parties with respect to their claims under Article 3 of the *SCM Agreement*. Moreover, in declining to rule on the Complaining Parties' claims under Article 3 of the *SCM Agreement*, the Panel failed to discharge its obligation under Article 11 of the DSU by failing to make 'such other findings as will assist the DSB in making the recommendations or in giving the rulings provided for in the covered agreements, namely, a recommendation or ruling by the DSB pursuant to Article 4.7. This constitutes false judicial economy and legal error. (para. 335)

Having found the Panel in error, the AB nevertheless did not go on to complete the analysis, i.e. to consider the claims that the Panel ought to have considered under the AoA.[16] The AB gave the following reasons for refusing to complete the analysis:

> In several previous disputes, the Appellate Body examined an issue 'not specifically addressed by the panel, in order to complete the legal analysis and resolve the dispute between the parties'. However, the Appellate Body has declined to complete the legal analysis where 'the factual findings of the panel and the undisputed facts in the panel record' did not provide a sufficient basis for the legal analysis by the Appellate Body. Moreover, as Article 17.6 of the DSU limits appeals to 'issues of law covered in the panel report and legal interpretations developed by the panel', the Appellate Body has also previously declined to complete the legal analysis of a panel in circumstances where that would involve addressing claims 'which the panel had not examined at all'. In addition, the Appellate Body has indicated that it may complete the analysis only if the provision that a panel has not examined is '*closely related*' to a provision that the panel has examined, and that the two are 'part of a *logical continuum*'.

16 In domestic legal systems, where an appellate tribunal has found errors of law in the judgment of a trial court, it may remand the matter to the trial level so that the trial court can apply the law as clarified by the appellate tribunal to the facts of the dispute. Under the DSU, the AB does not possess a comparable authority to remand a matter to the original panel. In these circumstances, the AB has engaged in a practice it calls 'completing the analysis.' This means that, having found errors of law in the panel ruling, the AB will not simply leave matters at reversing or modifying the panel's legal findings, but will proceed to apply the law as the AB has clarified it to the existing factual record of the case, as developed in the panel proceeding.

Turning to the specific case before us, we note that the Complaining Parties argue that their claims under the *SCM Agreement* are closely related to their claims under the *Agreement on Agriculture*. We are not persuaded, however, that Articles 3, 8, and 9.1 of the *Agreement on Agriculture*, on the one hand, and Articles 3.1(a), 3.2, and items (a) and (d) of the Illustrative List of the *SCM Agreement*, on the other hand, are 'closely related', because the issues presented under the two Agreements are different in several respects.

Furthermore, in the instant case, we note that the Panel made reference to the limited arguments made by the Complaining Parties under the *SCM Agreement*: [T]he Complainants [had] not set forth their claims under Article 3 of the *SCM Agreement* in quite as clear and unambiguous a manner as under the *Agreement on Agriculture*. Rather, [they] focused on their claims under the *Agreement on Agriculture*.

Although, on appeal, the Complaining Parties did argue their claims under the *SCM Agreement* to some extent, they did not address, in a sufficient manner, the question whether Article 3 of the *SCM Agreement* applies to export subsidies listed in Article 9.1 of the *Agreement on Agriculture* that are provided to *scheduled* agricultural products in excess of a responding Member's commitment levels. We believe that, in the light of Article 21 of the *Agreement on Agriculture* and the chapeau of Article 3 of the *SCM Agreement*, the question of the applicability of the *SCM Agreement* to the export subsidies in this dispute raises a number of complex issues. We also consider that, in the absence of a full exploration of these issues, completing the analysis might affect the due process rights of the participants.

Moreover, we do not have the requisite factual findings to complete the legal analysis. In particular, we do not have sufficient facts before us, as would be necessary to specify the period of time for withdrawal, as required by Article 4.7 of the *SCM Agreement*. We note in this respect that, when specifying what period would represent 'without delay', panels have taken into account, *inter alia*, 'the nature of the measures and the difficulties likely to be faced in implementing the recommendation'. Based on our reading of the Panel Reports and the Panel record, we fail to see any evidence therein regarding the nature of the measures that would be required to 'withdraw' the subsidy, which would permit us to make a recommendation under Article 4.7. Hence, *even if* we were able to examine the Complaining Parties' claims under the *SCM Agreement* and, *even if* we were to conclude that the *SCM Agreement* applies in the circumstances of this dispute and that the European Communities acted inconsistently with its obligations under the *SCM Agreement*, we would not necessarily be in a position to make a recommendation under Article 4.7 as to the time period for withdrawal of the subsidy.

Commentary

The existence of an explicit discrete remedy in the SCM Agreement not provided in the AoA made this a relatively easy case for rejecting the use of judicial economy. However, the underlying issue of principle, whether adjudicating a given claim is necessary to fully or adequately resolve a dispute, given that other claims have already been found to issue in violations, is a much trickier one. There are many instances where the violation of a particular provision of a covered agreement will not necessarily trigger a remedy that will achieve the complainant's objectives. Take, for instance, the SPS Agreement; a complaining Member may be challenging a measure as a violation of the national treatment and MFN provisions of SPS, as not based on an adequate risk assessment, as well as not least-trade-restrictive (5.6). If a panel were, for instance, to stop at a finding that the defending Member's risk assessment was inadequate under 5.1, a sufficient remedy would be for the defending Member to conduct a competent risk assessment (although there is always the possibility that such an assessment would not provide a basis for the measures and they would have to be withdrawn, this would not necessarily by any means be the case). However, if the panel went on to make findings on the other claims under SPS this might well result in the defending Member being required to alter substantive aspects of the measure itself, or withdraw it altogether. More generally, different aspects of a measure may raise different barriers to trade, each of which is of importance to the complaining Member. If these different aspects violate different legal provisions of the covered agreements, then judicial economy will undermine the legal rights of the complaining Member, since a finding limited to one or other of the aspects will only result normally in a requirement that the Member address those aspects, not withdraw the measure entirely.

In sum, to honor truly the underlying principle deployed by the AB in its ruling on judicial economy, panels will have to be much more careful in their decisions concerning judicial economy. A further systemic consideration here is that, where there is an action under DSU 21.5 concerning the adequacy of the defending Member's implementation of a panel ruling, the 21.5 panel will normally consider the consistency of the implementing measures, not only with those provisions of the covered agreements with which the original measures were found to be noncompliant in the first panel ruling, but with any other provisions that the complaining Member wishes to claim under in the 21.5 proceeding (provided, of course, they are within the terms of reference as established by the request for a 21.5 panel (*Canada – Aircraft 21.5* Report of the Appellate Body; *US – Shrimp 21.5*, Report of the Appellate Body)). This extends even to claims never made in the original proceedings and must surely include those that were fully argued but over which the original panel decided to exercise judicial economy. From this point of view, judicial economy may not be particularly 'economic' and only have the odd (and arguably undesirable) result of delaying the adjudication of certain claims to the implementation stage of the dispute.

5. Concluding remarks

Our analysis suggests that the arguments of the Panel regarding cross-subsidization can be defended on both legal and economic grounds. Indeed, the economic reasoning applied by the Panel is conservative in that it covers only a subset of the possible situations that can give rise to cross-subsidization in situations where only part of production benefits from support policies. Although the reasoning of the Panel – that support policies that create rents on a portion of a firm's output may allow for the cross-subsidization of exports – is quite general, the potential for similar arguments to be applied to instances involving non-agricultural products where governments have not made explicit export subsidy commitments is likely to be very limited. Arguments that it does not matter whether the cross-subsidies are in fact contingent on exports, but that what matters is whether *de facto* a policy generates incentives to cross-subsidize exports, must be limited to agricultural products for which export subsidy commitments have been made. Thus, this case does not open up possibilities for countries to argue for imposition of countervailing measures on the basis of alleged cross-subsidies, or to policies that generate rents on other crops or products than those that are exported by a producer (e.g., to multi-product firms). Nor can high border protection that is not associated with a formal support price system of the EC sugar type and export subsidy reduction commitments give rise to claims of illegal export subsidization.

While not relevant from a WTO-law perspective, an important aspect of this case, from an economic-development perspective, concerns the impact of the EC having to cut back exports significantly. Not only will domestic production have to fall substantially, the Panel/AB findings imply that the EC cannot re-export the amount of imported ACP sugar back on to the world market. To maintain the past levels of ACP imports, given a total export limit of 1.27 million tonnes, would require a very large cut in EC output. The needed cut is even larger if account is taken of the prospective additional sugar exports by LDCs to the EC under EBA. The 2006 CAP sugar reforms lowered intervention prices and will reduce output, and substantially diminish the rents available for ACP sugar producers. A number of ACP producers will be forced to exit sugar production because they are too high cost. This will give rise to adjustment costs in these countries. Although the CAP reform embodies significant adjustment assistance for affected EC producers, the amount allocated to ACP producers for this purpose is limited.

The fact that the EC did not 'safeguard' the ACP sugar export volume in the reform of its sugar regime is an exogenous shock for the ACP that they could not have foreseen, even though it had been clear for some time that the EC was likely to change the program in the context of its decision to negotiate reciprocal trade agreements to replace the Cotonou convention, and that there would also be some 'erosion' of rents as a result of the EBA initiative to grant duty-free, quota-free access to LDC exports of sugar as of 2009. Given that the source of the shock was the scheduling error (lack of scheduling of the ACP sugar quota), there would appear to be a case for the EC to make the ACP whole again.[17]

17 From a global-welfare perspective, the appropriate response is arguably to use non-trade instruments to provide financial assistance to the ACP, i.e. to offset the loss created by the Panel/AB decision.

References

Brownlie, Ian (2003), *Principles of Public International Law*, sixth edition, Oxford: Oxford University Press.

Fransden, Soren, Hans Jensen, Wusheng Yu, and Aage Walter-Jorgensen (2003), 'Reform of EU Sugar Policy: Price Cuts Versus Quota Reductions', *European Review of Agricultural Economics*, **30**(1): 1–26.

Gohin, Alexandre and Jean-Christophe Bureau (2006), 'Modeling the EU Sugar Supply to Assess Sectoral Policy Reforms', *European Review of Agricultural Economics*, **33**(2): 223–247.

De Gorter, Harry, David Just, and Jaclyn Kropp (2008), 'Cross-subsidization due to Infra-Marginal Support in Agriculture: A General Theory and Empirical Evidence', *American Journal of Agricultural Economics*, **90**(1): 42–54.

International Law Commission (2005), 'Eighth Report on unilateral acts of States', 57th session, A/CN.4/557.

Mitchell, Donald (2005), 'Sugar Policies: An Opportunity for Change', in M. Aksoy and J. Beghin (eds.), *Global Agricultural Trade and Developing Countries*, Washington, DC: The World Bank.

Sinclair, Ian (1995), 'Estoppel and Acquiescence', *Essays in Honour of Sir Robert Jennings*, Cambridge: Cambridge University Press.

Comment

EC – Export Subsidies on Sugar

Prepared for the ALI Project on the Case Law of the WTO

PAOLA CONCONI

European Centre for Advanced Research in Economics and Statistics (ECARES), Université Libre de Bruxelles, Avenue F.D. Roosevelt 50, CP 114, 1050 Brussels, Belgium
Email: prononi@ulb.ac.be

The dispute

In September 2004, a WTO Panel requested by Brazil, Australia, and Thailand concerning EU export subsidies for sugar found against the EU, a result upheld by the WTO Appellate Body in April 2005. In what follows, I will briefly discuss the main issues involved in this dispute and in the WTO ruling, before turning to some comments on the Hoekman–Howse paper. I will focus my attention solely on the economics part of the paper, since this is what was available when I was asked to write my comments.

The dispute concerned two main issues in the EU sugar regime: C sugar and ACP/India re-exports. Regarding the first issue, the EC sugar regime establishes production quotas for two categories of sugar, labeled 'A sugar' and 'B sugar'.[1] These are the maximum amounts of sugar that may be sold within the EC in a given year. Producers are required to export any surplus amounts, designated 'C sugar'. Domestic prices for A and B sugar are supported by an array of government measures and also receive direct export subsidies. EC sugar producers receive no additional funds from the EC if they export a large amount or no C sugar. The complainants argued that C sugar effectively benefited from a cross-subsidization from A and B quota sugar.

Regarding the issue of ACP/India re-exports, under the Sugar Protocol of the Cotonou Agreement, the EU grants preferential access to 1.3 million tonnes of

1 In what follows, I will use the present tense to describe the main features of the EU sugar regime at the time when this dispute arose. Notice, however, that some of these features have in the meantime been changed with the reform of the EU sugar policy introduced in February 2006, partly as a result of the WTO rulings. For further information, see the Commission website on sugar reform: http://ec.europa.eu/agriculture/capreform/sugar/index_en.htm.

sugar from African, Caribbean, and Pacific (ACP) countries. EU producers obtain export subsidies to re-export amounts of sugar equivalent to the imports of ACP-origin sugar. The EC has a similar sugar arrangement with India. The complainants argued that the EU should have included ACP/India re-exports in its calculation of total subsidized exports.

The WTO ruling

The Panel and AB reports found that the EU subsidies on sugar exports were beyond the level formally notified to the WTO – the so-called 'commitment schedule' – and were thus in violation of the WTO Agreement on Agriculture. The Panel finding was that both C sugar exports and ACP/India re-exports should be counted against the EU's WTO export-subsidy limits.

On the issue of C sugar, the Panel found that C-sugar exports benefited from a cross-subsidization from A and B quota sugar, effectively receiving an export subsidy. The Panel concluded that 'A, B, or C sugar are part of the same line of production and thus to the extent that the fixed costs of A, B, or C are largely paid for by the profits made on sales of A and B sugar, the EC sugar regime provides the advantage which allows EC sugar producers to produce and export C sugar at below total cost of production.'

On the ACP/India re-exports, the WTO Panel and AB reports found that the 1.6 MMT of sugar re-exports should be counted against EU's export-subsidy commitments. The EU argued that a footnote in its commitment schedule excluded this type of sugar from the scope of its subsidies-reduction requirements. The Panel dismissed this argument, holding that the footnote had no legal effect and could not enlarge or modify the EU's specified commitment levels.

Comments

The most controversial issue in this dispute, the one on which both the Hoekman–Howse paper and the other papers in the literature have mostly focused, involves the cross-subsidization of C sugar. This is also what I have decided to concentrate my comments on.

The general conclusion from the WTO Panel and AB reports is that below-cost exports of an agricultural product may, even in the absence of 'direct' export subsidies, represent proof of export subsidization if there is close linkage between these exports and domestic support programs.

To evaluate whether the argument of cross-subsidization is a valid one, we have to first be able to answer this question: 'What drives production of C sugar?' Hoekman discusses three possible answers: economies of scale, insurance motives, and the efficiency of some EU sugar producers.

The first answer is the one put forward by the WTO reports: given fixed costs, rents derived from quota production are used to cover below-cost C sales and enhance profits. As stressed by Gohin and Bureau (2006), this argument is not fully compelling. This is because 'in the beet sector, there are many opportunities to share machinery, to buy second hand equipment and to purchase contract work. Contract harvesting or planting costs are only slightly decreasing with the size of operation. The fixed component in the cost of contract work is not large enough to provide a significant incentive for producing C beet so as to spread this fixed cost on a larger output' (p. 230).

A second possible reason for the production of C sugar, which is considered by Hoekman, is that sugar producers may rationally overshoot production due to *ex ante* uncertainty about future harvests. The existence of rents associated with A and B quota sugar may strengthen the insurance motive, since producers may overshoot to make sure that they can capture the quota rents in the case of poor harvests. As stressed by Hoekman, one clear limitation with this argument is the fact that the EU sugar regime contains carry-forward provisions that allow for quota rights to be transferred to the next year, thus attenuating the incentive to overproduce.

The third possible reason for the production of non-subsidized sugar mentioned in the Hoekman–Howse paper is that some EU producers may actually be efficient and able to produce at world market prices. Indeed, some studies have argued that countries such as France, Germany, Austria, and the UK have a comparative advantage in sugar production and would be net sugar exporters even in the absence of any policy intervention (see, for example, the paper by Fransden, Jensen, Yu, and Walter-Jorgenson, 2003).

In his analysis of the possible reasons for the production of C sugar, Hoekman–Howse disregard a possible fourth explanation that has been put forward by the previous literature, i.e. expectations about future reform. The idea is that farmers may overproduce because they expect that historical reference levels would be used in future reforms. Indeed, in past reforms of various EU farm policies, quota allocations, premium rights, or compensation payments have been given on the basis of historical references. Under some expectations regarding future reforms, precautionary behavior involving the building up of potential reference levels would be rational (see Gohin and Bureau, 2006).

I find that the Hoekman–Howse paper does an extremely good job at explaining the complexities of the EU policy regime for sugar and the issues at stake in this dispute. My only criticism, if I have one, is that the paper does not go far enough in trying to answer the question of whether economies of scale are indeed the main reason behind the production of C sugar. Without a clear answer to this question, we are left with some serious doubts about the cross-subsidization argument put forward in the WTO Panel and AB reports.

A more critical assessment of the general reasoning of the panel in this dispute – that policies creating rents on a portion of a firm's output may allow for the cross-subsidization of exports – is of great importance, since this reasoning may lead to an increase in the number of future disputes. Other agricultural programs (e.g., US rice, corn, and soybeans programs) are particularly vulnerable to future dispute challenges, since Article 10.3 of the Agreement on Agriculture establishes the so-called 'reverse burden of proof'. According to this doctrine, a complainant must prove only that another country has exceeded its export commitments; the respondent must then prove that it did not grant an export subsidy on the excess exports.

References

Fransden, Soren, Hans Jensen, Wusheng Yu, and Aage Walter-Jorgensen (2003), 'Reform of EU sugar policy: price cuts versus quota reductions', *European Review of Agricultural Economics*, 30(1): 1–26.

Gohin, Alexandre and Jean-Christophe Bureau (2006), 'Modelling the EU sugar supply to assess sectoral policy reforms', *European Review of Agricultural Economics*, 33(2): 223–247.

Subsidization, price suppression, and expertise: causation and precision in Upland Cotton

ANDRE SAPIR

Professor of Economics, ECARES, Université Libre de Bruxelles; Senior Fellow at Bruegel and Research Fellow at CEPR

JOEL P. TRACHTMAN

Professor of International Law, Fletcher School of Law and Diplomacy, Tufts University

1. Introduction

The determination of causal linkage in trade-remedies cases – subsidies, dumping, and safeguards – has challenged WTO dispute settlement. There are two difficult questions in the context of determination of 'serious prejudice' under Articles 5 and 6 of the Agreement on Subsidies and Countervailing Measures (SCM Agreement). First, while theory indicates that subsidization of tradable goods may affect prices, and therefore cause 'serious prejudice' arising from 'significant price suppression', empirical validation and estimation of the magnitude of the effect is difficult. Second, the relevant treaty language does not explicitly specify the standard by which Panels must determine whether significant price suppression exists, or the standard by which Panels must determine whether this significant price suppression is caused by subsidies. These problems, combined with the institutional limitations on the ability of Panels to deal with economic evidence, make the outcome of these types of cases somewhat uncertain.

This paper analyzes the 'serious prejudice' component of the *Upland Cotton*[1] decision of the Appellate Body. It describes the reasoning of the Panel and of the Appellate Body in this phase of the case. It critiques this reasoning from the standpoint of the requirements of the SCM Agreement, from the standpoint of economic analysis, and from the standpoint of bureaucratic capacity. Section 2 describes the background and facts of the *Upland Cotton* case.

1 Appellate Body Report, *United States – Subsidies on Upland Cotton*, WTO Doc. WT/DS267/AB/R (Mar. 3, 2005) (adopted March 21, 2005) [hereinafter Appellate Body Report]. Reports of the Appellate Body and Panels are available at http://www.wto.org/english/tratop_e/dispu_e/dispu_status_e.htm.

Section 3 describes the legal reasoning of the Panel and Appellate Body on the issue of causation of serious prejudice, and, more particularly, significant price suppression. It examines the law of causation under the SCM Agreement, and critiques the *Upland Cotton* decision from the standpoint of the treaty text.

Section 4 examines the economic analysis of causation of 'serious prejudice' by virtue of significant price suppression. This is, of course, a combined legal and economic analysis, for the question of whether 'significant price suppression' exists is partially one of legal interpretation to determine the applicable measure, and partially one of assessment of facts, while the question of causation requires first a legal standard of causation, but also must utilize economic theory and methodology. Indeed, we suggest below that the question of the very existence of serious-price *suppression* includes an element of *causation.*

Section 5 examines the bureaucratic capacities of Panels, and of the WTO DSU mechanism, to carry out effective analyses of causation in this context, and recommends some alternative approaches. Section 6 briefly concludes.

2. Background

The US is the world's second-largest producer of cotton. In recent years, the US has exported an increasing proportion of its production, and is now the world's largest cotton exporter. Between 1991 and 2004, US subsidies for cotton production averaged $1.7 billion per year (Schnepf, 2005). Brazil is a major export competitor. In 2002, Brazil brought the *Upland Cotton* case to the WTO, attacking a number of components of the US cotton program.

Brazil made five major claims: (i) that US direct payments to producers are not in fact 'decoupled' income support, and therefore do not qualify for exemption from relevant reduction commitments; (ii) that payments under the 'Step-2' program to compensate US exporters and US mills for purchase of US upland cotton at high prices are illegal export subsidies and illegal import-substitution subsidies, respectively; (iii) that US export credit guarantees are prohibited export subsidies; (iv) that the four US cotton support programs that are contingent upon market price levels (loan deficiency payments, marketing-loss assistance payments, counter-cyclical payments, and Step-2 payments, collectively the 'price-based programs') caused serious prejudice by virtue of significant price suppression, and therefore must be discontinued or their effects removed; and (v) that the FSC-ETI Act of 2000 is a prohibited export subsidy. We focus on the fourth claim, and within that claim on the establishment of a causal link between a subsidy and significant price suppression.

3. The law of causation of significant price suppression and serious prejudice

3.1 *Articles 5(c) and 6.3(c) of the SCM Agreement*

Article 5 of the SCM Agreement prohibits WTO member states from causing 'serious prejudice' through the use of a subsidy. Article 5 of the SCM Agreement provides as follows:

> 5 No Member should cause, through the use of any subsidy referred to in paragraphs 1 and 2 of Article 1, adverse effects to the interests of other Members, i.e.:
>
> ...
>
> (c) serious prejudice to the interests of another Member.[2]

Article 6.3(c) of the SCM Agreement provides as follows:

> 6.3 Serious prejudice in the sense of paragraph (c) of Article 5 may arise in any case where one or several of the following apply:
>
> ...
>
> (c) the effect of the subsidy is a significant price undercutting by the subsidized product as compared with the price of a like product of another Member in the same market or significant price suppression, price depression or lost sales in the same market; ....

The reader will note that this provision does not explicitly specify that the subsidy at issue must be a sufficient (or 'but for') cause, or even a necessary cause, of serious prejudice.[3] However, if the subsidy need only be a contributory cause, or a cause that exacerbates existing serious prejudice, then an element of randomness is introduced to the regulatory structure, at least from the standpoint of the subsidizer. Under such a rule, for the subsidizer, even a subsidy with small effects, which would not by itself cause serious prejudice, may be actionable. The outcome would depend on other contributing factors.

This problem is somewhat analogous to the problem that exists in the safeguards context, with respect to causation of 'serious injury',[4] and in the anti-dumping duties context and countervailing duties context, with respect to

2 [original footnote 13 to SCM Agreement] The term 'serious prejudice to the interests of another Member' is used in this Agreement in the same sense as it is used in paragraph 1 of Article XVI of GATT 1994, and includes threat of serious prejudice.

3 An intermediate layer in the causation analysis is added by Article 6.3(c) itself. That is, Article 6.3(c) defines serious prejudice as potentially arising where 'the effect of the subsidy' is 'significant price suppression'.

4 See Appellate Body Report, *United States – Safeguard Measures on Imports of Fresh, Chilled or Frozen Lamb Meat from New Zealand and Australia*, WT/DS177/AB/R, WT/DS178/AB/R, adopted 16 May 2001, DSR 2001:IX, 4051; Appellate Body Report, *United States – Definitive Safeguard Measures on Imports of Wheat Gluten from the European Communities*, WT/DS166/AB/R, adopted 19 January 2001, DSR 2001:II, 717.

causation of 'material injury'.[5] In the safeguards and dumping contexts, the Appellate Body seems to have come to an interpretation that finds subsidies to be actionable where increased imports are merely a contributing cause, without being sufficient cause, of the requisite level of injury. However, this position is not immune from criticism, and these contexts may be different in important ways from the serious prejudice context. For example, 'serious prejudice to the interests of another Member' is different from 'serious injury'. As indicated in Article 6.3, the focus of this provision is on market effects, rather than industry effects. The criteria of Article 6.3 refer to displacement and price suppression, not to industry condition.

The Appellate Body has implicitly held in the safeguards context that if increased imports are merely a contributory cause of the 'seriously injured' state of an industry, they can be understood as satisfying the requirement for a causal link between increased imports and serious injury under Article 4.2(b) of the Safeguards Agreement.[6] However, to the extent that the existence of *serious* injury is dependent on another causal factor – say change in demand patterns – it seems inconsistent to find actionable serious injury in one context of increased imports but not in another otherwise identical context. But despite the attention to causation in Article 4.2(b) of the Safeguards Agreement, we might argue that safeguards law is responding not so much to causation as to existence of serious injury.

Can the same argument be made in the serious prejudice context under the SCM Agreement – that the subsidies law is responding not so much to causation as to existence of serious prejudice? Although it is not free from doubt, and the decision in *Upland Cotton* seems to hold otherwise, the better answer appears to be that it cannot. Serious prejudice seems to be required to be an exclusive result of the subsidies. The 'prejudice' is not injury – it is impairment of the right to a market undistorted by subsidies. Even if it is permissible that injury (or more properly, 'prejudice') that is not serious without supplementation by other causal factors can be the basis for a safeguards action, it seems impermissible that price suppression that is not significant without supplementation by other causal factors could be actionable as serious prejudice.

If this is true, then Panels are required to determine not simply whether significant price suppression exists and that subsidies are *a* cause, but that the subsidies alone have the power to, and did, cause significant price suppression: that they are *the* cause of the requisite level of price suppression. Of course, if other factors are causing price suppression at the same time, subsidies that alone could have caused

5 *U.S. – Hot Rolled Steel*, paras. 221–233 (antidumping duties); EC-DRAMS CVD panel, para. 7.404 (countervailing duties).

6 See Appellate Body Report, *United States – Safeguard Measures on Imports of Fresh, Chilled or Frozen Lamb Meat from New Zealand and Australia*, WT/DS177/AB/R, WT/DS178/AB/R, adopted 16 May 2001, DSR 2001:IX, 4051; Appellate Body Report, *United States – Definitive Safeguard Measures on Imports of Wheat Gluten from the European Communities*, WT/DS166/AB/R, adopted 19 January 2001, DSR 2001:II, 717.

significant price suppression would still be actionable. On the other hand, if supplementation by other factors is necessary to make the price suppression significant, then under this proposed analysis, no serious prejudice exists.

So the analogy to safeguards and dumping seems to fail. This leads to a conclusion that Panels faced with Article 6.3(c) cases must evaluate the extent to which the subsidies in question are sufficient, acting alone, to cause significant price suppression.

Most importantly, the plain meaning of Article 6.3(c) seems to call for a finding that the subsidy under investigation is sufficient, on its own, to cause significant price suppression. Eliding intervening language, 'the effect of the subsidy' must be 'significant price suppression'. It would require a powerfully counter-textual interpretative strategy – one that would be starkly inconsistent with the Appellate Body's consistent approach – to suggest that it would be acceptable for the subsidy under investigation merely to contribute to 'significant price suppression'. The very term 'price *suppression*' suggests that it is the action of the subject – the subsidy – that must cause it. In *Korea–Vessels*, the Panel stated that 'we view these terms [price suppression and price depression] as implicitly including a certain built-in concept of causation'.[7] The Appellate Body seems to agree in the present case.[8]

It is incumbent upon the Panel to make a finding of causation. Importantly, in contrast to the situation in connection with countervailing duties under the SCM Agreement, this is not simply a review of a national authority's finding, but *ab initio* investigation and determination.[9] So there is no possibility here for refuge in proceduralism: for making sure that the national authority considered all the required factors and prepared a reasoned and adequate report, without evaluating whether the requisite economic relationship actually exists.

While the Panel in the present case was correct to state that the SCM Agreement does not provide it with guidance as to how to proceed, this does not mean that there are no standards to apply to its determination. In fact, Article 11 of the DSU requires a complete 'objective assessment' where other parts of the WTO treaty are silent on procedure and requisite quality of determination. There may be a need, either through the work of the Appellate Body, or through the work of the political bodies of the WTO, to develop a set of administrative law-type standards for these types of determinations. There may be a further need for Panels to seek greater assistance of expert economists in their assessment of economic facts, just as they have sometimes done in connection with their assessment of scientific facts.

The implication of this understanding of the relevant portion of Article 6.3(c) is clear: a Panel must evaluate the extent to which the subsidy under investigation

7 Panel Report, *Korea – Measures Affecting Trade in Commercial Vessels*, WT/DS273/R, para. 7.534, adopted March 7, 2005.

8 Appellate Body Report, para. 433.

9 Appellate Body Report, para. 458.

caused significant price suppression. It has an obligation under Article 11 of the DSU to make an objective assessment of the facts. An objective assessment would seem to require the use of the best methodology reasonably available: the one most likely to reach an accurate judgment. It does not appear that WTO dispute settlement has yet developed a verbal measure for the standard of proof in these types of cases, such as the 'preponderance of the evidence' test generally used in US civil litigation.

3.2 *Defining the market: the a-index-based world market for upland cotton*

The first question under Article 6.3(c) is whether the effect of the subsidy was significant price suppression 'in the same market'. Brazil asserted that there were four relevant markets: (a) the world market for upland cotton; (b) the Brazilian market; (c) the United States market; and (d) 40 third-country markets where Brazil exports its cotton and where United States and Brazilian upland cotton are found.[10] The United States argued that the relevant market under Article 6.3(c) must be 'a particular domestic market of a Member', and that it cannot be a 'world market'. The Appellate Body agreed with the Panel to the effect that the scope of the market 'for determining the area of competition between two products, may depend on several factors such as the nature of the product, the homogeneity of the conditions of competition, and transport costs'.[11] The 'same market' need not be a specific geographic location. '[T]wo products may be "in the same market" even if they are not necessarily sold in the same place and at the same time, as long as they are engaged in actual or potential competition.'[12] The Appellate Body agreed with the Panel that this market could well be a 'world market'. Therefore, Article 6.3(c) does not exclude the possibility of the 'same market' being the 'world market'.

The US argued that the Panel's finding that a world market for upland cotton exists is inconsistent with the Panel's finding that the US price for upland cotton is different from the world price.[13] The Panel found that a world market exists, and is reflected in the A-Index.[14] The Appellate Body saw no reason to disturb this

10 Panel Report, para. 7.1230.

11 Appellate Body Report, para. 408 (citation omitted).

12 Ibid., para. 413.

13 Ibid., para. 411.

14 Panel Report, paras. 7.1260–7.1274. The Panel's 'four main reasons' were: prices of Brazilian and United States upland cotton are 'constituent elements' of the A-Index; 'key market participants' perceive the A-Index as reflecting the world-market price for upland cotton; the International Cotton Advisory Council treats the A-Index in a similar manner; and the Economic Research Service of the United States Department of Agriculture (the 'USDA') has itself referred to the A-Index as the world price. The 'A-Index' 'is a composite of an average of the five lowest price quotes from a selection of the principal upland cottons traded in the world market obtained by Cotlook, a private UK-based organization.' (Panel Report, para. 7.1264.)

finding.[15] The Appellate Body noted that the Panel concluded, as a matter of fact, that Brazilian and US upland cotton compete in the world market for upland cotton. The Appellate Body therefore concluded that the Panel did not err with respect to whether Brazilian and US upland cotton were 'in the same market'.[16]

The Panel used the A-Index as the world price, as the basis for its analysis of whether price suppression in the 'same market' existed. Here, the question before the Appellate Body was whether it was sufficient for the Panel to examine the world price, or whether it was required to analyze the price of Brazilian upland cotton in the world market.[17] The Panel had found that prices for upland cotton throughout the world are largely determined by the A-Index price, and therefore found that the A-Index adequately reflected world-market prices for upland cotton.[18] The Appellate Body agreed that it was unnecessary for the Panel to analyze actual sales prices of Brazilian upland cotton.[19]

Thus, the core question was whether the US subsidies caused significant price suppression in the A-Index.

3.3 Price suppression and causation

As suggested by the Panel in *Korea–Commercial Vessels*, price 'suppression' cannot exist separately from the causal agent being examined: the US subsidies. So to say, as Article 6.3(c) does, that the 'effect of the subsidy' must be 'significant price suppression' is to say that only reductions (or non-increases) in the price caused by the subsidy are to be considered. Reductions (or non-increases) resulting from other factors are not included in 'price suppression'.

However, the Panel in the present case made a separate analysis of the existence of price suppression, prior to its analysis of causation, and prior to its effort to address separate causes. In effect, the Panel engaged in a bifurcated analysis, separating price suppression from causation, as opposed to a unitary analysis of whether the US subsidies caused significant price suppression.[20] The Panel therefore implicitly understood 'price suppression' to mean 'price decline', excluding the causal criterion from its determination.[21]

The US complained about the Panel's order of analysis, but the Appellate Body found no legal error.[22] The Appellate Body pointed out that the serious-prejudice provisions of the SCM Agreement do not provide as much guidance on separating out causes as the trade-remedy provisions of the SCM Agreement.[23] The Appellate

15 Appellate Body Report, para. 411.
16 Ibid., para. 414.
17 Ibid., para. 416.
18 Panel Report, para. 7.1313.
19 Appellate Body Report, para. 417.
20 For a description of the difference, see Cass and Knoll, 1997.
21 The Appellate Body criticized the Panel's failure to separate fully price suppression from price decline. Appellate Body Report, para. 424.
22 Appellate Body Report, para. 431.
23 Appellate Body Report, para. 436.

Body pointed out that the definition of 'price suppression' implies a 'but for' or counterfactual analysis – but for the challenged subsidies, would price suppression have occurred? Therefore, according to the Appellate Body, some of the same factors that go into determination of price suppression go into determination of effects.[24]

In order to determine 'price suppression', the Panel looked at three considerations: (i) the relative magnitude of US production and exports in the world market, (ii) general price trends in the world market as revealed by the A-Index, and (iii) the nature of the subsidies at issue, and, in particular, whether or not the nature of these subsidies is such as to have discernible price-suppression effects.[25]

The Panel failed to contextualize its reference to the relative magnitude of US production and exports. Of course, the larger the role of the US in world markets, the greater the *possibility* that proportional changes in US supply would affect world prices. However, the Panel did not determine by how much the US subsidies resulted in increased production. So, if, as the US argued, the subsidies had little effect on production, they would have little effect on world prices, despite their size.

In fact, the Panel seemed to compare US production to Brazilian production.[26] But Brazilian production seems irrelevant: once the Panel had determined that the A-Index was the relevant 'price' for purposes of identification of suppression, the magnitude of Brazilian production became irrelevant to the determination of suppression and causation.

Similarly, it is hard to see how 'general price trends' tell us anything about 'significant price suppression' and its causation by a subsidy. Nor is it probative that US prices tracked world-market prices. As the Panel in *Korea–Commercial Vessels* stated, 'the existence of a flat or declining price trend, on its own, would not be a sufficient basis on which to conclude that prices were "suppressed" or "depressed". For such a conclusion to be reached, the causes of these observed trends would need to be examined'. That Panel concluded that price suppression and price depression 'concerns what the price movements for the relevant ships would have been in the absence of (i.e., "but for") the subsidies at issue.'[27] That Panel's perspective is worth quoting at length:

> the question to be answered in respect of the affirmative link between subsidies and prices is, in the case of alleged price depression, whether in the absence of the subsidies prices for ships would not have declined, or would have declined by less than was in fact the case. For price suppression, the question would be whether, in the absence of the subsidies, ship prices would have increased, or would have increased by more than was in fact the case. Such a framework implies also

24 Ibid., para. 433.
25 Panel Report, para. 7.1280.
26 Panel Report, para. 7.1284.
27 *Korea – Commercial Vessels*, supra note 7, at para. 7.537.

> analyzing the various factors contributing to the particular market situation forming the subject of the complaint, i.e., supply and demand factors, production costs, relative efficiency, etc.[28]

However, the Panel in *Upland Cotton* found an overall drop in prices 'relevant' but not 'conclusive'.[29] The Appellate Body agreed.

> [I]n our view, one would normally expect a discernible correlation between significantly suppressed prices and the challenged subsidies if the effect of these subsidies is significant price suppression. Accordingly, this is an important factor in any analysis of whether the effect of a subsidy is significant price suppression within the meaning of Article 6.3(c). However, we recognize that mere correlation between payment of subsidies and significantly suppressed prices would be insufficient, without more, to prove that the effect of the subsidies is significant price suppression.[30]

But both the Panel and the Appellate Body seem to confuse price suppression with price reduction. If subsidization caused a rise in prices to be less dramatic than it otherwise would be, this should constitute price suppression. Similarly, it is entirely possible for prices to decline for other reasons without any influence by a subsidy. So the evidence of a decline in prices is not only not conclusive, it is not relevant. On the other hand, it would be relevant if changes in the magnitude of subsidies were correlated with changes in the magnitude of price change, and if it could be shown to what extent causation ran from magnitude of subsidies to magnitude of price change, rather than vice-versa, in the context of price-based subsidies.

The Panel had found that 'except for a short period in MY 2000, the adjusted world price was *below* the marketing loan rate throughout virtually *the whole period from* MY 1999 to 2002.[31] This fact would suggest that farmers might be induced to plant on the basis of a marketing loan rate above the world price. The US argued that the Panel failed to address economic decisions of US upland cotton farmers at the time of planting. Specifically, the US argued that upland cotton prices would have supported a planting decision at the relevant times without the influence of the subsidies. The US presented evidence that at each of the times when farmers were making planting decisions, the expected world price realized at harvest was always higher than the marketing loan rate, meaning that the marketing loan rate-based subsidy would not have affected farmers' decisions, and therefore would not have affected quantities produced. However, the Appellate Body accepted the Panel's view that farmers might be induced to plant by the insulation from price declines provided by the marketing loan rate-subsidy

28 Ibid., para. 7.615.
29 Panel Report, para. 7.1288.
30 Appellate Body Report, para. 451.
31 Panel Report, para. 7.1294 (original emphasis).

program.[32] The Appellate Body determined that these are factual matters that the Appellate Body could not review.[33]

The US also presented data showing that US cotton-planted acreage responded to expected market prices, that US farmers changed acreage commensurately with changes made by cotton farmers in the rest of the world, and that the US share of world cotton production remained stable, demonstrating that US farmers respond to the same market signals as cotton farmers elsewhere. The Appellate Body simply noted that the Panel considered this data.[34]

Brazil submitted a report by Dr Daniel Sumner, and Sumner participated in several Panel meetings. Based on his modeling, Sumner found that but for the subject subsidies, the quantity of US production of upland cotton would have been an average of 28.7 % lower than actual, and US exports would have been 41.2 % lower than actual, from 1999 to 2002. He also found that but for the US subsidies, the A-Index would have been 12.6 % higher during the same period.[35] The US expressed several concerns regarding the model used by Sumner. The model itself was owned and operated by FAPRI, the Food and Agricultural Policy Research Institute, and was not available to Brazil, the US, or the Panel. However, the US argued and presented evidence to the effect that Dr Sumner had made inappropriate assumptions and otherwise used the model in ways that were improper. For example, the US argued that FAPRI and the US Department of Agriculture both found that the impact of decoupled payments on acreage under cultivation was negligible, while 'Dr Sumner's model produces results suggesting cotton acreage impacts as high as 15.9 % – that is, more than 50 times larger than what the FAPRI model would indicate.'[36]

It is fair to say that the Panel did not, in its report, attempt to deal with the concerns expressed by the US regarding the model presented by Brazil. Delphically, the Panel declared that:

> We have not relied upon the quantitative results of the modeling exercise – in terms of estimating any numerical value for the effects of the United States subsidies, nor, indirectly, in our examination of the causal link required under Articles 5 and 6.3 of the *SCM Agreement*.[37]
>
> [W]e have taken the analysis in question into account where relevant to our analysis of the existence and nature of the subsidies in question, and their effects,

32 Appellate Body Report, para. 445.
33 Appellate Body Report, para. 441.
34 Ibid., para. 446.
35 Panel Report, para. 7.1202.
36 *United States – Subsidies on Upland Cotton* (WT/DS267), Comments of the United States of America on Comments by Brazil on U.S. Comments Concerning Brazil's Econometric Model January 28, 2004, p. 2, available at http://www.ustr.gov/assets/Trade_Agreements/Monitoring_Enforcement/Dispute_Settlement/WTO/Dispute_Settlement_Listings/asset_upload_file156_5598.pdf.
37 Panel Report, para. 7.1205.

under the relevant provisions of the *SCM Agreement*, and have attributed to them the evidentiary weight we deemed appropriate.[38]

How is it possible to take this information into account, without saying why or where, and still perform an 'objective assessment' of the facts in accordance with Article 11 of the DSU? How is it possible to perform an objective assessment of the facts without engaging with the debate about the appropriate assumptions and parameters of these models? In this context, an objective assessment of the facts must use the best analytical tools available, which means using appropriately configured models. It is incumbent upon a Panel in this context therefore to evaluate the configuration of a model, and to use that model to determine causation of significant price suppression.

The Appellate Body has found a violation of Article 11 of the DSU when Panels have failed to ensure that a domestic competent authority evaluated all relevant economic factors and that the authority's explanation of its determination is reasoned and adequate.[39] It seems that, *a fortiori*, where a panel has an obligation itself to evaluate evidence, that this evaluation must be 'reasoned and adequate'.

The Panel also found that other studies prepared by non-governmental and governmental organizations, focusing on related issues but not addressing the specific legal issues salient to the Panel's work, and using assumptions that were not endorsed by the Panel, could only be used in the same way: 'we have taken the analyses in question into account where relevant to our analysis of the existence and nature of the subsidies, and their effects'.[40]

The Panel focused on price-contingent subsidies,[41] suggesting that the nature of these subsidies – their structure, design, and operation – is relevant to their effects.[42] The distinction between price-contingent and non-price-contingent subsidies was critical to the Panel's analysis of causal nexus.

- With respect to the marketing loan program, pursuant to which repayment was reduced by reference to declines in world market prices, the Panel concluded: 'We have no doubt that the payments stimulate production and exports and result in lower world market prices than would prevail in their absence.'[43] The Panel

38 Panel Report, para. 7.1209.

39 Appellate Body Report, *United States – Safeguard Measures on Imports of Fresh, Chilled or Frozen Lamb Meat from New Zealand and Australia*, WT/DS177/AB/R, WT/DS178/AB/R, adopted 16 May 2001. National authorities making similar determinations are held to a higher standard of explanation. Recall that Article 4.2(c) of the Safeguards Agreement requires a national agency making injury determinations to publish a 'detailed analysis of the case under investigation as well as a demonstration of the relevance of the factors examined'. Of course, there is no similar requirement applicable to Panels under Article 6.3 of the SCM Agreement. Yet the contexts seem similar, and presumably the requirement of the Safeguards Agreement can provide context by which to interpret the requirements of DSU Article 11.

40 Panel Report, para. 7.1215.

41 The Panel declined to aggregate the non-price-contingent subsidies with the price-contingent subsidies, because they are 'of a different nature and effect'. Panel Report, para. 7.1307.

42 Panel Report, para. 7.1289.

43 Ibid., para. 7.1291.

especially emphasized the structure of the US subsidy, linking payments to the A-Index. However, the fact that US subsidies are determined by reference to the A-Index does not by itself prove that these subsidies affected the A-Index. The Panel cited reports, provided by Brazil, of US Department of Agriculture economists to the effect that the structure, design, and operation of the program stimulated production and exports, and resulted in lower world-market prices than would prevail otherwise.[44] However, the Panel did not explain the basis for its judgment that the evidence presented by Brazil was more persuasive than the contrary evidence presented by the US. As noted above, in these cases, Panels are required to comply with the DSU Article 11 requirement of an 'objective assessment of the facts'. The Panel noted that the payments were 'very large'.[45] However, very large payments do not necessarily affect volume of production, or price.

- The Panel found that the user marketing (Step 2) payments contributed to artificially higher prices in the US.[46] The Panel inferred that these higher prices resulted in greater volumes of production that in turn had an effect on price.[47] However, again, this syllogism, and the magnitude of the effect, is dependent on a number of market conditions. While the Panel referred to information on the record about the *amount of the subsidies*, it made no attempt to quantify the effect on exports and world market prices. Again, the Panel merely asserted that the subsidies are 'a very large amount'.[48]
- The Panel engaged in a similar approach with respect to other price-linked payments. With respect to counter-cyclical payments (CCPs), the Panel stated that '[w]e have confirmed a strong positive relationship between upland cotton (base acre) producers receiving annual payments and upland cotton production'.[49] The portion of the Panel Report cited for this, Section VII:D, deals with the availability of the Peace Clause, and contains no analytical treatment of this issue. The availability of the Peace Clause is not dependent on the effects on production of the relevant measures.
- The Panel concluded as to the results of these three types of price-contingent subsidies as follows: 'In the particular facts and circumstances of this dispute, we consider that these three subsidies therefore [referring to price contingency] have a nexus with the subsidized product and the single effects-related variable – world price – that we are called upon to examine in our price suppression analysis under Article 6.3(c). The effects of these three price-contingent subsidies are, in our view, manifest in the movements in upland cotton prices in the same world market during the reference period.'[50]

44 Ibid., para. 7.1295.
45 Ibid., para. 7.1297.
46 Ibid., para. 7.1298.
47 Ibid., para. 7.1299.
48 Ibid., para. 7.1300.
49 Ibid., para. 7.1302, citing Section VII:D of the Panel Report.
50 Ibid., para. 7.1303.

The Appellate Body concurred: 'the Panel found that the price-contingent subsidies stimulated United States production and exports of upland cotton and thereby lowered United States upland cotton prices. This seems to us to support the Panel's conclusion that the effect of the price-contingent subsidies is significant price suppression.'[51] It should be noted that the Panel really made no factual findings to the effect that the US subsidies reduced, or prevented an increase in, US upland cotton prices.

The Panel declined to develop a definition of the term 'significant',[52] but determined that it was only required to 'filter out effects of insignificant degree or magnitude'. It might have drawn guidance on the ultimate purpose of examining whether 'significant price suppression' exists: a determination of 'serious prejudice'. It seems strange to suggest that 'significant' in this context means 'not insignificant', when the phenomenon examined must be constitutive of 'serious prejudice'. In addition, some would argue that the positive term 'significant' requires something more than effects that are 'not insignificant'.[53]

The Panel found that the step from 'significant price suppression' to 'serious prejudice' required no further analysis – there is no requirement for a separate finding of 'serious prejudice' once 'significant price suppression' is found.[54] If this is correct, then, as suggested above, the 'serious-prejudice' context should have influenced the understanding of the word 'significant' in this context. The Oxford English Dictionary defines 'serious' (in the relevant context) as '[w]eighty, important, grave; (of quantity or degree) considerable, not trifling'. Only the last of these terms is consistent with the Panel's understanding of 'significant' as 'not insignificant'. Furthermore, in determining that what it found to be 'significant price suppression' also constituted 'serious prejudice', the Panel traveled in the other direction: it determined that its finding that the price suppression was 'significant' was sufficient to constitute a finding that the prejudice was 'serious'.[55] By adopting a low threshold for 'significant' price suppression, and engaging in no further analysis to find 'serious' prejudice, the Panel magically transformed 'not insignificant' to 'serious'. This style of argument allowed the Panel to make no real findings of either causation or magnitude of effects.

While the Panel found that the question of 'significant price suppression' is one of degree of suppression,[56] it merely referred to (i) the magnitude of US production and exports, (ii) overall price trends, (iii) the market-price contingent,

51 Appellate Body Report, para. 450, citing Panel Report, paras. 7.1291, 7.1295–7.1296, 7.1299, and 7.1308–7.1311.

52 Following *Indonesia – Autos*, para. 14.254. *The New Shorter Oxford English Dictionary*, L. Brown (ed.) (Clarendon Press, 1993), defines 'significant' as: 'important, notable; consequential'.

53 In footnote 18 of the SCM Agreement, the treaty refers to effects that are 'not insignificant'. An interpretation based on *effet utile* would give effect to the difference between a reference to 'significant' and a reference to 'not insignificant'.

54 Panel Report, paras. 7.1376; 7.1389.

55 Ibid., paras. 7.1393–7.1394.

56 Ibid., para. 7.1328.

countercyclical nature of the US programs, and (iv) the 'order of magnitude' of the subsidies. On this basis – without ever looking at evidence of degree of price suppression – the Panel concluded that 'we are certainly not, by any means, looking at an insignificant or unimportant world price phenomenon'.[57] This begs the question.

Of course, the central question here is to what extent was the A-Index price suppressed by US subsidies (the 'effect of a subsidy' – not the subsidized exports). The Panel examined the existence of 'significant price suppression' prior to its examination of causation by challenged subsidies. This order of analysis seems comparable to the so-called 'bifurcated test' applied by some commissioners of the US International Trade Commission in injury determinations in connection with countervailing duty cases and dumping cases (see Sykes, 1996).[58] Under the bifurcated test, the ITC first determines whether the requisite material injury exists, and second examines the contribution of the dumped imports to the injury. The bifurcated test allows a finding of causation where other causes may play an important contributory role.

The Panel found a causal link between the price-contingent subsidies and the significant price suppression, for four reasons:[59]

1. The US exerts a substantial proportionate influence in the world upland cotton market. The Appellate Body stated that 'if the price-contingent subsidies increased United States production and exports or decreased prices for United States upland cotton, then the fact that United States production and exports of upland cotton significantly influenced world market prices would make it more likely that the effect of the price-contingent subsidies is significant price suppression. Accordingly, this fact seems to support the Panel's conclusion, when read in conjunction with its other findings.'[60] This seems a rather restrained endorsement.
2. The price-contingent subsidies were directly linked to world prices for upland cotton, thereby insulating US producers from low prices. The Panel found that Step 2 payments stimulated demand for US upland cotton by eliminating any positive difference between US internal prices and international prices, resulting in lower world-market prices than would prevail in their absence. The market loss-assistance payments and counter-cyclical payments were made in response to low prices for upland cotton, and stimulated US production by reducing risk associated with price variability. For the Appellate Body, this supported the Panel's conclusion that the effect of price-contingent subsidies is significant price suppression.[61]

57 Ibid., para. 7.1332.

58 There has been some recent criticism of the ITC approach to injury determination. See Bratsk Aluminium Smelter v. US, 444 F.3d 1369 (Fed. Cir. 2006).

59 Panel Report, paras. 7.1347–7.1356.

60 Appellate Body Report, para. 449.

61 Ibid., para. 450, citing Panel Report, paras. 7.1291, 7.1295–7.1296, 7.1299, and 7.1308–7.1311.

3. There is a discernible temporal coincidence of suppressed world market prices and the price-contingent US subsidies. The Appellate Body recognized that temporal correlation would be insufficient without more.[62]
4. US upland cotton producers would not have been economically capable of remaining in the production of upland cotton but for the subsidies at issue, *and* the effect of these subsidies was to allow US producers to sell upland cotton at a price lower than would otherwise have been necessary to cover their total costs.[63] While the Appellate Body accepted the US argument that a focus on variable costs may be more relevant than a focus on total costs, it did not find error.[64]

This causal link is itself rather circumstantial, and weak. Note that the burden of proof regarding the causal link is for the complainant to meet. Moreover, the Panel did not attempt to quantify the impact of the US subsidies on quantity produced or price, and so had no way of knowing whether the US subsidies caused 'significant price suppression'. There also seems little way to know the relative significance of the price suppression so caused. The Panel did not quantify subsidies, except to find that they were 'very large'. This goes to causation, especially as the US claimed that some of the expenditures went to farmers who did not raise upland cotton. It also goes to burden of proof – what is the standard of permissible inference from observations such as 'very large amounts'?

The Appellate Body found no requirement for quantification of the subsidy.[65] This seems strange, as it is difficult to see how a Panel could determine causation of 'significant price suppression' by the subsidy without knowing the magnitude of the subsidy. The Appellate Body did find that '[i]n the present case, the Panel could have been more explicit and specified what it meant by "very large amounts", beyond including cross-references to its earlier findings regarding certain subsidies. Nevertheless, the information before the Panel clearly supports the Panel's general statements regarding the magnitude of the price-contingent subsidies.'[66]

In *Korea–Commercial Vessels*, Korea argued that the following elements must be followed in order to analyze causation in this context:

> First, the subsidy must be quantified with respect to each subsidized producer. Second, the effect of the subsidy on the prices of the subsidized shipbuilder ('the subsidy effect margin') must be quantified, by estimating the non-subsidized cost of the product and comparing this with the producer's price for the product. Third, a 'price suppression and depression margin' must be quantified, i.e., the margin by which the prices of the complaining Member's like product have been suppressed or depressed. In this step, Korea argues, the effects of all other factors

62 Ibid., para. 451.
63 Appellate Body Report, para. 420.
64 Ibid., para. 453.
65 Ibid., para. 462.
66 Ibid., para. 468 (citations omitted).

on prices (including cost reductions, competition from other, non-subsidized, sources, etc.) also must be identified and eliminated.[67]

While this method of analysis seems appealing, albeit difficult to implement, neither the Panel nor the Appellate Body in the present case required anything approaching this level of social scientific precision.

Having found this rather speculative causal link, the Panel found that it was not broken by five alternative causes: (i) weakness in world demand for cotton due to competing low-priced synthetics, and weak world economic growth; (ii) burgeoning US textile imports, causing greater US exports of cotton; (iii) the tendency of a strong US dollar to have an inverse effect on the world price of cotton; (iv) Chinese subsidized cotton and the release of millions of bales of government stocks; and (v) upland cotton planting decisions driven by other factors such as the effect of technology on production, relative movement of upland cotton prices versus competing crops, and expected prices for the upcoming crop year.[68]

As to the first factor, the Panel asserted that increased US production belied the US argument that competition from synthetics was causing reductions in cotton prices. Yet, depending on existing capacity and the structure of variable costs compared to fixed costs, it is entirely plausible that the price effects observed were at least somewhat, or principally, due to low-priced synthetics, rather than the US subsidies supporting continued production.

As to the second factor, the Panel did not understand that imports of textiles and apparel to the US might reduce domestic demand for US-produced cotton, causing producers to seek export markets. Thus, US exports of cotton might rise without having a significant price effect, because the exports of cotton are replacing cotton used abroad in producing greater amounts of textiles and clothing for export to the US.

With respect to the third factor – the strong US dollar – the Panel declined to examine the contribution of this factor to price suppression of cotton, but merely asserted, seemingly irrelevantly, that the value of the dollar did not affect producer decisions. Yet the Panel's responsibility here was to provide an objective assessment of the facts. This would require the Panel to examine the degree to which a strong US dollar caused price suppression, in order to know whether the US subsidies were the cause of significant price suppression. Otherwise, it is not an 'assessment' of the facts, but a guess at the facts.

As to Chinese subsidies and exports, the Panel conceded that this would exert a downward pressure on prices, but stated that the additional Chinese supply was smaller than US exports, and that US production and exports either continued and/or increased. However, without examining the price effects of the Chinese cotton, it is not possible to know whether price-suppression effects observed were caused by US subsidies.

67 *Korea – Commercial Vessels*, Panel Report, supra note 7, para. 7.608.
68 Panel Report, paras. 7.1357–7.1363; Appellate Body Report, para. 421.

Finally, the US argued that technological and other price factors had more of an effect on US production decisions than its subsidies. The Panel concluded that 'United States producers continued to grow upland cotton due to United States subsidies rather than market prices or expected market revenue.'[69] But it was incumbent on the Panel to assess the relative magnitude of these effects in order to know whether the US subsidies caused significant price suppression.

Without evaluating the contribution to price suppression of these other causes, the Panel had no way of knowing the actual contribution of US subsidies to price suppression, or whether that contribution was 'significant'. The Panel begged the question of whether these other alternative causes of price suppression contributed enough to make any price suppression caused by the US subsidies not 'significant'.

The Appellate Body agreed with the Panel that it is necessary to ensure that the effects of other factors in prices are not improperly attributed to the challenged subsidies.[70] The Appellate Body compared the Panel's approach with respect to causation and non-attribution to the Appellate Body's jurisprudence under the Agreement on Safeguards.[71] 'Although the Panel found that some of them had price-suppressive effects, it did not attribute those effects to the United States's price-contingent subsidies.' But the Appellate Body's position on non-attribution in the safeguards setting has always been incoherent: the Appellate Body believes that separation is required, but cannot articulate a purpose for separation given that (in its view) there is no need to determine that the increased imports (in that context) are sufficient on their own to cause serious injury.

The Appellate Body quoted the Panel with respect to these other causal factors:

> Although some of these factors may have contributed to lower, and even suppressed, world upland cotton prices during MY 1999–2002, they do not attenuate the genuine and substantial causal link that we have found between the United States mandatory price-contingent subsidies at issue and the significant price suppression. Nor do they reduce the effect of the mandatory price-contingent subsidies to a level which cannot be considered 'significant'.[72]

The Appellate Body concluded: 'In sum, the Panel Report shows that it examined the other factors raised by the United States. Although the Panel found that some of them had price-suppressive effects, it did not attribute those effects to the United States' price-contingent subsidies.' Thus, the Appellate Body seemed to signal that it would follow its nonattribution approach developed in connection with safeguards and dumping.

69 Panel Report, para. 7.1362.
70 Appellate Body Report, para. 437 (citation omitted).
71 Ibid., para. 438.
72 Appellate Body Report, para. 457, quoting Panel Report, para. 7.1363

In the end, the Appellate Body was dissatisfied with the Panel's report with respect to these matters.

> Overall, the Panel evidently conducted an extensive analysis, but we believe that, in its reasoning, the Panel could have provided a more detailed explanation of its analysis of the complex facts and economic arguments arising in this dispute. The Panel could have done so in order to demonstrate precisely how it evaluated the different factors bearing on the relationship between the price-contingent subsidies and significant price suppression. Nevertheless, in the light of the Panel's examination of the relevant evidence, coupled with its legal reasoning, we find no legal error in the Panel's causation analysis.[73]

The Appellate Body seemed rather mechanically textualist in requiring of the Panel only what Art. 6.3(c) explicitly specifies, and little more. But the requirement to determine causation, combined with the DSU Article 11 requirement of an 'objective assessment', serves as a general 'requirement' that a reasonable determination be made, rather than that only the analysis specifically called for be done.

4. The economic analysis of causation of serious-prejudice and significant price suppression

So far there have been three serious-prejudice WTO disputes: *Indonesia–Autos*, *US–Upland Cotton*, and *Korea–Vessels*. In all three cases, the requesting parties based their claims at least partly on SCM Article 6.3(c), but *US–Upland Cotton* is the first and, currently, only serious-prejudice dispute where a party relied on economic modeling in presenting its claims and arguments.

One reason for the relatively small number of serious-prejudice cases is the difficulty to establish causation between subsidy and serious prejudice. In addition, putting forward a hypothesis of causation naturally entails the risk of Type I errors (rejecting the hypothesis when it is actually true) and Type II errors (accepting the hypothesis when it is actually false) since, as Robert Hudec had argued in the context of subsidies disputes: 'In the hands of a clever advocate, there is always some alternative explanation for events that have occurred, and even more ways to explain events that haven't' (Hudec, 1998). In other words, there are likely to be instances where governments financing subsidies that actually cause serious prejudice are found 'not guilty' and even more instances where governments financing subsidies that do not actually cause serious prejudice are found 'guilty'.

A legitimate question therefore is whether the risk of Type I or Type II errors in serious-prejudice disputes is such that the entire exercise is called into question. More generally, the question arises as to whether one can attach sufficient confidence in the determination of the effects of the domestic subsidies to actually trust the WTO domestic-subsidy regime.

73 Ibid., para. 458.

Steinberg and Josling recognize that the need to show causation for a successful case based on Article 6.3 SCM poses a challenge (Steinberg and Josling, 2003). In their view, however, this challenge can be surmounted by using two tools of economic analysis: regression analysis on subsidy and trade data, and simulation of the effect of subsidies by models. For Steinberg and Josling, these tools 'offer the only effective means of distilling whether subsidies are in fact causing "serious prejudice". Without using these techniques, the problem of hidden or spurious correlations [between subsidy and displacement (in Art 6.3(a) and (b) cases) or price (in Art 6.3(c) cases)] would render Article 6.3 virtually useless.'

Regression analysis is a statistical tool for the investigation of relationships between variables. It is the most common method used to estimate econometric models, which are used by economists to establish relationships between economic variables. The fact that econometric models are estimated with statistical methods implies that they can be subjected to various statistical tests to evaluate their accuracy and robustness.

Estimating econometric models can be of great use in trade-remedy investigations to determine whether subsidized imports (in countervailing duty cases), dumped imports (anti-dumping cases), or simply imports (in safeguard cases) have caused injury to domestic industry. A particular regression technique actually used in such investigations is the Granger-causality analysis, which tests whether one variable consistently precedes another.

In general, regression analysis requires many observations of the dependent and independent variables to be sufficiently statistically reliable. Granger-causality is even more demanding in terms of its data requirements. In practice, this means that establishing causality based on econometric estimation might be feasible in trade-remedy investigations where both the dependent (industry performance) and the independent variable (imports) can be observed on a quarterly basis or even more frequently. This is definitely not the case in disputes about actionable subsidies because here the independent variable is not subsidized imports but the subsidy itself, which normally is only observed on a yearly basis. It is not surprising, therefore, that parties have not submitted evidence based on regression analysis in any of the three serious prejudice disputes decided to date.

Leaving aside direct estimation, probably the best alternative to determine causation is the counter-factual or 'but for' approach. The basic idea of the counter-factual approach to causation is that a causal claim of the form 'event *c* caused event *e*' can be explained in terms of counter-factual conditionals of the form 'if *c* had not occurred, *e* would not have occurred'. The intuition that supports the counter-factual approach is the close association that is made between a cause of an event and a *sine qua non* condition of its occurrence. Here a cause is the condition 'but for' which the effect would not have occurred.

In this approach, the central problem is one of constructing the best possible counter-factual state of the world or 'anti-monde', i.e. what today's world would have looked like 'if *c* had not occurred'. Once the counter-factual has been constructed, it is then possible to compare it with the actual world to arrive at a view as to whether 'event *c* caused event *e*'.

In economics, there are essentially two ways to construct the 'anti-monde'. One is simply to use trend analysis and assume that today's world would have been a continuation of yesterday's world along past trends. The other is to use an empirical simulation model.

Broadly, there are two classes of empirical economic models: estimated econometric models and calibrated models. Like all models, they are based on assumptions. There is, however, a major difference between the two classes. Econometric models use statistical techniques to test their validity, whereas calibration models take them for granted, although some of the assumptions may in fact be based on econometric estimations. Calibration models are always calibrated so as to replicate the observed data. Hence, although they may incorporate some parameters that are econometrically estimated, other parameters are simply chosen to ensure that the model assumptions and the observed data are mutually consistent. These choices are not amenable to statistical tests. By contrast, econometric models do not perfectly replicate the observed data. They only provide a 'best fit' between the model assumptions and the observed data, but they allow testing the statistical validity of the assumptions.

In *US–Upland Cotton*, the Panel primarily used trend analysis to determine the existence of a causal link between some of the challenged US subsidies and the significant price suppression in the world cotton market. The Panel observed that the 'A-Index in MY 1999–MY 2002 was, on average, 29.5 per cent below its 1980–1998 average',[74] and implicitly assumed that the A-index of the world cotton price during the reference period 1999–2002 would have remained at the same level as during the period 1980–1998 in the absence of US subsidies. The difference between the counter-factual price of 73.54 and the observed price of 51.88 US-cents/lb, a fall of 29.5 %, was ascribed to the subsidies.

It is surprising that the Panel report contains no analysis of the behavior of the A-index during the period 1980–1998 other than the average level. Even a cursory examination would have shown that the A-index fluctuated substantially during the period and that the values observed during the period 1999–2002 were in fact not exceptional. The decline in the A-index started well before 1999: it went down from a peak of about 95 US-cents/lb in 1994/1995 to about 70 in 1998/1999 and to a trough of 45 in 2001/2002. A similar decline had occurred earlier. For instance, the A-index fell from a peak of about 90 US-cents/lb in 1979/1980 to a trough of about 50 in 1985/1986. There was no reason, therefore, to assume that the proper counter-factual for the period 1999–2002 was the average value of the period 1980–1998. The Appellate Body did not comment on this matter.

74 The original footnote 1463 reads: 'The A-Index averaged 73.54 and 51.88 US-cents/lb in the periods of MY 1980–1998 and MY 1999–2002, respectively. Exhibit BRA-209.' Panel Report, para. 7.1351.

As already noted, the Panel also 'took account' of the results of a simulation of an 'econometric model' submitted by Brazil in support of its claim of a causal link between US subsidies and serious prejudice in the form of price suppression. The simulation was performed by an external expert, Dr Daniel Sumner, using an adapted version of the Food and Agricultural Policy Research Institute (FAPRI) model. The simulation showed that 'but for' US-cotton subsidy programs providing direct price support, US exports would have declined on average by 41.2% and world cotton prices would have been on average 12.6% higher during the period 1999–2002. The United States objected to the changes made by Sumner to the FAPRI model, arguing that Sumner's adaptations and modifications made it different from the FAPRI system, introduced some errors, and exaggerated the results. The US argued that differences in the methodology for estimating US crop acreage exaggerated the US production response, and the choice of a more inelastic foreign-demand estimate exaggerated the world price change.

In the end, the Panel decided to take the 'analyses in question into account where relevant to [its] analysis of the existence and nature of subsidies, and their effects'.[75] However, the Panel did not rely 'upon the quantitative results of the modeling exercise – in terms of estimating the numerical value for the effects of the United States subsidies, nor indirectly, in [the] examination of the causal link'.[76] The Panel was willing to grant that the 'outcomes of the simulations are consistent with the general proposition that subsidies bestowed by Member governments have the potential to distort production and trade and the elimination of subsidies would tend to reduce "artificial" incentives for production in the subsidizing Member', but was not willing to go beyond that.[77]

This conclusion by the Panel seems to reveal an important impediment to the use of economic models in dispute-settlement cases pointed out by the WTO Secretariat: 'When disagreements about a model turn on many technical issues, and when economists themselves give conflicting views about the issues, a Panel may feel that it is not in a position to resolve those questions ... More fundamentally, a Panel may conclude that economic analysis is not necessary for the resolution of the dispute before it. In this respect, the *US–Upland Cotton* Panel found that the serious-prejudice provisions do not require a precise quantification' (WTO Secretariat, 2005).

The Panel in *US–Upland Cotton* did not, therefore, follow the reasoning of Steinberg and Josling (2003) that the need to show causation in Article 6.3 SCM disputes implies the use of empirical economic models. Instead, it based its conclusion that a causal link exists between the US subsidies and the significant price suppression it had found on three elements: the fact that the US 'exerts a substantial proportionate influence in the world upland cotton' market in view of the

75 Panel Report, para. 7.1209.
76 Ibid., para. 7.1205.
77 Ibid., para. 7.1207.

magnitude of its production and export of upland cotton; the magnitude and the price-contingent nature of US subsidies; and the 'discernable temporal coincidence of suppressed world market prices and the price-contingent United States subsidies', including the fact already referred to that the 'A-Index in MY 1999–MY 2002 was, on average, 29.5 per cent below its 1980–1998 average'. The Appellate Body remained silent on the use of empirical economic models in Article 6.3 SCM disputes.

Was the Panel right in ignoring the results of simulations of the 'econometric model' for the determination of the causal link? Our answer is yes, but not for the same reason as that given by the WTO Secretariat (WTO Secretariat, 2005). To our mind, the problem with the modeling exercise submitted by Brazil is not so much that it entailed disagreements among economists or that the Panel was unable to weigh the different views, but simply that it relied on a model that cannot possibly answer the question at hand.

Contrary to what the Panel, and Sumner himself (Sumner, 2003), asserted, the simulations submitted by Brazil are not based on an 'econometric model' but on a 'calibration model'. As already indicated, the difference between the two types of models is substantial. To quote the Economics Nobel Prize winner James Heckman, 'given the weak empirical foundations for [calibration] models, it is not surprising that the policy counterfactuals based on them are controversial and few outside the subfield take the estimates of the ... consequences of policies produced by this line of research very seriously. At the same time, the models are intellectually interesting frameworks and demonstrate what is logically possible' (Heckman, 2000).

It is right, therefore, to assert that the simulations prepared by Sumner indicate that a causal link between US subsidies and the world cotton price is 'logically possible'. But the simulations do not provide a sense of the degree of confidence that can be placed on this logical possibility, as would be the case with an econometric model. In reality, the problem with the calibration model is that it *assumes* from beginning to end that there is a positive relationship between US subsidies and the world cotton price;[78] it never tests it. However, if one is ready to accept the assumptions embedded in the model (including those made regarding the values of the different parameters), then the simulations can be very useful in quantifying the effects of the subsidies on the world price. Hence, the interesting result of the simulations submitted by Brazil is not that there is a causal link between US subsidies and the world cotton price, but rather that taking all the assumptions of the model for granted, world cotton prices would have been on average 12.6 % higher during the period 1999–2002 in the absence of US subsidies.

78 Obviously, the model does not posit a direct relationship between US subsidies and world cotton prices. Rather it assumes a complex set of relationships between large numbers of variables that imply an indirect relationship.

At the same time, one should not over-emphasize the fact that the calibration model was not estimated. For one thing, many of its key parameters, in particular demand and supply elasticities, are borrowed from econometric studies. In addition, it is possible to test the robustness of the model's prediction by running sensitivity analysis on these key parameters.

One of the principal arguments raised by the United States in its appeal against the Panel decision was that 'the Panel should have considered to what extent other market participants would increase supply or reduce demand in response to any alleged increase in cotton prices resulting from the absence of US payments'.[79] The Appellate Body noted that the dispute between the US and Brazil lies in whether the Panel took into account supply and demand elasticities of third countries 'as reflected in these model [simulations] or otherwise'.[80] However, the Appellate Body was unable to reach a verdict on what is ultimately an empirical inquiry. It simply noted that 'the Panel indicated expressly that it had taken the models in question into account. It would have been helpful had the Panel revealed how it used these models in examining the question of third country responses. Nevertheless, we are not prepared to second-guess the Panel's appreciation and weighing of the evidence before it.'[81]

In the *Upland Cotton* case, the Panel stated that it did not rely fully on these empirical studies. Rather, it seemed to develop a qualitative analysis, incorporating a similar logic in a less mathematically rigorous manner. But by failing to make clear its assumptions about the magnitude of the various components of causation of price suppression, and the magnitude of effects of other factors that would cause price suppression, the Panel failed to develop a convincing case. While the Appellate Body accepted this case, it did so reluctantly.

5. Institutional capacities to determine causation of serious prejudice and significant price suppression

At least in the context of serious prejudice cases, where the Panel is required to make the initial determination of the existence and causation of serious prejudice, it may be possible for Panels to use experts to assist.

5.1 Panel use of experts in economics, including econometrics

Just as biology provides the best tools available to determine whether there is a scientific basis for a sanitary measure, modern economics provides the best tools available in order to determine the effects of subsidies on prices. So, where the SCM Agreement calls for a determination by a Panel of whether a subsidy has caused significant price suppression, a Panel would be wise to use the tools

79 Appellate Body Report, para. 447, quoting Panel Report, United States' appellant's submission, para. 237.

80 Ibid., para. 447.

81 Ibid., para. 448.

provided by economics, or to engage expert economists, or to evaluate reports provided by expert economists.

Panels are permitted to establish 'expert review groups' under Article 13.2 of the DSU. This facility has not been used yet (see Pauwelyn, 2002), but it seems well-designed for use in cases where the Panel must make complex economic determinations such as the one required in the instant case. Panels have called upon individual experts in six cases: *Japan–Apples*, *Australia–Salmon*, *EC–Asbestos* (initial Panel and Article 21.5 Panel), *Japan–Agricultural Products*, *US–Shrimp*, and *EC–Hormones*. However, in none of these cases has the Panel consulted experts on economic issues. In *Dominican Republic–Cigarettes* and in *India–Quantitative Restrictions*, the Panels sought economic information from the IMF.

Article 24 of the SCM Agreement calls for the establishment of a 'permanent group of experts' in order to perform certain functions under that Agreement, including to assist Panels in connection with certain issues relating to prohibited subsidies. However, given the limited mandate under the SCM Agreement for its permanent group of experts, the more useful course would seem to be to utilize expert review groups under Article 13 of the DSU.

The determination of significant price suppression and its causation would seem amenable to a report from an expert review group comprised of economic experts in relevant disciplines, including trade economics and econometrics. Engaging expert review groups to work through the difficult issues of appropriate assumptions and modeling techniques would relieve Panels of a burden that they generally cannot bear. Article 13 of the DSU has been found to provide Panels with broad flexibility to utilize experts. So it is curious that economic experts have not been used.

It might be argued that it is better to have the litigants bring their own experts, and have the Panel determine which experts present the better argument. However, Panels generally lack the expertise to critique complex economic analyses. 'A non-expert cannot independently and directly check complex theoretical propositions that do not have simple observational consequences ... Whatever checking the non-expert can manage must rely on indirect devices like demeanor, credentials, and reputation' (Brewer, 1998).

In fact, in other trade-remedies cases, Panels and the Appellate Body have sought refuge in procedural criticism of national economic analyses. They might feel more comfortable engaging in a full review of national determinations of dumping margins and subsidization, injury, and causation, in accordance with the terms of the treaty, if they could rely on expert review groups.

Indeed, in a number of contexts relating to remedies, development, and other matters, experts in economics would appear useful. It may even be appropriate to develop a coherent 'economic jurisprudence' with respect to certain issues. While it might be objected that the WTO treaty does not contemplate rule or determination by economists, it appears reasonable to respond that where the treaty framers expressed rights and obligations in terms of economic concepts, they implicitly called for an accurate use of those economic concepts. The use of expert review panels appears to be a reasonable, treaty-specified method of achieving this goal.

5.2 Appellate review

The Appellate Body cautioned that '[t]o the extent that the United States' arguments concern the Panel's appreciation and weighing of the evidence, we note from the outset that the Appellate Body will not interfere lightly with the Panel's discretion 'as the trier of facts'.[82] However, '[w]hether the Panel properly interpreted the requirements of Article 6.3(c) of the SCM Agreement and properly applied that interpretation to the facts in this case is a legal question'.[83] Nevertheless, in several contexts, the Appellate Body declined to examine the Panel's appreciation and weighing of the evidence.[84]

Recall that in these cases, the Panel is the fact-finder, not the reviewer of a national administrative-agency record. There may be some need to develop an administrative law of the WTO, with a more fully articulated standard of review for these findings. The US claimed before the Appellate Body that the Panel had failed to 'set out the findings of fact, the applicability of relevant provisions and the basic rationale behind any findings and recommendations that it makes' as required by Article 12.7 of the DSU. At several critical junctures, the Panel's findings of facts can only be described as conclusory. Article 12.7 would seem to require not just a statement of the 'findings of fact' – the conclusions – but also the 'basic rationale' behind these findings. Here, the basic rationale was elided because the facts examined by the Panel do not indeed support a logical inference of causation. The Appellate Body declined to rule on the US claim that the Panel failed to satisfy the requirements of Article 12.7, because the US's Notice of Appeal did not provide adequate notice of this claim to Brazil.[85]

The US did not make a claim under Article 11 of the DSU.[86] Therefore, it did not allege that the Panel failed to 'make an objective assessment of the matter before it, including an objective assessment of the facts of the case' pursuant to Article 11. This is important, because part of the US concern was with the Panel's assessment of the facts. Under Article 17.6 of the DSU, appeals are 'limited to issues of law covered in the panel report and legal interpretations developed by the panel'.

5.3 Is determination of serious prejudice worthwhile?

Probably more than anyone else, Alan Sykes has taken a dim view of the WTO regime contained in the SCM Agreement. He has questioned whether the treatment of domestic subsidies under WTO law is actually desirable given that its

82 Appellate Body Report, para. 399 (citation omitted).
83 Ibid.
84 See, e.g., ibid., para. 448.
85 Ibid., paras. 492, 496.
86 Ibid., para. 398.

'criteria for determining which government programs are actionable ... are highly imperfect from an economic standpoint, and the challenges associated with efforts to do a better job are vast. It is by no means clear that general principles to sort unacceptable from acceptable domestic subsidy programs can be devised and administered successfully.'[87] This paper has not considered the broader question raised by Sykes about the possibility to determine what constitutes an undesirable subsidy from an economic standpoint. Instead, it has focused on a downstream issue, namely what should the role of economic models be in the determination of causation between actionable subsidies and serious prejudice by the Panel?

6. Conclusion

The *Upland Cotton* case illustrates the challenges that Panels face when they are required to evaluate complex economic matters. The serious prejudice provisions of the SCM Agreement call for an initial determination by the Panel, rather than the review of national agency determinations that is called for in the countervailing duty provisions. In the countervailing duty context, as in the safeguards and dumping contexts, the Appellate Body has seemed satisfied to have Panels engage in procedural review of national agency determinations, rather than substantive review. Although this position is subject to question, given the substantive requirements of WTO law, it is patently untenable in the serious prejudice context, where there is no initial national agency determination. In these cases, requirements to determine issues such as 'causation', 'price suppression', and 'significant' must be understood as requirements that Panels use the best analytical tools reasonably available to make such determinations.

References

Brewer, Scott (1998), 'Scientific Expert Testimony and Intellectual Due Process', *Yale Law Journal*, **107**: 1535–1681.

Cass, Ronald A. and Michael S. Knoll (1997), 'The Economics of "Injury" in Antidumping and Countervailing Duty Cases: A Reply to Professor Sykes', in Jagdeep S. Bhandari and Alan O. Sykes (eds), *Economic Dimensions in International Law: Comparative and Empirical Perspectives*, Cambridge: Cambridge University Press, pp. 126–165.

Heckman, James J. (2000), 'Causal Parameters and Policy Analysis in Economics: A Twentieth Century Retrospective', *The Quarterly Journal of Economics*, **115**(1): 45–97.

Hudec, Robert E. (1998), 'Does the Agreement on Agriculture Work? Agricultural Disputes After the Uruguay Round', International Agricultural Trade Research Consortium, Working Paper No. 98-2.

Pauwelyn, Joost (2002), 'The Use of Experts in WTO Dispute Settlement', *International and Comparative Law Quarterly*, **51**: 325–364.

Schnepf, Randy (2005), 'Background on the US-Brazil WTO Cotton Subsidy Dispute', Congressional Research Service Report, 11 July 2005.

87 For a useful and clear treatment, see Sykes, 2003.

Steinberg, Richard H. and Timothy E. Josling (2003), 'When the Peace Ends: The Vulnerability of EC and US Agricultural Subsidies to WTO Legal Challenge', *Journal of International Economic Law*, **6**(2): 369–417.

Sumner, Daniel A. (2003), 'The Impacts of US Cotton Subsidies on Cotton Prices and Quantities: Simulation Analysis for the WTO Dispute', Mimeo, Condensed and edited version of Annex I presented to the WTO cotton-dispute panel in September 2003.

Sykes, Alan O. (2003), 'The Economics of WTO Rules on Subsidies and Countervailing Measures', University of Chicago John M. Olin Law and Economics Working Paper No. 186.

Sykes, Alan O. (1996), 'The Economics of Injury in Antidumping and Countervailing Duty Cases', *International Review of Law and Economics*, **16**(1): 5–26.

WTO Secretariat (2005), 'Quantitative Economics in WTO Dispute Settlement', *World Trade Report 2005*, Geneva: WTO.

Comment

Upland Cotton Case

Prepared for the ALI Project on the Case Law of the WTO

HYLKE VANDENBUSSCHE

Université Catholique de Louvain, KULeuven, CORE, and CEPR

1. What was the case about?

In 2002, Brazil complained to the WTO Dispute Settlement mechanism that the US subsidies for upland cotton were depressing the price on the world market for cotton. According to Brazil, this price depression caused *serious prejudice* to the Brazilian producers of upland cotton. A WTO Panel was installed to investigate this complaint and to prepare an advice to the Appellate Body, the decision organ of the WTO. The Panel came to the conclusion that, indeed, US subsidies were a violation of the 'Agreement on Subsidies and Countervailing Measures (SCM)'. In line with the Panel's analysis, the Appellate Body decided that US subsidies were causing serious prejudice to Brazil and were therefore illegal in a WTO framework.

Sapir and Trachtman rightly point out that the case on upland cotton shows that from a legal and economic point of view the argumentation of the Dispute Settlement Panel was weak. The Panel insufficiently demonstrated a causal link between the US subsidies and serious prejudice required by law.

Sapir and Trachtman convincingly argue that under a correct interpretation of the law under Article 6.3(c) of the SCM agreement, it does not suffice to show that the US subsidies are *a* cause of serious prejudice (together with other causes), but it requires a demonstration that even taken in isolation, the subsidies cause serious price depression.

Therefore, from an economic point of view, the Panel should have tried to disentangle the effect of a US subsidy on world-market prices for upland cotton from other potential causes of price depression. This would have allowed the Panel to verify whether the US subsidies by themselves were a cause of price depression and how much the subsidies contributed to the price depression.

Sapir and Trachtman argue in favor of the application of more rigorous economic methods in the determination of *causality* in serious-prejudice cases like the

Upland Cotton case. Notably, the use of econometric and simulation techniques are considered necessary tools to disentangle different causes of price depression.

The purpose of my discussion below is to support this recommendation by Sapir and Trachtman by means of a graphical exposition that sheds some additional light on how economic analysis can be used for the causation analysis. The discussion will make evident that determining causality is not a simple task, which is why it should best be left to economic experts as will be argued below.

The weakness of the causality investigation in serious-prejudice cases like *Upland Cotton* is also prevalent in other types of cases. For example, the 'Antidumping Agreement', under Article 6 of the GATT, argues that in dumping cases a causal link is required between the *dumped imports* and the *injury to the domestic industry* of the importing country. At present, in most cases, this causality investigation is limited to a trends analysis. Whenever a rise in imports coincides with a fall in domestic-industry performance indicators this is often regarded as sufficient evidence of causality between dumped imports and injury to the domestic industry. Instead of this casual empiricism, the framework outlined below could also be used to determine causality in dumping cases as shown in Vandenbussche (1996).

2. Several causes for price depression are possible

The purpose of any quantitative analysis aimed at measuring the effects of US subsidies on world-market prices requires the construction of a counterfactual world. This counterfactual world gives an idea of what the price would have been in the absence of subsidies.

In the absence of any knowledge on the market structure for upland cotton, the simple assumption of a competitive market can be a starting point. This would suggest that prices are determined by the interaction between world supply and world demand, as illustrated in Figure 1. This in not an innocuous assumption but one that would need to be verified empirically before modeling the market structure, as explained more in Section 3.

Upland cotton, in view of its nature, is likely to be a homogeneous type of product, i.e. where it is hard for any customer to distinguish between different types of upland cotton. But again this is an assumption that would need to be verified empirically since product differentiation is likely to alter the analysis. For expositional purposes, we will assume that US and Brazilian upland cotton are perfect substitutes, i.e. consumers do not make a distinction between them.

In terms of supply, the case details suggest that the US is the largest exporter of upland cotton and that Brazil also is a major export competitor. From this it follows that both countries seem to account for a large share, if not most of, the world supply of upland cotton.

In order to construct a counterfactual world, it is necessary to have an adequate reference period that is a period where there was no price depression. In the

Figure 1. Price depression in the world market for upland cotton

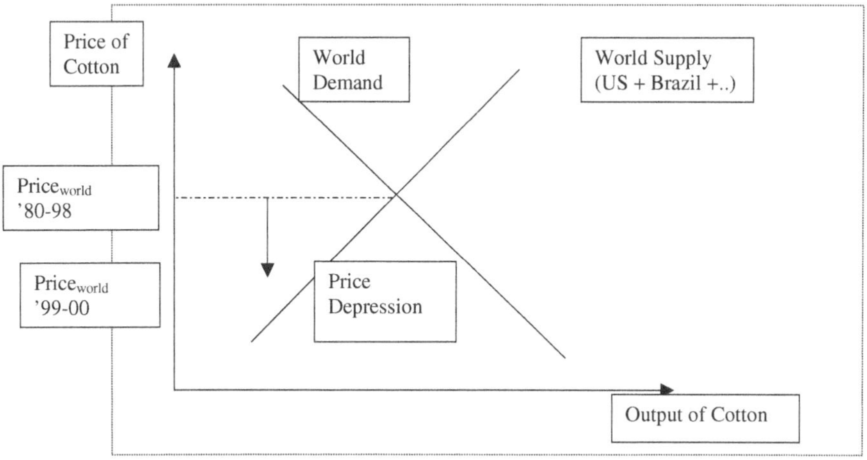

Upland Cotton case, the reference period used was the average world-market price for upland cotton over the period 1980–1998. This price was considered to reflect the price without US subsidization. Figure 1 shows how this reference price is given by the intersection of world demand and supply of upland cotton. The correct position and slope of the demand and supply curve is given by the elasticities of demand and the elasticity of supply respectively. These elasticities will prove crucial for the remainder of the exposition and are part of the essential information that the WTO Panel should have when analyzing the effects of US subsidies on prices.

Elasticities can be obtained through econometric techniques as long as one has a sufficiently long time span or a sufficiently high frequency of transactions data in a market.[1] Once the elasticities are known, the correct position and slope of the demand and supply can be inferred and a counterfactual world like the one in Figure 1 can be modeled using a structural equations model.

If a drop in the world-market price for upland cotton below the reference price is observed, as was the case in the period 1999–2000, either a shift in the supply curve of upland cotton or a shift in the demand curve or both will be the underlying cause.

A subsidy to a US farmer will imply that each US farmer will now supply more upland cotton to the export market for any given price. Or, in other words, the

1 See, for example, Angrist and Krueger (2001) for more details. The estimation of elasticities requires the use of instruments, i.e., demand and cost shifters that allow the identification of separate supply and demand curves respectively from using price and quantity data. A typical example of a demand shifter is the price of a substitute product. A typical example of a cost shifter of agricultural products is yield per acre. A demand shifter is used to identify the supply function and a cost shifter is used to identify the demand curve.

Figure 2. Cause 1: subsidy shifted the world-supply curve outward

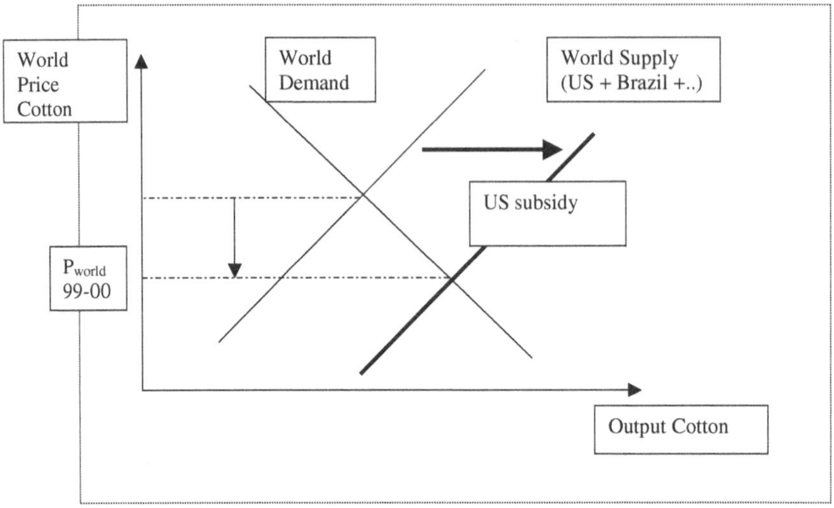

world-supply curve in Figure 2 is going to shift to the right. The extent of this shift will depend on the amount of the subsidy.[2] In Figure 2, we show a situation where the US subsidy is accountable for the total price depression in the world market observed in the market.

However, it is clear that demand factors could also have accounted for the fall in the world-market price in the period 1999–2000. This is illustrated in Figure 3. In fact, the price movements of substitute products like synthetic fibers, during that same period, may have resulted in an inward shift of the demand for upland cotton. In other words, rival products on the market may have reduced the demand for upland cotton. In Figure 3, we show a scenario in which the inward shift in demand completely accounts for the fall in the price of upland cotton observed on world markets.

The size of the demand shift will depend on the cross-price elasticity of synthetic fibers and upland cotton. The cross-price elasticity captures the extent to which the demand for upland cotton is affected by the price of substitute products such as synthetic fibers. Or, in other words, it captures the degree of substitutability between the two types of products and is another parameter that would need to be estimated econometrically after which its value could be inserted in a structural model such as the one presented in Figure 3.

A third possibility is that the world-market price for upland cotton has fallen due to a combination of demand and supply shifts.

2 For expositional purposes, we abstract from other variables that could affect the shift of the supply curve like the exchange rate of the dollar.

Figure 3. Cause 2: substitute products for cotton can shift the world demand for cotton inward

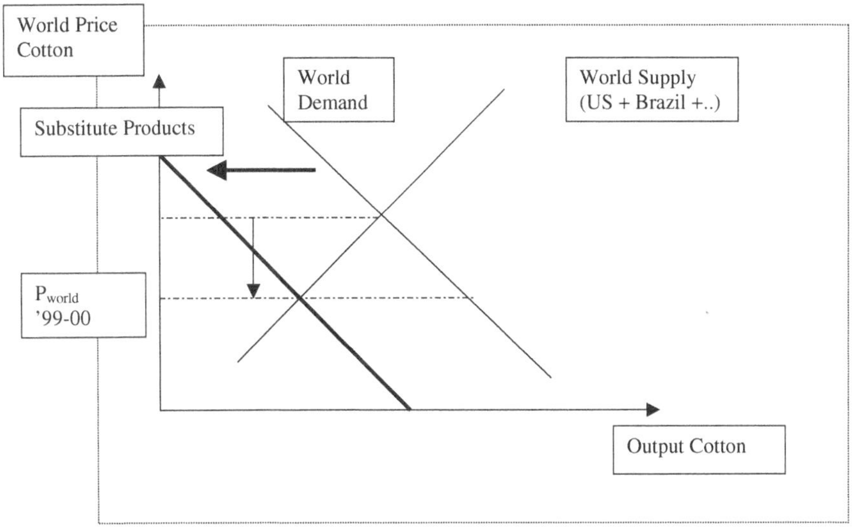

While Figures 2 and 3 above clearly indicate that several reasons could underlie the drop in the price for upland cotton, no attempt was made by the WTO Panel to disentangle the effects at work. Implicitly, a scenario such as the one in Figure 2 seemed to be what the Panel had in mind, i.e. that the US subsidy accounted for most, if not all, of the price depression.

A simulation model operating along the lines of the one presented above was put forward by Brazil. That model claimed to have disentangled the effect of the US subsidy on the world-market prices and argued that world price would have been 12.6 % higher in the absence of a US subsidy.

The US criticized the model saying that the elasticity of demand was assumed to be too inelastic, i.e. too steep a slope of the demand curve was assumed, thereby attributing too big a role to the effect of the US subsidy on the price decrease. Indeed, it can be seen from Figure 3 that if a steeper demand curve is assumed, an outward shift in the supply curve will result in a larger drop of the equilibrium price on the world market.

At the other extreme, in the case of a flat demand curve (with a demand elasticity of infinity), an outward shift of the supply curve would not affect the price at all, in which case the US subsidies would not be the underlying cause of the serious prejudice. With a flat demand curve, the only cause of a price reduction would be a downward shift in the demand curve.

The Panel's reply points out that without its own reliable estimates of the relevant elasticities, it is not in any position to counter arguments like the one raised by the US. The Panel replied that, in reaching its decision, it had not relied on the quantitative analysis prepared by the Brazilian party.

Whether or not the Brazilian estimates were the right ones is not the issue here. The heart of the problem is that the Panel did not have its own independent estimates, and may have found it hard to rest its case solely on evidence provided by one of the parties involved in the dispute. This lack of information makes the Panel's analysis look arbitrary and makes its decision process vulnerable to critique.

3. Causality determination is work for economic experts

Even from the sketchy outline above, it should already be clear that the estimation of a structural model with demand and supply parameters involving, amongst others, elasticities and cross-price elasticities is not an easy thing to do.

Moreover, for expositional purposes, we have made a number of simplifying assumptions that need not hold. The model used above assumes that the market for upland cotton is relatively competitive and that the price on the market is the outcome of joint demand and supply forces. Or, in other words, it assumes that farmers in the market are atomistically small such that their individual output has no effect on world markets. However, in reality, market conditions could be very different. In order to find out to what extent this assumption is true or violated, a thorough analysis of the market structure is required. Does the industry consist of many small farmers or are there large agricultural firms involved? This matters a lot in terms of industry structure and intensity of competition.

A related issue is the assumption on product differentiation. For simplicity, we have assumed that US cotton and Brazilian cotton are like products with little differentiation between them. However, this may not be a realistic assumption. In fact, in most markets, products are differentiated. Standard models from the literature in industrial economics point out that product-market competition is less fierce in more differentiated industries than in homogeneous products. Therefore, a US subsidy is likely to have larger price effects when upland cotton is a very homogeneous product than when the industry is characterized by differentiation.

The simple conclusion is that the causality investigation between subsidized exports and serious prejudice deserves a more in-depth economic analysis.

Sapir and Trachtman see a possibility for this within the context of the existing legislation, notably the use of Article 13.2, which foresees the possibility to install 'economic expert review groups'. The purpose of these experts would be to use various alternative methods, in the spirit of the one presented above, to address the causality issue on the basis of which the Panel could base its decision. With its own estimates of the relevant parameters involved, the Panel would be equally, if not better, informed than the parties involved. This would allow the Panel to include the quantitative estimates in its decisionmaking, which would largely improve the economic foundations on which it would rest its case.

I sincerely hope that the WTO takes this advice to heart and pursues the possibility of installing economic experts in future dispute cases. The 'outsourcing' of the causality investigation to economic experts will facilitate the decisionmaking by WTO Panels, and put them in a better position to defend their decisions *vis-à-vis* complainants and defendants involved in a case. It will also help them to better pursue the legal objectives of the WTO rules. Given that causality is also an essential element in the decisions surrounding antidumping cases and safeguard cases, WTO decisionmaking in those areas could also be improved. This, in turn, will result in the enhanced credibility and reputation of the WTO, which seems essential for its proper functioning in a more globalized world.

References

Angrist, J. D. and A. B. Krueger (2001), 'Instrumental Variables and the Search for Identification: From Supply and Demand to Natural Experiments', *Journal of Economic Perspectives*, **15**(4): 69–85.

Boltuck, R. (1991), 'Assessing the Effects on the Domestic Industry of Price Dumping', in P. K. M. Tharakan (ed.), *Policy Implications of Antidumping Measures*, North-Holland, pp. 99–141.

Vandenbussche, H. (1996), 'Is European Antidumping Protection against Central Europe too High?', *Weltwirtschaftliches Archiv/Review of World Economics*, **132**: 116–138.

US – Countervailing Duty Investigation of DRAMS

Appellate Body Report, United States – Countervailing Duty Investigation on Dynamic Random Access Memory Semiconductors (DRAMS) from Korea, WT/DS296/AB/R, adopted 20 July 2005

JOSEPH F. FRANÇOIS
Professor of Economics, Joseph Kepler University, Linz
DAVID PALMETER
Senior Counsel, Sidley Austin LLP, Washington, D.C.

1. Introduction

Paragraph 1 of Article 1 of the *Agreement on Subsidies and Countervailing Measures* (SCM Agreement) defines a subsidy as a 'financial contribution by government' that confers a benefit. A 'benefit' consists of something better than the market would provide.[1]

The governmental practices that would constitute a 'financial contribution' are set out in some detail in the first three of four subparagraphs of paragraph 1(a) of Article 1. These include grants, loans, equity infusions, and tax incentives. Subparagraph (iv) is an anticircumvention provision encompassing the financial contributions detailed in the first three subparagraphs when those contributions are made by a private body that a government 'entrusts or directs' to make them.

Paragraph 2 of Article 1 further provides that countervailing duties may be imposed only on subsidies that are 'specific' to an enterprise or industry, or group of enterprises or industries. Thus a subsidy is the provision of a financial contribution that confers a benefit to a specific enterprise or industry or group of enterprises or industries.

The scope, reach and interpretation of these provisions were the subject of the Appellate Body's June 2005 Report on *US – Countervailing Duty Investigation*

1 Appellate Body Report, *Canada – Measures Affecting the Export of Civilian Aircraft*, WT/DS70/AB/R, adopted 20 August 1999, DSR 1999:III, 1377, para. 157.

on DRAMS, a case that stemmed from the imposition by the United States of countervailing duties in the amount of 44.29% on imports of DRAMS, a type of semiconductor, from the financially troubled Korean producer, Hynix. The US authorities found that the Government of Korea (GOK) had entrusted or directed private Korean financial institutions to provide beneficial financial contributions, as defined in Article 1 of the SCM Agreement, to Hynix. The central issues in that Report concerned whether the Panel correctly interpreted the 'entrusts or directs' language of subparagraph (iv) in concluding that the countervailing duty measure imposed by the US was inconsistent with the requirements of that subparagraph, and whether the Panel properly reviewed the evidence on which the countervailing duty was based.

2. Procedural facts

The WTO dispute began when Korea first asked for consultations with the United States and then requested the establishment of a panel to examine the consistency of the countervailing duty order on DRAMS with the requirements of the SCM Agreement. The Panel found that the duties were inconsistent with both Articles 1 and 2 of the Agreement, the United States appealed, and Korea filed its own appeal on a procedural issue. The Appellate Body modified the Panel's Report by largely reversing its findings.

3. Procedural issues

Rare is the dispute that goes through the WTO process without procedural arguments, and almost as rare is the dispute in which procedural arguments make a difference in the outcome. The *DRAMS* case, in which the Appellate Body considered two procedural claims – and quickly disposed of them – was no exception. The first procedural claim was by the US, which argued that the Panel had erroneously concluded that Korea's original request for consultations was adequate. The second was the claim by Korea that the US notice of appeal with regard to the consultation request was defective. Since Korea's claim went to the jurisdiction of the Appellate Body even to hear the US claim of Panel error with regard to the consultation request, Korea's procedural appeal was considered first.

In its Notice of Appeal, the United States had said only that it sought review of the Panel's conclusion that 'Korea's consultation request provides a sufficient indication of the legal basis of the complaint within the meaning of Article 4.4 of the DSU'.[2] The request, therefore, identified both the issue (the Panel's conclusion with regard to the consultation request) and the legal provision (Article 4.4 of the

2 Para. 96. The DSU, of course, is the *Understanding on Rules and Procedures Governing the Settlement of Disputes* or 'Dispute Settlement Understanding'.

DSU) whose requirements the request allegedly failed to meet. This, the Appellate Body held, was sufficient, and Korea's jurisdictional appeal was denied.

The Appellate Body then considered the US argument regarding the alleged deficiency of Korea's consultation request on its merits. The consultation request dispute stemmed from the fact that, early in the process, Korea had filed an addendum to its original request. The initial request sought consultations only on the preliminary and final subsidy determinations of the US Department of Commerce and on the preliminary injury determination by the US International Trade Commission. The addendum sought additional consultations on the final injury determination and on the countervailing duty order – the 'measure' – itself. Two sessions of consultations in fact were held, one on the initial request and the other on the addendum.

Nonetheless, the US argued that, because the final injury determination and the countervailing order were not themselves part of the initial request, Korea was wrong to include them in its request for the establishment of a panel, and the Panel was wrong to consider them. The Appellate Body disagreed and upheld the Panel. It then moved on to the first key substantive legal question: the meaning of the words 'entrusts or directs' in subparagraph (iv) of Article 1.1(a) of the *SCM Agreement.*

4. The meaning of 'entrusts or directs'

We are trapped by our language. There is perhaps no better illustration of this than the effort of legal tribunals to interpret legal language, such as treaty language. Words are defined in terms of other words, a process that, in the end, is circular. But, as we proceed around the circle, emphasis, nuance, even meaning can change. Those changes in emphasis, nuance, and meaning often create difficulties when efforts are made to explain what a legal term requires.

The task of the Panel in *DRAMS* was to interpret the words 'entrusts or directs' in subparagraph (iv). The same task had faced the Panel in *US – Export Restraints*, and the *DRAMS* Panel simply followed the *Export Restraints* Panel's interpretation – an interpretation that was not appealed.[3] *DRAMS*, therefore, was the Appellate Body's first brush with the 'entrusts or directs' requirement, and it disagreed with both Panels.

Following the reasoning in *Export Restraints*, the Panel held that 'entrusts' contains the notion of 'delegation', while 'directs' contains the notion of 'command'.[4] The Panel, the Appellate Body said in disagreement, 'effectively

3 Panel Report, *United States – Measures Treating Exports Restraints as Subsidies*, WT/DS194/R and Corr., adopted 23 August 2001, DSR 2001:XI, 5767.

4 Panel Report, *United States – Countervailing Duty Investigation on Dynamic Random Access Memory Semiconductors (DRAMS) from Korea*, WT/DS296/R, adopted 20 July 2005, modified by the Appellate Body Report, WT/DS296/AB/R, para. 7.31.

replaced the terms "entrusts" and "directs" with two other terms, "delegation" and "command", whose scope it did not define, and went no further in clarifying the meaning of any of these terms'.[5] 'Entrusts or directs', it said, does not have the same meaning as 'delegates or commands'.[6]

'Delegation', the Appellate Body said, usually involves a formal action, while 'entrusts' connotes giving responsibility to someone.[7] Thus, it found too narrow an interpretation of 'entrusts' to mean simply 'delegation'.[8] Similarly, while governments can exercise authority by command, they are likely to have other, more subtle, means at their disposal. 'Thus, an interpretation of the term "directs" that is limited to acts of "command" is also too narrow.'[9]

The Appellate Body acknowledged, however, that identification of the kinds of government actions that could constitute entrustment or direction is difficult in the abstract. It noted in this regard that Korea admitted that 'in some circumstances "guidance" by a government can constitute direction'.[10] In the end, however, the Appellate Body did not rest its decision on abstract definitions. Instead, it said that a determination of entrustment or direction hinges on the specific facts of a case.[11] The facts of the *DRAMS* case, in particular the method of their evaluation, raised one of the more interesting issues in the Report: what is the correct way to evaluate circumstantial evidence?

5. Evidentiary issues

The evidentiary findings

Circumstantial evidence is indirect evidence. It does not go directly to the question at issue, but permits the answer to that question to be inferred by its consistency with a possible answer. The *DRAMS* case was all about circumstantial evidence.

In concluding that Korea had conferred a subsidy on Hynix within the meaning of Article 1 of the SCM Agreement, the US found that four financial contributions were made by both public and private creditors who were entrusted or directed to do so by the GOK. The contributions included an 800-billion-won syndicated loan, a 'Fast Track Programme' by the Korea Development Bank, and two restructuring packages. The objective of these contributions, according to the US, 'was the complete financial restructuring of Hynix in order to maintain the company as an ongoing concern'.[12]

5 Appellate Body Report, para. 109.
6 Appellate Body Report, para. 109.
7 Appellate Body Report, para. 110.
8 Appellate Body Report, para. 110.
9 Appellate Body Report, para. 110.
10 Appellate Body Report, para. 116.
11 Appellate Body Report, para. 116.
12 Panel Report, para. 7.7.

Some of the creditors were public bodies, others were banks that were owned or controlled by the GOK, while the remainder were private entities in which the Government had only a small interest or none at all. Korea conceded that financial contributions by public creditors were within the scope of Article 1 (although they did not agree that these met the specificity requirements of Article 2, which is discussed below). The core of the dispute revolved around whether the US finding that the GOK entrusted or directed the other creditors to make the financial contributions was supported by the evidence.

The Panel considered four items of circumstantial evidence that the US relied upon in finding a financial contribution: (1) Korea's policy of preventing the failure of Hynix; (2) its control of Hynix's creditors; (3) its coercion of those creditors; and (4) a prospectus filed by two Korean banks with the US Securities and Exchange Commission. The Panel did conclude that 'an objective and impartial investigating authority could properly have found that the GOK had a policy to save Hynix'.[13] However, while this policy could explain the participation of the public body creditors in the financial contributions, the Panel found that it was not sufficient to attribute to the GOK the participation of the other creditors. The 'existence of a GOK policy to save Hynix in and of itself could not properly be treated as evidence of government direction' of the non-public creditors, the Panel said.[14]

In evaluating the remaining three items of circumstantial evidence, the Panel found that, while the US had established that the GOK had regulatory control over the private creditors (including the government-owned or controlled banks), it had 'not properly established that the GOK actually exercised such influence or regulatory authority'.[15] Similarly, although the US demonstrated that one creditor had been coerced, it had not demonstrated to the Panel's satisfaction that others had been coerced.[16] Finally, it concluded that the prospectus filed with the US Securities and Exchange Commission did not establish that the filing institutions had been entrusted or directed to support Hynix.[17]

The Panel also rejected the US position that the four financial contributions at issue should be considered to be part of a single program, rather than four separate programs. Thus, in the Panel's words, 'although the [US] established that the GOK had a policy to save Hynix, and that the GOK had a certain capacity to influence [the non-public body] creditors … the [US] did not properly demonstrate that the GOK availed itself of that capacity to entrust or direct *all* [non-public body] creditors to participate in *all four* of the financial contributions at issue'.[18]

13 Panel Report, para. 7.51.
14 Panel Report, para. 7.51.
15 Panel Report, para. 7.176.
16 Panel Report, para. 7.176.
17 Panel Report, para. 7.176.
18 Panel Report, para. 7.177 (emphasis added).

Analysis of circumstantial evidence

A single piece of circumstantial evidence rarely, if ever, would be enough to justify a legal conclusion. Circumstantial evidence cases are built on the cumulation of evidence. The question before the Appellate Body was whether the Panel's approach to analyzing more than one piece of circumstantial evidence was correct. The Appellate Body concluded that the Panel's approach was in error.

It began its analysis with the observation that, although the Panel stated that it would follow the same approach that the US employed – that is, that it would base its conclusion on the totality of the evidence – the Panel actually did the reverse.[19] '[T]he Panel often appeared to examine whether each piece of evidence, viewed *in isolation*, demonstrated entrustment or direction.'[20] As an example, the Appellate Body noted that the US, in its countervailing-duty decision, had concluded that a GOK financial supervisory agency had increased credit limits for bank loans to single borrowers. The Panel concluded that, even though the US might have been correct in arguing that some of the creditors would not have been able to participate in a syndicated loan to Hynix without the waiver, the US could not 'properly have *inferred from this that the creditors were instructed or directed* to participate in the syndicated loan'.[21]

'We do not read the [US] to have inferred *solely from the waiver of loan limits* that entrustment or direction had taken place', the Appellate Body said. 'Nor do we consider that the [US's] reliance on this evidence suggests that "there is government entrustment or direction every time that a loan limit waiver is provided", for this would follow only if the [US] had based its finding of entrustment or direction *exclusively* on the waivers of loan limits.'[22] The waiver of loan limits had to be looked at in light of all of the actions the GOK took that had a bearing on its policy to save Hynix.

It is a legal truism that factual findings are to be made on the basis of an examination of the totality of the evidence, particularly circumstantial evidence. Even the Panel acknowledged this. Yet legal tribunals have seldom, if ever, explained why this is the case, and the Appellate Body's Report in *DRAMS* is no exception.

Despite its protestations to the contrary, the Panel, as the Appellate Body said, seemed to view each piece of evidence separately, in isolation, and if that piece – by itself – was not enough to establish entrustment or direction, it was put aside and the next piece was examined in the same way. The Panel correctly did not consider a process of addition, whereby evidence that fell short of the required level by itself would be added with similar pieces of evidence to reach a cumulative total. This apparently was the approach of Korea, which argued that it is 'a mathematical

19 Appellate Body Report, paras. 142, 143.
20 Appellate Body Report, para. 146 (emphasis in original).
21 Appellate Body Report, para. 146 (quoting from and adding emphasis to Panel Report, para. 7.101).
22 Appellate Body Report, para. 146 (emphasis in original).

truism that no matter how many zeros and negative numbers one adds together, the sum can never be a positive number'.[23]

Of course, adding zeros and negative numbers will not reach a positive number, but Korea's argument ignores the fact that the Panel *did* find some positive numbers. It found, for example, that Korea had a policy of preventing the failure of Hynix and that at least one non-public creditor had been coerced into participating in the rescue operation. But more importantly, if pieces of evidence are given a quantitative value, it is error to add them. To do so is to commit the error of the student who, after taking two examinations and receiving a 50% score in each, tells his parents that his score for the two exams was 100%.

When legal tribunals make factual determinations based on the totality of several pieces of circumstantial evidence, they are really engaged in an exercise in probability. There is one chance in two that a flipped coin will come up heads, but only one in four that it will come up heads twice in a row, one in eight that it will do so three times in a row, one in 16 that it will do so four times in a row, and so forth. If, after a single flip, a coin comes up heads, there is no rational basis for inferring that the coin has been altered in some way. But if it comes up heads a number of times in a row, an inference that the coin might have been altered would be reasonable.

Although evaluation of circumstantial evidence is based on an informal probability analysis, the process differs from simple coin-flipping probability because individual pieces of evidence, unlike coin flips, also have a qualitative value. One coin flip is no more important than another, but the importance and reliability of pieces of evidence can vary greatly. These factors can make an evaluation of the totality of the evidence difficult; nonetheless it is clear, as the Appellate Body concluded, that all of the evidence has to be looked at together and a judgment made as to how much the coincidence of the individual pieces supports a conclusion that none of them, alone, could support.

Other evidentiary issues

1. *Admissibility*

In its submissions to the Panel, the United States referred to evidence that was part of the record of its countervailing duty investigation, but had not been cited in its written decision to impose the duties. The Panel refused to consider this evidence on the ground that it amounted to an *ex post* rationalization.[24] The Appellate Body disagreed.

While Members may not attempt to defend countervailing duty decisions on the basis of evidence not contained in the investigative record, the evidence at issue concededly was contained in that record. And, while it is true that Article 22.5 of the SCM Agreement requires a final countervailing duty determination to

23 Appellate Body Report, para. 49 (quoting from Korea's appellee's submission).
24 Appellate Body Report, para. 159.

contain 'all relevant information on the matters of fact and law and reasons which have led to the imposition' of duties, it does not require Members 'to cite or discuss *every* piece of supporting record evidence for each fact in the final determination'.[25] In referring to the evidence at issue, the Appellate Body reasoned, the US was not advancing new reasons to support its decision, but was simply adding to the support of its reasons by referring to further record evidence. Accordingly, the Panel erred in refusing to consider this evidence.[26]

2. *Non-record evidence*

A claim by the US that the Panel itself had relied on non-record evidence was rejected in those terms by the Appellate Body, but, nonetheless, the Panel's conclusion with regard to the evidence was found to be erroneous.

Korea argued that, despite its ostensible control over the creditors of Hynix, its laws provided that any creditor not satisfied with proposed restructuring terms acceptable to a majority of the creditors could exercise an option to be bought out by the creditors who found the terms acceptable. If a buyout price could not be agreed to, the amount could be settled through mediation.[27]

A paragraph in Hynix's audit report, which was part of the record of the US investigation, stated that three creditors raised an objection to the terms of the proposed restructuring, but the paragraph gave no further information. The Panel concluded from this paragraph that the US should have understood that the three creditors had exercised an independent right to object and be bought out according to terms set through the mediation process. The Appellate Body, however, found that such a factual inference was not reasonably suggested by the text of the paragraph in question.[28] In fact, according to the Appellate Body, the US during its investigation had explicitly asked Hynix whether any creditors had exercised their buyout rights and received no indication from Hynix that this had occurred.[29] Accordingly, the Appellate Body found that, in reaching its conclusion on this issue, 'the Panel failed to "make an objective assessment of the matter before it" as required by Article 11 of the DSU'.[30]

3. *Standard of review*

The US appeal did not challenge the Panel's articulation of the proper standard for reviewing the countervailing duty determination; rather, it challenged the Panel's application of that standard. The Appellate Body agreed with the US.

25 Appellate Body Report, para. 164.

26 Appellate Body Report, para. 165. In footnote 303 to the Report, the Appellate Body referred to decisions under the *Anti-Dumping Agreement* that reached the same result.

27 Appellate Body Report, paras. 166–169.

28 Appellate Body Report, para. 179.

29 Appellate Body Report, para. 178.

30 Appellate Body Report, para. 179.

The only standard of review contained in the DSU is set forth in Article 11, which specifies that a panel 'should make an objective assessment of the matter before it, including an objective assessment of the facts of the case and the applicability of and conformity with the relevant covered agreements'. This general language was interpreted by the Appellate Body to mean that the 'objective assessment' called for by Article 11 requires a panel reviewing a Member's subsidy determination to 'be informed by an examination of whether the agency provided a reasoned and adequate explanation as to (i) how the evidence on the record supported its factual findings; and (ii) how those factual findings supported the overall subsidy determination'.[31] This means that a panel may not conduct its own *de novo* investigation or substitute its judgment for that of the Member.[32] A panel, the Appellate Body pointed out, acts 'as a *reviewer* of agency action, rather than as [an] *initial trier of fact*'.[33]

In reviewing an individual piece of evidence, a panel should focus on such items as its accuracy and whether it may reasonably be relied upon to support the inference drawn by the investigative agency.[34] In this dispute, however, the Panel not only failed to examine the evidence in its totality, it also 'examined whether certain pieces of evidence were sufficient to establish certain conclusions that the [US] did not seek to draw, at least solely on the basis of those pieces of evidence'.[35] Thus, in the view of the Appellate Body, the Panel failed to review the US determination, but reached 'its own view of whether entrustment or direction existed in this case'.[36] This *de novo* review of the evidence was contrary to the proper standard of review and the requirements of Article 11.[37]

6. Benefit

In its countervailing-duty investigation, the US rejected loan terms offered by private creditors of Hynix as market benchmarks, based on its finding that the creditors were entrusted or directed to offer those terms. The Panel concluded that, since the US erroneously found entrustment or direction with regard to these creditors, its rejection of them as market benchmarks was also erroneous. Since the Appellate Body reversed the Panel's findings on entrustment or direction, it found 'no basis for us to uphold the Panel's finding on benefit'. Accordingly, it reversed that determination.[38]

31 Appellate Body Report, para. 186.
32 Appellate Body Report, para. 187.
33 Appellate Body Report, para. 188.
34 Appellate Body Report, para. 188.
35 Appellate Body Report, para. 188.
36 Appellate Body Report, para. 188.
37 Appellate Body Report, para. 190.
38 Appellate Body Report, para. 205.

7. Specificity

The countervailing duty determination found that the financial contributions from all of the creditors were 'specific' within the meaning of Article 1.2 of the SCM Agreement because the program was directed toward a single enterprise, Hynix.[39] Because the Panel found no entrustment or direction with regard to the non-public creditors, however, it also found that the US finding of specificity with regard to these creditors was improper.[40] Following the logic of its reversal of the Panel's entrustment or direction, the Appellate Body also reversed the Panel's findings as to specificity with regard to the non-public creditors.[41]

8. No 'completing the analysis'

As is well known, the Appellate Body does not possess remand authority.[42] This means that when it reverses a panel's decision, the dispute usually is effectively ended, even though the nature of its reversal may leave crucial questions unanswered and may deny a complainant a decision on its claims.

A typical instance of this phenomenon occurs when a complainant asserts that the responding Member's measure is inconsistent with two or more of its WTO obligations. A panel may find in the complainant's favor in one instance, and – practicing judicial economy – conclude that it is unnecessary for it to decide the other. If the Appellate Body reverses the Panel's decision of a violation in the single decided issue, the second claim may simply be left undecided.

To avoid this situation whenever possible, the Appellate Body has developed a practice of 'completing the analysis'. When the factual findings of the Panel may provide an adequate basis for it to do so, the Appellate Body itself will supply the missing legal analysis on the undecided claim on the basis of those facts. But in some instances, the crucial facts have not been found by the Panel, and the record does not permit the Appellate Body to 'complete the analysis'. *DRAMS* was such an instance, even though it was not an example of the more typical two-claim case. In *DRAMS*, because the Panel employed the wrong methodology, it never decided some of the factual issues that it would have to have decided in order to employ the proper methodology.

The Appellate Body in *DRAMS* only reversed the finding of the Panel that the US was wrong in concluding that Korea entrusted or directed private creditors to provide benefit-conferring financial contributions to Hynix. However, the

39 See Panel Report, para. 7.204.

40 Panel Report, para. 7.208.

41 Appellate Body Report, para. 207.

42 The problem of the absence of remand authority is discussed in greater detail in David Palmeter and Petros C. Mavroidis, *Dispute Settlement in the World Trade Organization: Practice and Procedure*, 2nd edn, Cambridge University Press, 2004, pp. 227–233; David Palmeter, 'The WTO Appellate Body Needs Remand Authority', 32 *Journal of World Trade*, 51 (1) (1998).

Appellate Body did *not* decide the opposite. It did not decide that the US was correct in finding that Korea entrusted or directed the private creditors to provide those contributions. Whether the countervailing-duty order could have withstood a proper approach to reviewing the evidence is a question left unanswered. Because the evidentiary record was so sparse on issues that the Appellate Body felt it would need to examine to complete this analysis, it declined to do so and limited its conclusion on entrustment or direction, as well as benefit and specificity, to its examination of the Panel's legal conclusions, nothing more.[43]

9. Conclusion

The Appellate Body's legal conclusions in the *DRAMS* case seem sound. The Panel's consideration of the evidence was faulty, and this faulty consideration led to its failure to decide evidentiary issues that would have been relevant to a proper analysis. Consequently, after reversing the Panel on many points, the Appellate Body was unable to complete the analysis, could not remand the matter to the Panel for further proceedings, and, therefore, made no recommendation to the Dispute Settlement Body. The result was that, nearly two years after it invoked the dispute-settlement process, Korea was left without a decision on its claim that the US imposition of countervailing duties on exports of *DRAMS* from Hynix was contrary to the SCM Agreement. This hardly seems to square with the statement in Article 3.3 of the DSU:

> The prompt settlement of situations in which a Member considers that any benefits accruing to it directly or indirectly under the covered agreements are being impaired by measures taken by another Member is essential to the effective functioning of the WTO and the maintenance of a proper balance between the rights and obligations of Members.

It seems clear that the dispute-settlement process would be improved by granting remand authority to the Appellate Body.

43 Appellate Body Report, paras. 197–198, 208.

Comment

US – Countervailing Duty Investigation of DRAMS

Prepared for the ALI Project on the Case Law of the WTO

THOMAS J. PRUSA

Department of Economics, New Jersey Hall, 75 Hamilton Street, Rutgers University, New Brunswick, NJ, 08901-1248. Email: prusa@econ.rutgers.edu

Abstract: There are two compelling issues involved in *US – Countervailing Duty Investigation of DRAMS*. First, there is the question of whether creditors were 'entrusted or directed' to make financial contributions to Hynix, a large South Korean DRAM producer. This was the main topic addressed by the Appellate Body (AB) and is the focus of the François–Palmeter paper. Second, there is there is the question of injury assessment and nonattribution. Because the US did not appeal the Panel's decision, this aspect of the WTO dispute was not considered by the AB.

Background

In 1995, over $40 billion of DRAMs were sold worldwide. For the next seven years the DRAM market languished with sales revenue flat or declining year after year. In 2001, less than $10 billion of DRAMs were sold, even though the standard DRAM chip sold increased in capacity from just four megabytes (MB) to 256 MB. Prices were lower than industry experts predicted, and all DRAM manufacturers were losing money. As a result of this demand slump, by mid-2001 many DRAM manufacturers were on the brink of bankruptcy. Hynix, a large South Korean DRAM manufacturer, was perhaps the entity most precariously teetering on the ledge. Hynix, formerly a division of the giant Korean Hyundai Group, was an important part of the Korean economy, accounting for almost 4% of all Korean exports in 2000. Hynix was highly leveraged with billions in outstanding loans from both the Korean government (much of it dating back to when it was part of the Hyundai Group) and private creditors from around the world.

In 2001 creditors of Hynix agreed to a $7 billion bailout; the financing was comprised of new additional credit and a $2 billion debt/equity swap.

Participating creditors included government-owned banks, banks partially owned (but arguably controlled) by the Korean government, and a number of foreign banks.

Despite the promised bailout, Hynix remained the subject of numerous rumors of mergers with other DRAM manufacturers throughout 2001. The conventional wisdom was that there was excess DRAM capacity in the market and that Hynix was an ideal target for consolidation and rationalization. In early 2002, US-based Micron Technology Inc. offered $3.4 billion for Hynix's memory-chip business (the core of Hynix's business). The offer was rejected by Hynix's board in May 2002. When its takeover offer was spurned, Micron formally requested the countervailing-duty investigation with which it had been threatening Hynix. In 2003, the US determined that the bailout constituted a subsidy to Hynix and that the subsidized exports were the cause of material injury. The Korean government appealed the decision to the WTO. The panel ruled in favor of Korea on the vast majority of its claims, finding both the US's injury and subsidy calculations to be inconsistent with WTO rules. The US did not appeal the injury decision but requested the AB review the subsidy issues.

The issue of subsidy

As discussed by François and Palmeter, the key question before the AB was the whether creditors were 'entrusted or directed' by the Korean government to make financial contributions to Hynix. François and Palmeter discuss the idea that a series of events, taken together, can be construed to satisfy the 'entrusted or directed' standard even though any single incident is not definitive. In effect, the sum of the parts is greater than the whole.

One example of an event in a sequence of questionable acts is the allegation that banks waived loan ceilings to Hynix. Taken at face value, waiving the loan limit suggests that the government was going beyond standard practice to keep Hynix financially viable. This issue is incriminating evidence of special treatment. By itself, it was not evidence of a subsidy, but as part of a large number of other 'unusual' events, François and Palmeter argue that it can support a determination of government control.

A more subtle issue is whether the loan limits were truly waived. In particular, a key question not discussed by François and Palmeter is whether the preexisting loans were made to Hynix or to the Greater Hyundai Group and partially inherited by Hynix. If the latter, the US might argue that the loan ceiling was breached, while Korea might argue that additional loans to Hynix were below the ceiling (because it discounts the original Hyundai loans). The view that the sequence is demonstrative depends not just on the nature of each event, but also on the probative value of each claim. Without a better understanding of the underlying events, it is almost impossible to know whether the sequence is telling.

My own view is that, while the sequence discussion is interesting, the authors should also have tackled a more basic issue: is it likely that the government of Korea's intervention changed the market outcome? If so, then it is likely that the subsidy has affected the market in a way not desired by the WTO: this is the crux of the US's argument.

Korea's argument stressed the *ex post* outcome. That is, Korea argued that the foreign banks offered Hynix interest rates comparable to those offered to other companies at the same time period. According to Korea, there was no suasion, as foreign banks were treating Hynix no differently than they were treating other commercial clients. But the observed market outcome does not tell us about what the outcome would have been without government intervention.

To be a bit more precise, suppose for a moment that the market interest rate is i^M and that the return on a loan to Hynix is i^H. For argument's sake, let's suppose that without government intervention $i^H < i^M$; thus, without government intervention, banks will not provide the loan package. Now, let's also suppose that with government intervention $i^H = i^M$; and thus banks provide the loan package.

Korea argues that the fact that $i^H = i^M$ is an indication that the banks did not have 'their arms twisted' to make the Hynix loans; after all, they receive the same return as on other comparable loans. However, if the above scenario is true, the fact that we observe $i^H = i^M$ tells us nothing about what the return would have been without government involvement (assuming, that is, that there really was intervention).

The issue of injury

The US's injury determination suffered from many of the same shortcomings that have been discussed in other disputes. Two key flaws were noted by the Panel. First, the US did not separate the effects of Hynix DRAMs (i.e., the product subject to the investigation) from Samsung DRAMs (i.e., product not subject to the investigation). Second, the US did not properly assess the overall condition of the domestic industry in light of the weak market demand. In effect, Korea argued that Hynix was blamed for injury caused by Samsung (which accounted for the bulk of Korean DRAMs shipped to the US) and by weak demand. As it has done in the past, the US could not present any formal evidence that it had disentangled the various factors. The agency making injury determinations in the US, the US International Trade Commission (USITC), is reluctant to fully embrace economic inference and econometrics, as doing so would entail a loss of discretion.

The US did not appeal the injury analysis to the AB and instead requested the USITC to reconsider its determination in light of the Panel's comments. Always reluctant to acknowledge shortcomings in its analysis, the USITC simply re-affirmed its prior decision without any substantive changes in its analysis.

Postscript

This case highlights shortcomings of the WTO appeals process. On the one hand, the AB was unhappy with certain aspects of the Panel's determination and could not support the Panel's conclusions as written. On the other hand, the AB did not embrace the US position, either. Thus, what was really needed was the ability for the AB to remand the case back to the Panel. The need for a remand procedure is further highlighted by the seeming refusal of the USITC to incorporate the Panel's injury criticisms. Intransigence is hardly the basis for an appeal, but the unwillingness of the USITC to adjust its injury analysis is frustrating for foreign parties.

While Korea could have again filed an appeal to the WTO, two developments apparently changed the Korean government's calculus. First, a vast worldwide price-fixing scheme came to light in December 2003. As noted above, the Hynix bankruptcy crisis was caused primarily by persistent weak DRAM prices. Apparently, prices would have been even weaker had not all the major DRAM manufacturers regularly met to set prices over a three-year period. In light of the embarrassing disclosure, the Korean government may not have had the stomach for continuing its efforts on behalf of Hynix. Second, the duties on Hynix accelerated Hynix's efforts to build facilities in China. By the time the WTO AB made its decision, the US CVD orders were effectively moot, as Hynix either shipped the chips to China for processing or shipped DRAMs produced in its China facility to the US. Thus, there was substantially less commercial interest in the outcome by 2005.

United States – Sunset Reviews of Anti-Dumping Measures on Oil Country Tubular Goods from Argentina: a cloudy sunset

GENE M. GROSSMAN
Princeton University
JASPER WAUTERS
White and Case, LLP

Abstract: We review the WTO Appellate Body report on *United States – Sunset Reviews of Anti-Dumping Measures on Oil Country Tubular Goods from Argentina* (WT/DS268/AB/R, 29 November 2004). This dispute is one of several that deals with sunset reviews of antidumping-duty orders. In its ruling, the AB reasserts a rigid distinction between mandatory and discretionary law, and sets a very high standard for Member challenges to laws or practices that allow for violations of WTO obligations but do not mandate such behavior. We argue that this ruling is unfortunate, because it diminishes scope of and incentives for 'as-such' challenges to laws and practices, which have a potentially useful role to play in the world trading system. The AB ruling also overlooks the purpose and objectives of sunset reviews – to ensure that duty orders are not extended when their removal would generate no harm to an import competing industry – by failing to impose sufficient discipline on their conduct. We argue that a sunset review requires an evaluation of competitive conditions in the industry and of the reasons and incentives for dumping, in order that the investigating authority can judge whether the removal of a duty order would lead to a continuation or recurrence of dumping and injury. The Appellate Body's rulings in this and other similar cases have the effect of relieving the investigating authority of this responsibility and thereby render the sunset review process virtually meaningless.

1. The Dispute

This dispute concerns the 'sunset' review conducted by the United States of an antidumping-duty order it had imposed on imports of oil country tubular goods

This paper reviews the WTO Appellate Body report *United States – Sunset Reviews of Anti-Dumping Measures on Oil Country Tubular Goods from Argentina* (WT/DS268/AB/R 29 November 2004). It is prepared for The American Law Institute project on the case law of the WTO. The views expressed are those of the authors and do not necessarily reflect the views of their respective employers.

(OCTG) from Argentina and other sources. In a dumping investigation concluded in June 1995, the US Department of Commerce (USDOC) had found a dumping margin of 1.36% on exports by Siderca, the only Argentine exporter that had participated in its investigation. When the US International Trade Commission (USITC) found that dumped imports of OCTG from all sources had caused material injury to the domestic industry, the United States assessed an anti-dumping duty of 1.36% on all dumped imports of OCTG from Argentina. Siderca ceased to export OCTG to the United States following the application of that duty order.

In July 2000, five years after the order was issued, the USDOC initiated a so-called 'sunset review' to determine whether termination of the duty order on Argentine OCTG would likely lead to a recurrence or continuation of dumping, and the USITC investigated whether expiry of the duty order on all subject imports would likely lead to a continuation or recurrence of material injury to a US industry. When the investigating authorities found positively on both accounts and thus declined to revoke the duty order, Argentina complained to a dispute-settlement panel that the United States had failed to fulfill certain of its obligations under the *Agreement on Implementation of Article VI of the General Agreement on Tariffs and Trade 1994* (henceforth, the 'AD Agreement') by the manner in which it had conducted its sunset review.

Argentina's challenge included both claims against US laws and regulations 'as such' and against the application of such laws and regulations in the specific case of OCTG imports from Argentina. It argued before the Panel, inter alia, that Section II.A.3 of the US Sunset Policy Bulletin[1] (henceforth, the 'SPB') and USDOC 'practice' concerning determination of the likelihood of dumping in sunset reviews are inconsistent 'as such' with Article 11 of the AD Agreement governing the conduct of sunset reviews. Argentina also claimed that the USDOC had acted inconsistently with its obligations under various articles of the AD Agreement in the course of carrying out its sunset review of imports of OCTG from Argentina. In addition, it complained that the USITC had failed to obey the disciplines imposed by Articles 3 and 11 of the AD Agreement, which, it alleged, require an investigating authority to consider certain specific factors in the course of assessing the likelihood of recurrence or continuation of material injury. Moreover, it alleged impropriety in the US practice of cumulating imports from all subject sources in determining the likelihood of recurrence or continuation of injury. Of central importance in the case were Argentina's claims that certain provisions in Article 3 governing the determination of material injury in an initial dumping investigation also restrict the conduct of likelihood-of-injury investigations in sunset reviews.

1 'Policies Regarding the Conduct of Five-year ("Sunset") Review of Anti-dumping and Countervailing Duty Orders; Policy Bulletin', *United States Federal Register*, 63(73) (April 16, 1998).

1.1 *The SPB and USDOC practice on the likelihood of dumping*

Argentina pointed to Section II.A.3 of the SPB, which reads in relevant part as follows:

> The Department normally will determine that revocation of an anti-dumping order or termination of a suspended dumping investigation is likely to lead to continuation or recurrence of dumping where –
>
> (a) dumping continued at any level above *de minimis* after the issuance of the order or the suspension agreement, as applicable;
> (b) imports of the subject merchandise ceased after issuance of the order or the suspension agreement, as applicable; or
> (c) dumping was eliminated after the issuance of the order or the suspension agreement, as applicable, and import volumes for the subject merchandise declined significantly.
>
> The Department recognizes that, in the context of a sunset review of a suspended investigation, the data relevant to the criteria under paragraphs (a) through (c), above, may not be conclusive with respect to likelihood. Therefore, the Department may be more likely to entertain good cause arguments under paragraph II.C in a sunset review of a suspended investigation.

Argentina maintained that the 'normal' practice described in Section II.A.3 of the SPB constitutes a mechanistic formula for sunset reviews, in contradistinction to the requirements of Article 11.3 of the AD Agreement that the authorities must 'determine, in a review ... that the expiry of the duty would be likely to lead to continuation or recurrence of dumping and injury'. Argentina noted that the WTO Appellate Body (AB) had, in its ruling in *US–Corrosion-Resistant Steel* (para. 111), interpreted the words 'determine' and 'review' to 'suggest that authorities conducting a sunset review must act with an appropriate degree of diligence and arrive at a reasoned conclusion on the basis of information gathered as part of a process of reconsideration and examination'. A mechanistic practice could not fulfill this obligation. To bolster its case that the United States had failed to deliver the requisite 'diligence', Argentina provided evidence purporting to show that, in *every* sunset review previously undertaken by the USDOC, when the agency found that one of the three criteria outlined in Section II.A.3 had been satisfied, it had reached an affirmative finding of likely recurrence or continuation of dumping. Such a record, Argentina argued, could only result from a process in which the USDOC considers any of the three scenarios to be *conclusive* evidence of likely dumping. Therefore, the SPB and the consistent USDOC practices are not 'reasoned' but mechanistic, and accordingly should be ruled inconsistent with Article 11.3 of the AD Agreement.

The United States countered that, first, the SPB is not a 'measure' that can be challenged under the WTO dispute settlement process, and neither is it a government policy that has legal standing in US law. According to the United States, the SPB 'does not set forth rules or norms that are intended to have general prospective application'. Rather, it is meant 'simply as a transparency tool' to provide guidance to the public about evidence that normally would be considered probative. Inasmuch as the SPB does not *require* any particular process or finding by the USDOC in sunset reviews, the United States asserted, it cannot possibly breach any obligations under the AD Agreement, and so it should not rightfully be considered a subject for dispute settlement. In making these claims, the United States reiterated arguments it had put forth in *US–Corrosion-Resistant Steel*. The US argued that the USDOC sunset review practice cannot be challenged as a separate and independent measure under WTO law. Moreover, the United States added, even if the USDOC had never exercised its prerogative to rule negatively on the likelihood of continuation or recurrence of dumping in any case in which one of the three criteria of Section II.A.3 of SPB has been satisfied, that in no way would establish that it lacks the discretion to do so. The United States objected to a 'statistical analysis' that merely provides a 'correlation' between the scenarios set forth in Section II.A.3 and the outcomes of prior sunset reviews. According to the United States, Argentina had not fulfilled its obligation to prove that conformity with one of the three scenarios had determined the outcome of the sunset review of OCTG.

1.2 Likelihood of injury and the original injury determination under Article 3

A second main issue of dispute concerned the applicability of Article 3 of the AD Agreement, and in particular its mandates and tolerances for assessment of injury in an initial investigation of dumping to the procedures that could or must be used to assess the likelihood of continuation or recurrence of injury in the face of revocation of an antidumping-duty order.

Article 3 lays out the requirements for determining whether dumping has caused material injury to a domestic industry in the importing country. A footnote to the heading of Article 3 reads:

> Under this Agreement the term 'injury' shall, unless otherwise specified, be taken to mean material injury to a domestic industry, threat of material injury to a domestic industry or material retardation of the establishment of such an industry and shall be interpreted in accordance with the provisions of this Article.

Argentina argued that the disciplines of Article 3 of the AD Agreement with respect to 'injury' apply also to determinations of likelihood of injury in sunset reviews. The United States, it claimed, had not made a determination of likely recurrence or continuation of injury that complied with the requirements of Article 3. In particular, Argentina argued that the USITC did not fulfill the country's obligations under the AD Agreement in its investigation of likely injury in the review of OCTG to the extent that it did not provide 'an objective examination of ... the volume of the dumped imports and the effect of the dumped imports on prices in the domestic market for like products, and … the consequent impact of these imports on domestic producers of such products', that it did not provide 'evaluation of all relevant economic factors and indices having a bearing on the state of the industry' including the factors outlined in Article 3.4, and that it did not establish 'a causal relationship between the dumped imports and the injury to the domestic industry … based on an examination of all relevant evidence' available to it.

Argentina offered two arguments for its interpretation of the Agreement as regards the applicability of Article 3 disciplines to the likelihood-of-injury investigation in a sunset review. First, it noted, Article 11.3 requires that a member undertake a 'review' of the need for continued imposition of antidumping duties to 'determine' that the expiration of the duties would likely lead to a continuation or recurrence of dumping and injury. The AB had interpreted Article 11.3 in *US–Carbon Steel* and *US–Corrosion-Resistant Steel* to mean that the sunset review must have sufficient factual basis to allow the investigating authority to draw a 'reasoned and adequate conclusion'. According to Argentina, Article 3 of the AD Agreement provides the details of what should be considered a sufficient factual basis for such a conclusion.

Second, Argentina pointed to the text of the footnote to the heading of Article 3. This footnote provides a definition of 'injury' that should apply throughout the agreement. Since the injury that is to be investigated in a sunset review, as required by Article 11, is the same as the injury defined in Article 3, the procedures for assessing the injury ought to be the same in both instances, and the disciplines of Article 3 ought to apply directly to sunset reviews.

1.3 Cumulation in determination of injury in sunset review

Argentina also questioned the legality of 'cumulation' in the assessment of likely injury in sunset reviews. Argentina considered that, contrary to the remainder of Article 3, subparagraph 3.3 of the AD dealing with cumulation, applies only to original investigations of dumping. Article 3.3 provides that where imports of a product from more than one country are simultaneously subject to antidumping investigations, the authorities may cumulatively assess the effects of all such imports. It further spells out the conditions under which an investigating authority may cumulate. However, Article 11.3 states that 'any definitive antidumping duty shall be terminated on a date not later than five years from its imposition … unless the authorities determine … that the expiry of the duty would be likely to lead to continuation or recurrence of dumping and injury'. Argentina argued that the use of the singular term 'duty' in Article 11.3 precludes the use of cumulation in sunset reviews, which instead must consider whether the expiry of a duty, as applied to imports from a single WTO Member, would be likely to lead to a continuation or recurrence of injury. A 'duty', according to Argentina, refers to a single order that applies to imports from one country.

1.4 *The US response*

The United States refuted all of these claims. It pointed to the 'different nature' of original investigations and sunset reviews in asserting the different requirements for each. According to the United States, an original investigation must focus on extant conditions in the industry in order to assess the existence or threat of material injury. A sunset review, in contrast, necessitates a counterfactual analysis that addresses not the existing state of the industry, but the prospective state in the event of a removal of duties. Evidently, the different questions warrant different methods of analysis and consideration of different factors. Accordingly, the United States alleged, and notwithstanding the generally applicable definition of 'injury' in the footnote to the heading of Article 3, the disciplines imposed by that Article on initial investigations of injury cannot have been meant to apply also to sunset reviews.

Concerning the permissibility of cumulation in sunset reviews, the United States argued that the text does not speak to the issue and that 'Members are free to do that which is not prohibited.' The United States contested the significance given by Argentina to the singular use of the word 'duty' in Article 11.3, noting that the heading of Article 11 refers to 'duties' and that cumulation was a common practice by investigating authorities before the conclusion of the Uruguay Round, despite the use of the singular 'duty' in Article VI:6 of GATT 1994. Finally, the AD Agreement contains no cross-references that would link the prerequisites for the use of cumulation in an initial investigation, as outlined in Article 3.3, to obligations imposed by Article 11.3 for sunset reviews.

The parties disputed additional issues in this case having to do with the circumstances under which private parties are deemed to have waived their rights to participate in sunset reviews, the timeframe used by the USITC to assess the likelihood of recurrence of injury, and the appropriate standard for the term 'likely' in the matters considered in sunset reviews. However, we will limit our discussion in this paper to what we regard as the most important issues, which are the ones described above.

2. The Panel report and the parties' appeals

2.1 *The SPB – An Inconsistent Measure*

The Panel ruled that the SPB, indeed, is a measure that can be subject to WTO dispute settlement. It pointed for support to the AB report in *US–Corrosion-Resistant Steel*, which, it claimed, spoke directly to the issue.[2] The United States challenged this ruling on appeal, claiming that the AB's reversal of the Panel's ruling in the earlier case had been based on the insufficiency of the Panel's analysis.

2 The Panel referred to the AB's statement in para. 81 of *US–Corrosion-Resistant Steel* that 'any act or omission attributable to a WTO Member can be a measure of that Member for purposes of dispute settlement proceedings'.

Inasmuch as the AB did not go on to complete or correct the Panel's analysis in *US–Corrosion-Resistant Steel*, it did not intend to resolve the issue of whether the SPB can be the subject of a WTO complaint. The United States reiterated its position on appeal that the SPB has no legal standing in US law and that it is only a tool to provide information to the private sector. The United States argued that the Panel had neglected the status of the SPB within the municipal system of the country.

On the consistency of the SPB, as such, with Article 11.3 of the AD Agreement, the Panel also ruled in favor of Argentina. It observed that the AB had ruled out mechanistic or formulaic approaches to sunset review in *US–Corrosion-Resistant Steel*, and stated that, as a result, any scheme that attributes 'determinative value' to certain factors – as opposed to indicative value – is 'likely to violate' Article 11.3 of the AD Agreement.[3] The Panel reasoned that if any of the three scenarios in Article II.A.3 of the SPB is treated as conclusive for determining the likelihood of continuation or recurrence of dumping, then the SPB must be deemed inconsistent with Article 11.3. The Panel first examined whether the text of the SPB and the three scenarios set forth therein are meant to be 'determinative' or simply 'indicative' and concluded that the wording was ambiguous on this point. It thus proceeded to examine how the SPB had been applied in practice. The Panel concluded from the evidence provided by Argentina that the USDOC does indeed regard the provisions of Section II.A.3 of the SPB to be determinative regarding the likelihood of continuation or recurrence of dumping subsequent to the expiry of an antidumping-duty order. Thus, it ruled the SPB to be inconsistent with US obligations under the AD Agreement.

The United States challenged this ruling as well, claiming that the Panel's finding was based on a mere statistical analysis of prior sunset reviews and thus did not meet the standard for an 'objective assessment' in the current case. It reiterated that the USDOC has discretion to come to any conclusion it deems warranted about the likelihood of continued or recurring dumping, notwithstanding the correspondence of the facts in a case with the scenarios in Article II.A.3 and notwithstanding the pattern of findings in its prior reviews. The fact that the USDOC has not, as yet, exercised its discretion to deviate from the scenarios set forth in the SPB does not change the fact that it has such discretion. In sum, the Panel had failed to show that the text of Article II.A.3 of the SPB had *caused* the positive determination in the OCTG sunset review.

2.2 *Article 3 disciplines not applicable to sunset reviews*

In considering the applicability of the disciplines of Article 3 to sunset reviews, the Panel observed that in *US–Corrosion-Resistant Steel*, the AB had noted the differences between initial investigations and sunset reviews and had ruled that the investigating authority is not obliged to make a determination of *existing* dumping

3 WT/DS268/R (hereinafter, the 'Panel Report'), para. 7.143.

in a sunset review. By analogy, the Panel reasoned, it should not be obliged to make a determination of *existing* injury. Inasmuch as the authority is under no obligation to rule on existing injury (but only the likelihood thereof subsequent to a removal of duties), it need not follow the dictates of Article 3. However, the Panel ruled that if the authority does, indeed, undertake to determine the presence of injury in a sunset review, or relies on a past-injury determination in its sunset review, it would be bound to do so in the manner set out in Article 3.[4]

Argentina appealed this ruling, submitting that a rigorous and detailed examination of the issue of likely injury is mandated by the terms 'review' and 'determine' in Article 11.3. These words impose substantive disciplines on the conduct of an injury determination in any dumping investigation. Article 3 spells out what the Members considered to be necessary for such an examination. Therefore, Argentina claimed, these disciplines were meant to apply in sunset reviews as well. Argentina reiterated its claim that the footnote to the heading of Article 3 imposes a uniform definition of injury for the entirety of the AD Agreement, and that, by implication, any reference to injury in the Agreement must be interpreted in accordance with the provisions outlined in the remainder of Article 3. The investigating authority in a sunset review could not determine the likelihood of continuation or recurrence of injury following the removal of an antidumping-duty order unless it followed the steps outlined in Article 3, where 'injury' is defined and discussed.

2.3 Cumulation permitted in sunset reviews without disciplines imposed by Article 3.3

The Panel also ruled against Argentina on the permissibility of cumulation in sunset reviews. The Panel regarded the lack of an explicit statement in the Agreement as to whether cumulation is generally permitted to imply that investigating authorities are not prohibited from choosing this approach. It rejected Argentina's argument based on the use of the singular term 'duty' in Article 11.3, finding this attribution of 'far-reaching substantive meaning' to the use of the singular rather than the plural to be 'implausible'.[5] The silence of Article 11.3 on the question of cumulation was considered to imply a permission to cumulate also at the review stage. The Panel emphatically rejected Argentina's argument that, if cumulation is allowed in a sunset review, then surely the disciplines set forth in Article 3.3 for original investigations would apply at this stage as well. The Panel ruled that Article 3.3 governing the use of cumulation in initial investigations of dumping does not apply to sunset reviews, because Article 3.3 expressly mentions that the conditions are meant to govern investigations of the effects of *existing* dumping.[6] The Panel held that the text of Article 3.3 thus clearly

4 Panel Report, para. 7.274.
5 Ibid., para. 7.334.
6 Ibid., para. 7.336.

limits its applicability to original investigations. Argentina challenged these findings on grounds similar to its original arguments to the Panel. It claimed that the use of the singular term 'duty' was purposive, reflecting the Members' recognition that the changed circumstances over five years of application of a duty order, and the prospective nature of the likelihood inquiry, would render an investigating authority incapable of assessing the appropriateness of cumulation in a sunset review. For example, imports from a particular Member might no longer be present in the market, as was the case for imports of OCTG from Argentina. According to Argentina, the lack of a factual basis for assessing the appropriateness of cumulation explains why the authorization in Article 3.3 was meant to be limited to initial investigations. In any case, if cumulation is deemed to be permissible in sunset reviews, some constraints on its use such as those outlined in Article 3.3 certainly are implied, or else the investigating authorities would be free to use cumulation without discipline, which could not have been the Members' intended outcome.

3. The Appellate Body's decision

3.1 The SPB – a measure, but is it inconsistent?

The AB upheld the Panel's ruling that the SPB is a 'measure' subject to WTO dispute settlement. It regarded the United States's argument that the SPB is not a legal instrument under US law as irrelevant to whether it is a measure that can be challenged in the WTO, because the WTO dispute settlement bodies have no standing to opine on matters of US domestic law. Rather, the dispute settlement bodies must judge what policies are consistent with the provisions of the WTO Agreement and, for that purpose, they must consider 'acts setting forth rules or norms intended to have general and prospective application' as falling within their purview. The AB found that the SPB is a measure that can be subject to dispute settlement, because it has 'normative value' inasmuch as it 'provides administrative guidance and creates expectations among the public and among private actors'. Moreover, it is intended to have 'general' and 'prospective' application, because it is meant to apply to *all* sunset reviews conducted by the United States (para. 187).

However, the AB reversed the Panel's finding that Section II.A.3 of SPB is inconsistent, as such, with Article 11.3 of the AD Agreement. The AB endorsed the Panel's standard for assessing the consistency of the SPB with Article 11.3, namely that consistency hinged on whether the three scenarios of Section II.A.3 are determinative or merely indicative in the analysis of continued or recurring dumping. It also concurred with the Panel that the text of SPB is not dispositive of the question whether the three scenarios set out in the SPB should be regarded by the USDOC as conclusive. However, it differed with the Panel on the significance of the historical data provided by Argentina regarding the outcomes of prior sunset reviews.

First, the AB observed that the 'volume of dumped imports' and 'dumping margins' before and after the issuance of antidumping-duty orders are highly important factors in evaluating the likelihood of continuation or recurrence of dumping. Therefore, the scenarios described in Section II.A.3 of SPB have probative value. In the view of the AB, in order to determine whether the scenarios are regarded by the USDOC as conclusive, the Panel would have had to identify cases in which the conditions of one of the scenarios were met, and yet the probative value of other factors would have outweighed that of the relevant scenario and would have led to a different finding. In this instance, the Panel did not look for or identify such examples, but relied solely on the 'correlation' provided by Argentina. Since the Panel did not undertake a qualitative analysis of any of the cases included in the aggregate statistics, it could not know whether the determinations rested on factual foundations or whether they had been reached mechanistically. The AB concluded that, without qualitative examination of any of the cases underlying the aggregate statistics submitted by Argentina, it is 'not possible to conclude *definitively* that these determinations were based exclusively on these scenarios in disregard of other factors' (para. 212, emphasis added). The AB regretted that the United States had failed to identify cases in which other factors constituted the basis for the USDOC's determination or where the probative value of the scenarios outweighed that of other factors introduced by interested parties. In short, the United States had not challenged the factual correctness of Argentina's statistics, nor had it provided any evidence to counter the proposition that the USDOC applied the three scenarios in a mechanistic fashion. However, the AB considered that the lack of such assistance from the United States cannot excuse the Panel from conducting an objective assessment of the matter (para. 214). Finally, the AB emphasized that its ruling should not be taken to hold that Section II.A.3 of the SPB is in fact consistent with Article 11.3 of the AD Agreement, but only that the Panel had failed to meet the standards required for it to find a violation of the agreement.

3.2 Article 3 injury disciplines do not apply in sunset reviews

The AB upheld the Panel's decision that the investigating authorities are not bound to consider all of the specific factors mentioned in Article 3 of the AD when determining the likelihood of injury in a sunset review. The AB accepted Argentina's claim that the footnote to the heading of Article 3 defines 'injury' for the whole of the AD Agreement, but rejected its argument that the designation of a single definition implies that all provisions of Article 3 concerning the determination of injury in original investigations apply also to sunset reviews. According to the AB, a distinction can be made between the *definition* of injury and the *determination* of injury (para. 277). The Agreement further distinguishes between a determination of injury, addressed in Article 3, and a determination of likely recurrence or continuation of injury, addressed in

Article 11.3. These two determinations are different in nature and have different purposes, according to the AB (para. 279). Article 11.3 contains neither a cross-reference to Article 3 nor a textual basis for concluding that any of the specific provisions in Article 3 must be followed by the investigating authorities in a sunset review. While the words 'review' and 'determine' in Article 11.3 do require 'a reasoned conclusion on the basis of information gathered as part of a process of reconsideration and examination' (para. 283), they leave room for the investigating authority to design and implement an appropriate analysis that fulfills this obligation. In other words, such a requirement does not have to be satisfied through a specific methodology or the consideration of particular factors in every case, such as those mandated by Article 3 in the case of original determinations. Nevertheless, certain of the analyses mandated by Article 3 may prove to be probative or even required in order for an authority to arrive at a reasoned conclusion. For example, the AB considered that the fundamental requirements of 'positive evidence' and an 'objective examination' of Article 3.1 would be equally relevant to likelihood determinations under Article 11.3 (para. 284).

3.3 *Cumulation in sunset reviews – a permissible practice without disciplines?*

Finally, the AB upheld the Panel's ruling that Article 11.3 does not prohibit the use of cumulation in the likelihood-of-injury determination of a sunset review, nor do the conditions of Article 3.3 for the use of cumulation in an initial investigation necessarily apply to a sunset review. The AB rejected Argentina's argument about the significance of the use of the singular term 'duty', because the agreement uses the singular term also in other places (such as in Article 9.2) to apply to circumstances in which there are multiple sources of a dumped product from one or several countries. The mere use of the term 'duty' in the singular in Article 11.3 does not necessarily suggest that the likelihood-of-injury determination must be made on a Member by Member basis (para. 293). In addition to this textual argument, the AB observed that the rationale for allowing cumulation in original investigations is 'equally applicable' to likelihood-of-injury determinations. When considering the likelihood of continuation or recurrence of injury, the prospective injury in question might be caused by imports from multiple sources at the same time, just as the extant injury in an initial investigation might have multiple sources. Therefore, the reasons why cumulation might be potentially useful in evaluating the cause of existing injury are also reasons why it might be useful in evaluating the likelihood of future injury upon the expiry of an antidumping-duty order. The AB concluded that given the expressed intent of the Members to permit cumulation in injury determinations in the initial investigation and the rationale that exists for doing so, which applies also to the determination of the likelihood of future injury, the Members did not mean to preclude the use of cumulation in sunset reviews.[7] Nor did the AB accept Argentina's arguments that, if cumulation is permissible in sunset reviews, it must meet the conditions specified in Article 3.3 for initial investigations, or else there would be no discipline at all on such reviews. According to the AB, the text of Article 3.3 limits its applicability to original investigations. This does not imply that the authorities have carte blanche when deciding to cumulate, because sunset reviews must be based on a 'rigorous examination' leading to a 'reasoned conclusion' supported by 'positive evidence' and a 'sufficient factual basis' (para. 302). These requirements also govern the decision to resort to cumulation and thus impose substantive disciplines on the authorities.

4. Legal analysis

4.1 The SPB: 'measures' in the WTO

For a proper understanding of the issue, it is perhaps useful to recall the origins of the Sunset Policy Bulletin and its relationship to other instruments of US law. The United States did not have any sunset provision for its antidumping duties prior to the conclusion of the Uruguay Round and the introduction of the Uruguay Round Agreements Act.[8] Sections 751(c) and 752 to the Tariff Act, which were added to US law following the conclusion of the Agreement, provide for such reviews. Amendments to the Regulations further implemented the new regime.[9] Section 218 of Part 351 of Title 19 of the Regulations lays out the specific rules that the USDOC must follow when conducting a sunset review.

Before the United States began its first sunset review, the USDOC published the Sunset Policy Bulletin in the US Federal Register. In the Sunset Policy Bulletin, the agency sets forth 'policies regarding the conduct of five-year ('sunset') reviews … pursuant to the provisions of sections 751(c) and 752 of the Tariff Act of 1930, as amended, and [USDOC's] regulations'.[10] The Sunset Policy Bulletin is 'intended to complement the applicable statutory and regulatory provisions by providing guidance on methodological or analytical issues not explicitly addressed by the statute and regulations'.[11]

The question before the Panel and the AB in this case was whether such a 'policy document' can actually be challenged 'as such' before the WTO, i.e. independent

7 Since sunset reviews are to be based on existing facts, as well as projected events, the AB rejected Argentina's argument that cumulation in sunset reviews would not be appropriate for lack of a 'factual basis' (AB Report, para. 299).

8 Uruguay Round Agreements Act, Public Law 103–465, 108 Stat. 4809, which became law in the United States on 8 December 1994.

9 'Procedures for Conducting Five-Year ("Sunset") Reviews of Anti-dumping and Countervailing Duty Orders', United States Federal Register, 63(54)(20 March 1998), p. 13516, codified in Part 351 of Title 19 of the Regulations.

10 SPB, p. 18871.

11 SPB, pp. 18871–18872.

of its application in a particular case, and independent of the statute and regulations it is intended to complement. In prior cases, the AB had expressed the view, which was reiterated in this case, that, in principle, *any act or omission attributable to a WTO Member* can be a measure for purposes of dispute settlement proceedings. The acts or omissions that are so attributable are, typically, acts or omissions of the organs of the state, including those of the executive branch.[12] This clearly means that even nonbinding administrative guidance may be subject to challenge as a 'measure'.[13] The Panel relied on past statements of the AB in ruling that the SPB is a measure subject to dispute settlement and the AB logically upheld that decision.

In light of its previous rulings that 'anything goes', it is perhaps surprising that the AB felt it necessary to justify its ruling that the SPB is a measure that can be subject to dispute settlement on the basis that '*it has "normative value" and is intended to have "general" and "prospective" application*' (para. 187). If *any* act or omission attributable to the state can be challenged before the WTO, why should it matter that the SPB has normative value or that it is intended to have general and prospective application?

In our view, the issue of what constitutes a measure is much ado about nothing. Questions such as those that were addressed in this case confuse form with substance. Any act or omission attributable to a state is capable of engaging state responsibility, regardless of the form in which the act is expressed. This surely implies that a series of acts that reveal a *practice* may be challenged as well. Strangely, the AB has repeatedly stated – including in this case – that it has yet to pronounce on the issue of whether a practice may be challenged 'as such' in WTO dispute settlement.[14] Yet, at the same time, it considers the SPB, which is nothing more than the codification and documentation of an intended practice, to be a measure that can be challenged.

Indeed, the SPB is not a law or regulation. Rather, it announces the intentions of a governmental agency and explains how the agency will use the discretion

12 *US–Corrosion-Resistant Steel*, para. 82; also see AB Report, *Guatemala–Cement I* (footnote 47 to para. 69), where the AB ruled that in the practice established under the GATT 1947, a 'measure' may be *any* act of a Member, whether or not legally binding, and it can include even nonbinding administrative guidance by a government.

13 This view was based on the practice established under the GATT 1947 confirming that a measure may be *any* act of a Member, whether or not legally binding, and it can include even nonbinding administrative guidance by a government (see *Japan–Trade in Semi-Conductors*, adopted 4 May 1988, BISD 35S/116). It is clear that a measure can also be an *omission or a failure to act* on the part of a Member (see, for example, *India–Patent Protection for Pharmaceutical and Agricultural Chemical Products*, complaint by the United States, WT/DS50/R and WT/DS50/AB/R, adopted 16 January 1998, and also *India – Patent Protection for Pharmaceutical and Agricultural Chemical Products*, complaint by the European Communities and its Member States, WT/DS79/R, adopted 22 September 1998).

14 In para. 220, the AB wrote, 'Therefore, even assuming arguendo that a practice may be challenged as a measure in WTO dispute settlement – an issue on which we express no view here.' In *US–Gambling*, the AB stated that it 'has not, to date, pronounced upon the issue of whether "practice" may be challenged as such, as a measure in WTO dispute settlement' (para. 132).

left to it by the applicable legal instruments. A 'practice' may be regarded either as a string of individual cases or as a norm not expressed in a formal government document, or both. But is there any real difference between an unwritten norm and a written document such as the SPB? The expression of the norm in written form does facilitate the job of the complaining party, who can then point to the document to establish that a norm exists. When no such documentation of a practice is available, the complaining party may face a greater evidentiary burden in establishing the meaning and scope of the norm. But, in either case, there should be no difference for implementation purposes between a challenge to practice and a challenge to a particular instance in which the practice is used. When a practice is successfully challenged, the Member engaging in that practice must change its behavior and amend any written codification thereof. When a Member is found to have violated its obligations in a particular case, its good-faith implementation of the settlement ruling requires similarly that it change its behavior in any comparable situations that might subsequently arise. In other words, a Member that violates a WTO Agreement in some instance is obliged not only to right the wrong, but to change its practice as well.

So, why would a Member challenge a practice, when the evidentiary burden is greater in such a case and a successful challenge of a particular application ought to yield the same outcome? And why must the system tolerate such challenges to practice? The answers have to do with the realities of implementation. The recent disputes over US practice of 'zeroing' in calculating dumping margins are a case in point. In these disputes, the EC and Japan challenged the US practice of zeroing as such – in *US–Zeroing (EC)* and *US–Zeroing (Japan)* – presumably because they were not convinced that a ruling against zeroing in a particular instance would suffice to induce the United States to amend its general practice.[15] Given the persistence of US practice on this matter, their concerns apparently were warranted. And precisely because of this possibility for recalcitrant implementation, it is important that Members be allowed to challenge any measure, be it a law, a regulation, or a practice, and be it in written form or not.

In short, we believe that the AB was correct to consider the SPB to be a measure subject to dispute resolution, but not because it has normative value and is intended to have general and prospective application. Rather, the conclusion is warranted by the fact that the SPB represents an act of the US government that outlines its intended practice in sunset reviews.

15 In contrast, India challenged a similar zeroing practice by the EC in *EC–Bed Linen*, but in this case the challenge was made to a particular instance in which the practice was used, namely in the alleged dumping of bed linen. When the EC's method of calculating the dumping margin was found to be in violation of the AD Agreement in the bed-linen case, the EC proceeded to change its methodology for calculating dumping margins for all subsequent investigations.

4.2 *When does a nonbinding instrument or a 'practice' violate WTO obligations?*

The AB rulings on the SPB are important from a systemic point of view. In our opinion, they represent an unfortunate return to a strict application of the GATT distinction between mandatory and discretionary law. Hopes were raised following the Appellate Body's report in *US–Corrosion-Resistant Steel* that the end of this strict distinction was near. It appeared that the AB would be willing to accept that not only legislation *requiring* WTO-inconsistent behavior, but also laws that *allowed* such behavior could be found to violate a Member's obligations under the Agreement. Support for a less rigid interpretation of the old GATT distinction had been aptly expressed by the Panel in *US–Section 301*. We fear that the ruling in *US–OCTG from Argentina* closes the door once more and reveals the AB's intention to maintain a strict interpretation of the distinction. Evidently, the AB will consider only laws, regulations, and administrative measures that mandate WTO-inconsistent action to be in possible violation of a Member's obligations.

We recall that under general public international law, a State may challenge the particular application of a law or regulation, but State responsibility is not engaged by the mere existence of a law.[16] The situation is different in the GATT/WTO where the GATT Contracting Parties and WTO Members are allowed to challenge another Member's laws or regulations independent of their application in a particular case. The international trading system was structured this way, because the provisions of the GATT/WTO are meant not only to protect current trade but also to create a predictable environment for future trade. If Members could not challenge legislation that mandates actions at variance with the Agreement until the administrative acts implementing the legislation had actually been applied to their trade, the worthy objective of predictability would be defeated.[17]

Traditionally, however, the opportunity to challenge legislation on an 'as such' basis has been limited to legislation that mandates actions inconsistent with

16 This point was noted by the Panel in *US–Section 301*:

> Under traditional public international law, legislation under which an eventual violation could, or even would, subsequently take place, does not normally in and of itself engage State responsibility. If, say, a State undertakes not to expropriate property of foreign nationals without appropriate compensation, its State responsibility would normally be engaged only at the moment foreign property had actually been expropriated in a given instance. (para. 7.80).

17 GATT Panel Report, *United States–Superfund*, para. 5.2.2, referred to by the AB in *US–1916 Act*, para. 88. The Panel in *US–Section 301* also pointed to the indirect impact of trade laws on individuals as being the main difference between public international law and international trade law in order to explain this different approach to challenging legislation on an 'as such' basis:

> In treaties which concern only the relations between States, State responsibility is incurred only when an actual violation takes place. By contrast, in a treaty the benefits of which depend in part on the activity of individual operators the legislation itself may be construed as a breach, since the mere existence of legislation could have an appreciable 'chilling effect' on the economic activities of individuals. (para. 7.81)

the Agreement. Under this approach, only laws, regulations, and administrative measures that *require* behavior inconsistent with the trade agreement or that *impede* a country's compliance with its obligations under the agreement may constitute a violation as such. If a law leaves the administrative authorities with the *discretion* to act in a manner inconsistent with WTO obligations, such a law would not be considered in violation 'as such' with the Agreement. Rather, Members would need to challenge specific applications of such laws and show that the discretion left to the administrative authorities had been exercised in a manner that constituted a violation. The AB applied this distinction in a number of cases, most conspicuously in its report on *US–1916 Act*.[18]

Nevertheless, and surprisingly, the AB stated in its report on *US–Corrosion-Resistant Steel* that it had yet to make any determination as to the continued validity of this distinction in WTO law. In that case, which was the first to challenge the SPB, the AB overturned the Panel's decision for having applied the distinction between mandatory and discretionary law in a 'mechanistic fashion'. It considered the distinction to be an analytical tool, the importance of which would vary from case to case.[19]

The decision in *US–Corrosion-Resistant Steel* was hailed by some as an important reversal in the AB's approach. Howse and Staiger (2006: 34) conclude that 'by placing such emphasis on the status of the mandatory/discretionary distinction as an "analytical tool", the AB is telling us what the distinction is not: it is not a meta-rule that overrides or precludes the determination of state responsibility based on a reading of WTO treaty provisions.' They interpreted the AB as saying that a discretionary law could now be found to violate a Member's obligations under the WTO Agreement. In so doing, they suggested that the AB's arguments appeared to echo those of the Panel in *US–Section 301* and that the AB seemed to be endorsing, albeit implicitly, the jurisprudence of that Panel.

We recall that the Panel in *US–Section 301* made a convincing case for allowing discretionary legislation to be successfully challenged under certain circumstances. In that case, the Panel ruled that the traditional dichotomy between mandatory and discretionary law did not imply that discretionary legislation could never violate a WTO Agreement. Rather, the potential for discretionary legislation to contravene the Agreement would depend on the type of obligation that allegedly had been violated. For example, if the Agreement obliges a certain behavior, and thereby excludes administrative discretion, a law that allows such discretion presumably would constitute a violation of obligations.[20] The Panel gave the following instructive illustration to clarify its point:

> Imagine two farmers with adjacent land and a history of many disputes concerning real and alleged mutual trespassing. In the past, self help through force

18 AB Report, *US–1916 Act*, paras. 87–88.
19 AB Report, *US–Corrosion Resistant Steel*, para. 93.
20 Panel Report, *US–Section 301*, para. 7.54.

> and threats of force has been used in their altercations. Naturally, exploitation of the lands close to the boundaries suffers since it is viewed as dangerous terrain. They now sign an agreement under which they undertake that henceforth in any case of alleged trespassing they will abjure self help and always and exclusively make recourse to the police and the courts of law. They specifically undertake never to use force when dealing with alleged trespass. After the entry into force of their agreement one of the farmers erects a large sign on the contested boundary: 'No Trespassing. Trespassers may be shot on sight.'
>
> One could, of course, argue that since the sign does not say that trespassers will be shot, the obligations of the agreement have not been violated. But would that be the 'better faith' interpretation of what had been promised? Had they not pledged always and exclusively to make recourse to the police and the courts of law? (paras. 7.65–7.66)

We concur with the sentiment expressed by the Panel in *US–Section 301*. The potential for a discretionary law to be inconsistent with a WTO Agreement should vary with the type and nature of the obligation alleged to have been violated. If the motivation for allowing legislation to be challenged as such is to provide the predictability needed to plan future trade, then challenges to discretionary laws are essential tools to achieve this end. When the Agreement clearly requires a particular course of action, a law that authorizes the administrative authorities to behave differently should be regarded as inconsistent with the Agreement and a violation as such.

Unfortunately, the ruling in the case discussed here runs counter to the sentiments expressed by the Panel in *US–Section 301*. The AB appears to adhere still to a rigid distinction between mandatory and discretionary law. Its ruling reinforces the proposition that 'as such' claims will be held to a higher standard than claims against individual measures;[21] that an 'as such' claim can only succeed if it is firmly established that the law or norm being challenged *requires* a particular behavior contrary to WTO obligations; and that the preconditions for a successful 'as such' challenge are independent of the nature or scope of the obligation alleged to have been violated. It is now clear that the AB meant to say in *US–Corrosion-Resistant Steel* only that a law that appears to be written in a discretionary manner

21 The AB's outlook on the seriousness of 'as such' claims can be seen in the following quote from its report:

> '[A]s such' challenges against a Member's measures in WTO dispute settlement proceedings are serious challenges. By definition, an 'as such' claim challenges laws, regulations, or other instruments of a Member that have general and prospective application, asserting that a Member's conduct – not only in a particular instance that has occurred, but in future situations as well – will necessarily be inconsistent with that Member's WTO obligations. In essence, complaining parties bringing 'as such' challenges seek to prevent Members *ex ante* from engaging in certain conduct. The implications of such challenges are obviously more far-reaching than 'as applied' claims. (para. 172)

might nonetheless be *de facto* mandatory in nature.[22] But if the law or regulation in question does not mandate actions that are inconsistent with WTO obligations, there can be no violation of the Agreement, irrespective of the type of obligation allegedly violated.[23] For the reasons indicated earlier, we regret this rigid approach.[24]

Howse and Staiger were correct about one point: The AB will henceforth consider substance (and not just form) by allowing a complainant to argue that an apparently discretionary law or practice actually requires certain actions *de facto*. But the ruling in *US–OCTG from Argentina* makes clear that the evidentiary burden for this will be great. Evidently, it will not suffice to provide evidence that a certain pattern of behavior has been followed in more than 200 cases. Nor was the AB persuaded by the inability of the United States to provide a single counterexample to Argentina's claims that the three scenarios are jointly determinative. And the AB did not care that the SPB had been written by the executive authority itself to express how it intended to rely primarily, if not entirely, on the three scenarios. The AB considered none of this to be proof of a mandated action, because, after all, the repeated behavior by the USDOC could be coincidental and the absence of a counterexample could reflect only that appropriate circumstances had yet to arise.[25]

22 In the case discussed here, the AB considered the relevant question to be whether the three scenarios outlined in the SPB are in fact *conclusive* or only *indicative* for the USDOC in reaching a positive decision on likely continuation or recurrence of dumping. According to the AB, if a legal instrument does not *expressis verbis* indicate that a particular approach is required, the mandatory nature of the approach may nevertheless be established by the way the law operates and is implemented by the executive authority. But there is nothing revolutionary about that: in so doing the AB merely confirmed the generally accepted and oft-repeated notion that a Member's domestic laws are matters of fact and that the meaning of such laws cannot be established simply by looking at the legislative text. One should also examine the application and interpretation given to the text by the executive authorities and the courts. See AB Report, *US–Carbon Steel*, para. 157.

23 In contrast to the Panel's response in *US–Section 301*, the AB in *US–OCTG from Argentina* did not examine whether Article 11.3 of the AD Agreement rules out any behavior in a sunset review that the SPB allows. Evidently, the AB did not consider this to be germane to the decision. It would not consider the SPB to be in violation of the AD Agreement just because it allows the USDOC the discretion in a sunset review to act in a manner contrary to the United States's international obligations.

24 The AB stresses this point in *US–Carbon Steel*:

> The party asserting that another party's municipal law, as such, is inconsistent with relevant treaty obligations bears the burden of introducing evidence as to the scope and meaning of such law to substantiate that assertion. Such evidence will typically be produced in the form of the text of the relevant legislation or legal instruments, which may be supported, as appropriate, by evidence of the consistent application of such laws, the pronouncements of domestic courts on the meaning of such laws, the opinions of legal experts and the writings of recognized scholars. The nature and extent of the evidence required to satisfy the burden of proof will vary from case to case.' (para. 157)

25 It is interesting to compare this approach with the one followed in respect of the waiver provisions in this same case, and the one adopted in the *US–Zeroing (EC)* case. In both cases, the fact that the US was unable to come up with one example to rebut the allegation made was considered highly instructive. See

In rejecting Argentina's 'statistical evidence' (which, in this case, was 100% consistent with its hypothesis, not the usual 95% or 99% normally applied to statistical inference), the AB insisted on seeing examples of cases in which a USDOC ruling had corresponded to the indications of the three scenarios despite the existence of *convincing* evidence that the opposite outcome on dumping was likely. Moreover, Argentina would have had to show that the authorities had ignored the convincing evidence in deference to the applicability of one of the three scenarios. With this standard of evidence, there is not much chance for a claimant alleging an 'as such' violation to prevail except when the law or administrative measure expresses a clear mandate. The distinction between form and substance that the AB had identified in *US–Corrosion-Resistant Steel* apparently is one that makes little difference in practice: A Member will be able to challenge a measure that appears to be discretionary, but the challenge is most unlikely to succeed.

4.3 Factors to be evaluated in a likelihood-of-injury determination

Article 11.3 of the AD Agreement requires, *inter alia*, that the investigating authorities examine in a sunset review whether any dumping that is deemed likely to continue or recur following the termination of a duty order is likely to lead to a continuation or recurrence of injury to the domestic industry. The dispute in *US–OCTG from Argentina* addressed the question to the AB of what economic factors ought to be considered in such an examination, and, in particular, whether the disciplines imposed by Article 3 on the investigating authorities concerning injury determination in an initial investigation of dumping apply also to sunset reviews. The AB answered this question clearly and simply in the negative. According to the AB, the absence of any explicit cross-reference in Article 11.3 to the disciplines included in Article 3 and the oft-cited difference in the nature and purpose of an original investigation versus a sunset review are enough to resolve the issue in favor of a minimalist interpretation of the disciplines imposed by Article 11.3.

In the next section of this paper, we will argue that the obligation to conduct an examination of likely continuation or recurrence of injury asks quite a lot of the investigating authorities from an economic point of view. The authorities must address a counterfactual question of what industry outcomes would likely result from the removal of an antidumping-duty order, considering the likely pricing behavior by foreign firms and the associated strategic response by the domestic industry. In order to address this question rigorously and nonmechanistically, the authorities cannot avoid a rather detailed economic analysis. Here we shall argue

AB Report, *US–OCTG from Argentina*, para. 233 and Panel Report, *US–Zeroing (EC)*, para. 7.103, and the latter referred to with approval in the AB report, *US–Zeroing (EC)*, para. 201.

on legal grounds that a proper contextual interpretation of the term 'injury' in Article 11.3 should have led the AB to decide this aspect of the dispute differently and that, in fact, the types of disciplines imposed by Article 3 should apply to sunset reviews as well.

Argentina argued that the term 'injury' should be interpreted in a consistent manner throughout the Agreement, be it as a condition for imposing an anti-dumping duty or as a condition for failing to terminate a duty order after five years. Argentina pointed to footnote 9 to the heading of Article 3, which states, 'Under this Agreement the term 'injury' shall, unless otherwise specified, be taken to mean material injury to a domestic industry, threat of material injury to a domestic industry or material retardation of the establishment of such an industry *and shall be interpreted in accordance with the provisions of this Article*' (emphasis added). The AB accepted Argentina's argument that the injury referenced in Article 11.3 is 'material injury to a domestic industry, threat of material injury to a domestic industry or material retardation of the establishment of such an industry', but somehow overlooked the last phrase of the footnote when ruling that Article 3 does not set forth any *definition* of the term injury that applies to a *determination* of injury.

We see no basis for the AB ruling that Article 3 applies only to the determination of existing injury in an initial investigation, and not to the determination of likely continuation or recurrence of injury in a sunset review. After all, footnote 9 makes clear that, wherever the term 'injury' appears in the Agreement, unless otherwise specified, it must be interpreted in accordance with the provisions of Article 3. Article 11 contains no explicit statement that a different interpretation of 'injury' is required for sunset reviews. Accordingly, the provisions of Article 3 for determining injury ought to apply *mutatis mutandis* to the examination of injury required by Article 11.

According to the AB, the different nature and purpose of injury determinations in original investigations and sunset reviews justifies the possible use of different approaches in the two types of investigation. The AB has made similar statements about the different nature of sunset reviews and original investigations in other cases as well, but it has failed to explain why this difference implies a different set of disciplines and why it justifies reading out of the Agreement the last part of footnote 9. Of course, sunset reviews are different from original investigations; in an original investigation the relevant question is the existence or threat of injury, whereas in a sunset review it is the likely continuation or recurrence of injury. But the reason for an injury test presumably is the same in each case; namely, so as not to restrict trade unnecessarily when the actions of the foreign firms do not threaten or impose harm to domestic interests. Why would the signatories have meant this test to be weaker, and subject to less discipline, in a sunset review than in an initial investigation? If anything, the test in a sunset review should be stricter, and the disciplines greater, considering that Article 11.3 sets a presumption that the duty order *shall be* terminated *unless* a review finds circumstances to justify its continuation.[26]

In fact, the injury determination required in a sunset review may not be so different from that in an initial investigation of dumping. In an initial investigation, the authorities should first examine the *existence* of injury. But, where injury does not exist, they must then examine the *threat* of injury. In doing so, they must forecast future conditions in the industry, just as they must do in a sunset review. Article 3.7 lists factors that must be considered by the authorities when forecasting the future in assessing threat of injury. Why would they not need to look at a similar set of factors when forecasting the future following an assumed termination of the duty order? Moreover, as the Panel in *Mexico–Corn Syrup* (para. 7.132) correctly pointed out, the factors listed in Article 3.7 relate specifically to the likelihood of increased imports and not the resulting impact of the subject imports on the domestic industry. Their ruling implies that an examination of only the factors cited in Article 3.7 would not suffice for an investigating authority to determine that a threat of injury exists. Rather, the authority remains obligated to consider the impact of dumped imports on the domestic industry in accordance with the requirements of Article 3.4. By this reasoning, if the disciplines of Article 3.4 apply to an investigation of the *threat* of future injury in an initial investigation, they ought to apply as well to an investigation of the *likelihood* of future injury in a sunset review.

It is difficult to see how an investigating authority could fulfill its obligation from Article 11.3 to review the likelihood of continuation and recurrence of dumping and injury without obeying the disciplines of Article 3. Article 3 requires the investigating authority to examine the volume of dumped imports and the effect of these imports on the prices of competing domestic goods. Then it requires the authority to examine the impact of the dumped imports on domestic producers by evaluating all relevant factors that bear on the state of the industry. The list of factors in Article 3.4 includes basic measures of the health of the industry, such as sales, profits, productivity, market share, etc. Surely, the same set of factors is relevant for forecasting the health of the industry following the removal of a duty order. And when the AB states that some of the factors listed in Article 3.4 may not be so relevant in particular sunset reviews, depending on circumstances, this is no different from the fact that some factors may be less relevant than others in an initial investigation of dumping. For example, industry wages and

26 The AB in *US–Carbon Steel* has accepted that, in sunset reviews, the termination of the duty should be considered 'the rule' and its continuation 'the exception'. In that decision, dealing with the sunset review provision in the SCM Agreement (which is identical to that in the AD Agreement, *mutatis mutandis*), it wrote:

> An automatic time-bound termination of countervailing duties that have been in place for five years from the original investigation or a subsequent comprehensive review is at the heart of this provision. Termination of a countervailing duty is the rule and its continuation is the exception. (para. 88)

employment may not be such important factors in determining the health of a highly capital-intensive industry. Then this factor will not figure prominently in an initial investigation, even though Article 3.4 requires that it be considered. Why would not the same be true of a sunset review?

We see the role of Article 3 as being to ensure transparency and to impose discipline on Members that wish to introduce antidumping duties. The provisions require the investigating authority in the importing country to consider all relevant economic factors before it concludes that there has been injury and imposes measures that impede trade. We see nothing in the text of the Agreement, or in the economics of the situation, to suggest that such transparency and discipline is less important in a review of a longstanding order than in an original investigation of alleged dumping. If anything, we believe the opposite is true.

4.4 *Permissibility of cumulation in sunset reviews*

The AB ruled that the rationale for allowing cumulation in original investigations is 'equally applicable' to determinations of likelihood of injury following the removal of an antidumping duty. Although we have our doubts about the use of cumulation in general, the AD Agreement is clear on the permissibility of this practice in original investigations of injury. We can see no basis in the text for concluding that the Members meant for a different practice to apply in regard to cumulation in assessing likelihood of continued or recurring injury.[27]

However, it would seem that if the rationale for allowing cumulation is equally applicable to sunset reviews, the disciplines imposed by the Agreement to prevent abuse of this procedure ought to apply as well. The AB argues differently, however, focusing not on the *rationale* of the rule, but on a narrow, textual analysis. The AB points out that the text of Article 3.3, which sets forth such disciplines, refers to their applicability to antidumping 'investigations', and not to antidumping 'reviews'. But why would the term 'investigations' not be broad enough to cover both the original investigation of a claim of dumping and a subsequent review of the effects of removal of an antidumping order? The narrowness of the interpretation seems especially misplaced in light of the AB ruling that the same rationale for allowing cumulation applies in both cases.

One might well ask, why would the drafters of the Agreement have wished to impose disciplines on the practice of cumulation in original investigations, but not in reviews if, as the AB argues, the question in both cases is the same?

27 We note, however, that an economic argument similar to that made by Howse and Staiger (2006: 43–46) can be offered in favor of different procedures in the two types of determinations. Howse and Staiger argued that determining likelihood of continued or renewed dumping on an order-wide basis introduces a free-rider problem among the countries named in a dumping order, since each has limited ability to change its behavior in such a way as to rid itself of the order. Under a company-specific basis for determining likelihood of continued or renewed dumping, by contrast, each firm potentially can reap the rewards of its own 'good' behavior. Similarly, the use of cumulation in the determination of likelihood of injury from continued or renewed dumping may dampen the incentive for firms and countries to refrain from dumping that is likely to cause new injury.

In each case, the question concerns the impact of dumped imports on the domestic industry. Surely, if the disciplines on the practice of cumulation help us to assess accurately whether the dumped imports contributed to the existing state of an industry, they would also help us to assess accurately whether prospective dumped imports would contribute to the future state of the industry. But the AB does not even pose this question, let alone provide a reasoned answer.

The AB tries to reassure us that the inapplicability of the disciplines of Article 3.4 to sunset reviews does not mean that 'anything goes'. In such a review, the authority's decision to use cumulation still must qualify as a 'rigorous examination' leading to a 'reasoned conclusion' supported by 'positive evidence' and a 'sufficient factual basis' (para. 302). Apparently, the AB feels that these general terms are sufficient to impose the disciplines needed to avoid abuse. But if that is so, why did the Members feel the need to include the disciplines it did in Article 3.3? Shouldn't the general terms have been sufficient there as well? And besides preventing abuse, the listing of permissible procedures in a review helps to remove the uncertainty that parties face as to how they will be treated in a dumping investigation. Surely this rationale applies as much to sunset reviews as it does to initial investigations.

Alas, it is not even true that the AB remains faithful to the text in this part of its decision. First, it denies the applicability of disciplines for cumulation in a sunset review, because such disciplines are not to be found in Article 11.3. Then, it asserts the more general discipline imposed by the requirement for a 'rigorous examination', a 'reasoned conclusion', and a 'sufficient factual basis'. However, not only are these terms absent from Article 11.3, in fact they appear nowhere in the AD Agreement.

5. The economics of sunset reviews

Economic analysis of the sunset review provisions of the AD Agreement is complicated by the fact that the agreement as a whole lacks a coherent economic justification and interpretation. Several previous authors in this series have argued – and we concur – that the purpose and objectives of the condemnation of dumping and the provisions for antidumping duties are far from clear, as they do not seem to address any international externality or to curb noncooperative governmental behavior.[28] Without a clear understanding of why antidumping duties are tolerated by the international trading system in the first place, it is difficult to discuss the conditions under which they ought to be terminated.

There is no point in our rehearsing yet again the reasons why economists find fault with the AD Agreement as a whole. This issue has been discussed in great

28 See, for example, Janow and Staiger (2003), Howse and Neven (2003), and Horn and Mavroidis (2006).

depth elsewhere.[29] Instead, we will suspend our disbelief and take at face value that antidumping duties have some legitimate role to play in the world trading system and that the purpose of the sunset review is to determine whether 'expiry of the duty would be likely to lead to continuation or recurrence of dumping and injury'.

The AB has interpreted the words 'review' and 'determine' in Article 11.3 as requiring authorities in a sunset review to come to a 'reasoned conclusion on the basis of information gathered as part of a process of reconsideration and examination'.[30] The review cannot be mechanistic or formulaic. But it rejected Argentina's argument that the three scenarios of the SPB are determinative in US sunset reviews based on the historical record of findings in past reviews. Be that as it may, it is clear to us that the United States has not fulfilled its obligation to reach a 'reasoned conclusion' in this or any other sunset review.

Our claim is based on the failure of the United States to recognize, either in the wording of the SPB or in its current or past practice of sunset reviews, the nature of the questions that are posed by Article 11.3 of the AD Agreement. The questions are counterfactual:[31] What industry conditions are likely to prevail in the event that the duty order is lifted? Would dumping continue or resume in the absence of an antidumping-duty order? If so, would the dumped imports result in continued or recurring injury to the domestic industry?

To answer these questions requires, as Howse and Staiger (2006: 47) have pointed out, 'an understanding of two things: (i) what conditions led to dumping in the first place; and (ii) whether those conditions have changed in a way that removes the original reason for dumping'. As they further argue, 'neither of these two elements appears to play any real role in the USDOC's methodology for determining likelihood'. Ergo, the US practice as such (as described in the SPB or inferred from its repeated actions) and the US practice in this instance cannot have fulfilled the country's obligation to provide a reasoned conclusion to the counterfactual questions posed by Article 11.3.

A proper sunset review would begin with a description and analysis of competitive conditions in the industry in question. This analysis would address, *inter alia*, the reasons that dumping took place in the first place. Was there excess

29 See, for example, Boltuck and Litan (1991).

30 *US–Corrosion-Resistant Steel*, para. 111.

31 The United States acknowledged the counterfactual nature of the sunset review exercise in the Statement of Administrative Action that accompanied the implementing legislation. In *Uruguay Round Trade Agreements, Texts of Agreements, Implementing Bill, Statement of Administrative Action, and Required Supporting Statements*, H. Doc. 103–316, vol. 1, 103 Cong. 2 sess. (GPO, 1994: 884), it is written that 'under the likelihood standard, the Commission will engage in a counterfactual analysis: it must decide the likely impact in the reasonably foreseeable future of an important change in the status quo ... the revocation or termination of a proceeding and the elimination of its restraining effects on volumes and prices of imports'.

capacity in the industry that led foreign firms to price below their long-run average cost? Were international markets segmented and foreign firms attempting to gain additional oligopoly profits by practicing price discrimination? Did exchange-rate movements together with 'pricing-to-market' lead to different prices in two markets? Did the dumping have predatory intent? Although the AD Agreement does not in any way limit Members' rights to impose antidumping duties according to the motivation for this pricing behavior, an understanding of the reasons for the dumping is essential for properly addressing the issue of whether dumping and injury are likely to continue or recur if a duty order is allowed to expire.

Put differently, the investigating authorities need to develop a 'model' of the industry in question.[32] This model need not be a formal one, expressed in equations and complete with econometric estimates of important parameter values. Where feasible, such an econometric model could be valuable in assessing how changes in industry conditions are likely to affect pricing strategies and industry outcomes. But data limitations and time pressures will sometimes prevent investigating authority from conducting formal economic analysis. In some cases, the best feasible examination of the issue may involve the use of a more informal model – basically, a consistent 'story' about how the industry operates – in order to allow consideration of the relevant counterfactual issues. Certainly, the same model should not apply in every case; competitive conditions and market structure vary across industries, as do the importance of spare capacity, or exchange-rate shocks, and other factors that play a role in firms' pricing strategies. But without a conceptual model of the industry in question, any sunset review is bound to be formulaic and mechanical.

Once the investigating authorities have described the competitive conditions in the industry and identified the motive for the foreign firms' initial dumping, the next step in a proper examination of the likelihood issue requires them to consider how conditions in the industry have changed and to forecast what would be firms' pricing strategies under the new conditions and the assumed removal of the anti-dumping-duty order. If, for example, the root cause of the initial dumping is deemed to have been cyclical factors that created excess capacity, a relevant question is whether the conditions of spare capacity persist in the industry. If, alternatively, the initial dumping was associated with exchange-rate misalignment, the prevailing exchange values might be relevant. The counterfactual analysis that is mandated by the text of Article 11.3 of the AD Agreement can be formal or informal, depending on the available data and information. If, for example,

32 Boltuck and Kaplan (1998) make a similar argument in their template for the conduct of sunset reviews written before any such reviews had taken place. In particular, they advocate a counterfactual analysis that combines the use of a family of comparative static economic simulation models with more informal methods of industry analysis. They note, as we do, that conditions of competition will vary across different markets, and so a 'one size fits all' approach to the review process cannot be appropriate.

it is possible to describe industry conditions in a formal model with econometric estimates of key demand and cost parameters, then the likelihood question can be addressed by solving the model 'out of sample' using prevailing values of exogenous variables and an assumed change in the duty order applicable to subject imports.[33] If this is not possible due to data and time limitations, then an alternative would be to perform the necessary counterfactual experiments conceptually and possibly with the aid of industry experts. In either case, the goal should be to use the best available understanding of how the industry operates to address what outcomes are most likely in the event that the antidumping-duty order is terminated.

We would argue further that one element of the competitive condition in the industry is bound to have changed between the time of the initial investigation of dumping and the sunset review. Namely, at the time of the initial investigation, the foreign firms that engaged in the suspect pricing strategy may have been uncertain about whether their strategy constituted 'dumping' as legally defined and were certainly uncertain about whether their practice would lead to the filing of petitions of dumping and injury by the domestic industry. The firms presumably will have decided that the extra profits they could earn by pursuing a pricing strategy that might be challenged and then construed as 'dumping' outweighed the expected costs associated with the imposition of an antidumping-duty order. However, by the time of the sunset review, much or all of this uncertainty will have been resolved. If the duty order is revoked and these firms return to their prior pricing strategy, they can be reasonably sure that the practice will not go unnoticed. And, if challenged, they expect a similar finding to the first outcome unless industry conditions have changed substantially. It stands to reason that the temptation to 'dump' will be less, subsequent to the removal of a duty order, than it was before the initial investigation.

An analogy may help to clarify this point. Consider a criminal who has been arrested and convicted of theft. Before committing the original crime, the individual will have compared the perceived gains from the illegal activity with the expected cost of any ensuing punishment, taking account of the likelihood of being caught. Now suppose the thief is released from prison on parole. He may be unreformed in terms of social conscience and see the profits from thievery much as before. However, he will know that he is being monitored and that the probability of 'getting away with it' has diminished. The likelihood that he will resume a life of crime in the parole state, while not zero, normally will be reduced. The same is true for a firm that engages in dumping: it may see the profitability of this pricing strategy as being similar to what it was initially, but now choose to refrain in light of the anticipation of closer scrutiny.

33 See also Keck, Malashevich, and Gray (2006), who advocate the use of simulation methods to address the prospective determination that is required in the sunset review process.

It is interesting to note that our proposed analysis for sunset reviews fits comfortably with recent proposals made by Canada (TN/RL/GEN61) and Japan (TN/RL/GEN/104). The Canadian proposal, for example, provides the following list of factors that ought to be examined in sunset review of likely injury:

(a) the likely volume of dumped imports if the duty is allowed to expire, and, in particular, whether there is likely to be a significant increase in the volume of the dumped imports, either in absolute terms or relative to the production or consumption of the like product;
(b) the likely prices of the dumped imports if the measure is allowed to expire and their effect on the prices of the like product, and, in particular, whether the dumped imports are likely to significantly undercut the prices of the like product, or lead to price depression or price suppression;
(c) the likely performance of the domestic industry and of the foreign industry, taking into consideration their recent performances, including trends in production, capacity utilization, the potential for foreign producers to extend production to facilities currently used to produce other products, the employment levels, prices, sales, inventories, market share, exports and profits;
(d) the likely impact of the dumped imports on the domestic industry if the measure is allowed to expire, having regard to all relevant economic factors and indices, including any potential decline in output, sales, market share, profits, productivity, return on investments or utilization of production capacity, and any potential negative effects on cash flow, inventories, employment, wages, growth, including efforts to produce a derivative or more advanced version of the like product, or the ability to raise capital;
(e) changes in market conditions in the economy of the Member and internationally, including changes in the supply of and demand for the imports, as well as any changes in trends and in sources of imports into the Member; and
(f) evidence of the imposition of anti-dumping or countervailing duties by other Members in respect of like or similar products, and evidence that such duties are likely to cause a diversion of imports into the Member.

It should be clear that an investigating authority would need to look at a list of factors such as those contained in the Canadian proposal in order to address the counterfactual analysis about likely continuation or recurrence of dumping and injury that is mandated by Article 11.3. The incorporation of a list of factors such as this one into the AD Agreement would certainly clarify the required elements of a sunset review. But, we would argue that the AB should have no difficulty in interpreting the agreement *as currently worded* in a manner that recognizes the economic issues at stake.

6. Conclusions

This case is one of several that deals with sunset reviews of antidumping-duty orders. By its cumulative rulings, the Appellate Body has made clear that it does not expect very much from these reviews. Countries are free to assess the likelihood of continuation or recurrence of dumping without much regard for prevailing conditions in the industry, to assess the likelihood of continuation or recurrence of injury without any of the disciplines imposed on original dumping investigations, and to use whatever methods and procedures they see fit, provided that they can somehow claim to have reached a reasoned conclusion based on information gathered for the purpose. They can even rely repeatedly on a formulaic approach, provided that the other Members cannot show beyond a reasonable doubt that the approach has led to indefensible findings in earlier cases. In short, the AB has ensured that the sunset review process agreed to in the Uruguay Round has no teeth. Considering that sunset reviews were introduced to enforce a presumption that antidumping-duty orders ought to expire after five years except in particular and unusual circumstances, we cannot see this as a desirable or acceptable outcome of the jurisprudence.

Among the most important shortcomings of the AB ruling in *US–OCTG from Argentina* are two. First, the AB has reasserted a rigid distinction between mandatory and discretionary law. A law or executive order that *requires* an administrative authority to behave in a way that is inconsistent with a country's WTO obligations can be challenged 'as such' before the organization's dispute settlement bodies, and the complainant need only establish the existence of a requirement and its inconsistency with the agreement. A law or executive order that *allows* for behavior that is inconsistent with the agreement also can be challenged, but the standards for success are extraordinarily high. The complainant must then establish that the law or practice in fact has required the authorities to make decisions that run counter to WTO obligations; i.e., that the discretion to act legally or illegally in fact did not exist, and that such illegal action by the executive authority in the past was in fact mandated by the law or practice in question. This ruling is unfortunate, because it diminishes Members' incentives to challenge laws and practices as such, and forces them to wait for particular, disputable applications. As-such challenges could play a useful role in the trading system in helping to provide a stable and predictable environment for trade and in thwarting Members' efforts to continue illegal actions by a series of small changes in law with little change in practice.

Second, the AB failed to recognize the purpose and objectives of sunset reviews by failing to impose any discipline on their conduct. Surely the reviews have a purpose similar to that of original investigations – to ensure that duty orders are not imposed when their absence would not generate harm to an import-competing industry. Inasmuch as the Members saw fit to impose many disciplines on the conduct of original investigations in order to ensure that duty orders were not introduced when injury-causing dumping had not taken place, it is inconceivable that they could not have meant an analogous set of disciplines to apply in sunset reviews; all the more so because the reviews were presumptively intended to rid the system of obsolete orders.

It would have been possible for the AB to interpret the existing treaty language differently from what it has done. However, given the history of jurisprudence that has now accumulated, we would advocate an addendum by the Members that would clarify their intention to create a meaningful and disciplined sunset review process.

References

Boltuck, R. D. and R. E. Litan (eds) (1991), *Down in the Dumps: Administration of the Unfair Trade Laws*, Washington, DC: The Brookings Institution.

Boltuck R. D. and S. T. Kaplan (1999), 'An Economic Approach to ITC Sunset Reviews', in R. Lawrence (ed.), *Brookings Trade Forum 1998*, Washington, DC: The Brookings Institution.

Horn, H. and P. C. Mavroidis (2006), 'European Community – Antidumping Duties on Malleable Cast Iron Tube or Pipe Fittings from Brazil', in H. Horn and P. C. Mavroidis (eds), *The American Law Institute Reporters' Studies – The WTO Case Law of 2003*, Cambridge: Cambridge University Press.

Howse, R. and D. J. Neven (2003), 'Argentina – Definitive Anti-dumping Measures on Imports of Ceramic Floor Tiles from Italy', in H. Horn and P. C. Mavroidis (eds), *The American Law Institute Reporters' Studies – The WTO Case Law of 2001*, Cambridge: Cambridge University Press.

Howse, R. and R. W. Staiger (2006), 'United States – Sunset Review of Anti-Dumping Duties on Corrosion-Resistant Carbon Steel Flat Products from Japan: A Legal and Economic Analysis of the Appellate Body Ruling', in H. Horn and P. C. Mavroidis (eds), *The American Law Institute Reporters' Studies – The WTO Case Law of 2003*, Cambridge: Cambridge University Press.

Janow, M. E. and R. W. Staiger (2003), 'European Communities – Anti-Dumping Duties on Imports of Cotton-Type Bed Linen from India', in H. Horn and P. C. Mavroidis (eds), *The American Law Institute Reporters' Studies – The WTO Case Law of 2001*, Cambridge: Cambridge University Press.

Keck, A., B. Malashevich, and I. Gray (2006), 'A "Probabilistic" Approach to the Use of Econometric Models in Sunset Reviews', Staff Working Paper ERSD-2006-01, World Trade Organization Economic Research and Statistics Division, Geneva, Switzerland.

Comment

United States – Sunset Reviews of Anti-Dumping Measures on Oil Country Tubular Goods from Argentina

Prepared for the ALI Project on the Case Law of the WTO

EDWIN VERMULST

Vermulst Verhaeghe & Graafsma, Brussels, Belgium. Email: edwin.vermulst@vvg-law.com

Introduction

Gene Grossman and Jasper Wauters have provided an excellent analysis of and commentary on the AB report *United States – Sunset Reviews of Anti-Dumping Measures on Oil Country Tubular Goods* [OCTG] *from Argentina* with much of which I agree. As a result, my observations below are of necessity short.

1. The US: a victim of its transparency?

It seems hard to deny that of all active user countries of antidumping measures, the United States is the most transparent. US antidumping law tends to provide more detail than is required under the WTO Anti-Dumping Agreement [ADA]. In addition, the US agencies have published detailed guidelines on how they will apply the law. Third, US administrative determinations tend to explain in great detail how findings were reached and why arguments made by interested parties were accepted or rejected. Last, the system of disclosure of confidential information under an administrative protective order offers legal counsel of interested parties the opportunity to vet the findings of the agencies in detail.

The US system contrasts in this respect with the system of many other countries, whose antidumping legislation tends to be a carbon copy of the provisions of the ADA. Administrative guidelines, if they exist, tend to be internal documents that are not disclosed to the public or interested parties. Administrative determinations are relatively short and often full of conclusory statements that copy language from the ADA (e.g.: 'It was found that a pattern of export prices existed which differed significantly among different purchasers, regions or time periods, and that such differences could not be taken into account appropriately by the use of a weighted average-to-weighted average or transaction-to-transaction comparison.'). Nonconfidential summaries of confidential information and disclosures of findings and calculations by the agencies, notably on injury and the calculation of injury margins, tend to be so vague that they often leave interested parties, let alone the public (which does not have access to nonconfidential summaries and disclosures), guessing at how exactly the agencies arrived at their conclusions.[1]

This may – at least partially – explain why so many of the WTO cases in the antidumping area have targeted the United States.[2] It is easier to claim violations of ADA provisions when it is clear what the investigating authorities have done than if one first has to decipher what the authorities have done and on what basis and, even more importantly, obtain the evidence to prove it before a WTO panel.

Section II.A.3 of the SPB illustrates this point: It contains three scenarios that will 'normally' lead the DOC to determine that revocation of an antidumping order is likely to lead to continuation or recurrence of dumping. Within the weird world of antidumping, these scenarios make sense and probably are applied as a matter of practice by many other investigating authorities in sunset reviews, as long as the complainants are pushing for continuation of the duties. But they will not be written down, thereby precluding 'as such' claims.

Viewed in this broader context, it is perhaps understandable that the AB imposes a high evidentiary standard for 'as such' claims. Adoption of a low standard would punish countries such as the United States even more for their transparency and indirectly – and perversely – reward countries for maintaining nontransparent systems.

2. Applicability of Article 3 in sunset reviews

I agree with Grossman and Wauters that the injury disciplines of Article 3 ADA in general ought to apply equally to the determination of likely continuation or recurrence of injury in sunset (and interim) reviews, unless such application clearly does not make sense (see point 3 below).

If the focus in a sunset review is on the *continuation* of injury, this would appear to require a finding that injury, as defined in Article 3, is still occurring and that it would continue (or worsen) if the duties were to be lifted.

If the focus in a sunset review is on the *recurrence* of injury, there is no injury at present (possibly because the duties are 'working' or for other reasons), but there might be injury again if the duties were to be lifted. There is, in other words, a potential threat of injury. In such a case, the counterfactual analysis indeed should

1 In some jurisdictions, even the names of complainants are sometimes not disclosed because of confidentiality reasons!

2 Admittedly, the US is an aggressive enforcer of its antidumping legislation, but it is hardly the only one.

be similar to the threat analysis required by Article 3.7 ADA, which per the Panel in *Mexico-Corn Syrup* necessitates consideration of the Article 3.4 factors.

3. Applicability of cumulation and its conditions in sunset reviews

There appears to be no reason, legal or conceptual, why the cumulation concept of Article 3.3 ADA would not apply in sunset reviews.

As regards the disciplines imposed on cumulation by that Article, I believe that a distinction must be made between the first two conditions (under (a)) and the last condition (under (b)).

I would argue that the last condition that a cumulative assessment of the effects of the imports must be appropriate in light of the conditions of competition between the imported products and the conditions of competition between the imported products and the domestic like product applies equally in sunset reviews. If, for example, there has been a change in consumer preferences as a result of which the imports from country A no longer compete with other imports or with the domestic like product,[3] it would seem to me that imports from country A then would need to be decumulated.

On the other hand, the distinction between an original investigation and a sunset review would appear to justify nonapplicability of the *de minimis* dumping and negligible import volumes concepts in sunset reviews.

Indeed, the fact that duties were imposed in the original investigation entails that the imports during the original investigation period were dumped at more than *de minimis* levels and in nonnegligible quantities. A consequence of the imposition of the measures may well be that the dumping has dropped to a *de minimis* level or that the import volumes have become negligible. However, such developments do not guarantee that injurious dumping will not recur if the duties were to be lifted. Therefore, it would seem to me that such developments, in and of themselves, do not necessitate decumulation (in other words, automatic termination of the measures for the country concerned) in sunset reviews.

4. The economics of dumping and of sunset reviews

Grossman and Wauters start their analysis by pointing out that '[e]conomic analysis of the sunset-review provisions of the AD Agreement is complicated by the fact that the agreement as a whole lacks a coherent economic justification and interpretation'. While many will agree with this observation, the fact of life is that WTO Members have agreed that antidumping duties may be imposed if the conditions are met. The determination of dumping under the ADA is a mathematical-calculation exercise in which the reasons why exporters dump are

3 This could be the case, for example, if consumption of the product under investigation has moved to higher-end models while one country continues to supply low-end models.

irrelevant as a matter of law (indeed dumping may well be found *because of* the calculation methods authorized under the ADA) and not examined as a matter of practice. As long as this basic concept remains unchanged, any proposals to consider in sunset reviews what conditions led to dumping in the first place do not seem realistic.

Finally, I am not sure whether the imposition of antidumping duties has any deterrent effect in practice (and in fact may have the opposite effect in countries with prospective systems). It seems to me that firms' decisions on optimal pricing are based on an assessment of many elements, of which (the likelihood of) being subjected to antidumping duties is probably a relatively minor one. Perhaps a better analogy than the paroled thief who learns his lesson would then be the driver of a delivery van who regularly makes unauthorized stops to deliver his merchandise. The driver knows that he should not double-park or obstruct the sidewalk, but he really has no choice. Even if he is cited for a traffic violation, he will pay the fine and then do the same again the next day.

United States – Anti-Dumping Measures on Oil Country Tubular Goods (OCTG) from Mexico: a legal-economic assessment of sunset reviews

CHAD P. BOWN

Department of Economics and International Business School, MS 021, Brandeis University, PO Box 549110, Waltham, MA, 02454-9110 USA
Email: cbown@brandeis.edu, web: http://www.brandeis.edu/~cbown/

JASPER WAUTERS

White & Case International Trade (Geneva), 82 Rue de Lausanne, 1202 Geneva, Switzerland
Email: jwauters@whitecase.com

Abstract: This paper reviews the WTO Appellate Body Report on *United States – Anti-Dumping Measures on Oil Country Tubular Goods (OCTG) from Mexico* (WT/DS282/AB/R 2 November 2005). This dispute concerns the disciplines imposed by the Anti-Dumping Agreement on WTO Members seeking to extend their anti-dumping measures beyond the original five-year period through a so-called sunset review. Our analysis focuses on the Appellate Body's finding in this case that no causation analysis is required in sunset reviews, and addresses the AB's approach towards the legal instrument that provides for the US policy in terms of sunset reviews, the Sunset Policy Bulletin. We conclude that the Anti-Dumping Agreement, as interpreted by the Appellate Body in this and other similar cases, imposes only minimal disciplines of a general nature on Members wishing to extend the anti-dumping measure beyond its original five-year period. We argue that the 'textual' argument relied on to support this deferential approach is weak and has resulted in undermining the practical effect of, what was considered to be, one of the major achievements of the Uruguay Round Anti-Dumping Agreement: limiting the life span of an anti-dumping measure to five years. From an economic perspective, Panels and the Appellate Body are simply debating the wrong type of questions. The prospective nature required by a sunset review analysis raises questions such as why exporters engaged in dumping in the first place, and what the conditions of the industry were so that the dumped imports caused injury. At the moment, sunset reviews

This paper reviews the WTO Appellate Body Report, *United States – Anti-Dumping Measures on Oil Country Tubular Goods (OCTG) from Mexico* (WT/DS282/AB/R 2 November 2005). Thanks to William Davey and ALI conference participants in Geneva for useful comments on an earlier draft. The views expressed in this paper are those of the authors and should not be attributed to White and Case or any of its clients. All remaining errors are our own.

seem adrift as panels and the Appellate Body fail to give guidance to Members on how to do a more economically sound and informed review.

1. Introduction

This dispute concerns the disciplines imposed by the Anti-dumping (AD) Agreement on WTO Members seeking to extend their anti-dumping measures beyond the original five-year period. In essence, this dispute examines the question of whether the AD Agreement actually imposes certain substantive disciplines on authorities when conducting such sunset reviews.

By way of background, the AD Agreement provides for termination of AD duties after five years. AD duties can, in principle, remain in place for a period longer than five years. In other words, termination of the duty is the rule, and its continuation is the exception.[1] How much longer duties may remain in place depends on the outcome of successive reviews, called 'sunset reviews', in which authorities examine whether dumping and injury are likely to continue or recur in case the duty is terminated. The terms *continuation* and *recurrence* refer to two different factual situations: the first term presupposes that dumping and/or injury have not ceased to exist during the period of imposition of AD duties; the latter presupposes that the opposite has happened during the same period. The methodology used to demonstrate the likelihood of continuation or recurrence is not prejudged by the Article 11.3 AD Agreement, which is the only provision in the AD Agreement that specifically deals with such sunset reviews.

Mexico claimed that the way the US conducts such sunset reviews is inconsistent with the AD Agreement. Its complaint related to both US laws and regulations concerning sunset reviews and the specific application of such laws in the sunset review of an anti-dumping duty order imposed by the US on imports of oil-country tubular goods (OCTG)[2] from Mexico and other sources.

The facts

In August 1995, the US issued an anti-dumping duty order on OCTG from a number of countries including Mexico. The US Department of Commerce (USDOC), the authority responsible for determining the existence and amount of *dumping* in the US, calculated a dumping margin for the largest Mexican producer (TAMSA), and assigned margins based on this producer's rate to the other, non-investigated producers, such as Hylsa. Following the imposition of the anti-dumping duty, TAMSA stopped exporting to the US and thus was no longer

1 Appellate Body Report, *US–Carbon Steel*, para. 88. The experience over the last ten years with sunset reviews has actually been that the extension of the AD measure is the rule rather than the exception.

2 Such goods are used mainly for oil exploration and mining purposes.

dumping its products into the US. Yearly administrative reviews of the measure thus led to a zero dumping margin for TAMSA.

In the 'sunset review', USDOC and the US International Trade Commission (USITC), the US authority responsible for determining whether there is *injury* to the US domestic industry, examined whether termination of the duty on Mexican OCTG would be likely to lead to a recurrence or continuation of dumping and injury. Their conclusion was that it would. The likely dumping margin to prevail in case of termination of the duty was calculated to be 21.70 %, a figure that corresponds with the rate calculated in the original investigation, as amended.

As a result, instead of revoking the anti-dumping duty order on OCTG from Mexico, the anti-dumping measures were extended for another five-year period effective as of 25 July 2001.

Mexico's claims

Before the Panel, Mexico made a number of claims arguing that the US should have terminated the duty even before the sunset review in the course of one of the yearly administrative reviews. In the absence of dumping by the Mexican exporters, there was no need to maintain the duty 'in order to offset dumping'. In any case, according to Mexico, the duty should have been terminated at the end of the five-year period, and the US contrary affirmative determination of likelihood of dumping and injury recurring following expiry of the duty was flawed.

Mexico's claims related to the likelihood-of-*dumping* determination, as well as the standard for determining likelihood of *injury* in sunset reviews. With respect to the specific USITC determination of likely injury in the case of OCTG imports from Mexico, Mexico argued that the US failed to comply with a number of the disciplines set forth in Article 3 AD Agreement on injury, which it considers also to apply in sunset reviews.[3] In particular, Mexico alleged inter alia that the USITC did not examine all 15 factors of Article 3.4 AD, relied on a cumulative assessment of imports without legal basis and in a manner inconsistent with Article 3.3, and did not examine whether the likely injury would be caused by the dumped imports.

Against the background of this particular OCTG case, Mexico made a number of claims concerning the legal standards and requirements present in US law and US practice in respect of sunset reviews, which it considers to be inconsistent with the AD Agreement. In this respect, an important document challenged was the USDOC's Sunset Policy Bulletin in which this USDOC explains how it will determine the existence of a likelihood of dumping in sunset reviews.

3 According to Mexico, the definition of the term 'injury' in Article 3 and footnote 9 applies throughout AD Agreement and thus also in respect of a determination of likelihood of continuation or recurrence of injury under Article 11.3.

Mexico argued that Section II.A.3 of the US Sunset Policy Bulletin[4] (SPB) and USDOC 'practice' in the performance of sunset reviews are inconsistent, 'as such' with its obligations under Article 11.3. According to Mexico, it is clear from the SPB that the US authorities base their determinations on presumptions that dumping is likely to continue or recur in certain factual situations that are given decisive weight. The key elements in such factual scenarios are import volumes and dumping margins. If the situation described in any of the scenarios is met, likelihood will be found to exist without consideration of other relevant positive evidence.[5] Mexico argued that, by basing its sunset determination on such assumptions, the US is not complying with the obligation of the AD Agreement to base a sunset review determination on facts and evidence, rather than assumptions.

The United States response

The United States was of the view that nothing in the Agreement requires a WTO Member to terminate an anti-dumping measure following a finding of no dumping in the course of one or more administrative reviews.

The United States disagreed as to the applicability in sunset reviews of the disciplines of Article 3 AD Agreement relating to a determination of the existence of injury in original investigations. According to the US, a sunset review is concerned with the determination of the likelihood of recurrence or continuation of injury as a consequence of the termination of the measure, and because of this different nature and purpose, the disciplines of Article 3 do not apply. In the absence of a textual basis to import such disciplines into sunset reviews, the US argued that different questions warrant different methods of analysis and the

4 Section II.A.3 of the SPB reads in relevant part as follows:

> the Department normally will determine that revocation of an antidumping order or termination of a suspended dumping investigation is likely to lead to continuation or recurrence of dumping where—
>
> (a) dumping continued at any level above *de minimis* after the issuance of the order or the suspension agreement, as applicable;
> (b) imports of the subject merchandise ceased after issuance of the order or the suspension agreement, as applicable; or
> (c) dumping was eliminated after the issuance of the order or the suspension agreement, as applicable, and import volumes for the subject merchandise declined significantly.
>
> The Department recognizes that, in the context of a sunset review of a suspended investigation, the data relevant to the criteria under paragraphs (a) through (c), above, may not be conclusive with respect to likelihood. Therefore, the Department may be more likely to entertain good cause arguments under paragraph II.C in a sunset review of a suspended investigation.

5 This is what had occurred also in the sunset review concerning OCTG from Mexico. The USDOC concluded that there was a likelihood of dumping because the exports had stopped following the imposition of the antidumping order. A decline in import volume following the order is one of the factual scenarios which, according to the SPB, reveals a likelihood of dumping in the future as it allegedly shows that, without dumping, the exporter cannot sell its products in the US market. Mexico considered that such a presumption is inconsistent with the AD Agreement's requirements of making objective examinations based on positive evidence.

consideration of different factors. According to the US, any disciplines that may apply to sunset reviews are to be found in Article 11.3 AD Agreement. The US submitted that this implies, for example, that a cumulative assessment of likely injury of imports from several countries ('injury cumulation'), which is not mentioned in Article 11.3, is not prohibited in sunset reviews. It is permitted as a practice without the need to comply with the specific disciplines of Article 3.3 AD Agreement, as such disciplines apply only to original investigations. Similarly, there is no textual basis for introducing a requirement to establish a causal link between likely future dumping and likely future injury.

With respect to the challenge by Mexico of US sunset provisions as such, the US considered that the SPB cannot be challenged as such before the WTO. In particular, the US emphasized that the SPB is not a binding legal instrument in US law and is meant simply as a transparency tool. It cannot require any particular action and is, therefore, incapable of breaching the US's obligations under the AD Agreement. In any case, it argued, the three factual scenarios set forth in the SPB are not determinative or conclusive and do not require the USDOC to rule affirmatively on the likelihood of continuation or recurrence of dumping in any case in which one of the three criteria of Section II.A.3 of SPB has been satisfied. The USDOC has discretionary authority to examine other evidence and base its determination on such other evidence. According to the US, the fact that this has not happened so far does not imply that the authorities lack the discretion to deviate from the scenarios of the SPB.

2. The Report – Panel and Appellate Body

The challenge of the SPB

The Panel

The Panel first examined whether the Sunset Policy Bulletin was indeed a 'measure' that could be challenged through WTO dispute settlement proceedings and, if so, whether its provisions were inconsistent with the US's obligations under the AD Agreement.[6] The Panel was of the view that the first question had been answered affirmatively by the Appellate Body in previous cases such as *US – Corrosion Resistant Steel* and *US – Oil Country Tubular Goods Sunset Reviews*[7] finding that 'any act or omission attributable to a WTO Member can be

6 In this section, we discuss the most important issues addressed by the Panel and the Appellate Body in respect of Mexico's claims. An important number of Mexico's claims were addressed and rejected by the Panel but were not the subject of an appeal. We therefore did not include them in our discussion. In any case, most of these claims concerned issues already dealt with in previous sunset review cases and did not present any novel or systemically important question.

7 Appellate Body Report, *United States – Sunset Reviews of Anti-Dumping Measures on Oil Country Tubular Goods from Argentina* ('*US – Oil Country Tubular Goods Sunset Reviews*'), WT/DS268/AB/R, para. 189, adopted 17 December 2004, affirming finding of the Panel that the SPB is a 'measure' subject to WTO dispute settlement, Panel Report, *United States – Sunset Reviews of Anti-Dumping Measures on Oil Country Tubular Goods from Argentina* (*US – Oil Country Tubular Goods Sunset Reviews*),

a measure of that Member for purposes of dispute settlement proceedings'.[8] The Panel further referred to the Appellate Body's conclusions that any legal instrument under a WTO Member's law could also be challenged as a measure before a WTO panel irrespective of the way in which it operates in individual cases.[9] As the Appellate Body was dealing in both cases with the same SPB, the Panel, without any further ado, reached the conclusion that the SPB was a 'measure subject to WTO dispute settlement'.[10]

With respect to the question of what is required under the AD agreement, the Panel adopted the findings of earlier Appellate Body reports that Article 11.3 AD Agreement requires that a likelihood determination in a sunset review be made 'on a sufficient factual basis'. This implies that an investigating authority cannot base its determination on presumptions, to the exclusion of a full examination of the factual circumstances.[11] The Panel thus concluded that the relevant question to address was whether the scenarios based on the two factors (i.e., import volumes and historical dumping margins) are treated as determinative or conclusive, or merely indicative or probative.[12] If the latter was the case, no violation would exist.

The Panel examined the text of the SPB and came to the conclusion that it was not clear from the text whether the three scenarios based on import volumes and dumping margins were considered *determinative* or merely *indicative*. It thus decided to examine how the SPB had been applied in the past by the USDOC. In so doing, the Panel took to heart the warning given by the Appellate Body in *US – Oil Country Tubular Goods Sunset Reviews* case that such an analysis could not be based on 'mere statistical evidence'. The Panel decided that it would conduct a qualitative assessment of the evidence before it to see whether the affirmative determinations were made solely on the basis of one of the scenarios to the exclusion of other factors, in line with the guidance provided by the Appellate Body in *US – Oil Country Tubular Goods Sunset Reviews*.[13]

WT/DS268/R, at para. 7.136, adopted 17 December 2004 as modified by the Appellate Body Report, WT/DS268/AB/R.

8 Appellate Body Report, *United States – Sunset Review of Anti-Dumping Duties on Corrosion-Resistant Carbon Steel Flat Products from Japan* (*US – Corrosion-Resistant Steel Sunset Review*), WT/DS244/AB/R, adopted 9 January 2004, para. 81.

9 Ibid., para. 82.

10 Panel Report, 282/R, para. 7.24.

11 Appellate Body Report, *US – Corrosion-Resistant Steel Sunset Review*, paras. 178, 191.

12 Panel Report, 282/R, para. 7.30.

13 The Panel specifically recalled the following guidance by the AB in that case that:

> in order to objectively assess, as required by Article 11 of the DSU, whether the three factual scenarios of Section II.A.3 of the SPB are regarded as determinative/conclusive, it is essential to examine concrete examples of cases where the likelihood determination of continuation or recurrence of dumping was based solely on one of the scenarios of Section II.A.3 of the SPB, even though the probative value of other factors might have outweighed that of the identified scenario. Such an examination requires a qualitative assessment of the likelihood determinations in individual cases.

AB Report, *US – Oil Country Tubular Goods Sunset Reviews*, para. 209, as referred to in Panel Report, 282/R, para. 7.49.

Based on its analysis of 232 determinations, it came to the conclusion that despite the apparent recognition that it may do otherwise, USDOC has consistently based its determinations in sunset reviews exclusively on the scenarios, to the disregard of other factors. We quote from para. 7.63 of the report:

> In summary, our qualitative analysis of USDOC decisions reveals a clear picture. In almost all cases, USDOC begins with a recitation of the SPB scenarios. In the simplest cases, the determinations then recite facts fitting one of the scenarios, and USDOC concludes that there is a likelihood of continuation or recurrence of dumping. In other cases, USDOC seems clearly to have made its decision based exclusively on the SPB, without giving consideration to other potentially probative factors in evidence. We consider it telling that some of the determinations appear to indicate that the USDOC perceives the SPB scenarios as conclusive or determinative to the extent of obviating any necessity even to admit, let alone weigh, evidence as to other factors. In a few cases, USDOC appears at the outset willing to consider whether other factors may be relevant or probative, but does not ultimately rely on such factors, dismissing them summarily or not discussing them at all, and basing its final determination on evidence fitting the SPB scenarios. We emphasize that we are not focusing solely on the outcomes in these sunset reviews, but rather on our qualitative analysis of the determinations, and what we can discern about USDOC's decision-making process underlying those determinations. We therefore conclude that, despite the apparent recognition that it may do otherwise, USDOC has consistently based its determinations in sunset reviews exclusively on the scenarios, to the disregard of other factors. In our view, the actual determinations made, which in all cases ultimately conform to the results predicted by the SPB scenarios, belie the conclusion that USDOC does not consider them as conclusive or determinative in sunset reviews.

It thus concluded that the SPB established an irrefutable presumption of affirmative likely dumping in case one of the factual scenarios of the SPB was found to exist. The Panel found that, as Article 11.3 AD Agreement does not allow for such irrefutable presumption, Mexico had demonstrated that the SPB is, as such, inconsistent with Article 11.3 of the AD Agreement.

When it came to the specific determination of likelihood of dumping in case of OCTG imports from Mexico, the Panel was of the view that the USDOC, applying its policy of looking at the three specific scenarios, based its conclusions entirely on a decline in import volumes following the imposition of the order, and disregarded potentially relevant other evidence. Since the Panel was of the view that in a sunset review under Article 11.3 AD Agreement, an authority must act with an appropriate degree of diligence and arrive at a reasoned conclusion on the basis of information gathered as part of a process of reconsideration and examination,[14]

14 The Panel referred to the view expressed by the Appellate Body in *US – Corrosion-Resistant Steel Sunset Review*, paras. 111–115.

the USDOC determination of likely dumping was considered inconsistent with the requirements of Article 11.3 AD Agreement.[15]

The Appellate Body

The United States appealed the Panel's finding that Section II.A.3 of the SPB is, *as such*, inconsistent with Article 11.3 of the *Anti-Dumping Agreement*, contending that the Panel failed to correctly apply the applicable legal standard in its assessment of the consistency of the SPB. It did not appeal the findings of the Panel in respect of the specific case of Mexican OCTG imports.

The Appellate Body upheld the US's challenge of the Panel's determination of inconsistency of the SPB, and overturned the Panel in this respect. The AB examined the Panel's analysis and came to the conclusion that it failed to live up to the standard of a 'qualitative assessment' it had set for itself. What the Panel should have examined, in the AB's view, was whether, and how relevant and probative, factors outside the scenarios were considered by the USDOC. As the nature and extent of the evidence to rebut the presumptions of the scenarios varies depending on the applicable scenario, a Panel cannot conduct a 'qualitative assessment' without examining how such counterevidence was dealt with. The AB thus came to the overall conclusion that:

> the Panel's analysis does not reveal that the affirmative determinations, in the 21 specific cases reviewed by it, were based *exclusively on the scenarios to the disregard of other factors*. Nor does the Panel's review of these cases reveal that the USDOC's affirmative determinations were based solely on the SPB scenarios, when the probative value of other factors might have outweighed that of the identified scenarios. Accordingly, we conclude that the Panel did not conduct a 'qualitative assessment' of the USDOC's determination such that the Panel could properly conclude that the SPB requires the USDOC to treat the factual scenarios of Section II.A.3 of the SPB as determinative or conclusive.[16]

Having overturned the Panel's decision, the AB concluded that the Panel's statement of inconsistency of the SPB was 'moot and of no legal effect'.[17]

Likelihood of injury

The Panel

The Panel rejected all of Mexico's injury-related claims. The Panel considered that the Article 3 disciplines on 'injury' do not apply to determinations of 'likelihood of injury' in sunset reviews. It crucially relied on the reasoning of the AB in

15 The Panel noted for example that the USDOC did not rely on information concerning historical dumping margins, including the information on dumping margins calculated in administrative reviews during the period of time that the measure had been in place. Nor did USDOC otherwise consider any evidence relating to the amount of dumping originally found, the basis of that calculation, or whether changes in the underlying financial situation might affect the question of likelihood of continuation or recurrence of dumping. Panel Report, para. 7.78.

16 Appellate Body Report, para. 209.

17 Appellate Body Report, para. 211.

US – Corrosion Resistant Steel and *US – Oil Country Tubular Goods Sunset Reviews* concerning the difference between original investigations and reviews. The Panel considered that a determination of injury is not the same as a determination of likelihood of continuation or recurrence of injury in a sunset review, and that, consequently, requirements relevant to a determination of injury are not necessarily relevant to a determination of continuation or recurrence of injury. It concluded that an investigating authority is not required to make an injury determination in a sunset review, and that, therefore, the obligations set out in Article 3 AD Agreement are not directly applicable in sunset reviews.[18] Still, the Panel added, the provisions of Article 3 governing the determination of injury may provide useful guidance in the context of the analysis in sunset reviews.[19]

The Appellate Body

Mexico's limited appeal of the Panel's findings in respect of the applicability of Article 3 AD Agreement to sunset reviews concerned the Panel's interpretation of Article 11.3 of the *Anti-Dumping Agreement* and its failure to address the 'inherent' causation requirements under that Article. Referring to the underlying principles in the *Anti-Dumping Agreement* [20] and Article VI of the GATT 1994, Mexico argued that, even assuming that Article 3.5 of the *Anti-Dumping Agreement* (dealing with causation) does not apply directly to sunset reviews, the Panel failed to recognize the 'inherent' obligation to establish a causal link between likely dumping and likely injury in a sunset review determination under Article 11.3 of the *Anti-Dumping Agreement.*

The AB rejected Mexico's argument of an inherent requirement to conduct a causation analysis under Article 11.3 AD Agreement. On the one hand, the AB agreed with Mexico that the existence of a causal link between dumping and injury to the domestic industry is fundamental to the imposition and maintenance of an anti-dumping duty under the *Anti-Dumping Agreement.* In the words of the AB:

> an anti-dumping duty can be imposed and maintained *only* if the dumping (as properly established) causes injury to the domestic industry. Absent injury to the domestic industry, the rationale for either imposing the duty in the first place, or maintaining it at any time after its imposition, does not exist.[21]

On the other hand, the AB held the view that because the 'review' contemplated in Article 11.3 AD Agreement is a 'distinct' process with a 'different' purpose from the original investigation, a causal link between dumping and injury is not required to be established anew in a sunset review. The AB considered that in a sunset review, the nexus to be demonstrated is between 'the expiry of the duty' on

18 Panel Report, para. 7.117.

19 The Panel further rejected all of Mexico's arguments that the USITC did not base its 'likelihood of injury' determination on a sufficient factual basis. It considered that the USITC determination was based on positive evidence and supported by adequate reasoning.

20 Mexico referred to Articles 1, 3, 11.1, and 18.1 of the AD Agreement in particular.

21 Appellate Body Report, para. 117.

the one hand, and the likelihood of 'continuation or recurrence of dumping and injury' on the other hand. What is required under Article 11.3 is the effect of the expiry of the duty on the likelihood of continuation or recurrence of dumping and injury.[22] The AB did not consider that the requirement of establishing a causal link between likely dumping and likely injury necessarily flows into that Article from other provisions of the GATT 1994 and the *Anti-Dumping Agreement*. According to the AB, 'adding such a requirement would have the effect of converting the sunset review into an original investigation, which cannot be justified'.[23] The AB hastened to add that this did not imply that the causal link between dumping and injury envisaged by Article VI of the GATT 1994 and the *Anti-Dumping Agreement* was severed in a sunset review. It would only mean that reestablishing such a link is not required, as a matter of legal obligation, in a sunset review.[24]

Cumulation

The Panel

The Panel did not accept Mexico's arguments that, in sunset reviews, it is not permissible to cumulatively assess the effects of imports from various countries subject to the order. Neither did it consider convincing Mexico's alternative argument that in case such cumulation were permitted, the same disciplines as are imposed by Article 3.3 AD Agreement in respect of cumulation in original investigations would necessarily also apply in a sunset review context.

The Panel was of the view that the silence of the AD Agreement on the question of cumulation in sunset reviews is properly understood to mean that cumulation is permitted in sunset reviews. It referred to the finding of the Appellate Body in *US – Oil Country Tubular Goods Sunset Reviews*, which dealt with the exact same question. In that case, the AB concluded that cumulation is permitted in sunset reviews and that, since the disciplines of Article 3.3 AD Agreement are limited to original investigations, such disciplines do not apply in sunset reviews.

The Appellate Body

On appeal, Mexico argued that, irrespective of whether the specific obligations of Article 3.3 AD Agreement applied to sunset reviews, the USITC was under an obligation to ensure that cumulation was appropriate in light of the conditions of competition. It argued that, to do that, the USITC was required to make a threshold finding that the subject imports would be simultaneously present in the US market. According to Mexico, the Panel erred in declining to examine and make findings on this issue. In this respect, Mexico argued that nowhere in the USITC's analysis was there positive evidence demonstrating that imports from

22 Any such determinations under Article 11.3 must rest on a 'sufficient factual basis' that allows the investigating authority to draw 'reasoned and adequate conclusions'. See, for example, Appellate Body Report, *US – Oil Country Tubular Goods Sunset Reviews*, para. 311.

23 Appellate Body Report, para. 123.

24 Appellate Body Report, para. 124.

Mexico, and imports from Argentina, Italy, Korea, and Japan would be present in the United States market at the same time if the order were revoked. In any case, Mexico was of the view that having decided to cumulate Mexican imports with imports from four other countries, the USITC was required to do so consistently with the requirements of Article 3.3, regardless of whether that provision applies directly to sunset reviews.

The AB disagreed both with respect to the inherent 'simultaneous presence' argument and with respect to the general applicability of the disciplines of Article 3.3.

The AB failed to see why the USITC was required, under Article 11.3 AD Agreement, to follow the specific step of making a 'threshold finding' on the simultaneous presence of subject imports before resorting to cumulation,[25] given the fact that Article 11.3 does not prescribe any particular methodology with respect to cumulation in sunset reviews.[26]

In addition, the AB clearly established the fact that the disciplines of Article 3.3 relating to cumulation in original investigations do not apply per se in sunset reviews under Article 11.3. In its typical fashion, the AB added the following caveat:

> We do not, however, suggest that, when an authority chooses to cumulate imports in a likelihood-of-injury determination under Article 11.3, it is never necessary for it to determine whether such a cumulative assessment is appropriate in the light of the conditions of competition in the market place. In particular cases, a cumulative assessment of the effects of the imports may be found to be inappropriate and, therefore, inconsistent with the fundamental requirement that a determination rest on a sufficient factual basis and reasoned and adequate conclusions.[27] However, this fundamental requirement derives from the obligations under Article 11.3 itself, and not from the conditions specified in Article 3.3.[28]

25 Appellate Body Report, para. 152.

26 Typically, the AB offered the following attenuation of its statement that no such determination of simultaneous presence is required:

> This is not to say that it is never necessary for an investigating authority, performing a cumulative analysis of injury caused by imports from all sources, to examine whether imports are 'in the market together and competing against each other.' In order to arrive at a reasoned and adequate conclusion, an examination of whether imports are in the market together and competing against each other may, in certain cases, be needed in a likelihood-of-injury determination where an investigating authority chooses to cumulate the imports from several countries. But the need for such an examination flows from the particular facts and circumstances of a given case and not from a legal requirement under Article 11.3.
> Appellate Body Report, para. 153.

27 See Appellate Body Report, *US – Oil Country Tubular Goods Sunset Reviews*, para. 284.

28 Appellate Body Report, para. 171.

3. Analysis

Legal analysis

The case discussed in this report was the fourth and so far final one dealing with sunset reviews, and, not surprisingly, built on a number of such previous Panel and Appellate Body reports. We will, therefore, first provide a quick overview of the basic conclusions to draw from the sunset case law to date. Thereafter, we will briefly comment on the Appellate Body's finding in this case that no causation analysis is required in sunset reviews. Third, we address the AB's analysis of the Panel's decision in respect of the Sunset Policy Bulletin.

Sunset reviews – an empty box?

Only one provision of the AD Agreement explicitly deals with sunset reviews, Article 11.3 AD Agreement. It does not say much but simply sets forth two key principles: (1) that anti-dumping duties are to be terminated after five years; and (2) that by way of exception, duties may remain in place for a longer period of time if it is determined in a review that the expiry of the duty would be likely to lead to continuation or recurrence of dumping and injury. That is all that the text of the AD Agreement provides for in respect of sunset reviews.[29] All the sunset disputes dealt with by WTO panels and the AB revolved around the question whether some of the more detailed requirements about dumping and injury, as reflected in various provisions of the AD Agreement, as well as many of the procedural rules developed with respect to original investigations also apply to sunset reviews.

The commonsense argument is clear. A sunset review is more or less like a new investigation, and may take up to one year to conclude; it is about dumping and injury, terms defined in Articles 2 and 3 of the Agreement; an investigation is required, and the Agreement explicitly imposes respect for the procedural and evidentiary safeguards of original investigations also in the conduct of such review investigations. While the outcome of a review is different from the outcome of an original investigation, i.e. whether dumping and injury would be likely to recur rather than whether dumping and injury exist, the concepts used and the process followed are very similar. Nevertheless, the text of Article 11.3 does not cross-reference to these provisions of the AD Agreement in which dumping and injury are detailed. It does not contain any disciplines in terms of methodology to follow in sunset reviews. So the choice before the WTO panels and the AB was fundamentally the following: do we follow a strict textual approach or do we prefer a contextual approach based on common sense. The latter approach would inevitably lead to the introduction of a number of disciplines in sunset reviews, and thus limit the discretion of the investigating authority. Confronted with that choice on a number of occasions, the AB consistently opted for the strict textual approach and preserved to the maximum extent possible the investigating authority's

29 Article 11.4 adds that insofar as procedure and evidence are concerned, everything that was provided for with respect to original investigations also applies to reviews such as a sunset review.

discretionary authority in extending anti-dumping measures beyond the envisaged maximum period of five years.

The argument offered by the AB was basically that sunset reviews and original investigations are different processes with a different purpose,[30] to which different rules apply. The rules and disciplines for making a determination of dumping and injury that apply in original investigations, are not applicable as such in sunset reviews.[31] In respect of the likelihood-of-injury determination, the AB, in its report on *US – Oil Country Tubular Goods Sunset Reviews*, was of the view that no injury examination in the sense of Article 3 AD Agreement is required and that, therefore, the obligations set out in Article 3 do not apply in sunset reviews.[32] The same approach governed the likelihood of dumping determination. The AB was of the view that the silence on the methodology for determining likelihood of dumping in Article 11.3 suggests that no obligation is imposed on investigating authorities to calculate or rely on dumping margins in a sunset review. This is so because, in a sunset review, dumping margins may well be relevant, but will not necessarily be conclusive of whether the expiry of the duty would be likely to lead to continuation or recurrence of dumping. In an original investigation, however, a positive margin determination is a necessary condition for the imposition of a measure.[33]

It appeared that by taking this approach the Appellate Body was voiding of all meaning the need to conduct a sunset review. The hard-fought rule that duties could not stay in place forever, but were to be terminated after five years, becomes meaningless. If no disciplines apply to sunset reviews, such reviews become a formality; as has happened in practice in certain countries, an anti-dumping duty will in effect be extended quasi-automatically every five years.

Obviously concerned about this outcome, the AB decided to attenuate its hard line: it started to read things into a couple of the terms that appear in Article 11.3 and on that basis imposed some basic general limitations on an authority's freedom. While it refused to read the terms 'dumping' and 'injury' in context, the terms 'review' and 'determination' were interpreted as if they operated like Russian dolls containing a number of different obligations.

Based on the fact that a sunset 'review' requires a 'determination' of likely dumping and injury, the primary obligation the AB imposed on investigating authorities became to ensure that their determination of likelihood of recurrence or continuation of dumping and injury rests *on a sufficient factual basis that allows the investigating authority to draw reasoned and adequate conclusions*. The AB, in

30 Appellate Body Report, *US – Corrosion-Resistant Steel Sunset Review*, paras. 106–107; Appellate Body Report, *US – Carbon Steel*, para. 87.

31 Appellate Body Report, on *US – Oil Country Tubular Goods Sunset Reviews*, para. 359.

32 Appellate Body Report, *US – Oil Country Tubular Goods Sunset Reviews*, para. 280. Also see Panel Report, *US – Anti-Dumping Measures on Oil Country Tubular Goods*, para. 7.117.

33 Appellate Body Report, *US – Corrosion-Resistant Steel Sunset Review*, paras. 123–124.

its report on *US – Oil Country Tubular Goods Sunset Reviews* explained its reasoning as follows:

> In *US – Corrosion-Resistant Steel Sunset Review*, the Appellate Body emphasized the importance of the terms 'determine' and 'review' in Article 11.3, stating:
>
> > The words 'review' and 'determine' in Article 11.3 suggest that authorities conducting a sunset review must act with an appropriate degree of diligence and arrive at a *reasoned conclusion* on the basis of information gathered as part of a process of *reconsideration and examination*. (emphasis added)
>
> The Appellate Body also endorsed that Panel's description of the obligation contained in Article 11.3, which description the Appellate Body found 'closely resemble[d]' its own understanding:
>
> > The requirement to make a 'determination' concerning likelihood therefore precludes an investigating authority from simply assuming that likelihood exists. In order to continue the imposition of the measure after the expiry of the five-year application period, it is clear that the investigating authority has to determine, on the basis of *positive evidence*, that termination of the duty is likely to lead to continuation or recurrence of dumping and injury. An investigating authority must have a *sufficient factual basis* to allow it to draw *reasoned and adequate conclusions* concerning the likelihood of such continuation or recurrence. (emphasis added; original footnotes omitted)
> >
> > The plain meaning of the terms 'review' and 'determine' in Article 11.3, therefore, compel an investigating authority in a sunset review to undertake an examination, on the basis of positive evidence, of the likelihood of continuation or recurrence of dumping and injury. In drawing conclusions from that examination, the investigating authority must arrive at a reasoned determination resting on a sufficient factual basis; it may not rely on assumptions or conjecture.[34]

It is clear that suddenly the AB showed a great willingness to read a lot into two words. It imposed some important basic disciplines on sunset reviews. While we welcome in general such a development, we cannot help wondering why a similar approach in favor of importing some of the disciplines in terms of dumping and injury was rejected. To read such obligations into words as 'determination' and 'review' is not more textual than it would have been to do the same for dumping and injury. In other words, if one wanted to be consistent, the only solution would be to say that there simply are no disciplines imposed by the text of Article 11.3 and that the drafters had been sloppy by not cross-referencing the obligations that apply in original investigations.

At the same time, and in light of the lack of any serious economic justification for the use of anti-dumping, we do not want to be seen as suggesting that we disagree with the introduction of such disciplines by the AB. While consistency is certainly a virtue, one can also be consistently wrong. We should thus be happy with this lack of consistency by the AB in its approach to sunset reviews, which

34 Appellate Body Report, *US – Oil Country Tubular Goods Sunset Reviews*, paras. 179–180.

were starting to look very much like an empty box. At least the box is not completely empty now.

How full it is remains to be seen. While a requirement is introduced to base the determination on facts and positive evidence, a sunset review is by definition a forward-looking exercise. Even the AB thus admitted that some speculation about future events cannot be avoided.[35] Moreover, the demands on the type of evidence on which the determination is to be based are minimal. Limited observations, in the sense of small volume of export sales, might suffice for the purposes of conducting a lawful review.[36] More importantly, data that were evaluated in the original investigation may be used again and reevaluated at the review stage as 'a fresh determination, based on credible evidence'.[37] This implies that it may be justified to base a sunset determination of likely dumping on data from more than five years ago. At first glance, this seems troublesome. A prospective analysis as the one allegedly undertaken in a sunset review (i.e., will there be likely dumping and injury in case the duty is removed?) should be based on the most recent data, it would seem. One could argue that a prospective analysis based on data from more than five years ago can hardly be called meaningful. However, as we discuss in more detail below in the economics section, more recent data are not necessarily more relevant for the likelihood determination given that the data being used for comparison would be derived from a set of historical market conditions (under the order) that we anticipate would be quite different from the future market conditions (were the order to be removed).

Moreover, while the basic due-process rights applicable in original investigations have been applied to sunset reviews, the AB accepted one important exception: in sunset reviews, no individual determination of the need to maintain the duty with respect to the individual exporter is required.[38] This of course has the important consequence that a company can remain subject to an anti-dumping order even though it is no longer dumping. Its sales will continue to be monitored and remain under threat of anti-dumping action for another five years. But how can this be squared with the insistence on the need to have a sufficient factual basis for maintaining the duties; dumping is a practice of individual companies, it is not

35 Appellate Body Report, *US – Oil Country Tubular Goods Sunset Reviews*, para. 341.

36 Appellate Body Report, *US – Oil Country Tubular Goods Sunset Reviews*, para. 346:

> We endorse the Panel's view that '[t]he simple fact that the number of price comparisons was limited does not make this aspect of the USITC's determination inconsistent with Article 11.3 of the [*Anti-Dumping Agreement*]',

Also see Panel Report, *US – Oil Country Tubular Goods Sunset Reviews*, para. 7.303.

37 Appellate Body Report, *US – Carbon Steel*, para. 88.

38 In its report on *US – Corrosion-Resistant Carbon Steel Sunset Review*, the AB considered that paragraph 10 of Article 6, requiring the authority to calculate individual margins of dumping cannot apply in a review because, according to the Appellate Body, in a review, an authority is not required under Article 11.3 to calculate dumping margins in the first place. Appellate Body Report, *US – Corrosion Resistant Steel Sunset Reviews*, para. 155.

something countries engage in. Yet, if the facts support a determination that one or more exporters are likely to continue or restart dumping, all exporters remain subject to anti-dumping duties. The sunset review may well be based on facts in such circumstances, simply not necessarily on facts relevant to the exporter allegedly engaged in dumping. How does all this fit together? Only the AB knows.

Causation – required to keep the duty in place?

Dumping, injury, and the existence of causal link between the two are the basic conditions for any anti-dumping action. If there is no dumping, no duty may be imposed to offer protection to a domestic industry, even though it may be faring badly and could be said to be suffering 'injury'. Similarly, if imports are being dumped on the market, but the domestic industry in the importing country is healthy and profitable, no duties may be imposed, since the industry is not in a state of 'injury'. Likewise, imports may be dumped into a country, and during that same period of time the domestic industry may be going through a difficult period of loss of profitability and lay-offs, but still no protection can be offered through the imposition of anti-dumping duties unless it can be demonstrated that the dumped imports are the cause of this negative situation. The causation requirement thus plays an important role in preventing countries from passing on to exporting countries the costs of bad industrial management, lack of adequate investment in new technology, and a failed industrial policy in general.

In the case discussed in more detail in this report, *US – Anti-Dumping Measures on Oil Country Tubular Goods*, the Appellate Body confirmed, on the one hand, that a causal link between dumping and injury to the domestic industry is fundamental to the imposition and maintenance of an anti-dumping duty under the AD Agreement. However, on the other hand, and in line with the alleged textual approach outlined above, it also stressed the fact that the text of Article 11.3 does not require the establishment of a causal link between the likely injury and the likely dumping. It held the view that a sunset review is a distinct process with a 'different' purpose from the original investigation, and that therefore a causal link between dumping and injury is not 'required to be established anew in a review conducted under Article 11.3'.[39] According to the Appellate Body, 'adding such a requirement [of establishing a causal link between the likely dumping and likely injury] would have the effect of converting the sunset review into an original investigation, which cannot be justified'.[40]

The Appellate Body considered that the nexus to be demonstrated under Article 11.3 is not between dumping and injury, but between 'the expiry of the duty' on the one hand, and the likelihood of 'continuation or recurrence of dumping and injury' on the other hand.

39 Appellate Body Report, *US – Anti-Dumping Measures on Oil Country Tubular Goods*, para. 118.
40 Appellate Body Report, *US – Anti-Dumping Measures on Oil Country Tubular Goods*, para. 123.

However, to conclude on this basis that there is no need to establish a causal link between the likely future dumping and injury seems problematic to say the least. In our view, an examination of likelihood of recurrence or continuation of injury must refer to likelihood of injury *insofar as it is caused by* dumping, and not just any injury. Even under a strict textual approach, the Appellate Body erred by introducing such an artificial separation between injury and causation, since the only relevant injury under the AD Agreement is the injury *caused by* the dumped imports. Look at the text of the AD Agreement: injury and causation are both discussed in the same provision, Article 3 of the AD Agreement, entitled, *Determination of Injury*. So, there is no separate provision dealing with causation. While the requirement to establish a causal relationship between dumping and injury is expressed in one paragraph of Article 3, Article 3.5 AD Agreement, this is not the only paragraph of Article 3 linking injury to the dumped imports. Various other paragraphs of Article 3 such as for example Articles 3.1, 3.2, and 3.4, refer to the volume of dumped imports and the effects of such imports on domestic prices as well as the impact of these imports on domestic producers. In other words, such provisions do not simply set forth an analysis of the state of the domestic industry as such, quite to the contrary. They are all geared at establishing the existence of injury *caused by* dumped imports.[41] In our view, the Appellate Body's textual arguments separating injury from causation are misplaced, and its interpretation is not faithful to the text of the AD Agreement.

This being said, two additional comments are in place to put this error in the right perspective.

First, in practice, we wonder whether the Appellate Body's error will have much impact, as it seems that the AB was not willing to accept the consequences of its own ruling. It appears that a causation requirement was brought in through the back door: the need to establish a nexus between the termination of the duty and the likely dumping and injury that would follow.

Since it must be demonstrated on the basis of positive evidence that there exists a nexus between the expiry of the duty and the recurrence or continuation of dumping and injury, an investigating authority cannot simply ignore the intervening effect of an influx of imports from other sources, or an event such as a storm destroying a factory for example. The injury may continue, but it has nothing to do with the expiry of the duty, rather it is caused by an intervening factor, the non-subject imports, or the storm. In other words, it needs to be established that the expiry of the duty, which assumingly was protecting the industry from injury by

41 For example, Article 3.2 requires that it be examined whether there has been an increase in the volume of dumped imports. This is part of the 'injury' analysis, even though the volume of dumped imports is not informative of the state of the domestic industry as such. It is important in establishing the link between dumped imports and the injurious state of the domestic industry. In other words, an examination of the volume of dumped imports and their price effects are elements of a causation analysis, rather than an injury analysis *pur sang*. So, the relevant injury of the AD Agreement is a qualified 'injury caused by' dumped imports.

offsetting the dumping, is the cause of the recurring dumping and injury. If a storm or nondumped imports are the cause of the industry's problems, then the expiry of the duty cannot be blamed for such recurrent injury. Indirectly, therefore, the requirement of a nexus between the expiry of the duty and the likely dumping and injury imposes the establishment of a nexus between the dumped imports and the injury. So maybe the Appellate Body's sweeping statements about the absence of the need to establish a causal link between dumping and injury in sunset reviews is much ado about nothing ('Mucho ruido, pocas nueces', as the Mexicans would say).

This, of course, begs the question why the AB felt it was necessary to adopt such an overly restrictive and incorrect textual interpretation of the requirements of Article 11.3 and the term 'injury' in particular. The only explanation we can come up with is a fear of imposing disciplines and obligations on investigating authorities beyond what a strict, minimalist, and therefore incorrect reading of the text allows for.

A second comment is that, as we discuss in more detail below in the economic analysis section, it is not straightforward to establish an empirically and economically satisfactory causal relationship between future dumping and future injury. While that may be so, we note that it was not for such sound economic reasons that the AB concluded that causation was not an element to be established in a sunset review determination. Neither do we wish to suggest by this economic comment that the difficulty of establishing such a causal link would be a good reason for allowing the continuation of duties without further ado, quite to the contrary. The fact that it is difficult to come to any meaningful conclusion about such future events should be a reason for requiring termination of such measures. Any extension can only be based on speculation.

The SPB – the impossible task of demonstrating a violation

The Sunset Policy Bulletin (SPB) saga continued in this case. We recall that this was the third case to deal with the US Sunset Policy Bulletin, the ins and outs of which have been explained in the ALI report dealing with the dispute on *US – Oil Country Tubular Goods Sunset Reviews*. In essence, the SPB sets forth the USDOC's policy for determining whether dumping is likely to continue or recur when the anti-dumping duty expires. It provides for three factual scenarios centered around two criteria: import volumes and dumping margins. In case the facts are consistent with any of these scenarios, the SPB provides that the USDOC 'will normally' conclude that there is a likelihood that the exporters will continue or resume dumping their products into the importing country. A number of WTO Members have taken issue with the SPB as it sets forth certain basic assumptions on the basis of which the USDOC will reach its conclusions without regard to other evidence rebutting the validity of such assumptions. It was therefore argued to be inconsistent with the basic principle that a determination and review be based on facts and positive evidence, not assumptions.

The first Panel to deal with the consistency of the SPB in *US – Corrosion Resistant Steel Sunset Review* (DS 244) considered that the SPB was not a mandatory piece of legislation and concluded that, for that reason, it did not constitute a 'measure' that could be challenged through WTO dispute settlement proceedings. The AB overturned this decision stating that any act attributable to the State can be challenged as such before the WTO. It did not pronounce itself on the consistency of the SPB. A second Panel dealing with the SPB in *US – Oil Country Tubular Goods Sunset Reviews* followed the AB's jurisprudence and examined the SPB to find that it was inconsistent with the AD Agreement. But, this Panel, too, was overturned by the AB. The Panel's straightforward conclusion of inconsistency was based on consistent results of 232 affirmative sunset determinations all applying the three scenarios. The Panel was overturned by the AB because it failed to conduct a 'qualitative assessment' of the evidence and relied on 'mere statistical' evidence. The *US – Anti-Dumping Measures on Oil Country Tubular Goods from Mexico* case discussed in our report was thus the third case to deal with the SPB. The Panel was clearly aware of the errors committed by previous Panels, as it recalled the 'guidance' of the Appellate Body in terms of the legal standard for determining whether the SPB was inconsistent with the Agreement and the type of qualitative assessment a Panel is to undertake in order to establish any inconsistency based on the evidence before it. And yet, once again, the Panel got it wrong. At least, according to the AB.

We do not want to dwell on the comments of the AB with respect to the specific analysis of the Panel in this case. But we cannot but wonder why the Appellate Body wants to fault the Panel for not having examined in detail 206 of the 232 cases that were decided in an 'expedited' manner. After all, these were all cases decided on the basis of the US waiver provisions that the same AB in *US – Oil Country Tubular Goods Sunset Reviews* found to be inconsistent with the AD Agreement's requirement that a determination of likelihood of dumping and injury be based on positive evidence and not just on assumptions. If these determinations were all inconsistent with the AD Agreement and not based on evidence or arguments provided by the investigated exporters, why would the Panel have needed to examine these cases in more detail?

In any case, what we want to highlight is how difficult it is to demonstrate a violation in case the text of the legal instrument is prima facie discretionary, such as is the case of the SPB. The SPB provides that the USDOC 'will normally' reach its conclusion on the basis of the three scenarios, but allows parties to present, if good cause is shown, other evidence rebutting the presumptive conclusions reached on the basis of the scenarios. What the 232 affirmative determinations of the USDOC revealed, however, was how illusory such a possibility proved to be, as every determination had been based on one of the scenarios. But what the AB wanted was proof that evidence undermining the assumptions established under any of the three scenarios was offered by an interested party, that such evidence was rejected, and that it was rejected because the USDOC felt obliged by the SPB to reach its conclusion on the basis of one of the three scenarios. Only then would it be possible to conclude that the SPB mandated WTO inconsistent action, only then would the SPB be inconsistent 'as such' with the AD Agreement. This is of course a Herculean task.

It is doubtful whether the AB would have reached the same conclusions with respect to the evidence of a consistent application of the three scenarios establishing a presumption of likelihood of dumping had there not been an SPB. In other words, had the USDOC *practice* been examined as such, i.e. as a 'practice', the outcome would most probably have been different. It is clear that the fact that the USDOC always applies the three scenarios and has never to date been willing to accept data and arguments that did not fall inside the scope of these three factual scenarios should be sufficient to establish a violation. The zeroing case law and the way the zeroing 'methodology' was considered to be an 'as such' violation of the requirements of the AD Agreement stands in stark contrast with the overly rigorous mandatory/discretionary approach advocated in this case. Given the importance of sunset reviews as the door to an extension of the duty for another five years, and given the acknowledgment by the AB itself that termination of a duty after five years is the rule, and extension the exception, this deferential approach is all the more surprising and disappointing.[42]

It is for reasons of predictability and a stable trading regime that GATT/WTO jurisprudence allows challenges of laws on an 'as such' basis, thus even without the application of such laws, and without a need to wait for the damage caused by such legislative violations to occur. The direct impact of trade laws was an important consideration in allowing such 'as such' challenges. By denying Members a realistic possibility to challenge such quasi-discretionary measures as the SPB, the AB is undermining the objective pursued by such 'as such' challenges. Each Member will be forced to challenge the actual application of the SPB, although it is clear that USDOC will always base itself on these doubtful and overly simplistic assumptions, discarding alternative evidence.

This hard line is even more surprising in this particular case in light of the clear criticism expressed by the AB with respect to the assumptions underlying the three scenarios. The AB objected to the presumptions established under these three scenarios as being a sufficient basis for making affirmative determinations. It considered that there were certain cases where the presumption was quite forceful, but that for other scenarios the presumption was more doubtful. According to the AB, for example, a company's strategy and ability to increase or decrease its

42 So, after first having overturned the first Panel for not wanting to consider the possible violation contained in the SPB because it did not mandate any action, the AB has now *de facto* closed the circle making it clear that you may well be allowed to challenge such discretionary legislation 'as such', but you will never win the case. The evidentiary burden on a complainant is such that legislation that does not *expressis verbis* require WTO inconsistent action will never be found to be inconsistent as such with the WTO Agreement. The first Panel was right after all: let's not waste each other's time, this is a no-go from the beginning.

exports to particular markets would need to be examined to be able to say anything about the future likelihood of dumping to stimulate an increase in imports. It would require an examination of a variety of market conditions, such as, in particular, the opportunities available in different markets and the competitive conditions in the marketplace.[43] The USDOC never does such a thing but simply examines whether the facts of the case are covered by one of the three scenarios. If that is the case, it concludes that there is a likelihood of dumping. USDOC does not question the underlying assumptions.

In sum, it appears that many US sunset review determinations could be challenged before the WTO since all are based on the presumptions established by the SPB, yet the SPB itself remains untouchable. This is obviously not a desirable outcome.

We want to add one final systemic comment. The SPB saga demonstrates once again that the AB fails to introduce the expected predictability and uniformity in the dispute settlement process and does not clarify the legal obligations of the Agreement. Two Panels, both very much aware of what the Appellate Body had said in respect of the SPB and both expressly relying on the AB's statements in this respect, were overturned for having failed to correctly apply the Appellate Body's guidelines. Were both Panels too ignorant to understand what the AB was saying, or was the AB too vague in explaining what it considered to be required, and overly zealous in imposing respect for its own statements? We leave this to the reader to decide.

Economic analysis

This section provides an economic analysis of two key aspects of the Appellate Body's decision. First, we examine a role for causality between expected dumping and expected injury in the sunset review investigative process. Second, we provide an economic assessment of the use of cumulation in the likelihood-of-injury determination in the sunset review process. After addressing these issues in each of the next two sections, in the final section we return to the question of the economic importance of sunset reviews more broadly.[44]

Causation in sunset reviews

A key question at issue in the appeal is whether investigative authorities in the sunset review process are required to establish the existence of a causal link between likely dumping and likely injury. Before commencing our economic analysis of this question, we first review two foundational issues – what an economic

43 AB Report, *US – OCTG Mexico*, paras. 198–200. In fact, the scenarios are such that it will not be too difficult to reach affirmative determinations, which explains perhaps the fact that, unless the domestic industry was no longer interested in maintaining the order, every sunset review conducted by the USDOC has led to an affirmative finding.

44 There are a number of other economic issues associated with dumping involved in this dispute and decision that we choose not to address, given their substantial treatment in other contributions to this series.

analysis contributes *vis-à-vis* the question of how investigative authorities first make the likelihood-of-dumping determination during a sunset review; and how economics assesses the importance of causality in anti-dumping investigations more generally. After reviewing these issues separately, we then tie together our analysis below.

Likelihood of continued or renewed dumping. When examining the question of whether it is likely that a foreign firm will continue or renew its dumping if an anti-dumping order were removed, we first review the insightful analysis of Howse and Staiger (2006). A concise summary of their fundamental reasoning is simply that 'a meaningful assessment of the likelihood of continued or renewed dumping requires an understanding of two things: (i) what conditions led to dumping in the first place; and (ii) whether those conditions have changed in a way that removes the original reason for dumping' (Howse and Staiger, 53).

With this statement, we highlight the fact that Howse and Staiger rule out an alternative methodology – which is that the likelihood of dumping determination be based on evidence from pricing data and dumping calculations collected while the anti-dumping order was imposed.

Howse and Staiger rule out this (prima facie) attractive alternative by pointing out that evidence that a firm dumped while under an anti-dumping order is not necessarily a useful predictor of whether the firm would also dump in the absence of a such an order – i.e., in the sunset review scenario that the anti-dumping order would be removed. Blonigen and Park (2004) provide a theoretical framework and supportive economic evidence based on the behavior of firms under US anti-dumping orders that serves as a compelling explanation for the Howse and Staiger argument. Because the USDOC carries out its dumping determination retrospectively, i.e., by examining past dumping behavior, Blonigen and Park show how this can create a (counterintuitive) incentive for profit-maximizing firms to *increase* their dumping margins *because of* the presence of an anti-dumping order. Blonigen and Park not only illustrate this incentive within a theoretical economic model, but they also provide empirical evidence from a sample of pricing decisions made by firms under US anti-dumping orders that is consistent with the theoretical model's predictions.

The economics of causality in anti-dumping investigations. Before examining the question of causality in the specific setting of sunset reviews, we provide a brief discussion of the importance of the causality issue within the more general context of the link between dumping and injury.

While there may be evidence of dumping *and* evidence of injury to the domestic industry in an anti-dumping investigation, economists argue for the need for a causal link because of concern that other more compelling factors may have contributed to 'causing' the injury. For example, at the same time that dumping takes place, the domestic industry may face other economic shocks unrelated to dumped subject imports. Examples of such other factors include 'supply-side' shocks such as cost shocks due to unexpected changes in energy prices or other key inputs, labor shortages (strikes), poor managerial decisions, or natural disasters; 'demand-side' shocks such as fluctuations in income or tastes and preferences; or even shocks to the level of nonsubject imports.

Because of the presence of many theoretically compelling, and yet potentially *competing* explanations of the cause of injury to a domestic industry, economists have developed formal, empirically based methodological frameworks that investigative authorities can use to help sort between explanations. Two such examples are an econometric approach and a simulation approach.

A typical econometric approach to examine the causality question would have investigators use a multivariate regression analysis to examine the statistical relationship between movements in recent values of possible competing explanatory variables (e.g. subject imports, energy or other input prices, nonsubject imports, etc.) and movements in recent values of measures of industry injury (e.g. profits, revenues, employment, capacity utilization, etc.).[45] There are a number of reasons why, if there are no other constraints, the econometric approach can be the most compelling. For example, it is the most rigorous approach, as a properly specified regression framework allows the investigator to use data stemming from actual events to estimate how much of the injury is due to dumped imports, controlling for a number of other potential explanations for the injury. The drawback of this approach is that frequently there are realistic constraints to implementation, such as the fact that it may difficult or costly because it is very data intensive.

An alternative methodological framework that economists have developed to provide insight into the causation question is called a 'simulation' approach. The basic methodology is to use estimates of key economic parameters (e.g. demand, supply, and substitution elasticities) of the product market under investigation in combination with minimal data on changes in a few key market indicators (e.g. prices, domestic production, volume of subject and nonsubject imports, etc.) in order to come up with a rough, but economic-based assessment as to whether dumped imports are at least statistically a cause of injury.[46] While such simulation exercises rely heavily on assumptions of the model's market structure and the reliability of elasticity assumptions obtained from other sources, and they do not provide as much information as a multivariate regression analysis, such an approach can be an attractive and low-cost alternative useful for examining whether the basic economic facts are consistent with a scenario in which dumped imports contributed to injury. Indeed, such an alternative may be particularly appealing

45 See, for example, the approach of Prusa and Sharp (2001), as well as the discussion in Durling and McCullough (2004). Similarly motivated regression-based approaches to the related framework of assessing the relationship between imports and injury in safeguards law can be found in Grossman (1986) and Pindyck and Rotemberg (1987).

46 Economists at the USITC have developed such a model, frequently referred to as the COMPAS model (Francois and Hall, 1993). For applying a similar approach to related injury and import causality linkage cases in safeguard cases, see also Kelly (1988) and Irwin (2003).

when a more reliable though formal regression analysis is extremely difficult, perhaps because of lack of sufficiently disaggregated time series of data. This constraint is frequent when the scope of the investigation involves a few narrowly defined product categories and/or the period of investigation is a short time series.

The causal link in sunset reviews. In this section, we examine whether economist's arguments for the importance of a causal assessment, as well as the economic techniques to assess causality in anti-dumping investigations, more generally also apply to the case of *likely* dumping and *likely* injury determinations in sunset reviews.

The primary difference between the causation link in the injury-determination decision and one in a sunset review is that the latter is an assessment made *prospectively*. A sunset review decision is based on expectations of future circumstances relating two issues – the expected future pricing behavior of foreign firms and the expected future economic performance of the domestic industry in the presence of such expected foreign pricing behavior.

Because of the prospective nature of the assessment that is made in a sunset review, a regression-based analytical approach is not a useful exercise to assess the causality between any likely future dumping and any likely future injury. While the economic reasoning is quite intuitive, we do note that our arguments should not be misinterpreted as a statement condemning causation as a necessary component to anti-dumping more generally. It is simply that in the case of a sunset review, expected future market structure (e.g. number of competitors, degree of competition in the market, response of consumers) once the anti-dumping order is removed is an unknown, and this market structure is likely to be quite different from the market structure that exists empirically in the historical data that would be derived from a recent period during which an anti-dumping order was in place. Thus, even if a sufficiently disaggregated and long-time series of data were available (the usual constraint that can make even a desirable regression analysis impractical), drawing inference from such historical data derived from the period in which the order was in place is unlikely to accurately predict 'out of sample', future economic outcomes under conditions in which the anti-dumping order would not be in place.[47]

Would the alternative of an empirically based simulation approach be a useful exercise? Applying a simulation model could reveal useful insight as to the likelihood of future injury conditional on the likelihood of future dumping. Note, however, that use of such a model again requires information on a number of key parameters associated with expected future market outcomes – i.e., what would the demand, supply, and substitution elasticities 'look like' if the order were removed? Ultimately, an investigator would need to make an educated guess as to the size of these elasticities in a future state of the world and would therefore have

47 Indeed, this is one explanation for why Moore (2006) found little empirical relationship between traditional industry measures of injury (computed under the years of the order) and ITC sunset review injury decisions in the United States.

to confront the question of whether market conditions have changed from the most 'comparable' state of the world. This is likely the state of the world prior to the anti-dumping order being in place.

This economic analysis ultimately leads us back to an analogy to the original sunset review insight provided by Howse and Staiger, here applied to this follow-up issue of injury and causality, i.e. that a meaningful assessment of the likelihood of continued or renewed injury caused by likely dumped imports requires an understanding of at least two things: (i) what were the causes of injury in the first place; and (ii) whether the conditions surrounding these factors have changed in a way that removes them as likely future causes of injury.

Cumulation in sunset reviews

Our second area of economic analysis addresses the question of an anti-dumping investigator's use of cumulated imports in the sunset review injury determination. The fundamental economic concern with the discretionary use of cumulation is that investigators may face the incentive to use it strategically in order to 'manipulate' decisions – e.g. finding evidence of likely continued or renewed injury when there would not otherwise be such evidence.

The basic economic problem with cumulation is that its presence creates the possibility that one exporter's decision has 'externality' implications on other firms in an anti-dumping investigation. Whenever an exporter does not face the full cost or benefit of the actions it takes, the result is that its decisionmaking leads to distortions and outcomes that are inefficient. In the presence of such externalities, economists have noted that it creates an incentive to 'free ride'.[48]

Howse and Staiger (2006) examine a related issue of economic incentives affected by free-riding in the context of an anti-dumping investigator being confronted with the choice of calculating dumping on a firm-specific basis versus an order-wide basis. They argue that if the likelihood of dumping depends importantly on factors that are under the control of specific companies (e.g. technology choices, input costs) as opposed to factors that are common across firms (e.g. exchange-rate movements) then the analysis should be done on the company-specific basis. The intuition is that if margins are calculated order-wide, this can lead to free-riding behavior and ultimately inefficient outcomes. If a company's behavior affects the likelihood that its competitors will have an anti-dumping duty imposed or removed, then because the company does not face the full cost or benefit of its actions, it may decide to set prices or make other related choices that are inefficient. On the other hand, if the company knows that the decisions it makes only affect its own dumping margin (because the anti-dumping investigator has adopted a rule of calculating dumping on a firm-specific basis), all externalities are internalized, and there is no concern that this will lead to free-riding.

48 This assumes that the sunset review process would otherwise itself yield an efficient outcome. We do not address the broader possibility that the sunset review process itself is inefficient.

The question of whether or not to allow for cumulation in an injury determination creates a similar set of economic concerns over free-riding. Just as exporters may change their pricing behavior away from what is individually optimal in recognition that such behavior will affect the dumping decisions that are being made with respect to their competitors (e.g. if using the 'order-wide' method), exporters may also change their behavior away from what is individually optimal if they anticipate that their actions influence the injury determinations facing their competitors (e.g. if a cumulation rule is allowed).

If cumulation is left at the discretion of investigators at the sunset review stage, government authorities with a particular 'bias' (for or against domestic industry) will make the decision of whether to cumulate strategically to influence their *ex ante* preferred outcome. One concern is that investigators will have an incentive to cumulate multiple countries into their likelihood of continued or renewed injury determination simply because this increases the probability of free-riding on the part of each individual investigated country. For example, such a decision to cumulate in a sunset review may increase the probability that each individual exporter underinvests in its legal defense to have the order removed, as it does not stand to capture the full benefit of its litigation efforts. Furthermore, the exporter's decision not to adequately defend itself is undertaken in anticipation of the ability to 'free ride' on other exporters' legal defense, since the injury determination is likely to be cumulated. But since all exporters face this underinvestment incentive, too little is cumulatively spent on the legal defense. The lack of an adequately funded legal defense may lead authorities to use the prejudicial 'best information available' (BIA) in their ultimate injury determination, and the result is that the order is more likely to remain in place.

This concern over free-riding and the cumulation rule in injury determinations in anti-dumping *investigations* is supported by the findings of economic research. Early research on US and EU anti-dumping investigations documented a curious and unexplained 'superadditivity' effect in cases in which investigators cumulated imports. The empirically documented superadditivity effect is that the probability of a positive injury finding is higher when the number of defendants in the case is larger, holding constant their total market share.[49] Gupta and Panagariya (2006) provide a simple economic model to explain the empirically documented superadditivity effect. The Gupta and Panagariya explanation is that the larger is the number of exporters involved in the investigation, the smaller the incentive for each exporter to invest in its own defense, because there are positive externalities to them winning the case and not having a duty imposed.[50] Thus, the incentive of

49 For evidence on US cases, see Hansen and Prusa (1996); for evidence of the impact of cumulation in EU cases, see Tharaka, Greenaway, and Tharakan (1998).

50 A complementary explanation that Gupta and Panagariya attribute to Robert Staiger at the end of their paper, is that cumulation may have a super-additive impact on injury findings if the probability of a positive finding rises with the size of the dumping margin. Specifically, their explanation is that '[c]eteris paribus, the larger the number of firms exporting to the country in which dumping takes place the more

each exporter to 'free ride' leads to a smaller-than-optimal cumulative effort in putting up a legal defense, thus increasing the likelihood of a positive injury determination.

The economic intuition from cumulation, free-riding, and anti-dumping investigations extends to expected injury determinations in sunset reviews as well. Furthermore, exporters might not only have an incentive to free ride in sunset reviews, but certain exporters may have an incentive to try and (perversely) *increase* the probability of a continued or renewed likelihood of injury in the presence of cumulation, so that an anti-dumping order remains in place across numerous foreign competitors.

As one example to see the incentives behind this phenomenon, suppose that during the lengthy period that the anti-dumping order had been in effect, a firm that was originally simply an exporter had established a subsidiary within the investigating market, e.g. what is referred to as 'anti-dumping-jumping' foreign direct investment (FDI). Blonigen and Ohno (1998) present a model where the possibility of anti-dumping-jumping FDI creates incentives for foreign firms to act strategically *vis-à-vis* their other foreign competitors (e.g. increase dumping, causing injury) in anticipation of being able to subvert the anti-dumping order by becoming a 'domestic' producer through FDI. Because of cumulation, their actions will adversely affect other exporters, and the possibility of the FDI alternative also means that they will experience less of a consequence of their strategic actions if in the future much of their sales stem from local subsidiaries.

Furthermore, a second example could arise even without the need for FDI simply because of the *discriminatory* nature of the anti-dumping orders imposed. An important factor affecting an individual exporter's behavioral decision is the *relative* levels of anti-dumping orders that have been imposed. If an exporter's primary competition comes from other exporting firms, there are other potential scenarios in which even an exporter under an anti-dumping order may prefer the status quo of continued orders for all exporters relative to having all anti-dumping orders removed, as would be the case in a successful sunset review. Suppose the exporter has an extremely low margin, relative to the other foreign competitors, and that the domestic industry is either capacity-constrained or perhaps has even exited the market since the original order was imposed.

The overall implication is that even in sunset reviews, the cumulation rule allows for one firm's decisions to have substantial externality implications for other firms. This, in turn, leads to inefficient outcomes. A way to eliminate this inefficiency is to have firms internalize the implications of their decision, an outcome that is

intense competition is and hence the lower the price there is. As long as this does not impact the price charged by the exporting firms in their domestic markets, we will observe a larger dumping margin and hence larger probability of positive finding' (Gupta and Panagariya, 2006: 163).

more likely if anti-dumping investigators are not allowed to cumulate imports in expected injury sunset review determinations.

Do sunset reviews matter?

In this section, we provide a brief economic comment on the question of whether sunset reviews matter for the duration of imposed anti-dumping measures. Cadot, de Melo, and Tumurchudur (2007) empirically investigate a number of questions relating to sunset reviews. One of their results is that the change that has mandated sunset reviews during the WTO period has led to a stronger five-year cycle for the duration of anti-dumping measures, relative to the GATT period, during which there was no mandatory sunset review process.

Nevertheless, the authors present findings that there is still substantial heterogeneity in the duration of imposed anti-dumping measures across countries. For example, they find that the United States seems to have failed to comply with the spirit of the sunset review process, as it has continued to extend the duration of imposed anti-dumping measures beyond the five-year initial period. For a number of other countries, they find a higher likelihood of terminating measures after a sunset review at the five-year point. Nevertheless, even for these countries, the apparent evidence is that this action is undertaken 'voluntarily', i.e. it is not necessarily caused by the sunset review provisions of the ADA.[51] The implication is that such countries might have done so anyway, even if it were not mandated by the WTO agreements – thus, it is still an open question as to whether the mandatory sunset reviews have had an effect on the duration of imposed anti-dumping measures.

4. Conclusion

Two conclusions can be drawn from this case: First, the AD Agreement, as interpreted by the Appellate Body in this and other similar cases, imposes only minimal disciplines of a general nature on Members wishing to extend the anti-dumping measure beyond its original five-year period. This is problematic, as it seems to void much practical meaning from the rule that says that anti-dumping measures are to be terminated after five years. The very deferential approach towards sunset reviews taken by the Appellate Body is difficult to reconcile with its own statement that termination of a measure is the rule, and continuation the exception. That is certainly not true in the US. Yet, for 'textual' reasons, the Appellate Body has rejected almost all claims against the US laws and regulations that provide the framework for the US approach. As we tried to demonstrate in this paper, this 'textual' argument is weak and has resulted in undermining the practical effect of, what was considered to be, one of the major achievements of the Uruguay Round

51 This analysis is based on evidence that there seems to be little difference in how WTO members treat antidumping targets that are other WTO members (treatment group) versus targets that are WTO non-members (control group) in sunset reviews.

Anti-Dumping Agreement: limiting the life span of an anti-dumping measure to five years.

Second, from an economic perspective, it seems that Panels and the Appellate Body are simply debating the wrong type of questions. The prospective nature of the analysis that is to be performed in a sunset review raises particular questions in terms of the data to be used; it requires an overall approach that is different from the approach in an original investigation, which is retrospective in nature. Questions such as why exporters engaged in dumping in the first place, and what the conditions of the industry were so that the dumped imports were able to cause injury in the first place are important questions that are not answered in an original investigation. The answers to these questions are important however, as they could form the basis for a more meaningful prospective sunset analysis. At the moment, sunset reviews seem adrift as Panels and the Appellate Body fail to give guidance to Members on how to do a more economically sound and informed review. Unfortunately, this problem is not unique to sunset reviews, but is an inherent problem of the AD Agreement, and the use of anti-dumping as a trade policy instrument more generally.

References

Blonigen, Bruce A. and Yuka Ohno (1998), 'Endogenous Protection, Foreign Direct Investment, and Protection-Building Trade', *Journal of International Economics*, **46**: 205–227.

Blonigen, Bruce A. and Jee-Hyeong Park (2004), 'Dynamic Pricing in the Presence of Anti-dumping Policy: Theory and Evidence', *American Economic Review*, **94**: 134–154.

Cadot, Olivier, Jaime de Melo, and Bolormaa Tumurchudur (2007), 'Anti-Dumping Sunset Reviews: The Uneven Reach of WTO Disciplines', University of Geneva manuscript, February.

Durling, James P. and Matthew P. McCullough (2004), 'Teaching Old Laws New Tricks: The Legal Obligation of Non-Attribution and the Need for Economic Rigor in Injury Analyses under US Trade Law', in James Hartigan and E. Kwan Choi (eds), *Handbook of International Trade*, Vol. II, New York: Blackwell.

Francois, Joseph and Keith Hall (1993), 'COMPAS: Commercial Policy Analysis System', US International Trade Commission, May.

Grossman, Gene M. (1986), 'Imports as a Cause of Injury: The Case of the US Steel Industry', *Journal of International Economics*, **20**: 201–223.

Gupta, Poonam and Arvind Panagariya (2006), 'Injury Investigations in Antidumping and the Super-Additivity Effect: A Theoretical Explanation', *Weltwirtschaftliches Archiv/Review of World Economics*, **142**: 151–164.

Hansen, Wendy L. and Thomas J. Prusa (1996), 'Cumulation and ITC Decision-Making: The Sum of the Parts is Greater Than the Whole', *Economic Inquiry*, **34**: 746–769.

Howse, Robert and Robert W. Staiger (2006), 'United States – Sunset Review of Anti-Dumping Duties on Corrosion-Resistant Carbon Steel Flat Products From Japan: A Legal and Economic Analysis of the Appellate Body Ruling', in Petros C. Mavroidis and Henrik Horn (eds), *The WTO Case Law of 2003*, Cambridge: Cambridge University Press.

Irwin, Douglas A. (2003), 'Causing Problems? The WTO Review of Causation and Injury Attribution in US Section 201 Cases', *World Trade Review*, **2**: 297–325.

Kelly, Kenneth (1988), 'The Analysis of Causality in Escape Clause Cases', *The Journal of Industrial Economics*, **37**: 187–207.

Moore, Michael O. (2006), 'An Econometric Analysis of US Antidumping Sunset Review Decisions', *Weltwirtschaftliches Archiv/Review of World Economics*, **142**: 122–150.

Pindyck, Robert S. and Julio J. Rotemberg (1987), 'Are Imports to Blame? Attribution of Injury under the 1974 Trade Act', *Journal of Law and Economics*, **30**: 101–122.

Prusa, Thomas J. and David C. Sharp (2001), 'Simultaneous Equations in Antidumping Investigations', *Journal of Forensic Economics*, **14**: 63–78.

Tharakan, P. K. M., D. Greenaway, and J. Tharakan (1998), 'Cumulation and Injury Determination of the European Community in Antidumping Cases', *Weltwirtschaftliches Archiv/Review of World Economics*, **134**: 320–339.

Comment

United States – Anti-Dumping Measures on Oil Country Tubular Goods (OCTG) from Mexico

Prepared for the ALI Project on the Case Law of the WTO

WILLIAM J. DAVEY

Guy Raymond Jones Chair in Law, University of Illinois College of Law

In general, I thought that this was an excellent paper, with some very useful ideas on how to improve the rigor of the analytical process of determining whether dumping and injury are likely to continue or recur if antidumping duties are removed in the context of a sunset review. In this brief comment, I note some of my concerns with the entire process of sunset reviews – could there ever be an analytically satisfactory way of assessing the likelihood of recurring dumping and injury? In addition, I include a few comments on the overall approach of the WTO Appellate Body in the sunset review cases it has decided, to date, on the usefulness and proper interpretation of the so-called mandatory–discretionary distinction in 'as such' challenges to antidumping measures, and on the Appellate Body's treatment of the Panel's analysis of the US Sunset Policy Bulletin.

The paper essentially argues for a greater use of econometric models in the determination of whether dumping and injury are likely to recur. As noted, I think that this introduces more, desirable rigor into a process that would benefit therefrom. As such, it is a useful proposal. However, I think that there are very basic problems with the whole idea of the sunset review process. While improving the rigor of that process is laudable, it may be ultimately unsatisfying because the process itself is bankrupt. Essentially, the sunset review process tries to predict the likelihood that dumping and injury will recur if antidumping duties imposed five years earlier are removed. I think that is virtually unknowable, and any attempt at such a prediction is pure speculation. Consider the key factor in making such a prediction: How will the foreign producers/exporters behave if the antidumping duties are removed? While it would be interesting to know why they dumped in the first instance, the market conditions and other factors that led them to do so all occurred at least six years prior to the sunset review. Since there is no particular reason to believe, in this era of rapid change and globalization, that the market structure and the other relevant factors will be the same, any attempt to base a prediction of future behavior on the behavior that occurred six years ago has to be speculative. Consider the following: The market structure has likely changed. The advent of a globalized economy has meant that ownership structures are more fluid. Even industries like steel – the major users of antidumping actions historically – now have much different ownership patterns than they did only a few years ago, and, in particular, there has been a significant increase in cross-border holdings.[1] In many industries, technological innovation means that product cycles last less than six years. Even where ownership patterns and products have not changed, it is likely that there will be significantly different trade flows than there were six years earlier. This makes any attempt to base predictions on the past, pre-dumping duty period simply not realistic. Moreover, the prior behavior of the dumpers occurred at a time when the possibility of an antidumping investigation being initiated was unclear, a situation that no longer obtains. The mere fact of the sunset review indicates that domestic industry has an interest in preserving the antidumping duties and may well be expected to start a case if dumping behavior recurs. Thus, while it may be interesting to know what market conditions were present when the dumping initially occurred, I think that it can give only very limited insight into what might be expected in a post antidumping duty market six or seven years later. The period that the dumping duties were in effect also offers little guidance as to how the market will evolve if the antidumping duties are removed. It seems clear that different producer/exporters respond to antidumping duties in different ways – some abandon the market; others may behave strategically and attempt to use the existence of the antidumping duties to manipulate their prices so as to maximize their profits and/or market share. Thus, behavior in this period is also of little use in predicting the future. The fact is that the sunset-review process asks a question that is impossible to answer with confidence – how will businesses behave if antidumping duties are removed in a market that has never existed before?

As a policy matter, I think that five years of antidumping duty protection (not counting the market effects of the year-long investigation period prior to the imposition of duties) is sufficient for any injured industry. It is longer than the protection typically afforded to seriously injured industries in safeguards proceedings.[2] Accordingly, in my view the rule should be that antidumping duties terminate after five years. If dumping recurs, a new investigation can be initiated, and if dumping is found, perhaps the sunset policy should be suspended for that

1 The world's largest steel company, Arcelor Mittal, has significant operations in the US and Europe, as well as South America, Africa, and Asia. See www.arcelormittal.com.

2 The Agreement on Safeguards permits safeguards of up to eight years, but contains incentives so that the typical period is likely to be three years. Agreement on Safeguards, arts. 7–8.

product. But the basic rule should be automatic sunset. While this may sound utopian, I would note that Australia – one of the traditional major users of antidumping measures – once had a three-year sunset rule.

In their analysis of the Appellate Body's decision in this case, the authors express concern that its decisions have made sunset review an 'empty box', suggesting that the provisions on sunset review in the Antidumping Agreement have been interpreted so as to make them largely meaningless. In this regard, I would note that the authors may assume that a greater effect was intended for these provisions than may have been in the minds of at least some negotiators. The negotiations of the Antidumping Agreement were hotly contested, and the reality is that (i) different words were used in this provision than in the general provisions on dumping ('review' instead of 'investigation') and (ii) a sunset review certainly involves issues distinct from an original investigation. As a result, it is not so clear that the rules on investigations should be imported indiscriminately into the section on reviews. The suggestion that 'common sense' should prevail over the 'text' is not convincing, especially given the textualist approach generally applied by the Appellate Body. That said, I would concede that the Appellate Body seems to take a much more restrained view of the agreement as a control on antidumping authorities in the context of reviews than it has in other areas, most notably 'zeroing'. In its 'zeroing' cases, it has paid little heed to the text at times, while it seems fixated on the text in its sunset review cases. Why? Perhaps it is a matter of timing and politics. The first limiting view of the sunset rules[3] came shortly after the Byrd Amendment report,[4] which was quite severely criticized in the United States.[5] Perhaps the Appellate Body reacted by 'going slow' in the sunset review context. That would be consistent with the authors' view that the Appellate Body has given recent signs of tightening its control over national authorities' discretion in sunset reviews by suggesting there are (as of yet not clearly defined) requirements for such reviews embodied in such terms as 'review' and 'determination' and the need for a 'nexus' between continuing dumping and injury, even if not a need for a 'causal' relation.

The so-called 'mandatory–discretionary' distinction recognized in GATT/WTO dispute settlement allows mandatory government laws or regulations ('measures') to be challenged on an 'as such' basis. That is to say, if a measure, which the government is required to apply, necessitates a WTO violation, the measure itself may be challenged and not just its specific application. Initially, the distinction was used by Panels to reject challenges to measures that did not mandate a GATT violation, particularly where the government had discretion that it had not yet

3 *US – Corrosion-Resistant Steel Sunset Review*, WT/DS244/AB/R, adopted January 9, 2004.

4 *US – Offset Act (Byrd Amendment)*, WT/DS217 & 234/AB/R, adopted January 27, 2003.

5 US Senator Max Baucus referred to the Panel decision in *Byrd* as coming from a 'kangaroo court'. 'Baucus Sees No Interest in Repealing Byrd, as Senate Doubts WTO Panels', Inside US Trade (September 27, 2002).

exercised.[6] This made sense, as it was a sort of 'ripeness' requirement.[7] In recent times, the distinction has been perverted into a suggestion that no measure can be challenged on an 'as such' basis if the government has the discretion not to violate WTO/GATT rules. Thus, in the 'zeroing' cases,[8] the US argued that its practice of zeroing – a practice that it applied in every antidumping investigation where the issue arose (and it arose in most cases) – could not be challenged on an 'as such' basis since it was not required by US law to violate WTO rules, notwithstanding the fact that it always exercised its discretion so as to violate them. That makes no sense. Thus, while there is an open issue as how to define what sort of practice constitutes a challengeable measure, the mandatory–discretionary distinction should not be applied to prevent 'as such' challenges to consistent patterns of WTO violations.

In the instant case, the question was whether the US applied certain presumptions in a way that they were not rebuttable, such that they should be challengeable 'as such'. I tend to think that the Appellate Body may have been justified in finding that the Panel's examination of the US practice in the area had failed to establish such an irrebuttable presumption. While one can differ on this issue, it appears to me that there were some problems with the Panel's approach. Mexico had submitted evidence on 306 sunset reviews, but only 21 – or 7% – were considered to be relevant by the Panel in that they were contested. In seven of those 21 cases, no additional evidence was offered to the authorities; in five of them, no attempt was made to show that there was 'good cause' to consider additional factors. While one can wonder about the appropriateness of a 'good cause' requirement in this situation, it was not challenged, with the result that there were only nine cases on which the Panel could have based a finding that the presumption was irrebuttable. And even in respect of that handful of cases, for the most part the conclusion of the Panel was that the authorities' treatment of arguments that good cause existed was 'troubling'.[9] In any event, I think that it is arguable that the Panel did not give sufficient details of its examination of the individual cases to allow one to be satisfied that these nine cases showed that the presumption was irrebutable. In the end, the key fact for the Panel seemed to be that even though the US authorities sometimes said they were open to looking at other factors, in these few cases they did not. Thus, I was not surprised that the Appellate Body found that the Panel had not made the required 'qualitative' analysis. In any event, this issue seems quite

6 GATT Analytical Index 645–648 (6th rev. edn 1995), citing, in particular, *United States – Taxes on Petroleum and Certain Imported Substances*, BISD 34S/136, 163–164, para. 5.2.9; *United States – Measures Affecting the Importation, Internal Sale and Use of Tobacco*, BISD 41S/131, 174–176, paras. 118–124 (in both cases the discretion had yet to be exercised).

7 William J. Davey, Has the WTO Dispute Settlement System Exceeded Its Authority?: A Consideration of Deference Shown by the System to Member Government Decisions and Its Use of Issue-Avoidance Techniques, 4 *JIEL* 79, 101–103 (2001).

8 See, e.g., *US – Zeroing (EC)*, WT/DS294/AB/R, adopted May 9, 2006.

9 Panel Report, paras. 7.58–7.61.

minor. Even if the US had been found to have violated the WTO rules on an 'as such' basis, implementation would have involved either (i) a simple re-writing of the sunset policy bulletin to eschew firmly any irrebuttable presumptions or (ii) the elimination of the offending language and the adoption of more opaque procedures, common in almost all other WTO members that impose antidumping duties.

Mexico – Antidumping Measures on Rice

'Don't ask me no questions and I won't tell you no lies'

PETROS C. MAVROIDIS

Edwin B. Parker Professor of Law at Columbia Law School, Professor at the University of Neuchâtel, Research Fellow at CEPR

ANDRÉ SAPIR

Professor of Economics, ECARES, Université Libre de Bruxelles, Senior Fellow at Bruegel, Research Fellow at CEPR

1. Facts

This case (*Mexico – Antidumping Measures on Rice*)[1] concerns the manner in which dumping margins should be calculated for exporters who have not been individually examined during the investigation process. Mexico imposed anti-dumping (AD) measures on US exporters of beef and rice to its market. It did not take any particular steps in order to identify all exporters; it limited itself to an investigation of US exporters identified in the petition, as well as of US exporters who voluntarily presented themselves to the Mexican authority. Mexico imposed the highest individually calculated margin on all 'unknown'[2] US exporters, that is on all US producers who had not been investigated and exported beef and rice to the Mexican market in the years following the imposition of antidumping duties. The United States (US) protested. In its view, Mexico should have applied the *residual rate* (that is, a duty corresponding to the average individual dumping margin found, as opposed to the highest individual dumping margin found) to all noninvestigated exporters, and not the highest duty, as it did.[3]

The Panel and the Appellate Body (AB) did not explicitly disagree with the United States, but did not uphold its arguments either. The Panel found that the Mexican authority should have pursued the investigation more actively, whereas the AB found against Mexico because it used wrong data.

The Panel and the AB also entertained claims on the manner in which Mexico chose the period of investigation (POI). Although this was not the core issue of the dispute, we consider it necessary to discuss the relevant findings since this is an

1 WTO Doc. WT/DS295.

2 We will use the terms *unknown* and *unidentified* as synonyms throughout this paper.

3 The US government was *de facto* defending its own practice.

area where case law is still evolving and the legislative guidance is quite open-ended. Mexico arbitrarily (that is, without any justification) restricted the months in each calendar year during which it investigated the existence of dumping and injury; it also used data that were 15 months old. Both the Panel and the AB condemned the use of POI chosen by Mexico.[4]

In Section 2, we discuss the claim concerning the duty that unidentified exporters should be paying. Section 3 deals with the claims on POI. Section 4 introduces economic considerations, and Section 5 concludes with a specific recommendation to improve the process of AD investigation.

2. Who are the dumpers?

2.1 *A brief discussion of the legislative framework*

Before, we examine the case, an introduction to the issue is necessary for two reasons:

(a) the facts are highly complicated;
(b) the AD Agreement accepts on the one hand that dumping is *private* business practice, but allows countrywide AD orders;
(c) at the same time, the AD Agreement does not *adequately* define who should be investigated when countrywide AD orders are imposed. State practice has evolved in a nonlinear manner in this respect.[5]

Since dumping is private practice, an investigating authority will have to identify a source of supply and calculate an *individual* dumping margin. Because, on the other hand, there is at least an implicit suspicion that all *other* private entities originating in the same country might be dumping as well, an investigating authority might be calculating dumping margins for more than one exporter.

4 The AB entertained a third claim on the permissibility of using assumptions during an investigation. The claim was upheld since Mexico was found to be violating the requirements of Arts. 3.1 and 3.2 AD to base its findings on positive evidence, on procedural grounds. This was a side issue briefly discussed and better explained in other case law. This is why we decided not to discuss it in detail. For the record, however, we mention that the AB acknowledged that, within the bounds of this discretion, an investigating authority may be expected to rely on reasonable assumptions or draw inferences. In doing that, it must ensure that its determinations are based on 'positive evidence'. Although it is not impermissible to use assumptions, these assumptions should be derived as reasonable inferences from a credible basis of facts, and should be sufficiently explained so that their objectivity and credibility can be verified. WTO members (through their investigating authorities) who use a methodology premised on unsubstantiated assumptions are ipso facto violating Art. 3.1 AD. An assumption is not properly substantiated when the investigating authority has not explained why it would be appropriate to use it in the analysis. Mexico, in the Final Determination, did not explain why the assumptions on which the investigation relied upon were appropriate and credible in the analysis of the volume and price effects of the dumped imports, or how they would contribute to providing an accurate picture of the volume and price effects of the dumped imports (§§204–205).

5 As we will argue later in this Section, this is one case where there is need for legislative amendment in order to avoid similar problems in the future.

If there are many sources of supply identified, the investigation could be hampered in case each one of them was to be investigated: in such cases, an investigating authority can investigate only a *sample*, and apply a residual duty on all non-investigated exporters (following the disciplines enshrined in Arts. 6.10 and 9.4 AD). Finally, new exporters (considered shipments), that is producers who originate in the country being investigated *and* who did not export during the investigation process, will undergo an expedited review when they start exporting to the country that has AD duties in place against imports from the country at hand.

Assuming producers have been sampled, the AD Agreement suggests that only two rates of AD duties are permissible:

(a) an individually calculated duty for all sampled exporters and all other exporters who have come forward and requested to be investigated;
(b) the weighted average of the individually calculated duties will be applied to all other sources (originating in the same country).

In case no sampling took place, individual dumping margins will be imposed on all investigated exporters. The AD Agreement does not *explicitly* allow authorities to investigate only some exporters in a nonsampling scenario. This is, nevertheless, what happened in the present case: Mexico did not sample; it calculated dumping margins for those investigated, and then imposed the highest margin on all non-investigated exporters.[6] The Agreement does not *explicitly* regulate this transaction. Besides investigated exporters, the AD Agreement regulates the dumping margins to be imposed on one more category of exporters: new shipments (Art. 9.5 AD). With respect to new shipments, as briefly alluded to above, the AD Agreement requests that an individually calculated duty be imposed, but is silent on the amount of default duty (assuming one is WTO consistent), that is the duty that they have to pay until a review has been initiated. There are good arguments to support the thesis that new shipments have to pay a duty until their review has been initiated. The obligation included in Art. 9.5 AD (to start an expedited review of the duty *imposed* on products coming from new exporters in order to calculate an individual duty for such new exporters) implies as much. The context of Art. 9.5 AD makes this conclusion inescapable. Art. 9.5 AD talks of products on which duties have been imposed, and the need for expedited review on new shipments. If no duties were in place, why should the review be expedited? Actually if no duties were in place on new shipments and the review was expedited, new shipments would have been enjoying a less favorable regime than old shipments that profited from a *normal* investigation. This could raise MFN issues. It is legally impossible that the law is illegal, and the task of the interpreter is to interpret it in a manner that all provisions retain their scope. It seems to us that to do that, we must

6 Hence, the US claim that Mexico should have imposed the weighted average on noninvestigated exporters has no basis in the AD Agreement. There is an obligation to impose the weighted average on noninvestigated exporters only in case an authority has sampled exporters.

presume that the new shipments are burdened by duties before the expedited review takes place. Then comes the question of the duty to be applied to unidentified exporters, assuming for the time being that such exporters, who were exporting during the period of investigation, can exist. It seems that, in principle, the only existing possibility,[7] assuming a willingness to impose duties, is that such exporters come under the purview of Art. 9.5 AD. There is an inconvenience, however: the wording of Art. 9.5 AD seems to suggest that it covers only cases of exporters who were not exporting the product at hand during the period of investigation. Hence, an extension to cover producers that were exporting such product is arguably *contra legem*.

It could be, of course, that some exporters originating in the same country (with the exporters being investigated) are not known to the authority. They could be unknown for a variety of reasons: because they managed to hide (let us call this, *uncooperative behavior*), or because the authority did not take any reasonable efforts to identify them (for example, they continued to export and were never requested to appear before the authority), or for other reasons as well. With respect to such unknown exporters, that is exporters who were exporting to the country investigating at the time the investigation takes place but for whatever reason were not identified during the investigation process, the AD Agreement is silent as to how much duty they should be paying, assuming they should be paying at all. We know, nevertheless, that such exporters are liable to pay duties since countrywide orders are perfectly GATT consistent: WTO Members can lawfully impose duties on all producers originating in the country of the *dumper* (Art. 9.2 AD).

Two questions thus emerge:

(a) *First*, what is the extent of the obligation imposed on the investigating authority to identify exporters?
(b) *Second*, the related question, assuming that there is no obligation to identify all current exporters (that is, with the exception of new shipments), what is the amount of duty to be imposed on unknown exporters?

2.2 *Speculating about the responses*

Art. 6.10 AD, we recall, requests determination of individual dumping margins for all *known exporters*. The same provision allows for sampling of exporters, in case their number is large. The nonsampled exporters will pay a duty in accordance with Art. 9.4 AD (weighted average). The term *known exporters* is nowhere defined in the AD Agreement. Let us take the sampling scenario first: one way to understand this provision is that sampling will occur only after *all* exporters have been identified. Assuming this is the correct interpretation, there will be no room

7 As we argued before, Art. 9.4 AD cannot be functionally put into operation, absent knowledge of all exporters.

for unknown exporters, but only for new shipments (i.e., producers who did not export during the POI). The upshot of this approach is the elimination of the third category (unknown exporters). The downside is that this might incite strategic behavior on behalf of the investigating authority and might push up AD duties: an investigating authority will have the incentive to investigate individually those dumpers that, in its view, might be credited with the largest dumping margin and thus impose a high weighted average on the rest. Is there insurance policy against this risk? Yes, in principle: nonsampled producers who believe they dump less, or do not dump a lot, will come forward and ask to be individually investigated. The investigating authority can, nevertheless, thwart such requests pointing to the nonpracticability of a marginal investigation (Art. 6.10 AD).

Art. 6.10 AD could also be understood as meaning that, following a first review of the file, it appears that there are dozens of exporters. The investigating authority does not go all the way and identify all exporters. It does investigate a sample of those identified (although, *not* a sample of all exporters), and imposes a weighted average on all other exporters, identified or not. Here, there is room for unknown exporters, but it does not matter. Known nonsampled and unknown exporters alike, will pay the weighted average duty, as per Art. 9.4 AD.

A variant of this latter approach would distinguish between known nonsampled and unknown exporters: the former would pay the weighted average, and the latter something else. This is the EC approach, which is not challenged in the present dispute.

Does the Agreement privilege one over the other approaches? The Agreement is unclear. There are good arguments though, supporting the view that the negotiators had in mind the first and/or the second scenario, but not the third: Art. 6.10 AD states that a statistically viable sample must be investigated. This term has a particular meaning in statistical analysis and would require an active research by the investigating authority. The same provision, however, waters down this concept by adding that the sample should be statistically viable on the basis of information with the investigating authority. This last sentence could be a simple truism (how could it be otherwise? The investigating authority can judge only upon information it possesses), or could be understood as diluting the obligation imposed: it is not a statistically viable sample that must be investigated, but a statistically viable sample of the exporters known to the investigating authority. Depending on the number of known exporters, the number could be quite low. By the same token, Art. 6.10 AD requests from authorities to investigate the largest percentage of the volume of exports that can *reasonably* be investigated. Criteria such as administrative capacity could be quite relevant in quantifying this obligation.

And what about cases, like the one before us, where no sampling took place? Once again, an investigating authority must impose individually calculated dumping margins on known exporters (Art. 6.10 AD). Does this provision also entail that it must identify all exporters? There are good arguments in favor of this thesis. One could plausibly, for example, argue that the sampling scenario should be reserved for cases where there are dozens of exporters, and the nonsampling for cases where the number of exporters is limited. In that latter case, the investigating authority should be responsible for calculating individual margins. The counterargument here would be: what if an exporter is hiding during the investigation process? How credible is this counterargument? Recall that those hiding will pay the residual duty anyway in the US, and a higher duty in other markets (such as Mexico, or the EC). So, they would have little incentive to hide in the first place.[8] And how credible is it that they can hide in a scenario where only few exporters exist? The importing state could check the relevant data, and identify the sources of supply to its market one by one. This is more or less what the Panel, as we will see, requested from the Mexican authority to do.

To recap: sampling should be reserved to cases where it is not manageable to investigate individually all exporters; in other cases, individual margins must be calculated for all. Hence, if at all, unknown exporters will exist only in case sampling has taken place. There should be no room for unknown exporters in the nonsampling scenario: those that hide and do not export during the POI will be treated as new shipments; those that continue exporting but do not present themselves to the investigating authority will be detected through cooperation between the customs authority and the investigating authority. If their number is not large, they will be individually investigated; in the opposite scenario, the investigating authority can perfectly well proceed and sample.[9]

Let us see now how all these issues were addressed by the AB in the report under discussion.

2.3 *The AB approach*

In the past, the AB has, on a number of occasions, revealed a preference in favor of an active investigating authority. In *Mexico – Antidumping Measures on Rice*, the Mexican investigating authority had limited its investigation to two US exporters identified by the petitioner, and two that had *motu proprio* presented themselves to the Mexican authority. The Panel held the view that the Mexican investigating authority violated its obligations by not making a reasonable effort to identify exporters other than the four mentioned above. In the case at hand, the Panel felt

8 Only assuming that they dump more than other exporters, and they know that this is indeed the case, they would still have this incentive to hide. But, even in this case, they would have no incentive to hide if they export to Mexico or the EC.

9 Recall that for this approach to be workable, cooperation among two governmental functions, customs authorities and AD investigating authority, is required. This might prove a daunting task for some developing countries. Note also, however, that the size of this problem should not be overstated: first, many developing countries, active users of the system, like Mexico, for example, have efficient customs authorities. Second, all that is required to communicate from one agency to another is information about the origin of the goods, a rather trivial issue.

that one could reasonably expect that it is incumbent upon an *active* investigating authority to look for some easily available information.[10]

The AB disagreed, but *probably* ended up with a similar, if not more ambitious, result. For a start, it held, following a completely textual interpretation of Art. 6.10 AD, that the term *known exporters* appearing in Art. 6.10 AD does not include exporters that the investigating authority *should* have known when the investigation was initiated (§255). As a result, the term *known exporters* is limited to exporters identified by the petitioners and exporters who voluntarily identified themselves to the investigating authority. By inference, unknown exporters are not only those covered by Art. 9.5 AD (that is, new shipments: exporters who were not exporting during the investigation), but also those who were exporting during the investigation but were not identified (either by the petitioners or voluntarily).

The next question before the AB was whether the AD Agreement imposes any limits on the amount of the duty to be paid by unknown exporters (who are not considered new shipments). Recall that the AD Agreement is silent on this score. US practice[11] suggests that, indeed, the residual rate (weighted average) of the individually established dumping margins should be applied to new shipments, as well as other unknown exporters. The Panel was not convinced by this argument. In §7.159 it developed its rationale for rejecting this argument. We quote from §7.159:

> The US argument that the placement of this provision immediately preceding Article 9.5 of the AD Agreement dealing with new shipper reviews implies that its rules also apply to non-shipping exporters is not convincing, as we do not find that anything can be deduced in and of itself from the sequence of provisions in the Agreement, particularly when the provision in question relates to an exceptional situation, while the subsequent provision does not. The United States also argues that the non-sampled interested parties and the new shippers dealt with by Article 9.5 are in a similar position and that by analogy the same Article 9.4 methodology for the calculation of a residual duty rate should apply. We are not convinced that the text of the Agreement supports this view. In this respect,

10 US exporters were being identified in a commercial publication that was before the Mexican investigating authority.

11 It bears repetition that the US scheme is *contra legem*: the US authority applies the residual duty even in case of nonsampling, when the AD Agreement clearly reserves the possibility to apply a residual duty for cases where sampling has taken place. EC practice, as briefly alluded to above, suggests another, residual, rate that applies to imports from unknown or new exporters: exporters that are not new shippers and kept quiet during the investigation, or exporters that remained unknown during the investigation, the reasonable efforts of the EC authority to identify them notwithstanding, will see their exports burdened not with the weighted average, but with a residual rate. Assume that the EC authority has sampled three exporters who ship equal volumes to the EC market, and that they are found to be dumping by 10%, 20%, and 30% respectively. The EC authority will impose the duties mentioned above to the three investigated exporters; a 20% (weighted average) duty on all identified exporters; and a 30% (residual) rate on nonidentified exporters as well as on new shipments. It seems that the EC higher duty for unknown exporters is reserved for cases when sampling has taken place. The consistency of such practice with the multilateral rules has not been established as yet.

> we find particularly relevant, the absence of any cross-referencing in Article 9.5 of the AD Agreement dealing with new shippers to the calculation methodology of Article 9.4 of the AD Agreement. This absence of cross-referencing is particularly conspicuous if one were to accept, *arguendo*, the analogous situation of non-sampled and non-shipping exporters. Indeed, especially in such a situation, one would expect the drafters to have explicitly referred to Article 9.4 of the AD Agreement. As on other occasions, where the drafters intended to see obligations apply in similar circumstances, they explicitly provided for such cross-referencing. We recall in this respect that the Appellate Body also found that the absence of such cross-referencing to obligations contained in other provisions is revealing of the absence of such an obligation. We find that Article 9.4 of the AD Agreement does not refer to non-shipping exporters outside a sampling situation, and that there was therefore no obligation for the Mexican authorities to calculate a residual duty margin for Producers Rice based on the 'neutral' methodology set forth in Article 9.4 of the AD Agreement. We therefore reject the US claim in this respect. (Italics in the original).

The above-cited passage suggests that an investigating authority, when imposing duties on shipments coming from new exporters does not *have to* apply a duty equivalent to the weighted average. This does not mean that, if it does so, it will be violating the AD Agreement. The question, nevertheless, remains what is the maximum permissible duty under the circumstances?[12]

In *Mexico – Antidumping Measures on Rice*, the AB did not take a clear stance on the issue. Indirectly, however, it provided *some* answers. The AB did state that an authority is not permitted to impose a residual duty rate *based on facts available*. According to the AB, an authority that imposes a duty on unidentified exporters based on facts available, including facts from the petition, is acting in violation of Art. 6.8 and paragraph 1 of Annex II AD. We quote from §§259–260:

> The second sentence of paragraph 1 of Annex II conditions the use of facts from the petitioner's application on making the interested party 'aware' that, if the information is not supplied by it within a reasonable time, the investigating authority will be free to resort to these facts available. In other words, an exporter shall be given the opportunity to provide the information required by the investigating authority before the latter resorts to facts available that can be adverse to the exporter's interests. An exporter that is unknown to the investigating authority – and, therefore, is not notified of the information required to be submitted to the investigating authority – is denied such an opportunity. Accordingly, an investigating authority that uses the facts available in the application for the initiation of the investigation against an exporter that was not given notice of the information the investigating authority requires, acts in a manner inconsistent with paragraph 1 of Annex II to the Anti-Dumping Agreement and, therefore, with Article 6.8 of that Agreement.

12 The Panel, in its report on *Mexico – Antidumping Measures on Rice*, did not have to address this issue.

> ...
> The United States exporters that Economía did not investigate were not notified of the information it required. Notwithstanding this, Economía used facts available contained in the application submitted by the petitioner against these uninvestigated exporters.

According to the AB, putting exporters on notice that facts available will be used is a precondition for the use of facts available. This condition, for obvious reasons, can never be met in the case of unidentified exporters: one cannot notify the person that has not been identified.

The AB addressed a situation in which the residual rate was based on petitioner data, and was particularly adverse when compared to the margins of dumping calculated for the examined (known) exporters. But the need to inform exporters of the fact that, in the absence of cooperation, facts available will be used, applies in all cases, and not only when the data used are provided by the petitioner. To a certain extent, any margin based on information other than data provided by the exporter itself is based on 'facts available'. Logically speaking, the AB's statement could thus be read to imply that no residual duty can be imposed on such unknown exporters. A rate based on the highest margin of an exporter individually calculated, as is the EC's practice, is also a facts-available rate for the noninvestigated exporter, and hence, in this line of thinking, would, as well, be WTO inconsistent. If this reading is correct, the AB effectively closed the door to the possibility that unknown exporters exist when no sampling has taken place: since recourse to Art. 6.8 AD is impermissible in such cases, the investigating authority must identify all nonsampled exporters.[13]

To conclude on this score, the AB responded in the following manner:

(a) there is no obligation for the investigating authority, in a nonsampling scenario, to identify all exporters;
(b) an investigating authority cannot use facts available against nonidentified exporters;
(c) it follows that an investigating authority must calculate individual dumping margins in this respect;
(d) in this line of logic, the maximum duty for nonidentified exporters will be the duty that will be individually calculated.

So let us take a real-world example and see how the AB finding holds. In the instant case, Mexico identified only four exporters and calculated dumping

13 A very imaginative reading of the AB Report could lead to the conclusion that all the AB wanted to say was that facts available which are *adverse* may not be used to calculate a duty for unknown exporters. There remains a serious problem: when is the use of facts available (not) adverse? Is a residual duty based on the highest margin found for an investigated exporter less adverse than the use of information contained in the petition? Is a lesser duty (for example, weighted average) not so adverse? If this was the true intention of the AB, it could simply adhere to the position advanced by the US lawyers during the litigation. It did not.

margins for each one of them. Days or weeks later, a fifth exporter, who was exporting during the POI, exports to Mexico. Mexico must calculate a dumping margin for this exporter, since it cannot use facts available (data from the four exporters already investigated). Since this exporter is not considered a new shipment, Mexico cannot conduct an expedited review either. So, in this reading, Mexico must pay the price (assuming there is a price to pay) for not having actively investigated the transaction before it, and identified all exporters. Recall that nothing stops Mexico from sampling, in case it realizes during the investigation process that the number of exporters is quite large.

On the other hand, one could make the argument that all the AB wanted to say is that facts available (Art. 6.8 AD) will not be used against nonidentified exporters in a nonsampling scenario. What else, however, could be used? How could the Mexican authority impose duties on nonidentified exporters that it does not individually investigate *without* having recourse to the information it gathered by investigating the US exporters for which an individual dumping margin had been calculated? All the Mexican authority knows is the amount of dumping margin for those individually calculated. If it cannot use it through Art. 6.8 AD on nonidentified exporters, the only provision it might have recourse to is Art. 9.5 AD. Is that what the AD had in mind? Is the AB's view that nonidentified exporters should be considered new shipments? If yes, then the AB has effectively extended the coverage of this provision to transactions not envisaged by the legislator: recall that this provision covers cases of producers who were not exporting during the investigation period, and not cases of producers who were exporting but were not identified during the investigation process.

To conclude: the AB does not request from the Mexican authority, in a nonsampling scenario, to actively investigate all exporters. It does not allow it to use facts available against nonidentified exporters either. The only reasonable conclusion under the circumstances is that, if Mexico does not ask the right questions, it will have to pay the price.

3. The period of investigation (POI)

3.1 The issues raised

The complainant raised two issues:

(a) it complained that Mexico chose only the six months every year (in the three-year investigation period), where import penetration was high. It thus ignored the other six months every year where the domestic industry fared better. As a result, the comparison was unfair. Mexico replied that it chose the same months for dumping and injury investigations, otherwise the comparison would be unfair;

(b) it further complained that Mexico used 15-month-old data. Such data were inappropriate in light of the changes that occurred ever since.

Mexico replied that these are the best data it could have used under the circumstances.

3.2 *The legislative framework*

The AD Agreement does not regulate the length of the POI. It imposes a requirement for fair comparison (Art. 2.4 AD), but falls short of imposing specific obligations as to the choice of POI. State practice has moved in to fill this gap. State practice, however, is not completely uniform, although elements of overlap are quite substantial. Over the years, WTO Members have, in the context of the Committee on Antidumping Practices (ADP), managed to reach some common understanding on the requirements for an appropriate choice of POI. However, two points are appropriate in this context: *first*, the ADP recommendations do not constitute an exhaustive treatment of the POI, since many questions are still open; *second*, the legal value of an ADP recommendation is an open issue.[14]

The Panel Report in part relies on the ADP Committee recommendation on the length of POI to support its view as to the length of the injury POI (§7.62).[15] The use of ADP recommendations in this limited manner proved useful. The ADP recommendation, however, was of no use when the Panel and the AB tried to address the two questions asked by the complainant.

3.3 *Some months every year ...*

Recall that the United States claimed that the AD Agreement had been violated because the Mexican authority had analyzed only six months' worth of data for each of the three years of data collection. Mexico asserted that it was necessary to examine these particular six months of every year instead of the full year in order to ensure that the period of the injury analysis paralleled the six-month period chosen for the analysis of dumping, so as to avoid any distortions.

The Panel saw no a priori reason why a period of investigation on the injury analysis should be chosen to fit the period of investigation for the dumping analysis in case the latter period of investigation covers a period of less than 12 months, as there is nothing in the AD Agreement that would require such an approach; quite to the contrary, in its view, was true.[16] The Panel considered that the choice of the period of investigation is crucial, as it determines the data that will form the basis for the assessment of the impact of dumping, and that an examination or investigation can only be 'objective' if it is based

14 In general, there is nothing like a clear statement by anyone (legislator or adjudicator) as to the legal value of WTO secondary law. It seems safe to argue, however, that they constitute an interpretative element of the primary law since they have been used as such by Panels so far.

15 By the same token, previous reports, such as the Panel Report on *EC – Pipe Fittings*, have used a recommendation by the ADP Committee as a source of law to reach its conclusion that it is desirable that the period for dumping investigation and for injury determination substantially overlap (§7.321).

16 Panel Report, *Mexico – Anti-Dumping Measures on Rice*, §7.82.

on data that provide an accurate and unbiased picture of what it is that one is examining.[17]

Mexico chose a three-year POI, and restricted its investigation into the six months for each of the three years. In fact, Mexico upheld the POI proposed by the petitioner (interested, of course, in seeing AD duties imposed). In the Panel's view, for Mexico to legitimately restrict the POI in this manner, it would have to provide some justification why this was necessary in order to perform a fair comparison. Mexico did not do that. In fact, the only element before the Panel was the US claim that the six months chosen were the months of high import penetration. In the absence of justification for the restriction, the Panel condemned the Mexican choice in the following manner:

> In sum, we find that the injury analysis of the Mexican investigating authority in the rice investigation which was based on data covering only six months of each of the three years examined, is inconsistent with Article 3.1 of the AD Agreement as it is not based on positive evidence and does not allow for an objective examination, as it necessarily, and without any proper justification, provides only a part of the picture of the situation. In addition, we find that the particular choice of the limited period of investigation in this case was not that of an unbiased and objective investigating authority as the authority was aware of, and accepted, the fact that the period chosen reflected the highest import penetration, thus ignoring data from a period in which it can be expected that the domestic industry was faring better.[18]

The AB agreed that these two factors – the selective use of the information gathered and the fact that the authority accepted the POI proposed by the petitioner, knowing that the petitioner proposed that period because it allegedly represented the period of highest import penetration – *plus* the absence of any justification explaining why the use of data from the remaining six months would distort the picture, were sufficient to conclude that the data used by the Mexican authority did not provide an accurate and unbiased picture (§§181ff.).

It is difficult to find fault with the AB on this score. The data used seem to suffer from selection bias (assuming that it is factually correct that the six months chosen are those of the highest import penetration, a fact that Mexico has not disputed). Such data cannot provide the input for a proper evaluation of the dumping margin and the ensuing injury.

3.4 *How old can data be?*

The United States further claimed that the Mexican authority had used a POI for injury that ended more than 15 months prior to the initiation of the investigation.

17 Panel Report, *Mexico – Anti-Dumping Measures on Rice*, §7.79. The Panel added, however, that its ruling should not be read as to imply that there could never be any convincing and valid reasons for examining only parts of years. Panel Report, *Mexico – Anti-Dumping Measures on Rice*, §7.82.

18 Panel Report, *Mexico – Anti-Dumping Measures on Rice*, §7.86.

The Panel considered that while the AD Agreement does not contain any specific and express rules concerning the period to be used for data collection in an anti-dumping investigation, this does not mean that the authorities' discretion in using a certain period of investigation is boundless.[19] The Panel was of the view that there is necessarily an inherent *real-time link* between the investigation leading to the imposition of measures and the data on which the investigation is based. In spite of the fact that an antidumping investigation out of necessity relies on historical data gathered during a past POI, such information should be the most recent information reasonably available:

> Of course, it is well established that the data on the basis of which this determination is made may be based on a past period, known as the period of investigation. Nevertheless, because this 'historical' data is being used to draw conclusions about the current situation, it follows that the more recent data is likely to be inherently more relevant and thus especially important to the investigation. This, as a consequence, implies that the data considered concerning dumping, injury and the causal link should include, to the extent possible, the most recent information, taking into account the inevitable delay caused by the need for an investigation, as well as any practical problems of data collection in any particular case.[20]

This led the Panel to the following conclusion:

> The requirement of a time-consuming and sometimes complicated investigation to demonstrate the existence of dumping and the ensuing injury poses a practical impediment to a complete identity in time between the imposition of the measure and the conditions for such imposition, i.e. dumping causing injury. Although this practical problem may lead to the situation in which any determination of dumping causing injury has by the time of the imposition of the measure become more of a proxy than a real time assessment of the current situation, it would, in our view, not be correct to be led by the practical necessity to examine the past to assess the present to accept that an investigating authority could justifiably base itself on old data to the exclusion of more recent data which was available and usable. To the contrary, the fact that an investigation of up to 12 months may have to be conducted to determine dumping, injury and the causal link magnifies the importance of having a period of data collection which ends as closely as possible to the date of initiation, as by the time of the possible imposition of the measure another 12 months may have passed.[21]

The Panel thus considered that a 15-month gap between the end of the period of investigation and the initiation of the investigation is sufficiently long as to impugn the reliability of the period of investigation to deliver, for the purposes of a determination, evidence that has the requisite pertinence or relevance, thereby

19 Panel Report, *Mexico – Anti-Dumping Measures on Rice*, §7.57.
20 Panel Report, *Mexico – Anti-Dumping Measures on Rice*, §7.58.
21 Panel Report, *Mexico – Anti-Dumping Measures on Rice*, §7.63.

failing to meet the criterion of 'positive evidence' pursuant to Article 3.1 AD.[22] The Panel did not state that the AD Agreement imposed a requirement not to use 15-month-old data. It did interpret the Agreement, however, to impose a requirement to *at least* explain why, in case such data have been used, it still adequately explains the state of affairs when the imposition of AD duties is being decided. Mexico failed to do that.

Note that, in order to reach its conclusion, the Panel once again relied on the ADP recommendation on POI which, in pertinent part, states that that the period of data collection should end as close to the date of initiation of the investigation as is practicable.[23]

The AB fully upheld the reasoning of the Panel.[24] It emphasized the fact that the determination of whether injury exists should be based on data that provide indications of the situation prevailing when the investigation takes place, because the conditions to impose an antidumping duty are to be assessed with respect to the current situation. Mexico's failure to explain why historical data could still appropriately explain the state of affairs when duties were imposed was critical in the AB's finding.[25]

Here too, it is difficult to find fault with the attitude of the AB. Even in the absence of clear language to this effect, it is illogical to interpret the AD as allowing for imposition of duties based on historical data. The wording of Art. 11.1 AD is highly pertinent here: duties shall be in place as long as necessary to counteract injury caused by dumping. A necessary precondition is that injury is being caused at the moment when duties are being imposed. Knowledge that injury is being caused as a result of dumping can only be based on data that prove that this is indeed the case. There should be a presumption that this is indeed the case when the data used are as close as possible to the date when the imposition of duties is being decided. Older data could also suffice assuming that the investigating authority can prove that nothing has changed ever since.

The AB did not go all the way and establish a reversal of the presumption in case older data have been used. It would be hard to implement such a proposal as a rule of thumb since it is far from being an easy exercise to come up with an age for permissible and impermissible data that will make sense across transactions. Implicitly however, this is what its ruling amounts to. In fact, all the United States proved in this context was that the data were 15 months old. It sufficed for the

22 Panel Report, *Mexico – Anti-Dumping Measures on Rice*, §7.64.

23 Before the AB, Mexico complained that the Panel wrongly relied on the ADP recommendation. The AB rejected Mexico's argument, holding that the Panel relied on the recommendation only to confirm its own interpretation. This view seems to suggest that reliance on such instruments as a means to confirm already adopted interpretations is legally correct in the AB's view. If yes, this would ipso facto lead to classification of such elements as supplementary means of interpretation (in the sense of Art. 32 of the Vienna Convention on the Law of Treaties).

24 AB Report, *Mexico – Anti-Dumping Measures on Rice*, §§163–172.

25 AB Report, *Mexico – Anti-Dumping Measures on Rice*, §165.

Panel and the AB to reverse the burden of proof and request from Mexico to respond why such data were still appropriate.

4. The problem lies with the law, not the judges' ruling

With respect to the POI, it is difficult to find fault with the rulings by the AB. We will thus focus on the treatment of unidentified exporters. The AB seems to have limited the risk of abusing the investigation process by outlawing recourse to facts available in a nonsampling scenario. The AB, nevertheless, cannot undo the intrinsic inadequacies of the AD Agreement. The AB can, at best, try to rationalize aspects of the AD Agreement, while maintaining the balance of rights and obligations struck by the principals themselves, namely the WTO Members. In fact, however, the problem with the AD Agreement goes much deeper than the lack of clarity with respect to the treatment of unidentified exporters. It relates to whether it is countries or firms that are responsible for dumping and that should pay AD duties if they engage in injurious dumping. In what follows, we advance some thoughts on this issue, and argue that a fundamental incoherence must be removed from the AD Agreement, whereby it considers dumping as private practice on the one hand, and presumes that dumping is a countrywide practice on the other. If this incoherence remains, we risk seeing many other dumping cases being brought before the WTO adjudicating bodies. Our arguments, therefore, go beyond the present case by suggesting what we consider as a necessary legislative amendment to the AD Agreement.

Dumping is a pricing strategy whereby producers in one country charge lower prices in foreign markets than in their home market. As such it is practiced by firms, not countries. Yet Article 2 AD defines dumping in terms of countries with no reference to individual firms:

> For the purpose of this Agreement, a product is to be considered as being dumped i.e. introduced into the commerce of another country at less than its normal value, if the export price of *the product exported from one country to another* is less than the comparable price, in the ordinary course of trade, for the like product when destined for consumption in the exporting country.[26]

This definition would seem to imply that the pricing strategy of all exporting firms of a particular product is identical, with the same price differential between the home market and the importing country for all relevant firms. This, obviously, makes little or no economic sense. There is no a priori reason to believe that two (or more) firms behave identically in terms of their pricing in different markets simply because they happen to produce the same product in the same country – unless they operate under perfect competition in the home- *and* in the importing-country markets.

26 Art. 2.1 AD, emphasis added.

If perfect competition prevailed, it would be hard to understand how dumping could occur altogether. Since dumping is a form of price discrimination, it requires that firms be able to set prices in the different markets rather than take them as given, as it is the case under perfect competition.

If markets were perfectly competitive, the 'law of one price' would prevail and all identical products would have only one price – at least within the same geographical or national market. However, perfect competition is clearly an extreme case that is unlikely to prevail in many circumstances, and therefore 'the "law of one price" is no law at all' in fact.[27]

There are essentially two reasons why the 'law of one price' does not hold. The trivial reason is that products may not be identical either because they are differentiated or because differences in the services offered by competing firms might lead them to charge different prices for the same product. But even if products are truly homogenous, price dispersion is likely to be the rule rather than the exception to the 'law of one price'. As Nobel Laureate George Stigler argued more than 40 years ago, price dispersion is related to the existence of imperfect information and search costs of consumers.[28]

Product differentiation and imperfect information imply that firms might be able to exert some degree of market power and hence to price discriminate. Moreover, different firms can be expected to face different circumstances and to have different capabilities that result in different costs and therefore different prices – unless they operate under perfect competition in which case prices have to be the same for all firms and the different costs simply translate into different profits.

The AD Agreement actually recognizes in two places that firms which produce the same product in the same country do not necessarily behave identically. The first acknowledgment of this comes in Art. 5 AD on antidumping initiations and investigations, where the Agreement states that applications to national authorities by the domestic industry in the importing country for antidumping measures must contain:

> a complete description of the allegedly dumped product, the names of the country or countries of origin or export in question, *the identity of each known exporter or foreign producer* and a list of known persons importing the product in question.'[29]

Furthermore, Art. 6 AD on evidence in antidumping investigations states that:

> The authorities shall, as a rule, determine *an individual margin of dumping for each known exporter or producer* concerned of the product under investigation.[30]

27 Varian (1980: 651).
28 Stigler (1961). See Baye, Morgan, and Scholten (2006).
29 Art. 5.2, emphasis added.
30 Art. 6.10, emphasis added.

In other words, the Agreement makes it clear that each 'known exporter or foreign producer' must be identified and that the national authorities must determine individual dumping margins for each of them. There is no question of lumping them all together and assuming that they behave identically.

However, as already discussed supra, there are two possible interpretations of the expression 'known exporter or foreign producer'. One interpretation is to consider that only those exporters or producers from the country concerned who have been identified by the domestic industry in its application for AD measures have potentially engaged in injurious dumping. The other interpretation is to treat all exporters or producers from that country as if they potentially engaged in injurious dumping, and to treat those identified by the domestic industry in its application as a special subset of exporters or producers.

Art. 6 AD contains no indication as to which of the two interpretations is favored by the Agreement. However, Art. 9 AD on the imposition and collection of AD duties contains some language dealing with another category of 'unknown' exporters, those who were not exporting to the importing country during the period of investigation but did so later on, which provides the necessary clue:

> If a product is subject to anti-dumping duties in an importing Member, the authorities shall promptly carry out a review for the purpose of determining individual margins of dumping for any exporters or producers in the exporting country in question who have not exported the product to the importing Member during the period of investigation, provided that these exporters or producers can show that they are not related to any of the exporters or producers in the exporting country who are subject to the anti-dumping duties on the product. Such a review shall be initiated and carried out on an accelerated basis, compared to normal duty assessment and review proceedings in the importing Member.[31]

Hence any exporter or producer of a product and from a country subject to AD duties is to be viewed as potentially engaging in injurious dumping in the importing country, if it exported to the importing country *after* the period of investigation. *A fortiori* the same must hold for exporters or producers who exported to the importing country *during* the period of investigation.

The interpretation chosen by the Agreement implies that all firms producing the allegedly dumped product in the country in question engage in injurious dumping, unless proven otherwise. It puts, therefore, the burden of proving innocence on all exporters, both those who are 'known' and those who are 'unknown'.

It could perhaps be argued that this interpretation of the Agreement rests not only on Art. 9.5 AD, but also on the language in Art. 6 AD itself.

The text of the Agreement states that:

> All interested parties in an anti-dumping investigation shall be given notice of the information which the authorities require and ample opportunity to present in

31 Art. 9.5 AD.

> writing all evidence which they consider relevant in respect of the investigation in question.[32]

The Agreement also states that *interested parties* include:

> (i) an exporter or foreign producer or the importer of a product subject to investigation, or a trade or business association a majority of the members of which are producers, exporters or importers of such product.[33]

These two statements could be interpreted as saying that national authorities in the importing country must investigate all exporters or producers of the allegedly dumped product from the exporting country subject to investigation. This would imply that, indeed, they are all considered potentially guilty of injurious dumping. Such reading of Art. 6 AD is reinforced by the statement that:

> In cases in which any interested party refuses access to, or otherwise does not provide, necessary information within a reasonable period or significantly impedes the investigation, preliminary and final determinations, affirmative or negative, may be made on the basis of the facts available. The provisions of Annex II shall be observed in the application of this paragraph.[34]

In other words, all interested parties must participate in the investigation, and those who refuse may be subject to AD duties.

Whatever the exact legal basis for the interpretation chosen by the Agreement, the fact of the matter is that it runs counter to economic rationality. The correct economic interpretation would have been that firms producing the same product in the same country will typically behave differently because they face different economic conditions and because perfect competition does not hold. Such interpretation would have implied that investigating authorities should not presume that all firms engage in injurious dumping simply because some might or even do.

This leads us to conclude that the Agreement is internally inconsistent from an economic viewpoint. On the one hand, the Agreement supposes that all exporters or producers of an allegedly dumped product who produce in the country in question are potentially guilty of injurious dumping in the importing country. On the other, it recognizes that different exporters or producers may behave differently and should therefore be subject to different treatment in terms of AD duties.

Hence, with respect to the fundamental question of the burden of proof and, ultimately, whether it is countries or firms that should be held responsible for dumping, nothing short of a revision of the AD Agreement itself can be satisfactory from an economic viewpoint.

32 Art. 6.1 AD.
33 Art. 6.11 AD.
34 Art. 6.8 AD.

5. Lock the case law

The AB advanced an interpretation of the AD Agreement that seems to move dumping back to the realm of private practices, as it should be, and away from unprovable conspiracy scenarios on which the Agreement itself in part rests. By outlawing recourse to Art. 6.8 AD in the case of nonsampling, the AB effectively imposes a duty on national investigating authorities to establish individual dumping margins for all exporters, instead of presuming that they all dump in the same manner simply because of their common origin. This is one (small) step forward, and it would be desirable, indeed, to lock it somehow. Although the lawmaking function of the AB is highly disputed, it is probably advisable to proceed first in the context of the *ADP Committee* and secure a Recommendation[35] that would repeat the AB findings and clarify that investigating authorities:

(i) are under the duty to identify all exporters in a nonsampling scenario;
(ii) must calculate individual dumping margins for each exporter.

By the same token it would be helpful to also clarify issues (legitimately) not touched upon by the present case, such as:

(i) the fact that nonsampled exporters are not liable to pay duties until a review takes place;
(ii) the nature of such a review (whether it should be expedited or not);
(iii) the amount of duty to be paid by new shipments.

The fundamental problem that we have identified in this paper is the unjustified presumption that all producers originating in a country must be dumping because one of them does; it must be taken care of through legislative amendment.

References

Baye, Michael, John Morgan, and Patrick Scholten (2006), 'Information, Search, and Price Dispersion', in Terry Hendershott (ed.), *Handbook of Economics and Information Systems*, Amsterdam: Elsevier Science.

Stigler, George J. (1961), 'The Economics of Information', *The Journal of Political Economy*, 69 (3): 213–225.

Varian, Hal R. (1980), 'A Model of Sales', *The American Economic Review*, 70 (4): 651–659.

35 Although the legal status of Recommendations by WTO organs (and, indeed, of all secondary law) remains *in limbo*, dispute settlement practice evidences increasing reliance on such instruments: recommendations dealing with the length of the period of investigation offer an excellent illustration to this effect.

Comment

Mexico – Antidumping Measures on Rice

Prepared for the ALI Project on the Case Law of the WTO

CLAUDIO DORDI

Professor of International Law, Bocconi University, Milan

The main issues raised in the paper

This commentary deals with two of the main issues raised in the paper presented by Mavroidis and Sapir, as follows:

1. The consequences following the Appellate Body (AB) interpretation of the term 'known exporter or producer ... of the product under investigation' contained in Article 6.10 of the AD Agreement;
2. Some shortcomings of the AD Agreement, and in particular the one identified in Section 4 of the paper of the authors, where Mavroidis and Sapir point out that while '[d]umping is a pricing strategy whereby producers in one country charge lower prices in foreign markets than in their home market', Article 2 AD 'defines dumping in terms of countries with no reference to individual firms'.

The consequences following the AB interpretation of the term 'known'

It is worthwhile to summarize, first of all, the rationale of the two authors' point of view regarding the interpretation of the term 'known' in Articles 6.10 and 12.1 of the AD Agreement, as follows:

1. The AD Agreement lacks precision as it does not contain any provisions aimed at determining:

   (a) The extension of the powers mandated to the AD investigating authority in identifying the 'known' exporters;
   (b) The treatment to be reserved, during AD proceedings, to the third category of exporters identified by the Agreement, the so-called 'unknown exporters'.

2. The AB, in interpreting the term 'known', did not manage to come up with a reasonable construction of the AD Agreement, as:
   (a) It applied a 'completely textual' interpretation of Article 6.10, holding that the term 'known exporters' appearing in Article 6.10 does not include exporters that the investigating authority should have known, but did not know, at the time when the investigation was initiated:
   (b) The above-mentioned interpretation has the effect of widening the class of unknown exporters, and, as a consequence, the impact of duties imposed on this class.

The divergent interpretation of the term 'known' provided by the Panel and by the Appellate Body reflects a different conception of AD proceedings and of the nature of the AD investigating authority powers. As recognized in many WTO member States, the AD investigating authority is the administrative body responsible for the application of the rules and regulations on antidumping duties and countervailing measures. Normally, investigations by administrative agencies or officials have no parties as found in a lawsuit or criminal prosecution, and, usually, there is no need to give notice of the investigation. However, *de facto*, investigations of the AD authorities are 'against' some exporters and end with a penalty (the AD duties) imposed on specific products manufactured by enterprises located in a definite country. Moreover, the AD Agreement provides specific burdens for the investigating authority regarding the notice of the investigation. Therefore, the WTO AD proceeding is a sort of hybrid standing in the middle between a lawsuit and an administrative proceeding.

Nevertheless, the *Mexico – Antidumping Measures on Rice* reveals the radical, and opposite, point of view of the Panel and the Appellate Body regarding the nature of AD proceedings and the features of AD investigating powers.

According to the 'extensive interpretation' of the Panel, which is shared by the two authors, the investigating authority, when conducting an investigation, cannot remain entirely passive and must inform those interested parties of which it can reasonably obtain knowledge.[1] As a consequence, the term 'known exporter or producer' in Article 6.10 refers to the exporters or producers of which 'an objective and unbiased investigating authority properly establishing the facts and conducting an active investigation could have and should have reasonably been considered to have [obtained] knowledge'.[2] According to this line of thinking, the nature of the powers of AD investigating authority is similar to that of the administrative agencies above mentioned.

1 Appellate Body Report, para. 237.
2 Panel Report, para. 7.187.

However, this interpretation cannot be satisfactory from a legal point of view as:

- it does not eliminate the category of 'unknown exporters' who were exporting during the period of investigation but have not been identified;
- the fact that, as pointed out by the authors, 'this category would probably be insignificant' cannot be considered as a welcomed result, in particular when the products under investigation are manufactured by many small and medium enterprises;
- there are no indications in the AD Agreement about the possibility to extend the treatment provided for all 'new shipments' to 'unknown' exporters. The AD Agreement, as it stands, 'does not specifically deal with the case of exporters who can ... hide during the investigation process'.

The Appellate Body, on the contrary, held that the term 'known exporters' appearing in Art. 6.10 AD does not include exporters that the investigating authority should have known, but did not know, at the time when the investigation was initiated. According to the authors, the AB followed a 'completely textual' interpretation of Art. 6.10 AD.

It should be pointed out, however, that the interpretation of the AB cannot be qualified as either 'restrictive' or 'completely textual' if we adopt, as a benchmark, the frame of a 'lawsuit' or a 'criminal prosecution' proceeding. Normally, before the courts, 'known' persons are those involved in the procedure because they either have been formally summoned or they have decided voluntarily to participate in the trial. The term 'known' is a qualified term that has a common meaning in the procedural law of most of the countries of the international community: it is a sort of 'general principle of law', as specified in Article 38 of the International Court of Justice Statute. The term 'known' has not a 'substantive meaning' (i.e. how many persons are known in a generic way) but a 'formal meaning' (i.e. how many persons are formally involved in the procedure). As a consequence, 'known' is a fact for the court and not a result that must be obtained with an investigation.

The consequences following from the above-mentioned interpretation of the term 'known' by the AB should be evaluated in connection with the fact that, according to the AB, the duty to be paid by unknown exporters cannot be based on 'facts available.' According to the AB, an authority that imposes a duty on unidentified exporters based on facts available, including facts from the petition, is acting in violation of Article 6.8 and paragraph 1 of Annex II. The implications of the above-mentioned statement have been clearly described by the authors:

> According to the AB, putting exporters on notice that facts available will be used is a precondition for the use of facts available. This condition, for obvious reasons, can never be met in the case of unidentified exporters: one cannot notify the person that has not been identified.

> The AB addressed a situation in which the residual rate was based on petitioner data, and was particularly adverse when compared to the margins of dumping calculated for the examined (known) exporters. But the need to inform exporters of the fact that, in the absence of cooperation, facts available will be used, applies in all cases, and not only when the data used is provided by the petitioner. To a certain extent, any margin based on information other than data provided by the exporter itself is based on 'facts available.' Logically speaking, the AB's statement could thus be read to imply that no residual duty can be imposed on such unknown exporters. A rate based on the highest margin of an exporter individually calculated, as is the EC's practice, is also a facts-available rate for the noninvestigated exporter, and hence, in this line of thinking, would, as well, be WTO-inconsistent.[3]

The authors criticized the above-mentioned reasoning stating that if:

> all the AB wanted to say was that facts available which are *adverse* may not be used to calculate a duty for unknown exporters', '[t]here remains a serious problem: when is the use of facts available (not) adverse? Is a residual duty based on the highest margin found for an investigated exporter less adverse than the use of information contained in the petition?'

The criticisms formulated by the authors can be shared only partially. Article 6.8 and paragraph 1 of Annex II, in fact, contain 'due process' provisions. 'Due process' rules provide normally 'procedural rights' guaranteeing fundamental fairness, justice, and liberty, and they do not deal with the substance of the rule. In the situation above mentioned, for example, it is not relevant for the due process provisions whether 'facts available' are *adverse* for the exporters. The simple fact that the exporters have not been notified of specific information by the investigating authority is a sufficient element impeding the investigating authority to utilize such information: i.e. it is not important whether the 'facts available' are adverse for the exporters. This is a principle that is common to most of the national legal systems.

Anyhow, the AB interpretation of the term 'known', combined with the preclusion of utilizing the 'facts available' in the application for the initiation of the investigation against an exporter that was not given notice of the information the investigating authority requires, carry some important consequences, such as the following:

- Even if the investigating authority, when conducting an investigation, is not obliged to be 'active' (i.e. informing those interested parties of which it can obtain knowledge), it is *de facto* forced to behave in a proactive manner, as it is not anymore possible to apply antidumping duties towards 'unknown' exporters based on 'facts available' (this means, in practice, that it is not possible to apply antidumping duties against unknown exporters!). The

3 Mavroidis and Sapir, Section 2.3.

higher the number of exporters identified, the larger the possibility to utilize 'facts available' for calculating dumping margins for noncooperative exporters;

- The investigating authority maintains its features of 'hybrid' entity, between a prosecutor and a court;
- In the EC, the AB interpretation is consistent with Article 41.2 of the Charter of Fundamental Rights, which guarantees 'the right of every person to be heard, before any individual measure which would affect him or her adversely is taken', and 'the right of every person to have access to his or her file, while respecting the legitimate interests of confidentiality and of professional and business secrecy.'

Incongruences in AD Agreement

Another interesting issue raised by the two authors is that while dumping is a practice of firms, the AD Agreement defines dumping in terms of countries with no reference to individual firms (Article 2 AD). Moreover, the authors highlighted that the AD Agreement is internally inconsistent from an economic point of view, as '[o]n the one hand', it 'supposes that all exporters or producers of an allegedly dumped product who produce in the country in question are potentially guilty of injurious dumping in the importing country. On the other, it recognizes that different exporters or producers may behave differently and should therefore be subject to different treatment in terms of AD duties.'

We will try to provide a valid explanation justifying the above-mentioned incongruency of the AD Agreement.

As Sapir pointed out (in another writing):

> Dumping can only occur if two conditions are fulfilled. First, the industry must be imperfectly competitive, so that firms have market power. That is firms must be able to set prices in the domestic or foreign market rather than take prices as given in both markets. Second, markets must be segmented, so that domestic customers cannot easily purchase products sold at a lower price in foreign markets. Dumping is considered an unfair practice in international trade.[4]

However, the absence of a national competition policy may be a factor favoring the increase of the market power of a group of companies in a specific country. That's why many authors justify antidumping as a protective measure aimed at coping with the differences existing in national competition laws and in the regulatory standard between States.

4 Sapir, Some Ideas for Reforming the Community Anti-Dumping Instrument, Brussels, 2006, p. 1.

Other authors have a more general view and consider that dumping can occur because of the differences existing between 'different economic standards'. J. Jackson, for example, stated:

> As world economic interdependence has increased, it has become more difficult to manage relationships among various economies. This problem is analogous to the difficulties involved in trying to get two computers of different designs to work together. To do so, one needs an 'interface' mechanism to mediate between the two computers. Likewise in international economic relations, particularly in trade, some 'interface mechanism' may be necessary to allow different economic systems to trade together harmoniously.[5]

Moreover, the segmentation of the market (the second condition identified by Sapir as a prerequisite of dumping) can be obtained by raising barriers to trade limiting the import of foreign goods. As a consequence, companies in countries where the competition is not particularly protected from abuses and where there are high import barriers, potentially have more possibility to dump products in other markets than companies located in countries where the competition is strictly regulated and with lower barriers to import. Of course, this conclusion is not always valid, as in the case of AD duties applied against shrimps originating in countries with thousands of enterprises producing shrimps.

Some suggestions

From our point of view, the paper of Mavroidis and Sapir raises two interesting problems:

1. What are the instruments that can be utilized to reduce the number of 'unknown' exporters in AD proceedings?
2. Is it possible to limit AD duties only to enterprises that really dump products?

In regard to question 1, we think that there is a need to restructure the institutional system of AD in importing countries; the investigating authority should be separated from the agency empowered to impose AD duties. A procedure closer to a criminal proceeding (with the investigating authority as a 'prosecutor' and with a sort of court empowered with the right to decide whether to impose AD duties) would solve the problem of 'passive' investigating authorities (and the problem of 'unknown' exporters).

With regard to question 2, there should be a modification in the definition of 'dumping'. Moreover, the definition of 'injurious dumping' could be limited to enterprises exporting from countries not adequately regulating competition and with high barriers to import.

5 Jackson, World Trade and the Law of GATT, 1997, p. 248.